EXORCISING PHILOSOPHICAL MODERNITY

VERITAS
Series Introduction

". . . the truth will set you free" (John 8:32)

In much contemporary discourse, Pilate's question has been taken to mark the absolute boundary of human thought. Beyond this boundary, it is often suggested, is an intellectual hinterland into which we must not venture. This terrain is an agnosticism of thought: because truth cannot be possessed, it must not be spoken. Thus, it is argued that the defenders of "truth" in our day are often traffickers in ideology, merchants of counterfeits, or anti-liberal. They are, because it is somewhat taken for granted that Nietzsche's word is final: truth is the domain of tyranny.

Is this indeed the case, or might another vision of truth offer itself? The ancient Greeks named the love of wisdom as *philia*, or friendship. The one who would become wise, they argued, would be a "friend of truth." For both philosophy and theology might be conceived as schools in the friendship of truth, as a kind of relation. For like friendship, truth is as much discovered as it is made. If truth is then so elusive, if its domain is *terra incognita*, perhaps this is because it arrives to us—unannounced—as gift, as a person, and not some thing.

The aim of the Veritas book series is to publish incisive and original current scholarly work that inhabits "the between" and "the beyond" of theology and philosophy. These volumes will all share a common aspiration to transcend the institutional divorce in which these two disciplines often find themselves, and to engage questions of pressing concern to both philosophers and theologians in such a way as to reinvigorate both disciplines with a kind of interdisciplinary desire, often so absent in contemporary academe. In a word, these volumes represent collective efforts in the befriending of truth, doing so beyond the simulacra of pretend tolerance, the violent, yet insipid reasoning of liberalism that asks with Pilate, "What is truth?"—expecting a consensus of non-commitment; one that encourages the commodification of the mind, now sedated by the civil service of career, ministered by the frightened patrons of position.

The series will therefore consist of two "wings": (1) original monographs; and (2) essay collections on a range of topics in theology and philosophy. The latter will principally be the products of the annual conferences of the Centre of Theology and Philosophy (www.theologyphilosophycentre .co.uk).

Conor Cunningham and Eric Austin Lee, *Series editors*

Not available from Cascade

Deane-Peter Baker	*Tayloring Reformed Epistemology: The Challenge to Christian Belief.* Volume 1
P. Candler & C. Cunningham (eds.)	*Belief and Metaphysics.* Volume 2
P. Candler & C. Cunningham (eds.)	*Transcendence and Phenomenology*
Marcus Pound	*Theology, Psychoanalysis, and Trauma.* Volume 4
Espen Dahl	*Phenomenology and the Holy.* Volume 5
C. Cunningham et al. (eds.)	*Grandeur of Reason: Religion, Tradition, and Universalism.* Volume 6
A. Pabst & A. Paddison (eds.)	*The Pope and Jesus of Nazareth: Christ, Scripture, and the Church.* Volume 7
J. P. Moreland	*Recalcitrant Imago Dei: Human Persons and the Failure of Naturalism.* Volume 8

Cascade

[Nathan Kerr	*Christ, History, and Apocalyptic: The Politics of Christian Mission.* Volume 3][1]
Anthony D. Baker	*Diagonal Advance: Perfection in Christian Theology.* Volume 9
D. C. Schindler	*The Perfection of Freedom: Schiller, Schelling, and Hegel between the Ancients and the Moderns.* Volume 10
Rustin Brian	*Covering Up Luther: How Barth's Christology Challenged the* Deus Absconditus *that Haunts Modernity.* Volume 11
Timothy Stanley	*Protestant Metaphysics After Karl Barth and Martin Heidegger.* Volume 12
Christopher Ben Simpson	*The Truth Is the Way: Kierkegaard's* Theologia Viatorum. Volume 13
Richard H. Bell	*Wagner's Parsifal: An Appreciation in the Light of His Theological Journey.* Volume 14
Antonio Lopez	*Gift and the Unity of Being.* Volume 15
Toyohiko Kagawa	*Cosmic Purpose.* Translated and introduced by Thomas John Hastings. Volume 16
Nigel Zimmerman	*Facing the Other: John Paul II, Levinas, and the Body.* Volume 17

1. Note: Nathan Kerr, *Christ, History, and Apocalyptic*, although volume 3 of the original SCM Veritas series, is available from Cascade as part of the Theopolitical Visions series.

EXORCISING
PHILOSOPHICAL
MODERNITY

Cyril O'Regan and Christian Discourse
after Modernity

Edited by

Philip John Paul Gonzales

CASCADE *Books* · Eugene, Oregon

EXORCISING PHILOSOPHICAL MODERNITY
Cyril O'Regan and Christian Discourse after Modernity

Cascade Books
An Imprint of Wipf and Stock Publishers
199 W. 8th Ave., Suite 3
Eugene, OR 97401

www.wipfandstock.com

PAPERBACK ISBN: 978-1-4982-9712-7
HARDCOVER ISBN: 978-1-4982-9714-1
EBOOK ISBN: 978-1-4982-9713-4

Cataloguing-in-Publication data:

Names: Gonzales, Philip John Paul, 1981–, editor

Title: Exorcizing philosophical modernity : Cyril O'Regan and Christian discourse after modernity / edited by Philip John Paul Gonzales.

Description: Eugene, OR: Cascade Books, 2020 | Includes bibliographical references and index.

Identifiers: ISBN 978-1-4982-9712-7 (paperback) | ISBN 978-1-4982-9714-1 (hardcover) | ISBN 978-1-4982-9713-4 (ebook)

Subjects: LCSH: O'Regan, Cyril, 1952– | Christianity—Philosophy | Metaphysics | Theology | Apocalyptic literature—History and criticism

Classification: BT103 G66 2020 (paperback) | BT103 (ebook)

Manufactured in the U.S.A.   03/17/20

To Cyril in friendship:
"We learn only from those we love."
—Goethe

Contents

AUSEINANDERSETZUNG

Contributors

John Betz is Associate Professor of Theology at the University of Notre Dame. He is the author of *After Enlightenment: The Post-Secular Vision of J. G. Hamann* as well as being the co-translator of Erich Przywara's magisterial *Analogia Entis*.

William Desmond is the David Cook Chair in Philosophy at Villanova University, and Professor of Philosophy Emeritus at the Institute of Philosophy, Katholieke Universiteit Leuven, Belgium as well as the Thomas A. F. Kelly Visiting Chair in Philosophy, at Maynooth University, Ireland. He is author of numerous books and is most known for his trilogy of the *Between*. His most recent book is *The Gift of Beauty and the Passion of Being: On the Threshold between the Aesthetic and the Religious*.

Caitlin Smith Gilson is Associate Professor of Philosophy at the University of the Holy Cross New Orleans and the author of four books, the most recent being *Immediacy and Meaning: J.K. Huysmans and the Immemorial Origin of Metaphysics*.

David Bentley Hart is a fellow at the Notre Dame Institute for Advanced Studies. He is the author of numerous books, the most recent being *That All Shall Be Saved: Heaven, Hell, and Universal Salvation*.

Jennifer Newsome Martin is Assistant Professor in the Program of Liberal Studies with a concurrent appoinment in the Department of Theology at the University of Notre Dame. She is the author of *Hans Urs von Balthasar and the Critical Appropriation of Russian Religious Thought* and the co-editor of *An Apocalypse of Love: Essays in Honor of Cyril O' Regan*.

John Milbank is Professor Emeritus in Religion, Politics, and Ethics in the Department of Theology and Religious Studies at the University of Nottingham. He is the author of numerous books, the most recent being *The Politics of Virtue: Post-Liberalism and the Human Future*, co-authored with Adrian Pabst.

Cyril O'Regan is the Catherine F. Huisking Professor of Theology at the University of Notre Dame. He is the author of numerous books and articles and is most known for his multi-volume Gnostic return series. His most recent book is *The Anatomy of Misremembering (1): Balthasar's Response to Philosophical Modernity. Vol. 1: Hegel.*

Aaron Riches is Assistant Professor of Theology at Benedictine College. He is author of *Ecce Homo: On the Divine Unity of Christ.*

Sebastian Montiel is professor of mathematics at the University of Granada, Spain. He is the author of *Curves and Surfaces* and translator into Spanish of the works of Charles Péguy, John Milbank, and Fabrice Hadjadj.

D. C. Schindler is Professor of Metaphysics and Anthropology at The Pontifical John Paul II Institute in Washington, DC. He the author of numerous books, the most recent installment being, *Love and the Postmodern Predicament: Rediscovering the Real in Beauty, Goodness, and Truth.*

Christopher Ben Simpson is Professor of Philosophical Theology at Lincoln Christian University. He is the author of four books, the most recent being *Modern Christian Theology.*

Introduction

PHILIP JOHN PAUL GONZALES
Pontifical University of St. Patrick's College Maynooth

On "the other side of the Arno" (*Oltrarno*) in Florence—that unforgettable city forever marked and written upon by the ambiguous, contested, and alluring beauty of the Renaissance—in the inconspicuous Church of Santa Maria del Carmine, lies the Brancacci Chapel: that hidden gem of early Renaissance painting often referred to as the "Sistine Chapel of the early Renaissance." The theological theme of the cycle is fairly unique in Christian art. It commences with the fall of Adam and Eve, followed by the ensuing dramatic redemption of humanity by Christ—here is the unique part—rendered through the mediatory role played by St. Peter in Christ's reconstitution of humanity. The cycle thus begins with the temptation and expulsion of Adam and Eve from paradise (Masaccio's *Expulsion from the Garden of Eden* being the artistic highlight) and then moves on to depict thirteen (existing) episodes of the life of St. Peter (Masaccio's *Tribute Money* being the most celebrated work in the entire cycle).

Some of these episodes are taken directly from the New Testament, while others are from *The Golden Legend*, compiled by Jacobus de Varagine (c. 1260). It is one of the latter that theologically and symbolically interests me here.[1] The *Disputation with Simon Magus and Crucifixion of St Peter* by

---

1. I leave aside here the question of hagiography and historical veracity in order to concentrate solely on the dramatic theological and symbolic import of this episode taken from *The Golden Legend*. This image is thus interpreted as disclosing the dramatico-symbolic leitmotif of this volume, namely, the exorcism of the anti-Christic lie. If this were more than an Introduction, I would have to address the historical manifestations of this lie, as I do elsewhere. See my *Reimagining the Analogia Entis: The Future of Erich Przywara's Christian Vision* (Grand Rapids Eerdmans, 2019). Thus, I consign myself

Filippino Lippi is artistically inferior to Masaccio but, nevertheless, theo-logically significant. That this panel contains the penultimate and ultimate episodes of the dramatic Petrine cycle—beginning with *Peter's Calling* by Christ and ending with the eschatological confrontation of Peter with Si-mon Magus and the subsequent crucifixion of Peter—is more than telling. Being called by Christ entails a radical testimony of love that is inseparable from an equally radical confrontation that seeks to discern, dispel, uncover, and exorcise lies and the spirit of untruth. As soon as the dramatic act of redemption, reconciliation, and reconstitution of humanity is enacted by Christ, history becomes a battleground for love, an arena of testimony and counter-testimony, confrontation, and dispute. In short, as soon as Christ makes his apocalyptic appearance on the stage of history, so too does the spirit of anti-Christ. The purpose of this anti-Christic spirit, in its seem-ingly infinite versions of incarnation/reincarnations, figurations, and dis-simulations, seeks ultimately to bear false witness to the authentic witness of Christ and his witnesses, to the extreme point where one can no longer tell the true from the false and, if it is possible, even the elect will be deceived (Matt 24:24). The complexity of this eschatological drama is symbolically and pictorially attested to in Lippi's brilliant *Disputation with Simon Magus and Crucifixion of St Peter.*

In this fresco, Sts. Peter and Paul humbly, yet boldly, bear witness and defend themselves against the false/true accusation of Simon Magus before the emperor Nero. By appearance Simon Magus is calmer and more peace-ful than Simon Peter, whose gesticulation and facial expression is more urgent (Peter's passion and impetuousness), in this dispute of *two* Simons. (Paul is more a background figure, while Peter foregrounds the dispute.) Moreover, Simon (Magus) is an entirely regal, commanding, and attractive figure dressed in white and scarlet and possessed of great self-composure and confidence (some critics see the face of Dante) in his denouncing of Simon (Peter) and Paul before Nero. The denouncing clearly concerns the accusation that Peter and Paul are seeking to overturn—transvalue—the gods, as there is a toppled statue of a pagan god before the feet of Nero. This accusation is in one sense true and in another false: true because Peter and Paul are indeed toppling the ancient gods, and false because these gods are false idols and therefore must be toppled in service to the Lamb. The truth and the lie are mixed in the prideful accusatory denouncing of Simon (Magus).

---

here to a pictorial eschatological image, which I interpretively offer as the ensign under which the themes of this volume march.

This mixing is complexified when one turns to the dizzying movement of hand gestures in the painting. Simon's (Magus) gestures are double or two-fold. His right hand is pointing towards Simon (Peter) while his left is pointing towards the ground at the fallen god/idol. Yet, if one pays close attention to the god/idol in its seemingly toppled state—depicted as demonically cunning and impish—it is pointing (testifying) towards Nero. Nero is pointing, with his right hand, towards Simon (Peter), beyond whom is seen, in the background of the disputation, Simon (Peter's) upside down crucifixion. To complicate this circle of lies and accusation, Nero's left hand, which is holding a scepter, seems to be pointing, like Simon (Magus), towards the fallen god/idol (perhaps both in a veiled and subtle obeisance).

Who then, is the origin of these lies, Simon (Magus), the god/idol, or Nero? Only a superficial casual viewing could say that Simon (Magus) is the instigator, because he is denouncing Simon (Peter) and Paul *before* Nero. For Simon (Magus) is a false prophet and a false prophet is always testifying to, and for, another spirit of falsehood, and this latter spirit of falsehood is likewise not an origin in itself but another level, layer, and stage in the covering over of the lie and its occult origin. In these three deceitful figures, there is a dissimulating *circumcessio* of lies, where the origin is always already occluded, because the origin is the father of lies, which begets the anti-Christic spirit, which begets falsehood upon falsehood and counterfeit doubles upon counterfeit doubles in a mesmerizing gyre that is ever-quickening.

Thus, there is a kind of Satanic triumvirate at work in this symbolically and theologically charged painting, mirroring the counter-t/Trinity in the Book of Revelation (false prophet, Satan, anti-Christ). This trinitarian inversion and perversion reaches its apex, I would suggest, in the figure of the seemingly fallen—toppled—god/idol that mimes the Lamb slain by obtaining victory through defeat. That is, in this inverse mirroring, the image of the god/idol (note again that this is an image: who is the god behind the image of this god/idol?) is defeated by the preaching of Simon (Peter) and Paul, both of whom preach Christ crucified and risen. In its state of being-overthrown the god/idol kenotically imitates the going down of the Lamb (i.e., the passion, death, burial, and descent into hell), desiring a perversely inverted inverse proportion, a going down that in each instant achieves a great victory: for Christ, the overcoming of sin, death, and the demonic powers and thus the redemption of humanity; for the god/idol, the overcoming, through a false kenosis, of one of the central witnesses of the Lamb, Simon (Peter), through his violent crucifixion and thus silencing. Yet, this silence is only an apparent silencing, as Peter's death (along with Paul's and countless others) is a bearing witness to the already-and-not-yet community or *basilea* of the eschatological priestly kingship of the Lamb slain. Peter's martyrological witness overcomes the second false kenosis in a truly imitative kenosis. Each kenosis is an imitation, but one is a mimicry that seeks to deceive, while the other is an imitation of love.

Simon (Peter), lovest thou me? Peter's witness to the crucified and risen Christ, along with the post-Easter question put to him by the glorified Lord, is now inscribed into his very flesh—like the very flesh of his Lord—this time with one crucial difference, or so the tradition says: Peter does not desire to be crucified the same way as his Lord because he knows himself to be unworthy of being so. Thus, he requests to be crucified upside down. This radical humility of love radically exposes the lie of the false kenosis feigned by the god/idol in his helpless (humble) being toppled and going down. The first kenosis brings the peace of love, the second and false kenosis brings the violence of the lie or the lie which is violence. The first results in an agapeic community (to borrow from Desmond) of peace, while the second results in a community of the lie and thus a pseudo-community and a pseudo-peace. The history of the world, since the coming of the Lamb, is the history of the acceptance of triune love, which the Lamb reveals along with his community of witnesses, *or* its rejection, resulting in an upbuilding of a counter-*basileia*, which ever-learns to feign, more and more perfectly, modes of Christian love, which are integral to the grammar of the Christian story of creation, incarnation, redemption, and apocalypse. Theologically, philosophically, and politically, these miming transgressive disfiguration-refigurations of the biblical narrative—the spirit of which is dramatically and symbolically represented by the figure of the proto-arch-heretic, Simon (Magus), in our painting—must be exorcised for love of the slain Lamb.

The present volume, *Exorcising Philosophical Modernity: Cyril O'Regan and Christian Discourse after Modernity*, concerns this very exorcism of the anti-Christic lie. But there are even true and false exorcisms. In the latter, Satan casts out Satan in order to continue the possession by and through the lie in another guise and/or manifestation, which continuously seeks to occlude the occult and violent origin. The true exorcism has one and only one final aim: through the power of the Spirit of Truth, to allow the pleromatic visionary reality of the mysterious *apokalypsis* of the slain Lamb to be seen and received as it is, for the glory of the Father. This, in turn, requires bearing the foolishness of the *mysterium Crucis* in the very flesh of the visionary, in witness and testimony to the reality of the community or bride as she painfully makes her way to the Bridegroom amidst an intensifying history where the yes or no to triune Love is remembered, forgotten, or misremembered in a land of ever-multiplying counterfeits. This volume concerns, celebrates, and questions the greatest Catholic theological exorcist writing in the English language today—the Irenaeus *redivivus* of postmodernity—Cyril O'Regan.[2]

The volume is ordered in a tripartite structure or tryptic and comprises nine essays/chapters, the denouement being Cyril O'Regan's beautiful and eloquent response to the superb contributions in this volume. The first part is titled *Ghosts of the Gnostic Present* and is made-up of four essays/chapters: "The Menace of Being: Cyril O'Regan, Figural Metalepsis, and the Counterfeit Doubles of Gnosticism," by William Desmond, "Re-membering *Geist*: From Hauntology to Pneumatology," by Aaron Riches and Sebastián Montiel, "Deleuze and Valentinian Narrative Grammar," by Christopher Ben Simpson, and "Poetry and the Exculpation of Flesh," by Jennifer Newsome Martin. The second part is entitled *Apocalypse and the Land of Counterfeits* and consists of three essays/chapters: "The Apocalypse of the Modern Soul: Cyril O'Regan's Reading of Hans Urs von Balthasar," by D. C. Schindler, "Metaphysics and Apocalypse: Apocalyptic Motifs in the Late Work of Erich Przywara," by John Betz, and "The Heart's Spectacular Silence: Time and Memory in Paul Ricoeur and Cyril O'Regan," by Caitlin Smith Gilson. The third part, under the heading *Auseinandersetzung*, comprises two essays/chapters: "*Geist's* Kaleidoscope: Some Questions for Cyril O'Regan," by David Bentley Hart and "Orthodoxy, Knowledge, and Freedom," by John Milbank. As O'Regan's response to the essays/chapters is exquisite and detailed, I will limit myself to a barebone description of each essay/chapter, in order to avoid negative repetition, while hopefully offering just enough to whet the reader's intellectual appetite, so to speak. Readers should also note that in O'Regan's response the treatment and/or organization of the essays/chapters are different from my organization. I read this to be for a twofold reason. First, my organization is for systematic and thematic purposes, while O'Regan's is organized according to an orchestration of a dialogical response, according to connecting and interlaced themes. That is, his is a response to a response, thus far, to his life's work, or to "Reading and Being Read." Second, O'Regan is forever and always a master hermeneut, and he is thus always casting new light on how to read texts, even when it concerns the organization of a text on themes in his own work. The two organizations are thus intended to be mutually reinforcing and enriching from different angles and ends.

The first set of essays/chapters, *Ghosts of the Gnostic Present*, are bound-together by adherence to O'Regan's Gnostic return thesis (as seen most famously in his series on Gnostic return), insofar as all these essays treat this theme in various creative ways, extensions, and supplementations,

---

2. For my treatment of O'Regan's work, see *Reimagining the Analogia Entis*, 288–320.

as the reader will readily notice. Moreover, as an extension of this thesis, these four essays are also an implicit endorsement of O'Regan's theory of hauntology (beautifully set forth in *The Anatomy of Misremembering*), that is, the belief that there are no clear-cut discursive genealogical historical breaks (*à la* Blumenberg). Rather, each essay implicitly or explicitly holds that discursive ghosts appear and reappear in different guises and thus demand continual discernment and exorcism. Hence the inclusion of the word, *Present*, in the title, as this exorcism is continuous until the eschaton.

Readers of both O'Regan and Desmond know that the spirit that binds these two daemonically inspired—in the Platonic sense—Irish intellectuals is deep and true. It is thus no surprise that in "The Menace of Being" one finds Desmond confirming, from a more phenomenological-ontological-metaphysical slant, O'Regan's "grammatical-hermeneutical" thesis on Gnostic return in modernity. Desmond's tactic is to put the focus on Gnosticism being a phenomenon of counterfeiting and doubling. The recrudescence of counterfeiting Gnosticism flips from a world-denying *gnosis*, in the ancient world, to a world-affirming *gnosis*, in the modern world, which results in a regime of absolute immanence. Yet, this is a paradoxical affirmation because at the heart of this regime is a will-to-mastery and absolute sovereignty, which ultimately sees being as evil and violent because the world is not given to be by the Agapeic God of creation. In the regime of absolute immanence, the world is not really affirmed, because it is made into the image not of the kingdom of the Father but of primal man or a humanity of self-coronated-apotheosis. This is seen, for example, in modern political atheistic movements where those "in the know" understand the dialectical laws of history and how to bring utopian peace out of violence. But this is an impatience with the given being of the between that seeks to sit in judgement over history in the place of God. The modern Gnostic regime of absolute immanence becomes the abyssal underground of a demonic humanism. In the face of this Desmond asks us, in a profoundly Augustinian gesture, to live in the mixed chiaroscuro of the between and history, where the wheat and the darnel are always mixed. *Before* evil and the menacing equivocity of the milieu of the between one must not seek to overcome evil with evil or violence with violence, but to overcome both with the powerless power of the patience of being. Which is to say, an abnegation of the sovereign self and, in its place, a radically porous self of patient exposure and non-violence.

Aaron Riches and Sebastián Montiel, in "Re-membering *Geist*," enter into the haunted spaces or corridors of Hegel's discourse by offering an exhilarating reflection on the disincarnate similarity of the paternal ghost of Hamlet to Hegelian *Geist*. Along the way, they draw interesting parallels, as well as crucial differences, between O'Regan's Balthasar-inspired hauntology and that of the founders of Continental hauntology, Louis Althusser (*The Specter of Hegel*) and Jacques Derrida (*The Specter of Marx*). (The original title to the *Anatomy of Misremembering* was *Balthasar and the Specter of Hegel*.) In the end, Riches and Montiel show how exceptionally successful O'Regan's form of discerning hauntology is in exorcising the Hegelian *Geist* because, ultimately, this exorcising is a carnal remembrance of Christ; that is to say, a successful exorcism of Hegelian *Geist* must, in the end, be Eucharistic.

In "Deleuze and Valentinian Narrative Grammar," Christopher Ben Simpson shows the fecundity of O'Regan's isolation of a Valentinian Gnostic narrative grammar, as established in the seminal *Gnostic Return in Modernity*, by showing that this grammar applies to an at-first-sight unlikely, yet fascinating candidate: the great postmodern herald of difference, Gilles Deleuze. Ben Simpson persuasively deploys O'Regan's six episodes of Valentinian narrative grammar, thereby systematically showing the "isomorphism between Deleuze's thought and Gnosticism as presented by O'Regan." Along the way, Ben Simpson fascinatingly shows Deleuze's indebtedness to, and involvement with, both the French esoteric tradition of Martinism and such shadowy figures of European esotericism as Johann Malfatti de Montereggio, Hoene Wroński, and Francis Warrain. All of which can, in one way or another, be genealogically traced to the "alpha" figure or father of modern Gnosticism and esotericism: Jacob Boehme.

Jennifer Newsome Martin's "Poetry and the Exculpation of Flesh" focuses on a lesser known aspect of O'Regan's work, namely, his poetic work, which consists of "several lengthy collections of poems." She focuses on *The Companion of Theseus*, a youthful work written while O'Regan was a graduate student at University College Dublin between 1975 and 1978. Newsome Martin offers an intricately detailed and delicate reading of *The Companion of Theseus* that brings into play a chorus of voices ranging from the theological voices Irenaeus and Tertullian, to the poetic voices of Osip Mandelstam and Anna Akhmatova, to the philosophical and psychoanalytical voices of Merleau-Ponty and Julia Kristeva. It is suggested, through this chorus, that O'Regan's poetry is united to his theological work, through an anti-Gnostic gesture that is an exoneration and "exculpation" of the flesh. In this poetic exoneration of the flesh, Newsome Martin contends that O'Regan's poetry privileges the primordiality of bodily experience, which is pre-reflective. Poetry as a wording of the flesh, one might say. O'Regan's poetry is a confessing absolution of the "un-romanticized" wounded-fragility of the vulnerably exposed flesh of our humanity.

In *Apocalypse and the Land of Counterfeits*, the three essays/chapters are bound together because each essay, in its own manner, has garnered inspiration from O'Regan's apocalyptic turn. Thus, these essays are testimony to the fecundity and fertility of O'Regan's powerful musings on apocalyptic, and how a genuinely Christian apocalyptic (ultimately Johannine in O'Regan's view) is, and must be, the visionary answer to our land of counterfeits.

In "The Apocalypse of the Modern Soul," D. C. Schindler engages O'Regan's seemingly "eccentric" thesis, presented in *The Anatomy of Misremembering*, that Balthasar is, and should be understood as, an apocalyptic theologian. Schindler affirms O'Regan's apocalyptic thesis and believes it to be the hermeneutic key to unlock the integral continuity of the whole of the Swiss thinker's massively imposing oeuvre. On Schindler's reading, O'Regan's interpretation is so powerful precisely because it foregrounds the theological "style" of Balthasar as a theological theme. For Balthasar, then, Christianity is not a revelation of "something" but rather Christianity *is* revelation: *apokalypsis*. Schindler traces this revelatory light from its inchoate beginnings in Balthasar's first major work, *The Apocalypse of the German Soul*, to the mature understanding of *traditio* understood as trinitarian revelation in volumes 4 and 5 of *Theo-Drama*. The latter understanding allows for the whole of history to be read within an apocalyptic horizon. Especially, the "rupture" that is modernity can be read within this trinitarian horizon of *traditio* as a rejection of the gift of the Holy Spirit. And the most pristine form of this rejection is Hegel's speculative controlling of this gift, which is no longer freely given, and thus, no longer a *gift*.

John Betz's "Metaphysics and Apocalypse" seeks to bring together metaphysics, whose historical province arises from the exquisite and unsurpassable rationality of the Greeks, and apocalypse, which arises from that revelatory horizon of the Hebraic spirit and heralds interruption and the making-new of all things. Betz, in the spirit of Balthasar and O'Regan, proposes that the two must be brought together and, indeed, that they already have been twined in the metaphysically biblical work of the mentor of Balthasar: the great Erich Przywara. To show how metaphysics and apocalypse are brought together Betz focuses on two latter works of Przywara: *Crucis Mysterium* and *Four Sermons*, given during World War II. In his dealing with *Crucis Mysterium*, Betz focuses on the eschatological confrontation Przywara provokes between Ignatius of Loyola and Nietzsche. In *Four Sermons*, the overarching theme can be said to be the twilight of the West or, in the words of Tolkien, "the days have gone down in the West behind the hills into shadow." The titles of the sermons are "The Man of the West," "Old and New Reformation," "Old and New Church," and "Old and New God."

Betz concludes that if any metaphysics is to be viable today, then it must be apocalyptic and thus be judged by revelation, which then implies that the only style of metaphysics possible, in this vesperal hour, is the *analogia entis.*

"The Heart's Spectacular Silence," by Smith Gilson, goes in search of the "Patmos Soul," that is, the soul that dwells within and incarnates the memory of the immemorial event of Christ. Smith Gilson locates the thought of Ricoeur and O'Regan within this apocalyptic space. This is so because both thinkers are Christocentric and their very exegesis flows from, and within, this center to the point that both their work "codifies the uneasy reality that truth predicts the eclipse of truth, and that in that eclipse none can escape its eviction." But never does Smith Gilson fail to keep before us the great differences between the two thinkers, especially seen in the Kantian parameters of Ricoeur's thought. Nevertheless, both must be seen and celebrated as apocalyptic "actors" who enter deeply into the land of counterfeits all the while giving testimony to the reality of Christ, especially before the extreme functionalization of Christ in the Hegelian speculative odyssey of historical consciousness seeking to become absolute. Hegel steps outside the Christ-event, while Ricoeur stands fast and O'Regan takes us deeper into the steadfast fidelity to Christ's unsurpassable apocalyptic revelation in this time of eclipse.

The two essays of the third part of this volume, *Auseinandersetzung,* call into question O'Regan's Gnostic return thesis, amongst other things. This calling into question by Hart and Milbank is not a calling into question of the monumental importance and brilliance of O'Regan's work but is rather a testimony to it. This is to say, any work as sweeping, intricate, complex, and visionary in scope as O'Regan's is bound to raise questions for thinkers like Hart and Milbank that are also involved in their own comprehensive projects. Nor is it insignificant here that this disputation involves central representatives—arguably *the* English-speaking theological representatives—of three major Christian traditions: Catholic, Orthodox, and Anglican. In this *disputatio* the stakes are high, indeed. They concern nothing less than the following: (1) What are the bounds or borderlands of Christian orthodoxy in relation to heterodox currents or strains? (2) What is the meaning and understanding of the Christian tradition and its "development"? (3) What does or should a Christian genealogy of modernity look like; who are the friends and enemies; who are the genealogical targets and how do we interpret epochal figures like Boehme and Hegel, for instance?

"*Geist's* Kaleidoscope," by Hart, while in agreement with O'Regan on many major theological points, as well as exhibiting an elective affinity in theological style and verve, demurs in regards to crucial aspects of O'Regan's Gnostic return thesis, genealogy of modernity, and the limits and bounds of orthodoxy. I only offer highlighted points of contention here. First, Hart calls into question the entire Gnostic return thesis that arose in nineteenth century scholarship, especially in Germany in conversation with German idealism, the most famous proponent being the Tübingen theologian: Ferdinand Christian Baur. Hart interprets Baur's influence as disastrous for Christian theology insofar as it created an unfounded fiction concerning Gnostic return. Second, Hart calls into question a theogonic interpretation of ancient Gnosticism, which transitions too easily into a developmental understanding of the divine in German idealism, thus making possible a Gnostic ascription of the latter. Third, Hart further protests against O'Regan's genealogical placement of Jacob Boehme as the "alpha" point of Gnostic recrudescence in modernity. Rather, Hart reads Boehme as a strict Lutheran voluntarist. Fourth, Hegel is read, in line with the reading of Boehme, also as a Lutheran voluntarist. Hegel's thought then is read as compatible with a certain strain of Christian "orthodoxy" that is actually seeking to eradicate all Gnostic elements from Christianity. Hart provocatively suggests that there is a Gnostic kernel in authentic Christianity that must be retained if Christianity is to remain true to its original apocalyptic interruption. Lastly, Hart worries about any project that seeks to demarcate the borders of orthodoxy into an orthodox/heterodox divide, shifted out in an all-too-confident theory of Christian tradition. Hart asks us to exhibit more, and not less, postmodern suspicion.

Milbank's "Orthodoxy, Knowledge, and Freedom" seeks to mediate and temper some of Hart's questions put to O'Regan's Gnostic return project while, in the end, seeking to tip the scale in favor of Hart's demurral. Yet, Milbank ups the ante, if you will, by explicitly stating the major stake implicit in Hart's essay, namely, a tension that "concerns the nature of orthodoxy and orthopraxis themselves: just what are the essential bounds of Christian belief, experience, and performance?" To begin answering these questions, for Milbank, one has to ask what the genealogical targets or heterodox currents or candidates are that lie in the tense borderland between orthodoxy and heterodoxy, where the double looks so much like the original and vice-versa. To oversimplify: the question becomes the question of who the real enemy is. With O'Regan and Balthasar, there are four very strong genealogical currents and/or strains that haunt Christian revelation: Romanticism, Neoplatonism, Gnosticism, and apocalyptic (and Milbank would like to add the esoteric tradition). The most insidious of these doubles of Christianity, for Balthasar and O'Regan, is Gnosticism. But Milbank suggests that the real enemy is voluntarism. Thus, like Hart, Milbank reads both Boehme and Hegel as dependent on Christian and Lutheran voluntarism. Moreover,

Milbank makes the claim that Romanticism, Neoplatonism, and esotericism are more compatible with Christianity than Balthasar and O'Regan will allow.

I leave it to the reader, after reading O'Regan's response and all the essays in this volume, to decide about the nature of the anti-Christic lie and the true false doubles of Christianity. Who are the friends of Christ and Christian revelation and who are the foes? For counterfeit doubles are also and most especially light-bearers and, in being so, demand all the more urgently the true exorcism grounded in the love of the Lamb slain. It is my hope that this volume has moved in the direction of this needed exorcism or, at the minimum, started a conversation concerning a discernment of spirits in our time of ever-proliferating imposters. Our hope lies in the fact that the community of seekers in this volume are tied together by a two-fold bond. The first is a visionary belief that there are indeed counterfeit doubles of Christianity and that these must be discerned, sought out, and uncovered; for the occult origin must be laid-bare. Such a conviction, such a belief, should never be taken lightly, as the number of Christian thinkers who believe in counterfeit doubles grows fewer and fewer by the day. The second bond is likewise visionary, that is, it sees that the work of Cyril O'Regan is a lodestar, or better, an evening star in this vesperal time of doppelgängers. O'Regan's ceaseless searching out of the spirit of the lie is done out of love for the Lamb slain, and the result of his exorcism of love is nothing less than an anticipation of the wedding feast of the Lamb. This volume, as O'Regan prophetically notes in his response, is something of an anticipation of that eschatological-apocalyptic fulfillment that will be an eternal feast or banquet of conversation, love, and response, culminating in the angelic hymn of glorification: the *Trisagion*. Thank you, Cyril, for gifting all of us with the banquet that is your astounding and inexhaustible work.

GHOSTS OF
THE GNOSTIC PRESENT

1

The Menace of Being

Cyril O'Regan, Figural Metalepsis, and the Counterfeit Doubles of Gnosticism

WILLIAM DESMOND

Villanova University and KU Leuven

Nature devouring, nature devoured,
Butchery day and night smoking with blood.
And who created it? Was it the good Lord?

—Czesław Miłosz, from "To Mrs Professor in Defense of My
Cat's Honor and Not Only"

Gnosticism and Counterfeit Doubles

I would like to offer a reflection on Cyril O'Regan's concern with Gnosticism in general and with Gnostic return in modernity in particular. I will open with a few words about Gnosticism, then outline something of what O'Regan's project entails, and then offer some reflections from a slightly different angle in which I hope to supplement his work rather than criticize it. In communication with his engagement with Gnosticism, I want to center some reflection on what I am tempted to call the menace of being.

This is partly due to sometimes different emphases in our approaches, emphases that do not negate a greater convergence on a vision of fundamental importance in the matters at issue. My own orientation is predominantly ontological-metaphysical, while O'Regan's has a kind of grammatical-hermeneutical slant. These two orientations are not mutually exclusive, and I hesitate to speak too univocally of a grammatical-hermeneutical slant, since there are deeply informed historical dimensions to O'Regan's work, as well as operative systematic elements of a highly sophisticated theological and philosophical character. I will say something about the sense of grammar in due course, but when one surveys his work as a whole one is struck by the singularity of its spiritual and intellectual style. No one else writes like Cyril O'Regan and that is not just an endearing eccentricity but an incarnation of the unique aesthetic register of his work. Aesthetic here means not the orchestration of dispensable flourishes but the communication of a singularly embodied sense of things.

The definition of Gnosticism is fraught with controversy, but a temptation to something resembling Gnosticism seems to be recurrent in human affairs rather than being confined to one time alone. It occurs, it reoccurs, it will occur again. We commonly associate Gnosticism with various sects active in the Hellenized Near East, especially in the first and second centuries. Some of these sects had a relation to Christianity, a relation often tense and hostile. Our knowledge of these sects, at one time, derived from early Christian critics, the heresiologists, so-called, such as Irenaeus, Tertullian, and Clement of Alexandria. Some critics have said their record was shot through with "propaganda" that distorts the putative "enemy." Other critics find veracity in the portrayals, despite the polemical edge.[1] The modern discovery of the so-called Gnostic Gospels introduced intriguing detail to the story, allowing us to read some of the texts directly, as well as adding complexity to the story of early Christianity. The situation is a rather confused plurivocity: many religious voices vie with one another, none seems entirely dominant, sometimes there is a kind of a community in the plurivocity, sometimes an air of cacophony, sometimes those hostile to each other tend to mirror their opponents, but with divergent spiritual intents. It would be difficult to give a univocal definition, reducing it to one clear, distinct, and essential feature. Irenaeus, referring to the Valentinian school, uses the comparison of a Hydra. Its signs are perplexing and many-meaninged. Gnosticism often baffles us with a proclivity to persistent shape-shifting,

---

1. Hans Jonas makes such a point, confirming Irenaeus and others, in the second edition of Jonas, *Gnostic Religion*, 295, after having consulted the Nag Hammadi texts. English translation from Robinson, *Nag Hammadi*.

with the space between the human and divine filled by imagination, myth, ritual, magic, story, and speculation.

Gnosticism has been called "the religion of dualism," but I prefer to speak of *doubles* and *doublings*. Dualism tends to be fixed on rigid binary oppositions, but Gnosticism shows something more fluid and metamorphosing, even protean. The notion of doubling qualifies dualism by the equivocal sense of being. It thus allows us more supple ways of confronting dualism(s), as well as allowing the subversion of dualities and the surpassing of oppositions. A crucial notion here is what I call the *counterfeit double*.[2] A counterfeit double images an original, but something, often very subtle, is missing or reconfigured in the double, such that we find it hard to say what is image/double and what original, and even to identify the counterfeit at all and differentiate it from the original. Consider: orthodox Christians and Gnostics tended to be doubles of each other, but because of factors added or omitted, or transmuted or distorted, they were doubles in *intimate opposition*. Recall non-Christian Gnosticism, defined by considerations closer to Neoplatonism, and note Plotinus's wrath against Gnosticism—this is redolent of hostility to the *intimate double*, a double both very like yet deeply unlike. Mirroring a con-fusing plurivocity, Gnosticism is often an eclectic mixing from different sources and many ancient cultures: a religious equivocity with many voices but no simple unity or community.

Consider here the struggle within Christianity over the question of "orthodoxy": that the notion of the "heretical" appears at all reflects both a struggle for the ascendancy of a certain religious configuration of life, as well as the truth of that configuration.[3] That the Gnostics are thought to have lost the struggle makes some commentators see nothing in all of this but the *will to power* of the "orthodox." This judgment mirrors our reconfigured ethos as much as theirs, and we can overstate the point. Such an ethos of religious plurivocity has some similarity to our own time: fresh possibilities seem to open up in a time of ferment and transition; the old seems to lose its immemorial stability; a kind of saving knowing is sought, often coupled with dissatisfaction with public, institutional religion. Not entirely unlike

[marginal handwritten note: counterfeit double]

---

2. This is a notion central to my *Hegel's God: A Counterfeit Double?* It is very much in the spirit of O'Regan's own understanding of the "heterodox Hegel" and raises similar questions about Hegel as a putative "Christian" thinker. O'Regan, *The Heterodox Hegel*. See O'Regan, *Misremembering*.

3. Many of the second-century Gnostics saw themselves as Christians. St. Paul uses the word "gnosis" frequently, though not quite in the "Gnostic" sense. Dan Merkur in *Gnosis* offers a chapter on defining Gnosticism. He seems to accept some distinction between Gnosticism (large G), as defined by the Messina conference (1966), and gnosticism (small g), which is an esoteric tradition of unitive mystical practices. Williams, *Rethinking "Gnosticism."*

postmodern "spirituality," in Hellenistic times, the turn to mystery religions sought a relation to the divine more immediately personal than found in the public religion, with its institutionalized rituals. In the equivocal manyness, pagan, Jewish, Christian, Iranian, Hermetic, and occult considerations, and the Lord knows what, are all thrown together and stirred in the melting pot of religious possibility.

If the equivocity seems to engender Babel, the voicing of multiple possibilities also can generate its own heterogeneous fecundity. Many styles are mixed in Gnostic texts: the parabolic, the speculative, the incantatory, the oracular, and so on. In some Gnostic texts (for instance, *The Sophia of Jesus Christ*) one is startled to hear Jesus Christ speaking in tones reminiscent of a Neoplatonic philosopher.[4] Not a few of the Nag Hammadi texts remind one of the discourses of Nietzsche's Zarathustra. The tone is often hieratic: full of proclamation and higher say-so; obscure, but laced with hints and insinuations of deeper meaning, delivered to insiders but meant to impress, to awe, outsiders. The Gnostic gospels are for everyone and for no one. Nietzsche's Zarathustra is himself often a parodist, indeed more: a mocker of Christianity. If Gnosticism is often a double of Christianity, the "same" but "other," close to the line but other than orthodox, parody strikes one as a rhetorical strategy that enshrines the wording of a doubling, repetitive of the original yet potentially undermining of it at the same time. If there is something here of *parodia sacra*, the Gnostic texts often seem to be deadly serious—earnest utterances of original and last secrets. I find that Nietzsche's own Zarathustra slips in and out of that kind of seriousness. The original Zoroaster is one of the figures of praise in Gnostic discourse. Nietzsche's Zarathustra is an equivocal double, very like and very unlike the original. For Nietzsche the original Zoroaster was the inventor of the moral distinction of good and evil—the fateful double that sets in motion the moral counterfeiting of the world. For Nietzsche the truth of immoralism is now to be announced, and becoming is to be restored to its innocence. I am reminded of Gnosticism in the superior announcement to the enlightened few: the world both restored and transfigured, but in the going under of its old corruption by Jewish Christianity.

Elsewhere I have tried to address Gnosticism at more length, while developing a metaxological philosophy of God. This philosophy requires attendance on the plurivocity of being religious, and Gnosticism figures in that plurivocity.[5] One can hear recurrent voices in relation to the divine,

---

4. Robinson, *Nag Hammadi*, 206–29.

5. Desmond, *God and the Between*. I draw from some of the thoughts there articulated in connection with Gnosticism, chapter 10.

sometimes disagreeing, sometimes agreeing, as in a kind of family conversation or quarrel, and sometimes a philosophical finesse beyond philology is needed to attend on these voices. There is something heterogeneous about Gnosticism, but also something transitional and intermediate: an ambiguous mix of religion and philosophy, one and many, personal and transpersonal, monism and dualism, speculation and myth, concept and metaphor. One can come across a strong dualism in some versions, yet also a movement towards the God of the whole. Yet again we find a sense of a God beyond the whole that, on the one hand, is not the God of biblical personalism and that, on the other hand, makes remarkable use of elements of a more personal soteriology with certain Christian tonalities. The diverse forms of Gnosticism are characterized by certain styles of response to the equivocity of our being in the *metaxu*. I say styles of response, not a univocally homogenous set of doctrines.

One of the constant orientations that recurs is a strong sense of the aesthetic equivocity of finite being, as haunted by exposure to evil, and marked by a certain doubling between One and many, tending now downwards to dualism and now upwards to recuperated oneness.[6] I want to focus on this orientation in terms of what we might call the menace of being. This is not confined to the earlier forms of Gnosticism. Foreboding concerning the menace of being is, in my view, quite widespread in the culture of post-Hegelian philosophy, extending into our own time. Our secret sense of metaphysical menace, often not acknowledged, much less faced, is the outcome of the long unfolding of the divorce of good and being that marks the project of modernity. My point will not be to endorse a view that sees good and evil as equally primordial, for I think there is an asymmetrical priority to good. What I mean by the saturated equivocity of good and evil has to do with the half-light, half-dark in which we live, very often quite impenetrable to us, the signs of whose duplexity perplex us, shock us, torture us, jolting us into finesse in responding to the ambiguous signs. Finesse for the counterfeit doubles of the divine is inherent in finesse for the wording of God. The full tale of that metaxological finesse is beyond the terms of this present reflection.

---

6. In *God and the Between*, I show how that aesthetic equivocity can yield to a more explicit dialectical sense with the pan(en)theistic God of the whole (chapter 11), and then to a more metaxological sense with the theistic God of creation beyond the whole (chapter 12), and turn us again to the intimate universal of the mystic God (chapter 13).

Cyril O'Regan, Gnostic Return, and Apocalypse

The equivocity of the sacred is hospitable to a grammatical-hermeneutical approach, for it makes us ask: how to read the sacred signs? The scholarly study of Gnosticism is almost an industry unto itself, but now I turn to some of the distinctive characteristics and excellences of Cyril O'Regan's approach. I will pay particular attention to two volumes in his project dealing with Gnostic return in modernity, one of which outlines the project as a whole, the other of which gives us its exemplification in the work of Jacob Boehme.[7] These are two volumes in a seven-volume project outlining the return of Gnosticism in modernity. The first volume deals with a more general and anticipative statement of the project as a whole, as well as the methodological protocols that guide it. The second volume deals with the most significant of early modern Gnostics, whose legacy was to reverberate in important successors who will be the focus in subsequent volumes. Among these, Hegel and Schelling will each receive a volume to themselves, while the return of Gnosticism in German and English Romanticism will constitute another volume. There will also be volumes devoted to anti-Gnostic discourses in the nineteenth century (treating of Kierkegaard, and S. T. Coleridge, for instance), as well as to Gnostic and anti-Gnostic discourses in the twentieth century. His recent magisterial volume on Hans Urs van Balthasar represents something of this anti-Gnostic concern.[8]

His ambitious project is motivated by the belief that all efforts hitherto to justify labelling modernity, or a significant band of discourses in modernity, as Gnostic have failed. It attempts to offer that justification, and to redo in the twenty-first century (with qualification, development, emendation, and even undoing) what Ferdinand Christian Baur (1792–1860), developing the Hegelian legacy, had done in the nineteenth. There is a third band of discourses in the post-Reformation period, neither orthodox Christian, nor liberal, to be called Gnostic, but in what more exact sense remains to be determined. The term "Gnosticism" is often used in a broad and somewhat loose sense, and its study in the more specialized sense is confined to a relatively small group. O'Regan contests what he sees as the too loose usage of the term, for instance, by Eric Voegelin, who uses it to refer too widely to a diversity of movements and thinkers. O'Regan's question: Is such usage helpful enough for a more precise and determinate study of both ancient Gnosticism, and its modern "return"?

---

7. O'Regan, *Gnostic Return*; O'Regan, *Gnostic Apocalypse*. O'Regan has also written *Theology and the Spaces of Apocalyptic*.

8. O'Regan, *Misremembering*.

One should note that the first book is also a contribution to determining what the notion of "modernity" is and engages extensively with the writings of Hans Blumenberg on this score. "Return" implies a first or prior presence and O'Regan primarily locates the first coming of Gnosticism in its Valentinian form. He argues that Valentinian Gnosticism provides the appropriate template for the ancient form, as well as one that illuminates his claim of a modern return. He provides a very complex understanding of this ancient form and in this shows his outstanding scholarly skills to great effect. He does not stop at this, however, and seeks to give determinate outline to the shape of a kind of return of Valentinianism in modernity. This cannot be any univocal repetition but might well involve a number of significant departures from the first original. These departures could well be developments of reserves, perhaps recessive in the original form, perhaps not there at all relative to new developments in modernity, developments that bring forth mutations that still have a significant continuity with the earlier form, even in the admitted discontinuity. For instance, ancient Gnosticism can be seen as more dualistic and world-denying, while modern forms tend to be not dualistic thus, and oriented to a certain plerosis in immanence itself. Initially, they might seem quite opposite, and it is not evident how we might get to the second from the first. O'Regan accomplishes this task in a discourse that has intricate specificity, suppleness of application, and yet an overall structure of coherence.

What is crucially important is the *grammar* of a narrative, and specifically the notion of a Christian narrative grammar and, with respect to the thesis of "return," a Valentinian narrative grammar. A grammar designates an underlying set of rules of formation that allow a diversity of instantiations. A plurality of concretions may be possible according to that grammar, and yet the plurality may recognizably belong, more intimately or more dissidently, to a certain identifiable narrative. We are pointed to something both rule-governed yet allowing supple divergence and the arising of new unpredictable enunciations, albeit still conforming more or less to the grammar. Only with such a notion of narrative grammar do we have helpful access to public articulations of what is at stake, articulations that allow the precision and determinacy, as well as the suppleness, needed. O'Regan enters into discussion with many important figures in addition to Blumenberg, such as Foucault and Jonas. The latter, for instance, while held in high respect, is found wanting by relying on existential orientations that lack, O'Regan thinks, the public determinability, and hence "objectivity," that a more narrative-based account can supply.

Some repetitions of the narrative grammar may hew more closely to an established tradition, some developments may develop or depart from the narrative, so much so as to be defined as heterodox or unorthodox positions, or to constitute a new discourse that subverts the original form of the narrative. In the language O'Regan uses, the relation of Christian and Gnostic narrative can be understood in terms of disfiguration and refiguration. When the disfiguration and refiguration veers towards bringing to form a new narrative configuration relative to more orthodox positions and narratives of God, he speaks of a metalepsis. The language is technical and initially forged in his ground-breaking *The Heterodox Hegel*. But perseverance with the initial strangeness will yield great benefits. Relative to metalepsis itself, there can be many intermediate phases, and a sophisticated conceptual apparatus has to be available to define the continuities and discontinuities between extremes.

In broad outlines, *Gnostic Return in Modernity* pursues this project in Part I by diversely discussing the Baurian model of Gnostic return and the many challenges it must face and meet. In Part II, the book gives an account of what a Valentinian narrative grammar looks like. Irenaeus is a central character in this work, and while O'Regan does not want to demonize Gnosticism, his own preference for a non-Gnostic Christian narrative is not hidden. He is one who, with respect, mourns more than celebrates the return of Gnosticism in modernity, even though his major aim is to provide a model of Gnostic return that will be accepted by both celebrators and mourners.[9]

O'Regan wants to offer us what he calls a "figural Irenaeus." The following citation seems to me to sum up some major features of what O'Regan draws to our attention:

> A discussion of metalepsis provides the primary context for an appropriation and correction of Irenaeus with the aim of fashioning a figural Irenaeus. Irenaeus is the Christian thinker who has the clearest conceptual grasp of metalepsis as essentially consisting of disfiguration-refiguration of biblical narrative. Moreover, in an interpretive move whose genius can be fully appreciated in light of the Nag Hammadi texts, Irenaeus indicates how disfiguration-refiguration of narrative has surface and depth narrative dimensions: On the surface the biblical narrative is disfigured and refigured by an inclusive narrative that moves from an archeological divine perfection to its reconstitution after the contingent mishap of a divine fall that brings an anti-divine and/or the otherness of nature into existence. On the depth level, the biblical narrative is disfigured and refigured by an inclusive narrative where the divine perfection of omega

9. See O'Regan, *Gnostic Return*, 12, for instance.

is regarded as qualitatively superior to the divine perfection of alpha, and when it is understood teleologically to rehabilitate the accidental nature of fall and teleologically integrate the suffering attendant on the fall, thereby justifying both. A figural Irenaeus not only appreciates the doubleness of the Valentinian challenge, but also recognizes that in the modern period the challenge of the teleological rendition of inclusive metaleptic narrative will be much more to the fore.[10]

Since *Gnostic Return in Modernity* outlines the project in broad contours, the essential methodological instruments, as well as the ensemble of conceptual resources to be brought into play, by the nature of the case, it makes different demands on the reader than *Gnostic Apocalypse*. This second book deals in greater specificity with Boehme as the alpha figure of the return of Gnosticism in modernity, and hence it is not formal or propaedeutic, but has the character of a fully articulated study of an intriguing thinker. In the first book, the formal demands of the project as a whole are to the fore, and since it also anticipates subsequent volumes, it does not entirely stand on its own. Nevertheless, given the range of ambition of the author, it is indispensable, and while subsequent volumes, willy nilly, will resume some of its themes, to have them set forth in their own terms supplies the necessary framing of the project as a whole.

Jacob Boehme is an intriguing figure: for some he is too dense a figure; for others he is too fanciful a figure to be included in more respectable philosophies and theologies. O'Regan makes a persuasive case that, while a heterodox thinker, he should be taken seriously, not only in terms of his own inherent interest, but in terms of influences, overt and hidden, on major figures succeeding him. O'Regan begins by giving a succinct exposition of Boehme, and then goes on to offer his argument in confirmation of the thesis of Gnostic return. Hence, this work is both a study of Boehme and a demonstration of his pivotal role in subsequent thinkers with Gnostic characteristics, as well as a first confirmation of the overall thesis outlined in *Gnostic Return*.

The exposition and demonstration is too complex to summarize here, but overall we find in the thinking concerning the divine a decisive swerve towards a more erotic God. This is an erotic God in which kenotic and agonistic movements serve a teleological completion of divine self-becoming. While this God is not devoid of agapeic registers, finally the erotic figuration is in the dominant. The erotic, kenotic, and agonistic divine becoming places the God of the end as higher and more "complete" than the God

10. O'Regan, *Gnostic Return*, 230.

of the beginning. In between beginning and end is the fall of the divine, figured in such a way that points backwards to the Valentinian narrative and forward to successors like Hegel, where the erotic motif dominates far more inclusively. Boehme prepares the refiguration that a speculative thinker like Hegel completes.

The discussion is compelling and for me it is philosophically interesting that our languages of the divine are so tied to "metaphors" of love, be they erotic or agapeic, as in this instance. One is astonished at the intricacy of concern with perhaps something that, from another angle, has an elemental tang about it: what is the love that is the divine? O'Regan tends to veer off existential intonations, consistent with his stress on narrative grammar. But it is also an interesting question whether the issue of love can be addressed without something approximating more to an ontology of love, with both existential and systematic dimensions. O'Regan worries about subjectivism, and hence plumps for narrative. But if there is a certain elemental mystery at the center of it all, is the idiocy of the existential and ontological finally avoidable, even when approached with superbly articulated speculative or narratological protocols?

O'Regan shows an enviable knowledge of Boehme, as well as an admirable command of more orthodox positions, pre-Reformation and Reformation, as well as a command of apocalyptic, Neoplatonic, and Kabbalistic thought—not to mention German idealism and Romanticism, but these will be to the fore in volumes succeeding the present two. A summary of the structure of *Gnostic Apocalypse* will make evident how all these concerns are addressed. Part I is entitled "Visionary Pansophism and the Narrativity of the Divine." Here we find a succinct account of Boehme's views, accessible to the novice but of interest to the initiated. Part II is entitled "Metalepsis Unbounding." Here O'Regan discusses a number of "swerves" in Boehme, ranging from his recapitulation of minority traditions in pre-Reformation and post-Reformation Christianity, to swerves more individual to Boehme's own distinctive vision, and finally to swerves that go all the way to full Boehmean metalepsis. Part III is entitled "Valentinianism and Valentinian Enlisting of non-Valentinian Discourses." It explores the relations of Boehme's discourse and Valentinian narrative grammar. In successive chapters, there are here some remarkable discussions of Boehme's Valentinianism. Once again, the details are too intricate for summary here, but they repay close and serious study.

In sum, these brilliant volumes begin a project that sets a benchmark in the study of Gnosticism. They throw light on large movements, as well as being of detailed interest to scholars engaged with the specific interpretation of individual philosophers, theologians, and religious thinkers (and in later volumes to come, also poets). They are marked by immense erudition that offers to the reader an education in itself. They are written with rhetorical boldness that never sacrifices precision. In each of them, there surfaces a certain intellectual passion in O'Regan's overall engagement with the challenge posed by modern forms of Gnosticism. O'Regan offers as epigraph to each volume a poem of his own composition, showing genuine poetic powers, and confirming one's sense of him as an accomplished stylist, and in more registers than the mere proses of the academy.

The Menace of Being

What O'Regan does with "metalepsis" is very close to the spirit of what I intend in the notion of the "counterfeit double." The figural dimension and the reading of signs brings it also closer to our need of theological and philosophical finesse for the equivocity that saturates our being religious. As already indicated, what I want to say in the ontological-existential register I see as overlapping with, rather than departing from, O'Regan's narrative-hermeneutical approach. As we shall see, "Gnostic return" can be seen as ontologically constitutive in relation to the equivocity of evil—though here perhaps in a more "speculative" vein, in an ontological-metaphysical register, by comparison with O'Regan's meticulous grammatical-hermeneutical pursuit of Gnostic return.

Let me first say something about the ontological orientation that surfaces in many formations of Gnosticism and then I will return to the grammatical-hermeneutical pursuit. I take this ontological orientation to be seeded deep in the being of the human being and concerns a suspicion of the evil of being. Often today we think here too quickly of moral evil, but this is not what is primally at stake. It is something more ontologically elemental and is not a matter of evil as a choice or due to choice. It is closer to a primal foreboding that does not always find itself in fitting words. It might be more helpful to speak of the menace of being, just because menace signals something that is neither something simply determinate nor due to our self-determining. There is an indeterminacy in what menaces us, though we are often hard put to pin down exactly what makes us feel menace.

A father does not raise his hand to threaten the wayward son; a change in the tone of the voice can be enough; a look can do it. There are looks that, while entirely silent, are absolutely eloquent of menace. Nothing is said and yet the communication of the menace occurs as if in the instant. There are smiles that radiate on two levels of ontological orientation, one surface appearance being the greeting of the friend, the other surface, not surfacing, and yet there in the face by not being there, a grimace of pure malice.

A person may be actually threatening or not be threatening at all, but in our unstable anxiety we take the face of the other, in its mysterious ambiguity, as a sign of menace. A hidden worm has already turned in the soul and what comes towards it, even if it is with a smile, is received as a secret threat. True goodness can be experienced as a threat, indeed a menace, to a person living a lie. The possible relations between self and other are legion.

It is perhaps easy to grant the legion in ourselves, and we are easily inclined to say that there is no menace of being in itself or *per se*: we project our own anxiety on the thing itself, but the thing neither welcomes nor repulses. I think this way of thinking is too easy. To a degree it simply accepts the modern world picture where an all-pervasive objectification and neutralization and univocalization of being strips of things other to us all the qualitative charges of attractiveness and repulsiveness, of hospitality and hostility: a pure naked neutral "is." This univocal neutralization is not true to what gives itself, what shows itself. Things give themselves, show themselves in an idiotic and aesthetic happening. They are replete with the equivocity of aesthetic show. There is nothing univocal. The equivocity is the fertile ambiguity wherein the menace of being thrives.

How to describe a menace? The notion of being threatened has to be granted here. We find or feel ourselves under threat, but at the outset we cannot always pin down exactly what threatens us. We find ourselves, say, on a dark road, and we think something seems to move in the shadows, and the feeling comes over us that something in the darkness might be a menace to our being. Immediately we are put on our guard, though sometimes when we investigate we discover that the feeling was a false alarm. But a false alarm is a real alarm. That I am alarmed about an "I know not what" tells us perhaps more about ourselves than the source of the seeming threat. There is an ontological porosity in our being but in that porosity the menacing crystallizes and takes form. This deep porosity of our being means we are ontologically exposed, and hence always open to the possibility of the hostile (as well as the hospitable).

We might claim, of course, that there is nothing in the world or being as other that is menacing. The menace springs from our exposed finitude, our vulnerable frailty. No doubt this is true in part, but if there is a menace of being it cannot reside simply in us. Something about the otherness generates in us foreboding about the menacing. If this were not so, a simple taking of oneself in hand would soon dispel our baseless fears. But this is too simple. The child wakes to the play of shadows on the wall and the night terrors of the menacing. The parents will shush and re-assure the child that there is nothing there and call back again the balm of sleep. There is nothing there, and yet the child wakes to menace. A foreboding: one cannot quite say what exactly it is about, but it arouses a disquiet in us we cannot put to sleep. Menace is more threatening than foreboding, but both exist along the spectrum of relative indeterminacy. There are direct threats of course, but there is something not direct about foreboding and the feeling of being under threat. A menace is not always a direct threat, and yet we can feel it directly in the body. We can be invaded by foreboding that the source of threat is itself in the body of the world. Somewhat related: the feeling of stain in our bodies may not be entirely separable from the feeling that the world itself is stained. There is a pollution of something pure, perhaps; though there can be experiences of stain and nothing but stain, pollution that does not seem to refer to a purity, either before pollution or beyond it. We are then coming closer to a purer exposure to being, felt as evil.

I think we can find the insinuation of that menace, for instance in Shakespeare's *Macbeth*. Lady Macbeth invokes the dark powers of night: "Come seeling night. Scarf up the tender eye of pitiful day." Is there a sense of secret menace that hovers over the way God and Satan seem *together to toy with Job*? One thinks also of menace as bound up with temptation, now seductive, now foreboding, which is not evil yet, and yet is no longer purely good, somewhere between innocence and the irrevocable misdeed. I wonder if obsession with the menace of being is bound up with the erotic seduction of the woman, suspected as a mixed-up, indeed promiscuous equivocity, which gives rise not to an appreciation of beauty but to an obsessive witch-hunt that would kill the curse. But the hunter carries the curse. I am put in mind of striking experiences like that of William James, who, when speaking of the sick soul, mentions "the *green skinned youth* of black hair" that reduced the observer to horror and "a mass of quivering fear."[11] There is a similar account in Nietzsche: "What I fear, is not the horrible shape behind my chair, but his voice: it is also not the words, but the dreadfully inarticulate and inhuman sound of that shape. Yes, if he only could speak as human beings speak!"[12]

The ontological threat is in the *suggestion* of a possible violence to come—actual violence is not necessary. The thought of violence is already enough to be a violence—a violation. Just as a hint of violence is sometimes enough to violate a person, so also intimidation does not have to be

11. James, *Religious Experience*, 160.

12. Nietzsche, *Werke in Drei Bänden*, 148: "Was ich fürchte, ist nichts die schreckliche Gestalt hinter meinem Stuhle, sondern ihre Stimme: auch nicht die Worte, sondern der schauderhaft unartikulierte und unmenschliche Ton jener Gestalt. Ja, wenn sie noch redete, wie Menschen rede!"

overt—the intimation of it is often enough. Our complicity with possible evil is awoken in it. One might see the connection with original sin and our fallenness: something is not right about our being, and perhaps also about being as it now is.

Figural Metalepsis, Double Reading, and Counterfeit Doubles

I want to connect these thoughts with the ontological orientation often marking a Gnostic sense of the evil of being. Out of a heightened sensitivity for the menace of being can crystallize, not only trepidation before an essentially equivocal creation, but also a *regime of counterfeit doubles* that proliferates throughout the whole of immanence. I see this as relevant to O'Regan's narrative-hermeneutical approach, as well as his ambition to be a figural Irenaeus. One of the expertises practiced by some Gnostics was producing "alternative readings" to what were to be deemed canonical scriptures by those differing from them. These readings are doubles of the readings more normally accepted by the historical Christian community, but they are often not straightforward counterfeits because something in the re-interpretation *reverses* the other reading. One might see something quasi-dialectical in this reverse doubling: by a different reading something is turned into the opposite of what it is initially taken to be. That sacred scriptures are marked by constitutive ambiguity allows the reader, against "normal," orthodox interpretations, to venture heterodox versions.

Here are some instances of what I mean. The story of the fall: the "normal" reading claims a fall *into* evil with eating the forbidden fruit; the Gnostic alternative is not just a re-doubling of this reading but a reversal claiming that with this eating of the fruit begins our release from sleep in equivocal creation. This "fall" is the beginning of the *real reversal* of a fall, even more original, when the divine *pneuma* was entrapped in matter. The *serpent* solicits humans to knowing as a spiritual awakening.[13] By contrast, "God" is the figure of envy—the hoarding demiurge who begrudges us the divine knowing rightfully ours. To accept the serpent's solicitation to release from the jealous "God" is to initiate the reversal towards the true state of things: divinization through self-knowing. Here too, in reverse, our pride is good: we stand up, over against the despotic "God." Hence the element of

---

13. See *Apocryphon of John* in Robinson, *Nag Hammadi*, 110ff., for a counter narrative of creation of Adam and Eve; also *The Hypostasis of the Archons* in Robinson, *Nag Hammadi*, 155, where, by contrast with the carnal woman, "the Female Spiritual principle came [in] the snake, the Instructor; and it taught [them] . . . ."

anti-Judaism in some forms of Gnosticism. Moses is not the great prophet but the one who enchains humankind with law. The law oppresses spirit; the divine spark is beyond the law.

I remark on how seduction, temptation, and menace are, somewhat paradoxically, in the same family of equivocal in-betweenness. Temptation and seduction are at the core of the story of the first fall, but there seems no menace in them. To be tempted thus is to play (delightfully?) with possibility, or to be played with; seduction is to be groomed slowly for (sweet?) surrender, not to be hurried to forced submission; to be menaced is not to be hit with the fist of the foe, but to be made liquid with nameless trepidation, building to terror. How relate menace then to temptation and seduction? One has to ask: why is the seducer attractive? Part of the answer is to grant that the "logic" of the counterfeit double is at work. Only consider how the seducer doubles what is attractive: there is a show of love without the spirit of love, a show that mimics love but does not love. Such a show redoubles the equivocity: it offers an image that mimics what is not there—love—by presenting it as being there, but all in order to conceal that what is most of all not there is precisely love. Such self-concealing equivocity, self-concealing in revealing itself, constitutes something of a showing in the modality of the counterfeit double. (I am put in mind of Heidegger's self-concealing origin: concealing even in revealing.)[14]

A second instance, again connected with my theme of the menace of being: the Gnostic reversal is an "alternative reading" of the Creator's "It is very good." To the contrary: it is not at all good; it is blighted.[15] The aesthetic exteriority of the material world has the tinge of evil. One might interject the question: how think finite being as an evil, how think of the creation as an evil whole? Not easy. An image that comes again to mind is the thick night in *Macbeth* when King Duncan, "God's anointed," is about to be murdered. The night is sticky with sinister threat. The dark space around is full with foreboding—closing in, closing us in. The thickening night is stifling,

---

14. See my *Art, Origins and Otherness*, chapter 7. See also Jonas, "Gnosticism, Existentialism, and Nihilism" in *The Phenomenon of Life*, 211–34.

15. "Awakening" might recall what I call the resurrection of agapeic astonishment, but Gnostic awakening is *turned away* from the good of creation, hence from the "It is good." The postlapsarian opening of the eyes of Adam and Eve is not quite what I mean by posthumous mind, since this "opening" is a partial blinding, an obscuration of our porosity to the divine, and calls for a saving knowing that is posthumous to this fall: posthumous mind, recreated life after the death of our fall into evil. Posthumous mind is called to agapeic love of the mortal and the singular. Void of this love, there are doubles of agapeic astonishment and posthumous mind that might be counterfeit. On the sleep of finitude and the sticky evil in *Macbeth*, see my *Sabbath for Thought?* chapter 1; also "Sticky Evil."

congealing into a kind of evil stickiness. It is as if one has to strike back, resist the encircling darkness. We are struck by dread that the equivocity of being itself is *threatening and under threat*. Threatening: ominous, foreboding, as if over things an abysmal darkness sat brooding. Threatened: the life in which we are tempted to take joy seems radically insecure, held out to us, snatched back from us, when we reach to it and give our hearts over. As the ambiguity of the sacred is intensified, so also is our sense of ontological insecurity, all the way to the last apocalyptic war of the adversarial powers. If one demurs and objects that such thoughts are products of fancy, one has only to recall the horrors of the twentieth century. Prisoners of the concentration camps, inmates of the Gulag, lived and died in the belly of the beast: it was not feigned. In a striking utterance (that might have been uttered by Schopenhauer, for instance), "This world is a corpse-eater."[16]

Consider this further reverse doubling in an "alternative reading" of *the Tower of Babel*. The tyrannical "God" views with alarm as human beings, with one language, grow in power, and scale the heavens. The "God" of the lower world, threatened, sows confusion. This world is not abundant with generous gifts and good things; it is a mean economy of antagonistic lack and possession, deprivation and repossession. When "God" waxes, man wanes; when "God" wanes, man waxes. What humankind takes is taken away from "God"; there is no surplus of generous giving or allowance. The Tower of Babel read thus is like a repeat double of the fall. Divine envy is repeated in the second sowing of discord after Babel. The self-elevating power of humankind is divine, but it is cast into confusion, to perpetuate the dominion of the jealous "God" over the realm of the counterfeit doubles.

I mention here how the theme of *parodia sacra* is of relevance to O'Regan's figural metalepsis, as it is of relevance to the significance of the counterfeit double. I draw attention to how in the alternative scriptures one can find certain *sacred mimicries* between what is "below" and what is "above." The fallen Sophia mimics the higher. The divine Sophia herself mimics the Forefather, seeking to bring to be through herself alone. The false creation, the abortion, plagiarizes divine emanation. Counterfeit doubling begins to proliferate. The demiurge counterfeits the Forefather. Material making counterfeits spiritual emanation. Hylic creation parrots pneumatic. The lower Adam apes the primal Adam. A counterfeit Adam and Eve mime the true Adam and Eve, the archetypal Male-Female. The fullness of lack—the fallen creation—counterfeits the fullness without lack—the pleroma.

16. *The Gospel of Philip*, in Robinson, *Nag Hammadi*, 144: "This world is a corpse-eater. All the things eaten in it themselves die also. Truth is a life-eater. Therefore no one nourished by [truth] will die. It was from that place that Jesus came and brought food. To those who so desired, he gave [life, that] they might not die."

The father of lies mimics the serpent of wisdom. Bishops and deacons—said to be "dry canals"[17]—impersonate the initiated *gnostikoi*. The orthodox are forgeries of the true, though they brand the true as the heretic. It is as if the false visible church substitutes itself, like a cuckoo's egg, for the true invisible church of spirit.[18] From the other side, Irenaeus acutely warns his congregation that cut-glass and emeralds are deceptively similar.

There is sacred mimicry also in how the agonistics of the divine within itself are mimed in the antagonistics of the human and the divine. The aesthetic cosmos is a counterfeit double of the noetic cosmos, brought to be by this upstart "God." If God's in his heaven, all's unwell with the world. There is the One God, the true original, Godhead beyond god; then there is the God who claims to be the one God, the only God, the counterfeit double. The counterfeit double is proximately the source of the given aesthetic cosmos. This second "God" is not good, and his creation is essentially, divinely tainted with evil. It is as if everything appears in a mirror that reverses left and right, above and below, good and evil. It is as if Descartes's evil genius were the "God" of the world below, where now fair is foul and foul is fair. This counterfeit double, this demiurge, "Yaldabaoth," is a derivative "God" emerging with the primal fall.[19] Ignorant of the higher God and forgetful of Sophia, the female principle, thinking there is none but he and none above him, he is himself bewitched by the equivocal snare of counterfeit doubling as such. He is sometimes associated with the God of the Old Testament, but there the Creator celebrates the creation on giving it to be, seeing that "It is good, very good." If fair is foul and foul is fair, this "It is good" cannot be taken at face value here. There is no face value, for every face is a mask that might be the opposite to what it shows itself. From such a perspective, this

---

17. Apocalypse of Peter, in Robinson, *Nag Hammadi*, 343.

18. See *The Second Treatise of the Great Seth*, in Robinson, *Nag Hammadi*, 335 on Adam as a "laughingstock" and "counterfeit type of man," on Abraham and Isaac as "counterfeit fathers," Solomon and Moses as "laughing stocks," the twelve prophets as "imitations" and "counterfeits." One thinks: with the false God goes the false prophet, the false Messiah, the false church, the anti-Christ (see *Sabbath for Thought?* chapters 4 and 6, also 183 ff.). *The Gospel of Judas*: Christ and Judas as twins, intimate doubles. The Bogomil belief: The Devil was the eldest son of God: God had two (twin) sons, the devil the oldest, Jesus Christ the younger—see Stoyanov, *Other God*, 158. When in his *History of Philosophy* Hegel comments on Jacob Boehme, he seems to endorse Lucifer as the firstborn of light—Lucifer "falls"—the necessary moment of being-for-self—to be replaced by Christ. There is a paragraph to that effect also in his *Phänomenologie des Geistes*, 538; *Phenomenology of Spirit* par. 776. O'Regan is very sensitive to what these passages betray about Hegel, what Hegel himself betrays. See his superb account of the transition from religion to absolute knowing, O'Regan, "Impossibility of a Christian Reading."

19. Yaldabaoth, *Apocryphon of John* in Robinson, *Nag Hammadi*, 104.

divine affirmation becomes a counterfeit "Amen." The face of affirmation is itself a duplicitous mask. The "It is good" is a ruse of the counterfeit "God" of creation intended to tempt and entrap us.

Equivocal Creation: A World of Duplicity

To recall O'Regan's themes of Gnostic return and apocalypse, under such a dominion of the counterfeit doubles, we seem to be in a prison, and this pris- on seems far worse than Plato's cave. We are not *in* prison, we ourselves *are* prison, and we are in the prison of ourselves. The divine spark is prevented from escape, but we do not know it, bewitched as we are by the enchantment of the counterfeit doubles. How do we wake from such a bewitchment? Can we awaken ourselves? If we are in an enchanted slumber and under the *spell of ourselves*, must the delivery come from *beyond* ourselves? Compare this with the overall rational confidence of Neoplatonism and Plotinus, on the one hand, and with the affirmation of the goodness of creation of biblical theism. Gnostic orientations are overshadowed by the equivocity of evil. A baleful light is felt to fall on being, a light darkening rather than enlighten- ing, for it generates counterfeit doubles of the divine that entrap the true light. The menace of being communicates the fundamental equivocity of immanent being, haunting the human condition, touching us in the flesh itself. It is impossible to say in a univocally clear way that being as given is good. Rather, it seems unequivocal—paradoxically so since creation seems to be essentially equivocal—that being is *not* good. Equivocal being, like dark matter, seems to spread a malign spell that paralyzes our transcending powers. We are in a prison with *no outside* and any outcry for freedom on the other side seems like a pointless appeal.

In such a regime of the counterfeit double, immanent discord reveals itself as a kind of radical opposition nested in all union.[20] The creation shows itself as "in the way" and we must do away with what is in the way to find the way. The given world is an intermedium of adversity; it might *appear* as beautiful, but attractive guile can be more hostile in its hidden effect than overt aggression is. The beauty of the world calls to us achingly, tempting us, winning us, making us tarry with the gloriously mortal. But the mortal things come to be as destined not to be. They are sweet nothings. There is reversal in this. Beauty itself must be taken in the opposite sense to our immediate attraction to it: it shows itself as the swindle that ensnares. If we apply this to the woman, her beauty becomes the seduction of menace that blinds us to the menace. In a more total sense, creation as seeming to

20. For example, *The Gospel of Philip* in Robinson, *Nag Hammadi*, 132–33.

communicate the beauty of the finite whole must be treated as a danger. It is the intermedium of adversity that shows itself now as the intermedium of the adversary.[21] In return, we must be hostile to this intermedium, because its beauty hides hostility itself. We must hate ourselves as of the world, for it is our being its creatures that is repellent. I would say that our being a creature is to be between, often *torn* between evil and good. But here when we love the beauty of the world, we are betrayed by our love. Being created at all is the first guilt, the guilt that hides itself in everything else seductively second. In anguish, we are forced to ask: Is that all there is? Life as a swindle that grooms us only for death?

These seem like extreme positions, and they are, but they are persistent in human existence. I think in recent centuries of Schopenhauer's agreement with the Silenus, companion of Dionysus, who tells Midas, "Best not to be at all." I think of how the meaning of eros is said to be the death drive. I think of the democratization in our time of the feeling of the absurdity of existence, once confined to the cultured few, now extended to the consuming many. The absurdity and the menace are cousins in the same family of darkness. This is not to deny that the perplexing equivocity persists. If the given creation intimates itself as (a counterfeit) double—as both hospitable and hostile—we can respond with a "yes" or a "no": "yes," if we find the hospitality sufficiently welcoming; "no," if the hostility proves too sharp. In practice there is always more of mixture, with much of "perhaps." We do find that if we open ourselves, we protect ourselves; if we surrender ourselves, we take care to secure ourselves; if we give ourselves, we also grab for ourselves. Equivocal creation can foster a mentality of dualism, which seeks unity in a hyperbolic One, beyond equivocal creation. The absolute Forefather (*protē Pater*) of the Gnostics answers to this hyperbolic One. The saving search for this One can fix its terms in a variety of dualisms (perhaps inherited philosophically from Platonic sources, religiously from Iranian sources). This can contribute to a redoubling of immanent creation as a domain of counterfeit doubles: not univocally hostile but equivocally; hostile but as hospitable—again like the welcome of a seducer who leads us to woe through perilous pleasure. ("Samael," "venom of God," "accuser," "angel of

---

21. See *The Gospel of Philip* in Robinson, *Nag Hammadi*, 140: "Either he will be in this world or in the resurrection or in the places in the middle. God forbid that I be found in them! In this world there is good and evil. Its good is not good, and its evil not evil. But there is evil after this world which is truly evil—what is called 'the Middle.' It is death. While we are in this world, it is fitting for us to acquire the resurrection for ourselves, so that when we strip off the flesh, we may be found in rest and not walk in the Middle. For many go astray on the way. For it is good to come forth from the world before one has sinned."

death," can also be translated as "seducer.")[22] How are we to "see through" the seducer? It would seem we need a knowing of finesse rather than of geometry or system. We need to be awakened to the difference between the true divinity and the counterfeit double. The theme of the idol here presents itself. But which is the true original God and which is the counterfeit double? Gnosis itself, as a knowing, is said to be this awakening to the true God, beyond all counterfeit doubles: awakening to the divinity imprisoned in ourselves, our flesh, gnosis inaugurates our passage through and beyond the counterfeits. In this Gnostic orientation to being, equivocal creation is itself the seductive but misleading double of the true God. Awakening, as it were, reverses the locus of the counterfeiting: it is not the "above" world that counterfeits but the "below" world of the fallen.

It is worth remarking that the regime of counterfeit doubles takes somewhat opposite shapes in ancient Gnosticism and more modern forms. There is a dialectical reversal from transcendence to immanence, a reversal speculatively developed by thinkers like Hegel. This is something that deeply engages O'Regan.[23] Notice, too, the reversal of the post-Hegelian thought, which reduces theology to anthropology: the "above" world falsifies the "below" world; if there is no "above" world, then there is no "below" world, and supposedly we are released, say, to history as class war, or to the innocence of becoming. Nevertheless, there is no escape from equivocal becoming, and no escape into innocence either. In a kind of Gnosticism, the human being is the Primal Being: a reversed Gnosticism, since Primal Adam is more ultimate than any Primal Father or Fore-father. In ancient Gnosticism the absolute One is utterly beyond the counterfeit creation, for this world here and now is the domain of the mimicry of spirit, hence the need of a world-denying flight. In more modern forms, it seems all but the opposite, in that the absolute One as utterly transcendent must be re-doubled in *absolute immanence*, which is now the pleroma to be realized through the self-becoming of the absolute One (Hegel again). The flight to hyperbolic transcendence as world-denying in the ancient form is mirrored and reversed in the flight from transcendence to utter immanence in the modern form.

Of course, the Gnostic view has much in common with other religious views. In many, if not most, religious traditions, the inner way is seen as more suitable to the soul's journey to God than is nature's exteriority. Everything

22. In the *Apocryphon of John*, in Robinson, *Nag Hammadi*, 104, Samael is the third name for the demiurge. His other names are Yaldaboath and Saklas. Samael also has the meaning of the "blind god."

23. We find this concern in O'Regan's *The Heterodox Hegel*, as well as his recent book, *Anatomy of Misremembering*.

turns on the interpretation of the self-recovery and the precise relation of the inner to the divine itself. The way out is a way in and a way upwards. The important point here is that the return to the divine in self is the return of the divine to itself. In the end, this is not the self gathered together with the divine, not even the self gathered into the divine, but the *self-gathering of the divine in itself.* Ancient Gnosticism looks to this as absolutely beyond and other, but in the modern Gnosticism of someone like Hegel, this self-gathering of God into Godself is the absolute whole of wholes and the end of time in immanence.

In the modern form, the "inward way" becomes utterly immanent: history becomes the dialectical process of realizing the divine spark initially implicit in, sleeping in, the process of equivocal becoming. The ancient form reflects, so to say, an ascetic "Platonic" response to the suspicion of the given world as a counterfeit double. The modern form expresses a non-ascetic "Hegelian" response to the counterfeit double of an alien transcendence. One is a version of "Christian" gnosis as world-denying, the other a version of "Christian" gnosis as world-affirming. But the terms in both are more or less set by dualism and dialectic, with the equivocal double as a fall from, or immanent self-alienation of, the absolute One. One has to wonder how all of this relates to the menace of being, the goodness of given being, and if there is agapeic creation in either form. The God beyond creation of Gnosticism seems like a dualistic version of the God of the whole of immanent pan(en)theism, which can take more overt dialectical form.[24]

We see here the sense of ontological menace extended to the worry that we risk being hemmed in by a dubious, even evil whole. Secretly, and sometimes not secretly, our response reveals a desperate need to be saved from the seeming dissembling of given creation. There is a deep doubleness marking the human being as metaxological, but Gnosticism both reflects and deflects this in a certain direction, impelled by the menace of ontological ambiguity, inflected painfully in our encounter with the equivocity of evil. We embody the struggle of powers; we participate in the struggle of powers; we sometimes seem to be instruments of the powers. In this we can also become the rivals of God. One could say that the pride of the dubious "God," the demiurge, can be redoubled in the wrath of the domineering human being who, in turning against the menace of being, initiates a movement of terror against being. One doubles down in one's rejection of given being. Doubling back out of being becomes a redoubling war on the evil of

---

24. The theme of the double can be linked with a more dialectical holism: it can lead to a God of the whole: dialectic beyond equivocity. Thus the Gnostic traces in Hegel—though transformed by speculative dialectic. Desmond, *God and the Between,* chapter 11 turns to the God *of* the whole, chapter 12 to the God *beyond* the whole.

being—there is no acceptance of any good as given. This redoubling can take the form of return to the origin that is hard to separate from an exit into the future. Return to the origin merges with apocalypse as turn to the future. This can span the spectrum: the modern apocalypse of radical Islam which would destroy the false creation, or that of revolutionary politics that would usher in the kingdom of perfected humanity on earth. For both revolutionary terror of left and right, atheist and Islamic, the good will be there at the end. Otherworldly terrorizing and this-worldly terrorizing are at one in their hatred of the evil of given being. Could we say that the modern inflection of apocalypse turns the will to life of *eros* into the death drive? The menace of being calls forth the will to destroy the menace rather than simply to escape it. There is nothing good about it; exterminate it in a final solution. The unmenaced middling self-satisfaction of the last men is asleep to the more extreme menace, which these last men thus help along, by allowing its undisturbed incubation.

The terrorizing of given being is not antithetical to a kind of aristocracy of knowing that goes with Gnosticism, whether ancient or modern. Those enlightened have seen into the heart of things and are elevated to a more ultimate status by means of this gnosis. This elevation can be a recoil from the messiness of the many-too-many, a secret irritability at the mess itself, an antipathy to the otherness of the world as one mess of a place. The Gnostic Christ is not the God-man but a duplex being: divine Christ, human Jesus, for suffering is not allowed to touch "God," nor is flesh. One wonders if the following, with different combinations of factors, point to a family resemblance to Gnosticism. One thinks of the modern formation of *atheistic politics*: here we have witnessed an inner circle of dominant revolutionaries who claim to be the ones "in the know" about the inner dialectic of historical development, and who act accordingly from this purportedly higher more ultimate standpoint.[25] One thinks of those who are more *scientistically minded*: they can be convinced that their scientific precedence over those not "in the know" licenses them with superior cognition vis-à-vis all areas of life. One thinks of the *revolutionary terrorist*: before the revolution, he must operate in secret in enemy territory, the land of the foe, but he must look normal; in a dangerous land, he must counterfeit the foe to defeat him. The menace of being puts one in mind of being a spy in alien territory: one must lead a *double* life; be what one is not; not be what one is—a double

---

25. On Gnosticism and politics, see Voegelin, *Science, Politics and Gnosticism.* Voegelin's phrase "the immanentization of the eschaton" seemed to have even the cachet of academic chic at the time of its formulation—conservative chic, if that is not an oxymoron.

agent, a traitor who is faithful.[26] After the revolution, the mask is off, and it is not now the desire for justice that is to the forefront but the thirst for revenge against the enemy, all now elevated less by superior knowing as unbridled will to power.

By contrast, the saving knowing of gnosis seems like a kind of catharsis of the toxins of equivocal creation, a purge of spirit that is beyond the temptation of counterfeit doubles in the finite world itself (vide Catharism). In the ideal it would seem to offer a purity no longer touched by mortal trash. But is such an untouched untouchability secure against its own dialectical reversal? One could venture that the posture is tempted to turn that which is other to the pure self into the impure other, on whom, in turn, pure power can be unleashed. One worries that this divine humanity metamorphoses into a demonic humanism when the flesh of creation ceases to touch it. The sweet will to power ferrets out wily ways to serve itself, even as it avers it serves its "God," or even claims to be a god itself. This can occur in *any* religious orientation. It has occurred in the atheistic political projects of modernity. Instead of the birth of the man-god who perfects all things, our outsoaring will to power has been colonized by the monstrous.

One worries too about a *further* doubling of reversal, just in our claim to have achieved spiritual sovereignty. If the first reversal is from being a slave of the lower to being master of the higher, this second reversal would reflect a claim to a *higher sovereignty* that is really a fall into spiritual evil, not now "below" but on the heights. What is at issue is the spiritual pride that claims itself to be divine.[27] Does release from the counterfeit double of God "below" create its own counterfeit double of God "above"? A "higher" counterfeit double, that is a more evil counterfeit double, just in the claim to be beyond all counterfeit doubles, and all evil? If so, then escaping evil's equivocity is so fraught with ambiguity that the escape from evil seems just another evil. Beyond good and evil, we do not meet Nietzsche's "innocence of becoming," but an outlaw evil masquerading as the higher good. Gnostic awakening claims to release the light in us, but here in a kind of reversed Gnosticism, what is released is not the light but the darkness. And it is not the darkness of God. This rejoinder to the menace of being menaces given being with non-being. Its outlaw saving saves nothing in being as given. It "works" to undo the work of creation, though always in the name of

26. One thinks of the occultation of secret traditions. Consider too the *The Gospel of Judas*: Judas is the double agent; he is the "betrayer" who is the truer "insider," whose "treachery" intimately furthers the higher work of salvation; this again epitomizes reversal in the reading of the role of Judas in the redemptive sacrifice of Christ.

27. One recalls Solovyov's "Tale of the Anti-Christ"; on this see my *Sabbath for Thought?* chapter 5.

completing that creation by "making a difference." Its doing is an undo-ing. Its response to the menace is to uncreate being. It has created itself by uncreation and metamorphosed into the devastating menace of non-being.

In light of the menace of being, one need not deny that an ambiguous truth glimmers in Gnosticism, in its equivocal response to our equivocal condition between good and evil. Its search for a transforming knowing is both a mediation and attempted transcendence of that equivocity. It responds to dimensions of our middle condition we cannot deny. Does it embody the spiritual finesse to glean the traces of the divine in the equivoc-ity of the between—as itself the chiaroscuro of the good—rather than the impenetrable night of a counterfeit creation? Gnosis seems to want release from the between, not the "yes" to it that affirms in its finite goodness the gift of the divine. Is there any hope for a saving knowing in the equivocal matrix of finite creation? I think there is a metaxological mindfulness and way of being that is not a betrayal of the equivocal dimension of things. But it is not also duped into untrue denigration of the genuine worth of finite things. We must make true peace with the milieu of being in which the mixture of things grows, and not impatiently, prematurely, and violently claim to separate the wheat from the tares. Metaxological mindfulness does not usurp the prerogative of the final judgment. The equivocal intermedium of things must be allowed in its mixture, in a patience that for us borders on the divine. When this patience is exposed to the menace of being it does not set out to conquer evil with counter-evil.

Bibliography

Desmond, William. *Art, Origins and Otherness: Between Art and Philosophy*. Albany, NY: SUNY Press, 2001.

———. *God and the Between*. Oxford: Blackwell, 2008.

———. *Hegel's God: A Counterfeit Double?* London: Routledge, 2003.

———. *Is There a Sabbath for Thought? Between Religion and Philosophy*. Bronx, NY: Fordham University Press, 2005.

———. "Sticky Evil: On *Macbeth* and the Karma of the Equivocal." In *God, Literature and Process Thought*, edited by Darren Middleton, 133–55. Aldershot, UK: Ashgate, 2002.

Hegel, G. W. F. *Phänomenologie des Geistes*. Edited by J. Hoffmeister. Hamburg: Meiner, 1952.

———. *Phenomenology of Spirit*. Translated by A. V. Miller. Oxford: Clarendon, 1977.

James, William. *The Varieties of Religious Experience*. New York: Penguin, 1985.

Jonas, Hans. *The Gnostic Religion: The Message of the Alien God and the Beginnings of Christianity*. 2nd, rev. ed. Boston: Beacon, 1963.

————. *The Phenomenon of Life: Toward a Philosophical Biology.* Studies in Phenomenology and Existential Philosophy. Evanston, IL: Northwestern University Press, 2000.

Merkur, Dan. *Gnosis: An Esoteric Tradition of Mystical Visions and Unions.* Albany, NY: SUNY Press, 1993.

Nietzsche, Friedrich. *Werke in Drei Bänden.* Edited by Karl Schlecta. München: Hanser, 1956.

O'Regan, Cyril. *Anatomy of Misremembering: Von Balthasar's Response to Philosophical Modernity. Volume 1: Hegel.* Chestnut Ridge, NY: Crossroad, 2014.

————. *Gnostic Apocalypse: Jacob Boehme's Haunted Narrative.* Albany, NY: SUNY Press, 2002.

————. *The Gnostic Return in Modernity.* Albany, NY: SUNY Press, 2001.

————. *The Heterodox Hegel.* Albany, NY: SUNY Press, 1994.

————. "The Impossibility of a Christian Reading of the *Phenomenology of Spirit*: H. S. Harris on Hegel's Liquidation of Christianity." *The Owl of Minerva* 33.1 (2001–2) 45–95.

————. *Theology and the Spaces of Apocalyptic.* Milwaukee, WI: Marquette University Press, 2009.

Robinson, James M., ed. *The Nag Hammadi Library in English.* San Francisco: Harper and Row, 1978.

Stoyanov, Yuri. *The Other God: Dualist Religions from Antiquity to the Cathar Heresy.* New Haven: Yale University Press, 2000.

Voegelin, Eric. *Science, Politics and Gnosticism.* Chicago: Regnery, 1968.

Williams, Michael Allen. *Rethinking "Gnosticism": An Argument for Dismantling A Dubious Category.* Princeton: Princeton University Press, 1996.

2

Re-membering *Geist*

From Hauntology to Pneumatology†

AARON RICHES AND SEBASTIÁN MONTIEL

ἅ ἐστιν σκιὰ τῶν μελλόντων, τὸ δὲ σῶμα τοῦ Χριστοῦ.
—Colossians 2:17

Thus while he spake, each passion dimmed his face,
Thrice changed with pale—ire, envy, and despair;
Which marred his borrowed visage, and betrayed
Him counterfeit, if any eye beheld.

—John Milton, *Paradise Lost*

The carnal action of *Hamlet* springs from the provocation of a spectral
return, not to life but to memory: "Hamlet. Remember me" (I.v.91).
The encounter of young Hamlet with this Ghost precipitates in the son a
mode of memorialization that, in the context of his life, sets the stage of an
apocalyptic catastrophe in which he is assigned a messianic role:

Rest, rest, perturbèd spirit . . .

. . .

The time is out of joint. O cursèd spite,

That ever I was born to set it right.[1]

The spectral return of the father in a shadowy likeness (a "σκιά") to his carnal body (his "σῶμα") sets the word "out of joint" and opens a field of historical and ontological disjunction. This drama sets the stage for Jacques Derrida's idea of *hauntologie*.[2]

Offered in his *Specters of Marx*, the heart of the Derridean idea of *hauntologie* problematizes a series of liminal experiences of memory and memorialization—the fearful indeterminacy of the relation of sonship with the paternal "origin," the unstable boundary between identity and memory, the porosity of dying and living, the agony of delineating presence and absence. The idea is constitutive and masterfully deployed by Cyril O'Regan in his monumental offering, *Balthasar and the Specter of Hegel*[3]—or *The Anatomy of Misremembering: Von Balthasar's Response to Philosophical Modernity*, volume 1, *Hegel*.[4]

I. Derridean Hauntology and Hegelian Hauntotheology

In *Balthasar and the Specter of Hegel*, O'Regan reconfigures the theological study of Hegel, responding with a definite *Nein!* to the still lingering question as to whether Hegel's philosophy is in fact "Christian"—or, if not, can perhaps be made to serve Christian orthodoxy. The program rests in part on an invocation of a book by the French Communist and structuralist Louis Althusser. *The Spectre of Hegel*[5] is the English edition of the first half of Althusser's *Écrits philosophiques et politiques*, a selection of the "early" Althusser. The key theme of the collection is the haunting presence of Hegel, in a double sense.

In "Man is the night" (1947),[6] Althusser clarifies the dual manner of the Hegelian haunting. In the first place, Hegel himself is haunted, he is a

---

†. An earlier version of the essay appeared as "On Re-membering *Geist*: Hegelian Hauntotheology and O'Regan's Anatomy of Misremembering." *Modern Theology* 32 (2016) 268–78.

1. Shakespeare, *Hamlet*, I.v.190, 196–97. All quotations from Shakespeare's *Hamlet* are taken from Hibbard, *Oxford Shakespeare*.

2. Derrida, *Specters of Marx*, 1–60.

3. "Balthasar and the Specter of Hegel" is the original and more telling subtitle of volume 1 of *The Anatomy of Misremembering*. It is the subtitle intended by O'Regan, which appeared in some online advertisements, but was finally replaced before publication with the simpler but less precise "Hegel."

4. O'Regan, *Misremembering*.

5. Althusser, *Spectre of Hegel*.

6. Althusser, *Spectre of Hegel*, 173–76.

thinker "dismantled, torn to pieces, trampled underfoot, and betrayed," he is a prince Hamlet, whose legacy yet "profoundly haunts and dominates an apostate age."[7] The "profoundest themes of the Romantic nocturne haunt" Hegel's thought,[8] he is torn apart by the void of the human nothingness and the ideal of being, that is, of spectral realization. This, for Althusser, is the basic dynamic at the heart of Hegel: carnal being ("σῶμα") is nothing, but the spectral is a shadowy thing (a "σκιά") waiting to be realized. If this is the dynamic heart of Hegel, it is also his allure, his haunting power. Dismantled and betrayed, because of this, Hegel haunts and dominates not only the apostate age of Althusser, but the thought of Althusser's great master, Karl Marx.

In his master's thesis, "On Content in the Thought of G. W. Hegel" (1947),[9] Althusser makes a comment that foreshadows the trajectory of his mature Marxist project. Hegel, Althusser argues, understood the contradiction, the tearing apart, of the essence of philosophy, the seeming impossibility of thinking the alienation of thought without oneself "becoming the prisoner of the essence of one's own thinking."[10] And herein lies the trouble of Marx. According to Althusser, as a philosopher, Marx too was the prisoner of an apostate age and so of Hegel. Hegel haunts Marx to such an extent that Marx is imprisoned by the injunction of the dead master. And in a telling comment, Althusser writes, "Marx succumbed to the necessity of the error he wished to retrace in Hegel, in that Hegel had exposed this necessity in the philosopher, while overcoming it in himself so as to engender the Sage. Marx's error lay in being a sage."[11] Herein lies Althusser's impossible later program: to exorcise Marx of the specter of Hegel. That is, to recover the carnal and material intuition of the Marxist body of thought in order to purge it of this spectral overdetermination of Hegel's ghostly presence. By a different mode, and in a different way, what O'Regan offers in *Balthasar and the Specter of Hegel* is diagnostic of how Balthasar, for modern theology, is the sage Althusser recognized Marx could not be. In any case, the Balthasar we receive from O'Regan is no less determined than Althusser: to resist the spectral presence of Hegel is the task of the sage of modern theology. The genius of Balthasar is to have realized that to do so one must perform, not a mere exorcism, but an anatomy of misremembering.

---

7. Althusser, *Spectre of Hegel*, 174.
8. Althusser, *Spectre of Hegel*, 172.
9. Althusser, *Spectre of Hegel*, 17–172.
10. Althusser, *Spectre of Hegel*, 132.
11. Althusser, *Spectre of Hegel*, 132.

For O'Regan's Balthasar, Hegel represents "a constitutive act of mis-remembering of the Christian tradition and what grounds it."[12] To this end, the sage of modern theology must perform an "anatomy of misremember-ing" coupled with a great symphonic rehearsal of the Christian tradition, more colossal and more robust than Hegel's. That a constitutive resistance to Hegel should be understood as "complimentary of Balthasar's . . . defense of the validity of the Christian tradition as a milieu of compelling memory" is neither obvious nor can it be "simply read off of Balthasar's text."[13] O'Regan is accordingly commissioned with the task of "excavating" the evidence for this claim, which he carefully, patiently, and decisively executes over the course of this massive tome. O'Regan shows that Balthasar is as much ap-prehensive of Hegelian thought as he is engaged by it. But more fundamen-tally, O'Regan shows that, if Hegelian thought is a primary contributor to the overdetermination of Enlightenment forgetfulness, the misremember-ing that accompanies such an overdetermination poses a more dangerous threat, "since it more surreptitiously liquefies and ultimately liquidates Christianity, while seeming to enact a kind of memory that is difficult to distinguish from the memory that constitutes Christianity."[14] Indeed, ac-cording to O'Regan, "from Balthasar's point of view Hegelian memory (*Er-innerung*) constitutes the most blatant form of the misfiring of memory or misremembering in the post-Enlightenment era."[15] Thus incited, Balthasar confronts and diagnoses this "colossal act of misremembering that puts us out of touch with the intellectual, moral, and practical gifts of the tradition, and the gift of creation, redemption, and sanctification, which renders the triune reality of God, on which they depend."[16]

O'Regan's analysis of Hegel thus concerns the problematic "half-life" by which Hegel "refuses to be totally impertinent."[17] This is to argue that Balthasar's resistance to Hegel is a work in the field of *hauntologie*, and so internally bound up with something of the wrestling of Althusser and Der-rida: Balthasar's hauntology speaks not only to Hegel's haunting of contem-porary discourse, but also to his discourse itself being haunted. It is haunted because in its post-Enlightenment discursive mansion it houses the ghosts of Christianity's premodern others, among whom one finds apocalyptic, Neoplatonism, and Gnosticism. And when it becomes an issue as to how

12. Althusser, *Spectre of Hegel*, 46.
13. Althusser, *Spectre of Hegel*, 17.
14. Althusser, *Spectre of Hegel*, 33.
15. Althusser, *Spectre of Hegel*, 521.
16. Althusser, *Spectre of Hegel*, 33.
17. Althusser, *Spectre of Hegel*, 46.

hostile the ghosts are to Christianity, attention falls on Gnosticism as the ghost that is truly a *Doppelgänger*, and equally on the responsibility of the theologian to detect and to refute it.[18]

In this way *Balthasar and the Specter of Hegel* develops one of O'Regan's earlier works, *Gnostic Return in Modernity*,[19] but now with a new attention to how, like the Ghost of Hamlet, the specter of Gnostic return through Hegel necessitates theological resistance, and what form that resistance must take.

Hegel's thought itself is born of resistance to Enlightenment forgetfulness. Here O'Regan quotes the *Phenomenology*: "When the Enlightenment becomes dominant, 'memory alone . . . preserves the dead from the Spirit's previous shape as a vanished history.'"[20] Hegel indeed offers "an illuminating diagnosis of the Enlightenment as constituted by a particularly aggressive form of amnesia."[21] Against the forgetfulness of Enlightenment, Hegel judged that the inheritance of the Christian memory cannot, in fact, be simply forgotten (history always haunts the present), but even if it could be forgotten, it should not be. The question, then, concerns *how* the haunting presence should be remembered. Thus Hegel's critical diagnosis of the Enlightenment was coupled with an alternate thought: "a singularly powerful system of 'recollection' (*Erinnerung*) in which much that is dismissed by the Enlightenment [i.e., Christian *dogmata*] is retrieved as worthwhile and is rationally justified."[22] But this retrieval is not performed in the name of fidelity to mainline Christianity, but rather in the service of constituting "Hegel's narrative ontotheology of Spirit (*Geist*),"[23] a heterodox re-imagining of Christian theology, reminiscent of various forms of peripheral Christianity: Valentinian, Joachimite, Neoplatonic, apocalyptic, German mysticism, etc.[24] Here Christian ideas are "recollected," in spectral fashion, in exchange for the sublation of the real and carnal body, the "σῶμα" of historical, sacramental, and ecclesial Christianity.

The aim of Hegel's project thus was to liberate the spiritual essence of Christian doctrine from its material incarnation, to unshackle the spectral idea from the carnal fact, in order to re-member it for a new and shadowy end. The insights of Christian doctrine, dissociated from their antique and

18. Althusser, *Spectre of Hegel*, 47.

19. O'Regan, *Gnostic Return*.

20. O'Regan, *Misremembering*, 10; citing *Phenomenology* # 546.

21. O'Regan, *Misremembering*, 14.

22. O'Regan, *Misremembering*, 14.

23. O'Regan, *Misremembering*, 217.

24. Cf. O'Regan, *Heterodox Hegel*, passim.

naïve form (i.e., from the bodies of history, sacrament, and *ecclesia*), were restored to thought in purely spectral form. Christ, the Trinity, the Spirit, the end of history, all re-appear in Hegel, but with a merely syntactic correspondence to the grammar and carnal significance of traditional theology. Nothing short of a radical reallocation takes place, insofar as the history of *this* first-century Palestinian Jew is dissociated from Hegel's new "Christology," just as the Blessed Sacrament is de-coupled from the epiclesis of Hegel's *Geist* and the *totus Christus* is divorced from his new idea of the "end of history." The specter of a laboriously disincarnated Christianity, summoned against the forgetfulness of the Enlightenment, entailed therefore a colossal re-imagining of Christian thought, life, and practice in terms basically in accord with its opposite.

Hegel's performance clarifies that to his mind the only way to rescue Christian thought from the *damnatio memoriae* imposed upon it by the Enlightenment is to refuse the "real presence." There cannot be in history either a visible or comestible divine body. Above all, Christology must be reallocated. If Hegel writes of "Christ," he writes not at all of his sacramental body, of the historical man "Jesus of Nazareth," and much less of the *corpus verum*, the church. Accordingly, this reallocation of Christology radicalizes the mediaeval inversion between the Christological poles, *corpus verum* and *corpus mysticum*.[25] Whereas the traditional ascription of *corpus verum* to the church and *corpus mysticum* to the Eucharist was inverted in the Middle Ages, with the effect of making the church less concrete and more spectral, Hegel's reallocation achieves a new sublimation of every concrete reference to a divine bodily presence of Christ (ecclesial, historic, or Eucharistic).

Reallocations within Christology are bound in Hegel to wider reconfigurations of Trinitarian thought that undermine the traditional Christocentric heart of Christianity in favor of what O'Regan calls "pneumatic displacement."[26] The three divine persons, the concrete determinacies of the Christian God, are blended by Hegel into an impersonal and imperial ghost: the totalizing *Geist* that encompasses and swallows paternity and filiation in the final process. As Hegel puts it:

> God is spirit: no darkness, no coloring or mixture enters into this pure light. The relationship of father and son is drawn from organic life and is used in representational fashion. . . . We say that God eternally begets his Son . . . but at the same time we must know very well that God is himself this entire activity. God is the beginning, he acts in this way; but he is likewise simply the

25. Cf. de Lubac, *Corpus Mysticum*, 13–19 and 34–39.

26. O'Regan, *Misremembering*, 195 and 523.

end, the totality, and it is as totality that God is the Spirit. Merely
as Father, God is not yet the truth.[27]

Whereas for mainline Christianity the Spirit sent is the "guarantor"
of the ultimacy of the promise of the Incarnate Son,[28] the "comforter"
(παράκλητος) who binds the Christian *communio* to the Lord,[29] the *vin-
culum amoris* who eternally binds the Son to the Father, for Hegel the procession and subsequent effusion of the divine Spirit is subsumed into the
dialectic evolution of a "holy ghost" that, as much as it is essentially Germanic, should be invoked as *der wahre Geist*. In this regard a critical com-
ponent of Hegel's colossal act of misremembering is prepared by Joachim de
Fiore, who in the twelfth century had already elided the ultimacy of Christ
with his theology of the third age of the Spirit.[30]

Likewise, the "spirit" of Hegelian thought implies a new overdetermination of the old Christological inversion of *corpus verum* and *corpus
mysticum*, now in favor of pure *Geist* and an imperial "end of history." In
this way, Hegelian thought concedes to *Hamlet* that the carnal genealogy
of paternal-filial transference must yield to an ultimate (but unverifiable)
spiritual reminder. In other words, genealogy must be replaced by memory,
and so anatomy by (para)-psychology. Taking into account how Hegel's
thought is thoroughly theological—in what O'Regan has clarified as "ontotheology"—this shift is nothing but a further reflection on the previous
Hegelian submersion of the three divine persons into the new impersonal
and imperial *Geist*:

> The German Spirit is the Spirit of the new World. Its aim is the
> realization of absolute Truth as the unlimited self-determination
> of Freedom—*that* Freedom which has its own absolute form it-
> self as its purport. The destiny of the German peoples is to be the
> bearers of the Christian principle.[31]

It is noteworthy that Hegel associates the Germanic more with an attribute
of a ghostly Spirit than with any concrete people. Along with the inter-
changeability of the Germanic with Christendom, this will make possible
a new theopolitical imagination: the new divine *corpus verum* on the earth
will become the state.

---

27. Hegel, *Philosophy of Religion*, 284n93.

28. Eph 1:14.

29. John 14:15–31.

30. Cf. de Lubac, *Joachim de Flore*, 359–78.

31. Hegel, *Philosophy of History*, 358.

II. Hauntotheological Anthropology, or the Semantic Incompleteness of Ghosts

The foregoing leads to the deep and complex *hauntological* question of the relation between reality and memory, carnal integrity and ghostly re-membrance. The question is a variant of the problem of the relation of sameness and difference.[32] In the case of *Hamlet*, it amounts to the overwhelming question of the Shakespearian drama: is the Ghost really the King, Hamlet's father? or is he an "unreal" image of the father, a counterfeit? or is he some mysterious third, some kind of *tertium quid*? In the case of Hegel, the question is this: is *der Geist* the Christian God? Is it humanity? or some kind of equivocal in-between?[33] The return of such a ghost is always a provocation to memory, an injunction against forgetfulness. And it is in this way that Hegel comes on to the scene of the Enlightenment: as a young Hamlet who has received an injunction to set right the time, to remind: to re-call European thinking to her paternal origin, which is Christian. Against the sanction of forgetfulness the Enlightenment imposes, Hegel recalls the Christian tradition, which "is not simply a cornucopia of memories held by the church to be faithful to the primal mystery, but a memory of memories that critically sifts through individual memories for their aptness, their particular qualities, their relation to other perspectives, and their relevance for the moment."[34]

In this sense, Hegel appears and presents himself as a friend of theology and a rescuer of the Christian tradition, but he does so in a ghostly way. He does not propose a new carnal relation to the origin, but a spiritual representation. As such, he proposes in the place of the carnal origin a specter that by definition lacks a body and so provokes a form of dis-membered memory, a re-minder that finally fails to re-member the forgotten real and corporeal presence. And so, what Hegel generates is a *mis*-re-membering, a memory that distorts and cuts us off from the principal current of the tradition, the carnal filial belonging. And so, like Hamlet, Hegel does not discover a carnal belonging to the Father, but an ambiguous inherence in relation to a carnal absence, the identity of which cannot be felt but must be established through a pure spiritual "decision," an axiom: the Ghost is the Father.[35]

---

32. See Milbank, *Beyond Secular Order*, 19–113.

33. O'Regan, *Misremembering*, 15.

34. O'Regan, *Misremembering*, 8.

35. *Hamlet* I.iv.23–24.

The voluntaristic identification of the Ghost with the Father constitutes, as John Milbank puts it, "a decision against a middle in *being* between identity and difference."[36] Here not only is carnal mediation overcome, but even the univocity of postmodern "Scotism." All that remains is a dialectical "counterfeit mediation which involves a constant agonistic shuttle between sameness and difference."[37] The apparent novelty of the Spirit's dialectic results both in "a swallowing of the different by the same and in an abjection of pure difference as totally contingent and irrelevant for the comprehension of truth."[38] Consequently, the three persons of the divine Trinity are fused: the Father is the singularity of *Geist* and the incarnation of the second person is reduced to the "understanding of history as the 'becoming' of the Trinitarian life."[39] We can say that the "Hamletian" transition—living-remembering-rotting—now develops into a "Hegelian" shift: living-law-state. The evolution from genealogy to forensic surgeon passing through (para) psychology results in the passage from anatomy to law passing through logic, or in the field of mathematics, from semantics to syntax passing through axiomatization.

It might seem somewhat strange that the evident semantic incompleteness—in the sense of logical formal systems—of *Hamlet*'s Ghost and of Hegel's *Geist* allows a pure free choice of identity, rather than preventing identification *tout court*. The last novel of Luigi Pirandello, *Uno, nessuno e centomila*, published in 1926, clarifies this strange phenomenon.

Provoked by a completely irrelevant remark of his wife about his nose, the protagonist of *Uno, nessuno e centomila*, Vitangelo Pirandello (note how the vowels of his first and last names are shared), begins to suffer an insuperable crisis of identity. He discovers that everybody he has ever met has constructed a different and credible "Vitangelo" and that none of these *personae* coincide with his own image of himself. After a process of internalization of these different identities, the protagonist's confusion increases to such a point that each time he looks into a mirror, the latest image of "Vitangelo" recalls to him the figure of a stranger. And thus, the carnal Vitangelo discovers inside himself "one hundred thousand" images of himself, and ends up becoming "no one." He declares:

> Maybe now you would admit that a minute ago you were another one. Of course, my dear, think about it! A minute ago, before this case worried you, you were another one; no, no, instead of

36. Milbank, *Beyond Secular Order*, 51.
37. Milbank, *Beyond Secular Order*, 51.
38. Milbank, *Beyond Secular Order*, 52.
39. Milbank, *Beyond Secular Order*, 84.

this, you were one hundred other ones, one hundred thousand other ones. And, believe me, this has not to do with any wonder. Rather, tell me if you can ensure that you will be tomorrow the same you, you imagine you are today.[40]

Vitangelo realizes that a true living mind does not possess a definitive identity, because it does not cease to be born and to die at every moment. In other words, he comes to believe that carnality is irrelevant to the determination of the identity of a person, and so identity becomes construed as a pure and spectral fluidity. So, if released from every carnal fact, the spirit becomes a flow of changing and changeable identities. Vitangelo's "discovery" is the problem of Hamlet.

The most pressing anxiety of *Hamlet*'s Ghost is convertible with that of Hegel's *Geist*: not that they have no identity, but that they are the host of any identity. They are *semantically undetermined*, like human beings in the Pirandello anthropology. And this occurs because this anthropology is a theological anthropology abstracted from every relation to a carnal fact. Herein the essence of a human being is not revealed by Pilate's indication "*ecce homo*," that is, by reference to a precise suffering Jew in whom God is incarnate, but rather by an ultimate fulfillment of "spirit" in the legal framework of a German Reich: a ghostly *Geist* that can be constituted as the bearer of all our identities. It is a theological anthropology unable to distinguish people from ghosts, since it is associated with a Hegelian Gnosticism making it impossible to distinguish between Jesus's Father and Germany's *Geist*. The point, for us, here concerns the absolute difference between the spectral genealogy of nihilism and the incarnate genealogy of concrete truth, between a shadowy abstraction and a concrete universal: if Spirit is anywhere, Spirit is nowhere; but if Spirit is somewhere, Spirit is everywhere.[41]

---

40. Pirandello, *Uno, nessuno e centomila*, 43.

41. Cunningham, *Genealogy of Nihilism*, xviii: "The 'discovery' that nihilism offers the possibility of a doctrine of creation should not wholly surprise us, for was it not Newman who spoke of the 'dispensation of Paganism'? Consequently, Paganism was an ore to be mined for the truth it contained. Indeed, this caused Newman to move away from an approach that was 'either/or,' to one of 'both/and.' This is certainly to be encouraged. Yet it may be fair to suggest that Radical Orthodoxy deepens this principle. For it too calls us to move from 'either/or' to 'both/and.' Yet this move is somewhat radicalised, to the degree that it becomes an approach of 'both/and—either/or.' For is it not true, that if God is said to be anywhere, God is nowhere; but if God is somewhere, God is everywhere?"

III. Ghosts, Shadow People, and Doppelgängers

Most people, if they believe in ghosts, think of ghosts and "shadow people" as basically the same thing. Initiates in the paranormal sciences or in occult arts know very well that they should not be confused.[42] Both tend to the malevolent and share certain demoniac qualities, but witnesses maintain that shadow people are more baleful and sinister than "normal" ghosts. A ghost is a spiritual remnant of a person who has died, while a shadow being enjoys a certain fuzzy materiality, which may grow or intensify with the passing of time. What is more, shadow people generally haunt a determinate living person in the form of a double. Making use of ancient Germanic and Danish mythologies, the famous Romantic writer Jean Paul designated them by a neologism successfully adopted as a loanword in many languages: a shadow being is a doppelgänger (literally, "double-goer"). Such as they are described in some stories, these doppelgängers are a kind of paranormal parasite, whose haunting is really a feeding on a "host" being. In some cases, shadow beings kill the person whose identity they are absorbing; and in these cases, the victim is erased from existence, and history rewritten as though he/she were never born.[43]

    Maybe the most significant and brooding literary example of a doppelgänger is that depicted in *The Shadow* (1847), a tale fittingly set in another "Hamletian" state. Composed by Hans Christian Andersen, the story is an evidence of Andersen's aspiration to be remembered as a poet and thinker.[44] In *The Shadow*, Andersen tells the story of a learned young man from a northern country who once travelled to an exotic, warm region where the sun shone from early morning till evening. The heat was almost unbearable; only when the stars came forth did the man go outdoors onto his balcony to take the air. From the house opposite where the learned man was staying, the sound of music always could be heard; but nobody had ever seen the mysterious dweller of that house. One day, taking his evening air on the balcony, listening to the music and thinking of the enigma of its source, the man observed his own shadow falling on the wall of the opposite house and jestingly asked his shadow to step in through the half-open door of the balcony from where the music flowed. The shadow nodded and departed into the opposite house, while the learned man turned and re-entered his room.

    The next morning, the man went out to take his coffee and read the paper. Standing in the sunshine he realized that he had lost his shadow. Vexed

42. Ahlquist, *Life After Death*, 122.

43. See Bergin, "John Dies at the End."

44. It is at least curious to remember that one of Andersen's most philosophically pretentious tales was titled *At vaere eller ikke vaere*, "To be or not to be" (1857).

by this, he consoled himself that in warm and sunny climates everything grows quickly, and so a new shadow would shortly grow. After a few weeks he had grown his new shadow, and thus he returned to his northern home, where "he wrote books about the true, the good, and the beautiful, which are to be found in this world."[45]

Many years passed, until one night there was a knock at the learned man's door. It turned out to be his old shadow. Though thin, "the shadow was, in fact, very well dressed, and this made a man of him."[46] An intermittent relationship begins between the shadow and the learned man. In one of their meetings, the learned man complains of the futility of his work, "writing about the true, the beautiful, and the good; but no one cares to hear anything about it. I am quite in despair, for I take it to heart very much."[47] The shadow responds: "That is what I never do," he does not concern himself with the transcendental and the question of ultimacy. Rather: "I am growing quite fat and stout, which everyone ought to be. You do not understand the world . . . you will make yourself ill about it."[48]

Over time illness does come upon the learned man. "Sorrow and trouble pursued him, and what he said about the good, the beautiful, and the true, was of as much value to most people as a nutmeg would be to a cow."[49] Having fallen quite ill and unsubstantial, his friends begin to tell him, "You really look like a shadow."[50] The shadow proposes to the old master that he take him to a resort, so the old master can convalesce and take the waters. The shadow offers to assume all the expenses of the vacation, with one stipulation: that the shadow now act as "master" and the learned man act as "shadow." The old master agrees.

The two figures take their vacation. At the resort, the shadow meets a princess, who falls in love with him. On the night the princess and the shadow are to be married, the shadow offers his old master a position at the palace, but on one condition:

> "Listen, my friend," said the shadow to the learned man; "now that I am as fortunate and as powerful as any man can be, I will do something unusually good for you. You shall live in my palace, drive with me in the royal carriage, and have a hundred thousand dollars a year; but you must allow everyone to call you

45. Andersen, "The Shadow," 268.
46. Andersen, "The Shadow," 554.
47. Andersen, "The Shadow," 556.
48. Andersen, "The Shadow," 556.
49. Andersen, "The Shadow," 557.
50. Andersen, "The Shadow," 557.

a shadow, and never venture to say that you have been a man.
And once a year, when I sit in my balcony in the sunshine, you
must lie at my feet as becomes a shadow to do."[51]

The learned man rejects the ridiculous proposition and threatens to tell the princess everything. The old shadow has him arrested and put in prison. When the princess asks her groom later what has become of his wise shadow, he bitterly feigns: "I have gone through the most terrible affair . . . imagine, my shadow has gone mad; I suppose such a poor, shallow brain, could not bear much; he fancies that he has become a real man, and that I am his shadow."[52] That evening, before the city is lit for the wedding, the learned man is executed.

This summary of Andersen's allegoric story, along with Pirandello's novel, helps us throw light on our two principle ghostly characters: *Hamlet's* Ghost and Hegel's *Geist*. The dissimilarities of our two principal "spirits" (or "shadows"?) notwithstanding, they share significant features: they are both figures semantically incomplete, shadowy and ambiguous in relation to their carnal origin, which they purport to represent but may in fact, like Andersen's shadow, feed off and kill. As much as our two principal "spirits" haunt a stage (one dramatic, the other philosophical and historical), the question of their status as possible "doppelgängers" haunts them—Is the Ghost the spirit of Old Hamlet? Is Hegel's *Geist* Christian in any authentic sense? This agonizing ambiguity sets in motion, in both cases, a mechanism of remembrance that nevertheless threatens the legitimacy of the social body and carnal origin they purport to represent and defend, whether the carnal genealogy of the Danish dynasty (lost ultimately to Fortinbras), or the body of the church swayed by the spirit of the Enlightenment. The respective dénouements of Shakespeare's tragedy and Hegel's theo-logical implementations suggest that these acts of remembrance are not ultimately acts of memory, but acts of mis-re-membering, counterfeits of an unattended reality.

IV. Mis-re-membering the Father, or Failing to Restore the Danish Dynasty

When Derrida first read James Joyce's *Ulysses* in the late 1950s, he was struck by the book's resonance with Hegel.[53] Just as Joyce had re-membered the

51. Andersen, "The Shadow," 560.
52. Andersen, "The Shadow," 560.
53. Derrida, *Deconstruction in a Nutshell*, 25.

odyssian narrative of homecoming in an attempt to gather "totality" into a single book, so Hegel's re-membrance of Christian semantics had attempted to gather the "whole" in a single philosophical system. Derrida's observation is prescient, and more so in light of the significance O'Regan has given to Hegel's evocation of the *Odyssey* in the Preface of the *Phenomenology*. According to O'Regan, the "narrative matrix" of the *Phenomenology* is "supported by the odyssian figure," and so determines how Hegel's thought "shapes a perfect circle."[54] Remembering the "odyssian figure" allows Joyce and Hegel to attempt the "impossible task of precisely gathering in a totality, in a potential totality, the potentially infinite memory of humanity . . . to reach absolute knowledge through a single act of memory."[55]

The homophonic evolution of *memorari* and *membrum* in English is here felicitous insofar as it unfolds one way by which memory might aim at re-collecting a "totality." The evolution puts into play the meaning of words etymologically unrelated in Latin: *memorari*, "to be mindful of"; and *membrum*, "member," as in part of a body. This phonetic proximity helps us see the metaphysical reciprocity between words as diverse as "member," "membership," "dismember," and "remember," "remembrance," "misremember." While alternative terms such as "remind" or "reminder" refer to mental or spiritual shifts, we might naïvely read the former with hyphens in strategic places, to say "re-member," "re-membrance" or "mis-re-member," endowing the terms thus with carnal density. The latter genealogy suggests that memory activates not only a mental restoration but the possibility of a corporal recovery. To remember a ghost, in this light, is to attempt to give the spectral something "carnal," a corporeal "presence." In the same way, to recall to life a once living *corpus*, reduced now to a shadow existence, amounts to something like a reanimation of the body. All this being so, the accusation of "mis-re-membering" implies either a kind of abortion (spontaneous or otherwise) or a reconstituted counterfeit "body," that of a doppelgänger. Here we pass beyond the (para)-psychology of ghosts to a strange new science: the "anatomy of specters," or the "anatomy of misremembering."

Shakespeare's tragedy and Hegel's philosophical oeuvre are both conceived as works of remembering intent on restoring corporeal patrimony. Through specters, they attempt to achieve something like an odyssian homecoming, to "shape a perfect circle." In the case of *Hamlet*, the aim is the carnal restoration of the paternal lineage against a (putative) usurper; in the case of Hegel, the act aims to restore the rational legitimacy of the Christian

---

54. O'Regan, *Heterodox Hegel*, 59.
55. Derrida, *Deconstruction in a Nutshell*, 25.

corpus against the Enlightenment *novum*. Both accounts can be respectively read as constitutive of a strange new science.

In the Scylla and Charybdis episode of *Ulysses*, Stephen Dedalus offers a now famous reading of *Hamlet* in which Shakespeare, playing the Ghost in the original 1601 production, reveals himself to be the true father of his own recently dead son, Hamnet:

> *Hamlet, I am thy father's spirit,*
>
> bidding him list. To a son he speaks, the son of his soul, the prince, young Hamlet and to the son of his body, Hamnet Shakespeare, who has died in Stratford that his namesake may live for ever.[56]

In *Ulysses*, the question of paternity and filial memory of the father is, of course, bound up with the theme of usurpation and cuckoldry; and in this sense, the question of the counterfeit and authentic memory is a key Joycean theme. Specifically, these questions coalesce, in both cases, around the filial question of authentic paternity, and so questions of memory, misremembering, validity, and counterfeit. For Stephen, the Ghost in *Hamlet* begs filial remembrance in the face of a usurper father figure, Claudius, who has made the authentic father a cuckold, before murdering him and stealing his paternal and kingly rights.

If the injunction of the Ghost is one on behalf of memory of the dead father, the ghostly cry for memory is well juxtaposed against the forgetfulness urged by the usurper himself. As Claudius councils Hamlet to forget:

> You must know your father lost a father;
> That father lost, lost his; and the survivor bound
> In filial obligation for some term
> To do obsequious sorrow. But to persever
> In obstinate condolement is a course
> Of impious stubbornness.[57]

The dramatic tension here unfolds within the filial soul between a "new father" who recommends forgetfulness of the carnal father and a "ghostly father" who recommends a form of radical re-membrance: fidelity to a spectral image of the father. And this brings us to the deep question of re-membrance in *Hamlet* and the agonizing risk of the counterfeit and of *mis*-remembering, which animates the tension of Shakespeare's drama.

---

56. Joyce, James *Ulysses*, 282.

57. Shakespeare, *Hamlet*, I.ii.89–94.

The Ghost is first encountered in I.i. Before he enters the stage, the spectral presence already haunts the drama in the memory of the guard: "Has this thing appeared again tonight?" Marcellus asks Bernardo and Francisco.[58] The "dreaded sight twice seen" is not yet named or identified,[59] it is simply referred to as a "thing," until Bernardo observes how it comes "in the same figure like the King that's dead."[60] The "likeness" of the Ghost and the King is then noted variously, by Horatio and Marcellus.[61] But the likeness remains "strange" and not one of certain unity and identity with the dead King.[62] The ambiguity of the phantasmal presence notwithstanding, the friends resolve to report the apparition to young Hamlet. It is thus that Horatio explains the perplexity of their night vision to Hamlet, of a ghostly presence, that is again described in terms of a likeness.[63] Hamlet's first response is to concede that it is "strange,"[64] while he determines to declare it "my father's spirit, in arms!"[65] A determination he resolves on when he meets the Ghost in I.iv, declaring in the form of an axiom: "I'll call thee Hamlet / King, father, royal Dane."[66] That this is an axiomatic decision is highlighted by the fact that it is announced in the very speech in which Hamlet has wondered if the Ghost is a "spirit of heath or goblin damned" and conceded that it "com'st in such a questionable shape."[67]

The risk of Hamlet's axiomatic decision to identify the Ghost with his father is underlined by the fearful warnings of Marcellus and Horatio not to follow the Ghost. Nevertheless, Hamlet settles to obey the ghostly bidding to a private interview, in which now the Ghost identifies himself as "thy father's spirit."[68] The Ghost then explains that he is "Doomed for a certain term to walk the night, / And for the day confined to fast in fires, / Till the foul crimes done in my days of nature / Are burnt and purged away."[69] This purgatorial plight highlights moreover the strangeness of the mysterious apparition, since "the foul crimes" to which the Ghost refers are not it would

---

58. Shakespeare, *Hamlet*, I.i.21.

59. Shakespeare, *Hamlet*, I.i.25.

60. Shakespeare, *Hamlet*, I.i.41.

61. Shakespeare, *Hamlet*, cf. I.i.44 and 58.

62. Shakespeare, *Hamlet*, I.i.64.

63. Shakespeare, *Hamlet*, I.i.212.

64. Shakespeare, *Hamlet*, I.i.220.

65. Shakespeare, *Hamlet*, I.i.260.

66. Shakespeare, *Hamlet*, I.iv.23–24.

67. Shakespeare, *Hamlet*, I.iv.19, 22.

68. Shakespeare, *Hamlet*, I.v.9.

69. Shakespeare, *Hamlet*, I.v.10–13.

seem his own, but those of his putative murdered Claudius. On orthodox Christian grounds, there are strong reasons to suspect the authenticity of this story: purgatory is a zone of penance, where dead sinners are granted a new time of penance on the way to bliss. It is not a zone from which spirits return to the living with requests for vengeance, as if their purgatorial stay was the result of unpaid crimes committed against them. And yet this is precisely what the Ghost of *Hamlet* demands: "Revenge his foul and most unnatural murder."[70] And not only so, the drama of the play unfolds under the supposition that action will prove fidelity to this memory. It is thus that the Ghost takes his leave from Hamlet: "Adieu, adieu, Hamlet. Remember me."[71] Memory will be proved by the deed of revenge, a point the Ghost repeats in his second encounter with Hamlet: "Do not forget. This visitation / Is but to whet thy almost blunted purpose."[72]

The anxiety that overshadows Hamlet hinges on the fact that the identity of the Ghost is indeterminable, and so must reduce to a mere "decision."[73] The experience of dislocation that this semantically indeterminate identity provokes calls into question the boundaries according to which identity and memory, presence and absence, death and life, normatively function. In this way *Hamlet* dramatizes the hauntological, that is, reveals how the ghostly presence provokes the threat of misremembering by virtue of the fact that the ghostly is precisely a semantically underdetermined being. A ghost can appear as any "one" (and so can appear anywhere and nowhere). Likewise, in Hegel, the three persons of the Holy Trinity, the determinate identity of the Christian God, are fused into undetermined *Geist*, just as the incarnation is reduced to the "understanding of history as the 'becoming' of the Trinitarian life."[74]

It may seem at first strange that the semantic incompleteness of *Hamlet*'s Ghost and Hegel's *Geist* allows for this radical free choice of identities, and not a delimiting identification *tout court*. But this is the point. The pressing problem of the *Hamlet* Ghost and the Hegel *Geist* is not that they are void of every identity, but rather that they represent a pure possibility of identity because they possess no carnal, paternal, or historical density. And herein lies the deep anxiety of hauntology: is the Ghost really Hamlet's father? Or is he a simulacrum? Is *der Geist* the Christian God? or is it what William Desmond calls a "counterfeit double"?[75]

70. Shakespeare, *Hamlet*, I.v.25.

71. Shakespeare, *Hamlet*, I.v.91.

72. Shakespeare, *Hamlet*, III.iv.102–103.

73. Cf. Shakespeare, *Hamlet*, I.v.18–24.

74. Milbank, *Beyond Secular Order*, 84.

75. Desmond, *Hegel's God*.

The hazard of misremembering, the risk of axiomatic fidelity to a "counterfeit double," is underlined by the spectral demand: "Revenge this foul and most unnatural murder."[76] Memory must prove itself, thus, in a carnal deed. To be sure, Hamlet is anxious to resolve the threat of mis-re-membering, but the *Mousetrap* proves insufficient. For while the play-within-the-play may elicit evidence of Claudius's guilt, it nonetheless bears not at all on the identity of the Ghost. The bloody ending of the real play, by contrast, suggests a spectral counterfeit: a dramatic revelation of the end of fidelity to a mis-re-membered patrimony. The remembrance enjoined by the Ghost does not reestablish the paternal-Danish lineage; rather it brings the son of the king's body to death and realizes the loss of the kingdom to a Norwegian dynasty, more remote to Hamlet's paternal origin than the "carnal likeness" of Claudius.

V. *Geist* as a Doppelganger of *Pneuma*, or Why the Reich Is a Parody of the Church

At this point, it should be clear that *Hamlet* is an *avant la lettre* dramatization of the dynamic O'Regan adroitly uncovers in Balthasar's trenchant "anatomy of misremembering." What is more, this dynamic deepens the complex drama of hauntology: the specter haunting post-Hegelian thought and culture, a specter that is as much a specter of Hegelianism as it is of young Hegelianism, of Joachimite Christianity as it is of Valentinian Gnosticism. The dynamic of hauntology, expounded by Derrida in terms of *Hamlet* and so internal to the nature of Hegelian *Geist*, as both Derrida and Althusser have elaborated it, is critically advertised by O'Regan as a key basis of *The Anatomy of Misremembering*.

In his oeuvre, Balthasar offers a cathedral of these two kinds of re-membering against the forgetfulness of the Enlightenment inheritance. And so, Balthasar must, as O'Regan shows, simultaneously offer an "anatomy of misremembering" in which he resists not only forgetfulness but also the misremembering tendency that usurps carnal memory. Instead of being a faithful memory of memory, instead of "knitting together of Christ's body by the participation of Many in his sacrifice,"[77] Hegel has conjured a powerful system of "recollection" of Christian tradition, symbols, and practices in a mode that subtly distorts and transforms them into a counterfeit double. While Hegel speaks of the Trinity, of Christ, of the Spirit, in each case these are "ghostly" terms that return in the haunting guise of the concrete figures

76. Shakespeare, *Hamlet*, I.v.25.

77. Cavanaugh, *Torture and Eucharist*, 229.

they pretend to represent. In Hegel these are finally goblins damned, evil spirits, and doppelgängers. Hegel's theology is, as O'Regan puts, "gloriously awry" and constitutes an "epic deviation":

> Hegel's Christology disappoints: the unique singularity of Christ is less important than Christ as illustrative of a general principle of reality; the folding of resurrection into cross suggests resurrection's eclipse rather than it being a feature of a Christological paradox; and finally the cross itself is reduced to its capacity for its meaning being made transparent to human being, and appropriated by them. . . . Even more important are the trinitarian distortions, for Hegel's trinitarianism comprehends and represents a synopsis of the epical narration of the divine in and through which the divine develops and actualizes itself. . . . Hegel has to be seen to be romancing the tradition instead of taking it seriously. . . . Hegel abolishes the immanent Trinity-economic Trinity distinction by making the immanent Trinity a function of the economy, and eternity a function of temporality . . . , the history of suffering is instrumental in the constitution of the divine. The excision of the inexplicable is also a place when Hegel not only avows divine possibility, but demonstrates its necessity.[78]

Alongside the threat of forgetfulness runs the parallel, more dangerous threat of *mis*-remembering: a pseudo-*ressourcement* of traditional memories that, in fact, misconstrue the original forms of thought, modes of feeling, and ways of life of Christianity, now at the service of an end (or ends) that essentially distorts (or makes opaque) the "primal mystery." Mis-remembering is more dangerous than forgetfulness.

Forgetfulness, if it is not easily countered, is countered nevertheless in a rather straightforward way: dynamic acts of *ressourcement*. The example of Balthasar, here, is eminent. His oeuvre is a grand example of Christian remembrances in the face of modern forgetfulness. In O'Regan's words, Balthasar provides us with a "symphonic rehearsal of the tradition of discourse, action, and form of life of the 'catholic tradition' and also the way in which they involve conversation with other discourses and negotiations with non-Christian practices and forms of life."[79] But if this is Balthasar's primary task, his secondary (but no less critical) task is to perform a radical deconstruction of misremembering; indeed this is the essential complement to Balthasar's symphonic rehearsal, according to O'Regan.

78. O'Regan, *Misremembering*, 39.
79. O'Regan, *Misremembering*, 22.

If resisting misremembering is the essential complement to Balthasar's symphonic rehearsal, this secondary task has gone largely unrecognized. The clearest evidence of this is the very ambiguous and contradictory treatments of Balthasar's use of Hegel (and to a lesser extent Heidegger) in the secondary literature. The massive exception here, the one work O'Regan highlights as really anticipating his own "anatomy of misremembering," is David Hart's *The Beauty of the Infinite*.[80] In this regard, *The Anatomy of Misremembering* is a vindication of the depth of insight of the *The Beauty of the Infinite* into the heart of Balthasar. Hart understands Heidegger and Hegel as the basic roots of postmodern thought, roots that put into question the very possibility of Christian faith in the most dangerous of ways. This, on Hart's depiction, was clearly grasped by Balthasar, who, despite some recent Anglo-Saxon readings of him, was absolutely clear in his judgment against Hegel and Heidegger. O'Regan confirms Hart's judgment here. But as much as there is a profound proximity here between *The Anatomy of Misremembering* and *The Beauty of the Infinite*, and as much as O'Regan owes a substantial debt to Hart on this count, there is an important distinction to be drawn. O'Regan writes:

> *The Anatomy of Misremembering* distinguishes itself from Hart's text in being essentially a double reduction: a reduction, on the one hand, to a textually specific Balthasar and, on the other, a reduction to more focused consideration of the capacity of Hegel and Heidegger to subvert as well as influence the theological enterprise.[81]

Whereas Balthasar is largely only evoked by Hart, in O'Regan there is an abundance of textual evidence, which gives the argument now a carnal intimacy. The second point of distinction between *The Anatomy of Misremembering* and *The Beauty of the Infinite* is more important, not because it contradicts anything that Hart argues, but because it adds a new layer, which answers a critical perplexity that Hart's judgment raises.

For Hart, Hegel is theologically unredeemable. His relation to Christianity is essentially negative: "At best [Hegel's thought] runs interference on Christian discourse and at worst puts into question its very possibility."[82] By contrast, for Rowan Williams, for example, the figure of Hegel is decidedly ambiguous and ambiguously intertwined in the thought and thinking of Balthasar. Hegel may be a problematic figure, but he can be mobilized and read in a hopeful direction—especially, for Williams, as read through

80. Hart, *Beauty of the Infinite*.
81. O'Regan, *Misremembering*, 23.
82. O'Regan, *Misremembering*, 23.

Gillian Rose.[83] And so, whatever his commitment to traditional Christianity, and whatever is yet problematic in his thought, Hegel can be made to
serve an authentic Christian purpose.[84] Whereas for Williams, Hegel is (at
least at key points) an unwitting ally in a Balthasarian recovery of Christian
memory against Enlightenment forgetfulness, for Hart this is impossible.
What O'Regan helps us to see is how these two seemingly contrary judgments are sustainable, even if that of Hart finally must be given priority:

> [Even while] Hegelian thought demonstrates a capacity to
> disfigure and refigure Christian symbols and narrative so as
> to present a plausible facsimile of the sort offered by historical
> Gnosticism . . . Balthasar concedes that Hegel can and should be
> appreciated for elevating Christianity not only above other reli-
> gions, but also above just about all cultural discourses, for put-
> ting Christ and the cross at the center of an adequate account of
> reality and for suggesting that the Trinity should be regarded as
> an encompassing horizon. But the trilogy shows . . . that Hegel's
> thought should be submitted to a diagnostic in order to assess
> the degree of positive correlation between it and the mainline
> theological tradition. The results Balthasar believes are not
> Christianly bearable. Hegel revises the entire set of doctrines
> that articulate salvation history, that is, creation, incarnation,
> redemption, sanctification, and eschaton, as he also revises the
> relation between the divine milieu and the milieu of salvation,
> essentially making the former depend on the latter.[85]

O'Regan shows, thus, that if Balthasar is as much concerned by Hegelian thought as he is engaged by it, and if Hegelian thought can be an ally in
the overdetermination of Enlightenment forgetfulness, the misremembering Hegel entails poses, finally, an ultimate threat, "since it more surreptitiously liquefies and ultimately liquidates Christianity, while seeming to
enact a kind of memory that is difficult to distinguish from the memory that
constitutes Christianity."[86] Indeed, according to O'Regan, "from Balthasar's
point of view Hegelian memory (*Erinnerung*) constitutes the most
blatant form of the misfiring of memory or misremembering in the

83. Williams, "Between Politics and Metaphysics" in *Wrestling with Angels*. Cf. Gilliam Rose, *Hegel Contra Sociology*.

84. See Williams, "Hegel and the Gods of Postmodernity," "Logic and Spirit in
Hegel," and "Balthasar and Difference," in *Wrestling with Angels*, 25–34, 35–52, and
77–85.

85. O'Regan, *Misremembering*, 21 and 24.

86. O'Regan, *Misremembering*, 33.

post-Enlightenment era."[87] Balthasar is thus moved to confront and diag-
nose this "colossal act of misremembering that puts us out of touch with
the intellectual, moral, and practical gifts of the tradition, and the gift of
creation, redemption, and sanctification, which renders the triune reality
of God, on which they depend."[88] And so O'Regan sets himself the task to
outline and interrogate the substantive and formal disagreements Balthasar
brings to bear against Hegel and Hegelian thought. Substantively this concerns a "structural resistance" to Hegel's theological-philosophical revision
of "the grammar of Christian belief, and relatedly the practices and forms of
life that deserve 'Christian' and philosophical sanction."[89] Formally it concerns the "univocal developmental view of the tradition of artistic, religious,
and philosophical discourses" as they develop to find their synthetic realization in Hegel's system, an essentially "self-mediating structure of concepts."[90]

VI. After Reading: On the Sacramental Consummation of Re-membering

The word for remembrance in Hebrew is *zîkrôn*, meaning also memorial.
It comes from the root word *zākar*, which includes both the sense of "to
remember" and "to mention." Other variations of the word include *zākor*,
"remember," and *zeker*, "in remembrance of," "being mindful," "bringing to
remembrance," "calling to mind." In Hebrew, being verbs such as "remember" always denote an action. Remembering is not just a state of being; in
Hebrew tradition one remembers in order to act, to make a carnal gesture.
And so, it is also for Christianity.

The Eucharist is the heart of Christian remembrance. The apostles and
early believers were instructed by their Guide: "Do this in remembrance
(ἀνάμνησιν) of me." The word ἀνάμνησις ("remembrance," "recollection")
occurs a number of times in the New Testament and the Greek Old Testament. It is mostly used in the context of sacrificial rites,[91] which have
to do with ritual acts of remembrance. The root of the word comes from
ἀναμιμνήσκω, "to remember," from ἀνα- + μιμνήσκω, "to remember more to
mind." In these cases, the term *anamnesis* can be translated "memorial por-
tion," "memorial offering," or "memorial sacrifice." Thus, in the remaining

---

87. O'Regan, *Misremembering*, 521.

88. O'Regan, *Misremembering*, 33.

89. O'Regan, *Misremembering*, 36.

90. O'Regan, *Misremembering*, 36.

91. Cf. Heb 10:3; Lev 24:7; Num 10:10; Pss 37 and 69.

two occurrences of *anamnesis*,[92] Christ's words "Do this in remembrance of me," the Eucharist is offered as the event when remembrance of the Master is renewed, and remembered carnally. But recalling that the Christian rite is specifically a remembering of his cross, of the moment of his broken body, the *anamnesis* takes on its fuller resurrectional sense: remembering Christ is literally an act of re-membering, of gathering his body together and recognizing that he is not a ghost, he is carnal fact, a bodily presence.

In 1933, under the shadow of the Third Reich, Karl Barth issued the challenge that the most radical Christian resistance is simply to practice "theology and only theology," and to practice it "as though nothing had happened."[93] In one way, Barth's wager amounted to the claim that fidelity to the Christian memory is enough. O'Regan overwhelmingly shows us that Balthasar's wager is more radical: only a symphonic rehearsal of the tradition, that includes within it a ruthless criticism of misremembering, can hope to resist the most dangerous peril of anti-Christian modernity. Ultimacy here lies not in theoretical argumentation but in apocalyptic focus on the *Agnus Dei*, the concrete, sacramental, and Paschal fact to which the *anamnesis* of the Eucharist returns. As O'Regan writes, "In the eucharist, Christ remains the indispensable actor who comes to us and forms the very community that would receive him."[94] The Eucharist, then, is the final and ultimate resistance to mis-remembering the Christian tradition and to the "counterfeit double" that is Hegelian *Geist*. The real presence of the *verum corpus* is a scandal that cannot be mis-remembered.

The return of a ghost is always a provocation to memory, an injunction against forgetfulness; Hegel comes on the scene of the Enlightenment as would a young Hamlet receiving the injunction of a ghostly father: "Adieu . . . Remember me."[95] Against forgetfulness, he recalls the Christian tradition, which "is not simply a cornucopia of memories held by the church to be faithful to the primal mystery, but a memory of memories that critically sifts through individual memories for their aptness, their particular qualities, their relation to other perspectives, and their relevance for the moment."[96] The "*mis-*" of Hegel's remembering lies hidden under the critical guise of his disingenuous aptness, on the one hand, and the irreducible fecundity of the primal mystery, on the other. This concealment allows Hegel to appear as a shadowy friend of theology, the old learned man who still studies the good,

---

92. Luke 22:19; and 1 Cor 11:24.
93. Busch, *Karl Barth*, 226.
94. O'Regan, *Misremembering*, 199.
95. Shakespeare, *Hamlet*, I.v.91.
96. O'Regan, *Misremembering*, 8.

the true, and the beautiful. But as O'Regan shows, fastidiously and elegantly, the spectral ambiguity of Hegel is ultimately a simulacrum of the primal mystery. No shadow or ghost can take the place of the Father.

Bibliography

Ahlquist, Diane. *The Complete Idiot's Guide to Life After Death.* New York: Penguin, 2007.

Althusser, Louis. *The Spectre of Hegel.* Translated by G. M. Goshgarian. London: Verso, 1997.

Andersen, Hans Christian. "The Shadow." In *Hans Andersen's Fairy Tales*, translated by Mrs. H. B. Paull, 550–61. London: Warne, 1930.

Bergin, Nicholas. "'John Dies at the End' has limited showing in Omaha." *Lincoln Journal Star*, March 7, 2003, online at http://journalstar.com/entertainment/movies/john-dies-at-the-end-has-limited-showing-in-omaha/article_3110e9ad-f575-5fc7-b561-37597da78fda.html.

Busch, Eberhard. *Karl Barth: His Life from Letters and Autobiographical Texts.* London: SCM, 1975.

Cavanaugh, William. *Torture and Eucharist.* Oxford: Blackwell, 1998.

Cunnigham, Conor. *Genealogy of Nihilism: Philosophies of Nothing and the Difference of Theology.* London: Routledge, 2002.

de Lubac, Henri. *Corpus Mysticum: L'Eucharistie et l'Église au Moyen Âge.* Paris: Aubier, 1949.

———. *La postérité spirituelle de Joachim de Flore.* Paris: Cerf, 2014.

Derrida, Jacques. *Deconstruction in a Nutshell.* Edited by John D. Caputo. New York: Fordham University Press, 1997.

———. *Specters of Marx: The State of the Debt, the Work of Mourning and the New International.* Translated by Peggy Kamuf. London: Routledge, 1994.

Desmond, William. *Hegel's God: A Counterfeit Double?* Aldershot, UK: Ashgate, 2003.

Hart, David Bentley. *The Beauty of the Infinite.* Grand Rapids: Eerdmans, 2003.

Hegel, G. W. F. *Lectures on the Philosophy of Religion*, vol. 3, *The Consummate Religion.* Edited by Peter C. Hodgson, translated by Peter C. Hodgson et al. Berkeley: University of California Press, 1985.

———. *Philosophy of History.* Translated by J. Sibree. Kitchener, Ontario: Batoche, 2001.

Joyce, James. *Ulysses.* New ed. New York: Everyman's Library Classics, 1992.

Milbank, John. "On Modern Ontology." In *Beyond Secular Order: The Representation of Being and the Representation of People*, 19–113. Oxford: Wiley-Blackwell, 2013.

O'Regan, Cyril. *The Anatomy of Misremembering: Von Balthasar's Response to Philosophical Modernity, volume 1: Hegel.* New York: Herder & Herder, 2014.

———. *Gnostic Return in Modernity.* Albany, NY: SUNY Press, 2001.

———. *The Heterodox Hegel.* Albany, NY: SUNY Press, 1994.

Pirandello, Luigi. *Uno, nessuno e centomila*, Libro Secondo, V, "Fissazioni." Torino: Einaudi, 1994.

Rose, Gilliam. *Hegel Contra Sociology.* Cambridge: Cambridge University Press, 1981.

Shakespeare, William. *Hamlet.* In *The Oxford Shakespeare*, edited by G. R. Hibbard. Oxford: Oxford University Press, 1987.

Williams, Rowan. *Wrestling with Angels: Conversations in Modern Theology*. Edited by Mike Higgton. London: SCM, 2007.

3

Deleuze and Valentinian Narrative Grammar

CHRISTOPHER BEN SIMPSON

My counterintuitive contention in this essay is that such a would-be world-affirming materialism as Deleuze's is in odd proximity to Gnosticism. Part of what is so strange about this critique is that what is most objectionable in Deleuze's work for the confessional theologian is not his atheistic materialism but the presence in his thought of elements of a Gnostic religious narrative that functions as a parody and an inversion of Christianity. My conclusion regarding persistent and pervasive Gnostic themes in Deleuze comes in part from a recognition of a plausible genealogical account of how this strain of thought could have come down to Deleuze (depending largely on the work of Christian Kerslake) and in a larger part from seeing the consistent structural similarities between the thought of Deleuze and Gnosticism as presented in the work of Cyril O'Regan.[1]

---

1. This essay is excerpted from my *Deleuze and Theology* (London: Bloomsbury, 2012). The material is used by kind permission of T. & T. Clark.

1. Deleuze, the Esoteric Tradition, and Valentinian Narrative Grammar

Thinking in terms of "a somewhat speculative genealogy,"[2] Deleuze stands in a certain relation to minor authors[3] like Johann Malfatti de Montereggio (1775–1859), Hoëne Wronski (1776–1853), and Francis Warrain (1867–1940), who were key in the revival of the modern European esoteric, occult, "heretical" tradition with ties to the Gnostic return in modernity.[4] Malfatti and Wronski were especially influential in, indeed providing the "theoretical foundations" for, the French esoteric movement of Martinism, "one of the main currents of occultism in the nineteenth century."[5] Today (as in Deleuze's time) Malfatti and Wronski "remain almost unknown, and," Kerslake notes, "Deleuze was unusual for referring to them at all."[6]

Deleuze mentions Wronski in the context of his discussion of the "esoteric" use of calculus in *Difference and Repetition*.[7] Beyond specific mention, it is evident that Deleuze "ended up appealing to [Wronksi's] ideas to ground his philosophy of differentiation"[8] and his formulation of the distinction between the virtual and the actual—where, for Wronski, "knowledge and Being are opposed as creation to inertia, as spontaneous calculation versus preservation and petrifaction. Given this context, we can imagine the creative principle and the preservative principle combining in a principle of transformation."[9]

---

2. Crockett, *Radical Political Theology*, 135. Crockett is speculating about another genealogy, for the record.

3. Deleuze, *Abécédaire*.

4. Kerslake, "The Somnambulist and the Hermaphrodite"; Bonta, "Rhizome," 62–63; D. Smith, "Univocity," 167–68.

5. Martinism "originat[ed] in the thought of Martinès de Pasqually (?–1774), and his follower Louis Claude Saint-Martin (1743–1803). The former, a Spanish or Portuguese Jew, had inaugurated a number of secret societies in France devoted to theurgic ritual, while his follower Saint-Martin was the author of mystical tracts (including one entitled *L'Homme du désir*) which gave primacy to the mystical task of interior transformation over ritual. . . . By the end of the 19th century, a number of Rosicrucians, Freemasons, Illuminati, and theosophists inhabited Paris and assembled to form a new movement of French Martinism, in which Papus and Stanislas de Guaita were the intellectually dominant figures. The theoretical foundations of late French Martinism were provided by Malfatti and Hoëne Wronski" (Kerslake, "The Somnambulist and the Hermaphrodite").

6. Kerslake, "The Somnambulist and the Hermaphrodite."

7. Kerslake, "Wronski," 168–69.

8. Kerslake, "Wronski," 168.

9. Kerslake, "Wronski," 178.

Francis Warrain—who "published several major studies of Wronski, as well as editing the collection of papers by Wronski to which Deleuze refers in *Difference and Repetition*"[10]—expanded Wronski's thought toward a metaphysical vitalism that focused on the idea of a "non-organic life" as having to do with the "pulse of differentiation," of intense "vibrations" (repeated differences).[11] Such a mathematical vitalism Warrain also connected to cabbalist mysticism working toward a "rational" (not revealed) religion in an esoteric mode.[12]

One of Deleuze's first publications (when he was twenty-one) was an introduction to a new edition of Johann Malfatti's *Mathesis: or Studies on the Anarchy and Hierarchy of Knowledge* published "by a small publishing house, 'Griffon d'Or', which published books mostly on occult themes in the immediate aftermath of the war, including a number of books on Martinism."[13] Malfatti's *Mathesis* combined esoteric mathematics with theosophical thought. Seeing theosophy as tracing back to origins in Hindu mysticism, Malfatti (a heterodox physician) found an "occult anatomy, in which the vital forces that rule the body were ordered hierarchically in polarities, potencies and planes."[14] Malfatti and Wronski stand as central figures in nineteenth-century esoteric, occult, theosophical Martinism that stands in a line of descent (focusing on an esoteric, secret tradition of "initiates") originating with the ancients, passing through Jakob Boehme in modernity, and revived in their own day.[15]

Mark Bonta observes the "rather startling resonance" between Deleuze and Jakob Boehme. Boehme's vision of the divine as highly complex and radically anti-hierarchical and the world as a "manifestation of a drama

---

10. Kerslake, "Wronski," 170.

11. Kerslake, "Wronski," 170–71, 183.

12. Kerslake, "Wronski," 171–72.

13. Kerslake writes of Malfatti, an Austrian physician—highly respected in his time, Beethoven's doctor, perhaps his poisoner, unintentionally (using alchemical elements like arsenic and lead medicinally) and/or intentionally (as an agent of the Austrian government)—that "his ideas are frankly so strange that a basic reality-check on his existence and movements needs to be carried out before any further examination of his work" (Kerslake, "The Somnambulist and the Hermaphrodite").

14. Kerslake, "The Somnambulist and the Hermaphrodite".

15. "Malfatti is more reckless in suggesting that there is one universal philosophy which emanates first of all from Indian mysticism, and then repeats itself in different forms throughout the history of religion, through the Neo-Platonism of Proclus and Dionysius the Areopagite, down to Boehme and Saint-Martin. This conviction that something eternal is repeated by various 'initiates' throughout history is a background assumption of Malfatti's book, as well as of the esoteric and occult traditions in general" (Kerslake, "The Somnambulist and the Hermaphrodite").

taking place in God himself" represent the kind of "subterranean mystical currents" subject to the nineteenth-century occult revival to which Deleuze was indebted.[16] With Boehme—"a highly plausible candidate for designating the alpha point of the genealogy of Gnostic return in modernity"[17]—we can see the revivification of a "hidden, or heretical, tradition"[18] that mutated in the European occult tradition fostered by Malfatti, Wronski, and Warrain. It is of this strange, esoteric teaching that one may hear something of "the last, dying and frenzied echoes" in the equally strange work of Deleuze.[19]

For an understanding of this Gnostic return, I depend upon Cyril O'Regan's seminal work, *Gnostic Return in Modernity*[20] from which I trace an uncanny systematic coherence or isomorphism between Deleuze's thought and Gnosticism as presented by O'Regan.[21] O'Regan defines Gnosticism in terms of a Valentinian narrative grammar and the rule-governed deformation of classical Valentinian narrative genres. The Valentinian narrative grammar is "an invariant sequence of episodes" in the story of "the becoming of the perfection of the divine," of the loss and recovery of divine perfection.[22] This "invariant sequence of episodes" mimics, doubles, and "transgressively interprets" the central episodes of the biblical narrative,[23] such that in this counterfeit doubling of Christianity contrary positions are taken on: "the nature of the divine, the value of creation, the interpretation of the fall of human being, Christ and his redemptive mission, and finally the nature of salvation."[24] The six narrative episodes of the Valentinian narrative grammar are:[25]

1. A realm of pure and undisturbed divine perfection, presumptively immune from change and narrative adventure.

16. Bonta, "Rhizome," 62–63, 66; Kerslake, "The Somnambulist and the Hermaphrodite."

17. O'Regan, *Gnostic Return*, 8.

18. Albert, "Impersonal, Hylozoic Cosmology," 193.

19. Kerslake, "The Somnambulist and the Hermaphrodite."

20. While O'Regan sees something of twentieth-century Gnosticism in the radical, secular theology of Altizer and Tillich, Deleuze is not mentioned in the book (O'Regan, *Gnostic Return*, 5, 36).

21. My reading of Deleuze along these lines coheres, at least in part, with Hallward's reading.

22. O'Regan, *Gnostic Return*, 138, 141.

23. O'Regan, *Gnostic Return*, 138.

24. O'Regan, *Gnostic Return*, 101. On William Desmond's understanding of the counterfeit double see Simpson, *Religion, Metaphysics and the Postmodern*, 103.

25. O'Regan, *Gnostic Return*, 133, 138.

2. The introduction of fault into the realm of divine perfection and the fall from the divine, that is the fall *of* the divine and the emergence of the creative capacity that parodies the creator God of Genesis.

3. The positing of a source in and from the divine that reveals itself as non-divine and the emergence of evil as associated with the creation of the material and psychic world.

4. The fall of human "pneumatic being" through a kind of forgetfulness.

5. The appearance of "a redeemer figure who is associated with Jesus" who delivers liberating knowledge apart from any saving activity of an atonement.

6. Salvation as "the realization of a human perfection, associated with knowledge, and the full-scale reconstitution of divine perfection."

The "systematic deformations" of the classical Valentinian genre are the "theogonic [regarding the origin of God/gods], pathetic, and world-affirming figuration[s]."[26] Deleuze, we will suggest, echoes all six narrative episodes and two of the three common modern "systematic deformations" of the Valentinian narrative grammar (the theogonic and the world-affirming). Deleuze's reversed Platonism ends up entailing something like a strange Gnosticism—without an *archē*, without a One—an orthodox heterodoxy in which, as Hart observes, the "mirror preserves the image it inverts."[27]

2. Virtual Life and the Dark Pleroma

The notion of the virtual as a power of which the actual world of our experience is an expression displays the connection between the virtual and "virtue" in the sense of power—as Hallward notes, "the older, now archaic meaning of the word, which relates it to the possession of inherent virtues or powers."[28] This can be seen against the background of a genealogy tracing from late medieval voluntarism (focusing on Divine will and power as "the only explanation for the way things are"[29]) to the modern focus on the autonomous power and will of the human person to the late modern focus on a thoroughly inhuman impersonal power beneath the human person—such that we, as William Desmond writes, "participate in living

---

26. O'Regan, *Gnostic Return*, 45.

27. Hart, *The Beauty of the Infinite*, 38.

28. Hallward, *Out of This World*, 30; See the OED for "virtual" and "virtue."

29. Pickstock, *After Writing*, 123; Milbank, *Theology and Social Theory*, 381.

in an organic nature alive with a darker, sublimer energy."[30] One thinks of Schopenhauer, but also Spinoza, Bergson, and Nietzsche. (I imagine the descent of mad power from the heavens to the proud mortals to the darkly rumbling earth itself beneath them.) As with Wronski's "creative virtuality" proper to the Absolute as a "continuous self-differentiation of creative becoming," Deleuze's virtual is a fundamental autogenic power,[31] such that, as Hallward writes, "existent individuals are simply so many divergent facets of one and the same creative force" or power.[32] This fundamental movement of power is the divine game—"that is, the game of unqualified creation as such, behind which there lies only the pure potential of absolute constituent power or play."[33]

Deleuze's thought can be presented as a kind of pantheism, emphasizing the becoming of the divine as, in Desmond's terms, an erotic origin, a divine self-origination, "self-determining eternity that determines itself in its own temporal productions."[34] Such a "dialectical monism," as Desmond tells the story, is a version of human self-determining self-transcendence.[35] Reflecting, as Hallward observes, "the notion that the universe and all it contains is a facet of a singular and absolute creative power," Deleuze "annuls the difference between God and world . . . in favour of God, not world"[36]— that is, instead of installing a dualism between God and the world, Deleuze sees the world as a function of God, or the divine power or game: "dualism is therefore only a moment, which must lead to the re-formation of a monism."[37] Here Deleuze's philosophy generally parallels Boehme' theosophy in which "the course of the world," Kerslake writes, is "understood as the manifestation of a drama taking place in God himself."[38] In this, Deleuze follows the general thrust of the Gnostic narrative of "the becoming of the perfection of the divine."[39]

---

30. Desmond, "From Under the Ground of the Cave."

31. Kerslake, "Wronski," 176, 182.

32. Hallward, *Out of This World*, 16–17.

33. Hallward, *Out of This World*, 54, 143.

34. Desmond, *God and the Between*, 106.

35. Desmond, *God and the Between*, 92.

36. Hallward, *Out of This World*, 4, 10.

37. Deleuze, *Bergsonism*, 29. Hallward writes: "one of the most characteristic features of Deleuze's work is his tendency to present what initially appears as a binary relation in such a way as to show that this relation is in fact determined by only one of its two 'terms'" (Hallward, *Out of This World*, 156).

38. Kerslake, "The Somnambulist and the Hermaphrodite"; Bonta, "Rhizome," 68.

39. O'Regan, *Gnostic Return*, 141, 136.

Seeing difference in itself as the divine, unknowable, "transcendent," inexplicable—a difference that "withdraws from thinkability"[40]—Deleuze represents, for David Bentley Hart, a postmodern "narrative of the sublime" for which the unrepresentable (here difference itself) *is* and is more true than the representable.[41] The visible world is the effect of an invisible potential.[42] Here, as Milbank writes, the "ungrounded 'mythical' content of difference," Deleuze's positive difference as the sole transcendental, is "the 'original' and continuous variation of a primordial 'unity'" as "always, endlessly, 'other' to itself."[43] Reflecting modern Gnosticism's different understanding of difference in the absolute as a change "in the meaning and function of the Trinity,"[44] Deleuze's fundamental reality is a deified "non-relational difference"—a self-differing power, "a differing [that] differs itself by itself."[45] With such an absolute, Hallward observes, "there can be no 'substantial' difference between a purely self-differing unity and a purely self-scattering multiplicity, since in either case there is no place for any relational conception of 'self.'"[46]

The Deleuzian divine is a God rendered unrecognizable,[47] in Desmond's terms, a dark origin. Behind Nietzsche's Dionysius, "the system behind Nietzsche's anti-system,"[48] is Schopenhauer's Will—a "dark self-expressing energy," a dark origin, "out of which all comes to be and into which all things pass, as into an ultimately inarticulate night"—with which "there is no point to its striving beyond itself," the apotheosis of the autonomous self into a blind Will at the root of the world.[49] Likewise, Deleuze's

40. Davies, "Thinking Difference," 84.

41. Hart, *The Beauty of the Infinite*, 52, 56.

42. Clark, "A Whiteheadian Chaosmos," 190.

43. Milbank, *Theology and Social Theory*, xiii, 301, 306, 314. Milbank notes that Deleuze's philosophy of difference cannot so easily (as with Heidegger or Derrida) fit the claim that it is an ontology of violence (Milbank, *Theology and Social Theory*, 314).

44. O'Regan, *Gnostic Return*, 2.

45. Hallward, *Out of This World*, 152–53.

46. Hallward, *Out of This World*, 156. "By 'relation' I mean a process that operates between two or more minimally discernible terms, in such a way as to condition or inflect (but not fully to generate) the individuality of each term. A relation is only a relation in this sense if its terms retain some limited autonomy with respect to each other. A relation is only a relation if it is between terms that can be meaningfully discerned, even if the means of this discernment proceed at the very limit of indiscernment. In other words, the question is: can Deleuze's theory of difference provide a coherent theory of relation between terms" (ibid., 152).

47. Bonta, "Rhizome," 7.

48. Desmond is here referring to Christopher Janaway's work.

49. Desmond, "From Under the Ground of the Cave." Desmond, *God and the Between*, 24–26.

axiomatic decision to think difference is a decision for that which "over-reaches thought," which is invisible, imperceptible, and immeasurable, and is not thinkable.[50] The will to power in Deleuze as the power of difference itself is indeed a reversed Platonism, with the absolute not as the Sun in the sky above but as that under the ground of the cave—for, Desmond writes, "Will is no sun, is no good, but a dark original, darker even than the shadow land of representation."[51] Such a dark divine, "a dark origin more primordial than the half-light half-darkness of the Cave," is more like Lovecraft's Cthulhu—a madness underneath our shadowy sanities—for in this reversal "the good God has flipped into its opposite and shows a face more like the evil genius disporting with itself."[52] The Deleuzian "One," then, is a chaotic "One"—a fecund Chaos that "stands in the place of the One," an eternal becoming that stands in the place of an eternal unity.[53] Instead of a transcendent divine will violently imposing order upon the world, Deleuze's is an essentially chaotic, problematic, agonistic, "violent" will or power.[54] This, in Desmond's terms, accords with Gnosticism's own "immanent divine agonistics" as "an equivocal agon within the divine as such."[55]

The first narrative episode of O'Regan's Valentinian narrative grammar presents "the fullness of the divine as both the alpha and the omega of a drama in which the aboriginal integrity of the divine is lost and regained."[56] Deleuzian life as virtual difference follows the pattern of this becoming divinity. Life in the Gnostic Valentinian narrative grammar "is ascribable to the pleroma and is a property of any being who participates in it" such that the "extrapleromic realm is the realm of death."[57] The divine life in Deleuze, likewise, is not as much one being as a domain of being, difference itself, a dark pleroma.

For Deleuze, after Wronski and Warrain, life itself is internally plural, dynamic, problematic, and differential—such that life itself as difference itself is the "vibration," the "ultimately non-organic pulse of differentiation" of a virtual "transcendental calculus."[58] "The endless, goalless, production of

50. Desmond, *God and the Between*, 24–26; Hallward, *Out of This World*, 36; Davies, "Thinking Difference," 85.

51. Desmond, "From Under the Ground of the Cave."

52. Desmond, "From Under the Ground of the Cave."

53. Hart, *The Beauty of the Infinite*, 57; Balthasar, *Cosmic Liturgy*, 45.

54. Hart, *The Beauty of the Infinite*, 64; Milbank, *Theology and Social Theory*, 278–79; Sherman, "No Werewolves in Theology?" 13–14.

55. Desmond, *God and the Between*, 218.

56. O'Regan, *Gnostic Return*, 133.

57. O'Regan, *Gnostic Return*, 131.

58. Kerslake, "Wronski," 170–71, 185. "On Warrain's Wronskian architectonic, life

Difference" for Deleuze is a fundamental plurality of "innumerable forces at play"—"multiple 'little divinities' effecting random syntheses of differential elements."[59] The divine life for Deleuze is a virtual movement of being in itself as an "infinitely powerful" creativity.[60] The internally multiple "One," the Deleuzian dark pleroma, is virtual difference itself becoming itself in its own creative generation.[61]

3. Degenerative Pantheism and the Moral Lobster

The picture of transcendence that Deleuze rejects in favor of immanence is something of a caricature. In Desmond's terms, it is God as the static, univocal eternity—absolute in its immutability and stasis beyond time and becoming, and so unable to relate to the world—that generates an equivocal oppositional dualism between God and the world.[62] Deleuze's problem with transcendence as hegemonic is not in relation to an orthodox Christian understanding of transcendence but to something at once "pre-Christian" and a "recurrent temptation" in the Christian tradition "to construe divinity over against or parallel to the universe."[63] The understanding of God as "the world's infinite contrary" is not the best representation of the Christian tradition but is the product of theological decline. God and creatures are not in competition with each other, for God is not a being; as Hart writes, the "God who gives of his bounty, not a God at war with darkness."[64]

---

is composed of a series of levels of reality, each a rhythmical and dynamic compromise between continuity and discontinuity, each with its own 'universal problem' [problème universel] (how to find a dynamic equilibrium for opposing forces), each with its own secret harmonies. For Warrain, this 'life' is the true matter of the transcendental calculus" (ibid.).

59. Clark, "A Whiteheadian Chaosmos," 192; Bonta, "Rhizome," 65. Kerslake writes: "Warrain's metaphysics of vibration and rhythm appears to be *both* immanently philosophical *and* esoteric, and suggests a way in which the potential clash of principles between philosophy and the 'esoteric' might be resolved. Warrain illustrated his chapter on Wronski's Law of Creation in *Concrete Synthesis* with a diagram which correlates the elements of Wronski's system one-by-one with the cabbalistic sephiroth of Jewish mysticism" (Kerslake, "Wronski," 171).

60. Hallward, *Out of This World*, 1, 4, 8, 10.

61. Hallward, *Out of This World*, 16, 55, 164.

62. Simpson, *Religion, Metaphysics, and the Postmodern*, 103–4; Desmond, *Ethics and the Between*, 42–44.

63. Burrell, *Freedom and Creation*, 60; McCabe, *God Still Matters*, 6–7.

64. Hart, *The Beauty of the Infinite*, 258; Burrell, *Freedom and Creation*, 62. Hart writes: "And this state of theological decline was so precipitous and complete that it even became possible for someone as formidably intelligent as Calvin, without any apparent embarrassment, to regard the fairly lurid portrait of the omnipotent despot of

Deleuze's "enthusiastically neo-Spinozist" pantheism reflects an aversion to hierarchy, echoing the occultist desire to escape from the judgment of God.[65] Yet in endeavoring to affirm this world by affirming an impersonal and immanent process as ultimate, he ends up with something other than the actual and concrete world of our experience, now subordinated. Embracing an immanent monism in order to escape from dualism and transcendence, in the manner Deleuze does, does not ultimately escape another kind of dualism.[66] Deleuze's actual and virtual are both real, but the virtual (as Hallward writes, the "virtual creating" as "the reality that lives in any actual creature," like an immortal soul[67]) is ultimately more real, the "'good' transcendental creative factor" having a definite privilege and priority over the "'bad' static and representable created element," over "the illusory solidity of the actual."[68] In this way, Deleuze's reversed Platonism yet reflects a Neoplatonic or Gnostic dualism—in Desmond's words, a "hyperbolic monism" that yet maintains "a strikingly strong dualistic sense."[69]

Over against an understanding of God as transcendent creator,[70] Deleuze's immanent, creative God follows the Gnostic narrative of "the becoming of the perfection of the divine" in the world-affirming variety (or "modern systematic deformation" in O'Regan's terms).[71] As such, Deleuze's God coheres with Desmond's idea of the dark origin—the apotheosis or "decomposition" of the "god" of the autonomous self into a blind Will at the root of the world,[72] a Dionysian origin, a dark "erotic absolute," "a blind, insatiable striving" prior to reason.[73] The Gnostic god is such a dark origin, relative to which "the world as a counterfeit double or dissembling medium is coupled with an equivocal *agon* both within the divine as such and between the divine and what comes to be relatively 'outside' the divine."[74]

---

book III of his *Institutes* . . . as a proper depiction of the Christian God." (Hart, *The Beauty of the Infinite*, 134).

65. Hallward, *Out of This World*, 4, 10, 12, 156; Kerslake, "The Somnambulist and the Hermaphrodite."

66. Milbank, "Immanence and Life," 18, 21.

67. Hallward, *Out of This World*, 35.

68. Milbank, "Immanence and Life," 16–17; Hallward, *Out of This World*, 32; Justaert, "Évaluation Théologique," 532.

69. Desmond, *God and the Between*, 211; Pickstock, "Theology and Post-modernity," 77; Milbank, *Theology and Social Theory*, 380.

70. Hallward, *Out of This World*, 3, 6, 12–14, 54.

71. O'Regan, *Gnostic Return*, 45, 141.

72. Desmond, *God and the Between*, 24–26.

73. Desmond, *Art, Origins, Otherness*, 165; Desmond, *God and the Between*, 25.

74. Desmond continues: "Immanent divine agonistics: Sophia, emanation of the

In O'Regan's Gnostic Valentinian narrative grammar, there is a moment in which the pleroma, the divine fullness, creates through its own fault, its own fall. There is, as O'Regan writes, the "introduction of fault into the realm of divine perfection and fall from the divine that is the fall *of* the divine and the emergence of the creative capacity that parodies the creator God of Genesis" as "the almighty and good creator of all that is."[75] The dynamic divine fullness overflows as a kind of fall that yields an ontological deficiency in the lower levels of being—a generation that is a degeneration in which "the divine itself in the spark of light has become trapped in the dissembling medium of material; hence the lower agonistics is a continuation of the highest breach within divinity."[76] Deleuze's movement of actualization in which, as Anthony Paul Smith writes, "identity is formed at the cost of losing the processes from which it arises," represents just such a fall.[77] This complex process of actualization reflects the plural levels of generation or degeneration that are found in Gnostic narratives, such as Boehme's.[78] The unilateral radiation of the virtual, the primary, dynamic "active or creative *naturans*," generates the actual, the secondary, "passive or created *naturata*."[79] Life as virtual power devolves into its actual, material embodiment as an estranged mutant progeny, something that wraps and swaddles and smothers, as something that is to be escaped.[80] This fallenness of the actual, in which things "fall into their allocated place,"[81] reflects the "negative estimate of the creator" in Gnosticism with its "negative consequences for an evaluation of the created order."[82] The virtual here is an abstract, ghostly force that never appears, is never presented or given.[83] When there is a personal God that shows up in Deleuze's writings that is not the positive impersonal God as the power of life, this God, the God of judgment, is something like the Demiurge, the evil creator God that the Gnostics often equated with the Old Testament God. In such a Gnostic disfiguration of the biblical narrative, this tyrannical voluntarist deity is the creator of

---

Alien God as absolutely pleromatic, beyond pleroma, so hyperbolic in light as to be, in a way, a dark origin" (*Art, Origins, Otherness*, 218).

75. O'Regan, *Gnostic Return*, 138, 162.

76. Desmond, *God and the Between*, 59, 218.

77. A. Smith, "The Judgment of God and the Immeasurable," 80.

78. Bonta, "Rhizome," 65, 70; Desmond, *God and the Between*, 221.

79. Hallward, *Out of This World*, 1, 29–30, 37, 47, 162.

80. Hallward, *Out of This World*, 25; Desmond, *God and the Between*, 221.

81. Hallward, *Out of This World*, 31.

82. O'Regan, *Gnostic Return*, 151.

83. Hallward, *Out of This World*, 22, 27.

imprisoned, hierarchical actuality, the enslaving moral master, the monstrous lobster enforcing identity.[84]

Deleuze makes an axiomatic decision for immanence over transcendence. His insistence on the univocity of being follows from and reinforces this choice for immanence. It is from this perspective that Deleuze, in his (in Hart's words) "excruciatingly unsophisticated" understanding of analogy, then sees analogy as something lukewarm, as trying to have it both ways, both univocity and equivocity, supporting a hierarchy of being—thus equivocity—and a stable sameness within that same hierarchy—thus univocity.[85] In fact, Deleuze's disdain for analogy is less a critique of analogy in itself than unfolding the consequences of Deleuze's axiomatic commitment to immanence. As Deleuze writes in *Difference and Repetition*: "Univocity signifies that being itself is univocal, while that of which it is said is equivocal, precisely the opposite of analogy."[86] But this simply misses the point of analogy, or, as Milbank writes in response to the above quote: "Of course, precisely not."[87] Analogy need not so much be, as Deleuze insists, "complicit with identity, presence and substance" as it may be rooted in a different understanding of genuine difference. "Analogy," Milbank writes, "does not imply 'identity,' but identity and difference at once" and so recognizes "the primacy of mixtures, *continua*, overlaps and disjunctions, all subject in principle to limitless transformation."[88] When Deleuze asserts that "to claim that being is said in one and the same sense of God and of the flea is a terrible thing, we must burn people like that,"[89] he misses that an orthodox Christian understanding of analogy and participation entails just this intimacy—analogy does not function to insulate God is his transcendence, it makes God more immanent to the flea than the flea is to itself. Analogy sees genuine difference in relation as ultimate. Analogy is also an attempt to be true, as Hart writes, to "the way in which difference concretely occurs, in sequences of positionings, interdependencies, and analogies that make room for one

---

84. O'Regan, *Gnostic Return*, 150–51; McCabe, *God Matters*, 17.

85. Hart, *The Beauty of the Infinite*, 62; Kaufman, "Klossowski, Deleuze, and Orthodoxy," 54. Deleuze sees the supporters of analogy as "those who are between the two [univocity and equivocity]" who are also "always those who establish what we call orthodoxy"—regarding Thomas: "historically he won"(Kaufman, "Klossowski, Deleuze, and Orthodoxy," 54). But is this true? Perhaps he "won" until only shortly after his death in 1277. When his work was reinstated, it was with a modern univocal framework towering in the background.

86. Deleuze, *Difference and Repetition*, 304.

87. Milbank, "The Soul of Reciprocity (Part Two)," 505.

88. Milbank, *Theology and Social Theory*, 306–7.

89. Kaufman, "Klossowski, Deleuze, and Orthodoxy," 54.

another."[90] As Milbank writes, Deleuze's "transcendental univocity, being entirely empty of content, and indeed the medium of a sheerly differentiated content, cannot possibly appear in itself to our awareness, but can only be assumed and exemplified in the phenomena which it organizes. Yet if Being remains in itself unknowable, always absent and concealed, then how do we justify the characterization of Being as univocity?" In the end, "nothing grounds a preference for this coding."[91] This reflects the Gnostic Valentinian "discursive paradoxes of an aporetic kind" in which the dark pleroma, "the Unknown God is revealed as unrevealed," as unrevealable.[92] The analogical, as with Desmond's metaxological, is the "middle realm" that "allows for a space of movement and reversal that escapes the pitfalls Deleuze locates in the dialectic."[93] The genuine difference that is given is not the pure difference of a relationless dispersal, but an irreducibly plural, different, and yet interrelated metaxological between. Without relation, Oliver Davies writes, "difference retreats into itself and thus withdraws from thinkability. It is only the thinking of a relationality between difference and ourselves . . . that can offer a dialectic in which thinking as a thinking beyond thought becomes meaningful."[94] The immanent middle of difference in relation need not be dominated or reduced to a flat sameness (a not-difference) by transcendence, and, as Milbank writes, "in order to avoid monism collapsing into a hierarchical dualism, or else an inverted hierarchical dualism . . . one needs . . . a philosophy of mediation. But mediation is, within immanence, always vanishing."[95]

4. The Human and the Inhuman

The understanding of the human as something deficient, a kind of prison to be escaped, echoes or coheres "the fall of pneumatic being" in Gnosticism.[96] The result, as Desmond writes, is that "we ourselves are the prison, and we are in the prison of ourselves."[97] The "fallen" human condition arises in Gnosticism in a manner that "depends directly or indirectly on the

90. Hart, *The Beauty of the Infinite*, 281.

91. Milbank, *Theology and Social Theory*, 306.

92. O'Regan, *Gnostic Return*, 146–48.

93. Kaufman, "Klossowski, Deleuze, and Orthodoxy," 47.

94. Davies, "Thinking Difference," 84.

95. Milbank, "The Mystery of Reason," 77.

96. O'Regan, *Gnostic Return*, 138.

97. Desmond, *God and the Between*, 221.

fallen divine,"[98] a deficient humanity tied to a deficient divinity. "Creation devolves from the fallen, disfigured aspect of the pleroma that is the fruit of misrecognition and failure to acknowledge limits."[99] The cause of the fall of spiritual being within the divine (with the distorted or confused element of the divine) is maintained in human beings by a forgetfulness—by a striving to be something one cannot be while forgetting the true nature of pleromatic life. For humans, Deleuze's true world—the "rhizomatic, connected world of pure desire"[100]—is another world, as the anthropological strata of meaning, the human world in which we live, is a degenerate projection. For the human, the unconscious and inhuman life of the world is "unlived," and indeed, for humans, "unlivable."[101] For Deleuze, the human world is a world of illusion, of *doxa*. We are not only ignorant about ourselves and about the world, but our humanity (the illusion of our humanity) seems to be at odds with a genuine appreciation of what we are—such that we are "trapped in ignorance, impotence and slavery."[102] Our attachment to the human strata of our "creatural delusions" is so consistently "obstinate" that it can be said that, for Deleuze, "humanity is the form that creation takes when it denies or turns against itself."[103] What we need to do is to become something other than our actual humanity, to escape the judgment of God, as the dominion of some evil divinity such that genuine pneumatic being (Gnostic true humanity) is at once "superior to the creator and his creation."[104]

5. The Christ of Philosophers

Deleuze's understanding of Spinoza as the Christ of philosophers follows the esoteric nineteenth-century impulse in figures like Warrain toward a "rational" (not revealed) religion.[105] Such a rational, Spinozist religion that has no need for atonement follows the Gnostic refusal "to understand the passion and death [of Jesus Christ] as the mystery of atonement."[106] But more deeply, the function of the Deleuzian Christ of philosophers resembles the fifth narrative episode of the O'Regan's Gnostic Valentinian Narrative Grammar

98. O'Regan, *Gnostic Return*, 138.

99. O'Regan, *Gnostic Return*, 133.

100. Shaviro, "God," 13.

101. Hallward, *Out of This World*, 92

102. Hallward, *Out of This World*, 55.

103. Hallward, *Out of This World*, 20, 62–63.

104. O'Regan, *Gnostic Return*, 151.

105. Kerslake, "Wronski," 172.

106. O'Regan, *Gnostic Return*, 151.

in which "a divine being, either explicitly or implicitly associated with Jesus Christ, enters the extrapleromatic world to recall human beings to their true destiny."[107] Deleuze's philosophy is faithful to Spinoza as an immanent Gnostic savior whose philosophy is the secret liberating knowledge that the world is not as we think it is. Here the gnosis is the philosophy of Spinoza as the Christ of philosophers whose *Ethics* awakens us from "the spell of ourselves" and recalls us to the virtual plane of immanence, the domain of spirit, of divine life—the good news of the crowned anarch-ingdom.[108] Here Spinoza resembles the Socratic teacher in Kierkegaard's *Philosophical Fragments*—the teacher who does not uniquely reveal something that one could not have come to otherwise, but is merely the passing occasion for one's realization of the answer that is immanent, that was always in one's midst. The immanent gnosis/gospel (the gospel of Spinoza, according to Deleuze) is such that, as Hallward notes, "redemption from the human," the overcoming and undoing of the human strata, "is the task of the human alone."[109] Philosophy, philosophers—and therefore supremely Spinoza, the Christ of philosophers—provides immanent assistance in seeing through the illusions of the actual.[110] Associated with Christ, but as a parodic reversal of the work of Christ, Spinoza stands to recall humanity to its true, inhuman destiny—only a philosopher can save us.

6. Stuck in the Desert, Saying Yes to the Ocean

As Deleuze's philosophy develops, especially in his partnership with Guattari, the actual world comes to be viewed as pervaded by structures of illusion and oppression that are to be escaped. Hallward sees in this "subtractive" move something implicitly mystical—a "mechanics of *dis*-embodiment and *de*-materialization" that continually leads out of the actual world as the site of entrapment toward the virtual as the site of life and creation.[111] We humans must transcend the actual as we experience it to achieve non-human immanence. Philosophy, for Deleuze, is to serve as a vehicle for the spirit's escape from its confinement in matter.[112] This reflects the Gnostic understanding of the world with its smothering intermediate layers/strata as a place of estrangement—in which "spiritual" humanity is enclosed and

107. O'Regan, *Gnostic Return*, 133.

108. Desmond, *God and the Between*, 221.

109. Hallward, *Out of This World*, 64, 90.

110. Hallward, *Out of This World*, 35–36.

111. Hallward, *Out of This World*, 3, 21, 44–45, 164.

112. Hallward, *Out of This World*, 7, 20.

would escape.[113] Here the spiritual, true humanity, in a reversal of the biblical narrative, would show a superiority to the creator and his creation.[114]

Indeed, in affirming the virtual, and advocating a return to the living, creative virtual, Deleuze reflects the final narrative episode of the Gnostic Valentinian Narrative Grammar, that of "the full-scale reconstitution of divine perfection"—the "narrative closure or *synclasis* [which is] a wished-for symmetry between narrative alpha and omega, such that ontotheological narrative essentially shapes a circle."[115] To gain access to reality, we must dissolve the obstructions of actuality, to see through them, and so return to their virtual, generative origin.[116] To overcome man and to return to the divine creativity as "a kind of becoming-God of the human"[117] is quite similar to a Gnostic salvation as, in Desmond's terms, "an 'awakening' to one's identity with the divine."[118]

The liberation and affirmation that are the substance of Deleuzian salvation have a spectral quality. Justaert argues that Deleuze's "liberation"—as seeing through the illusion of consciousness and discovering the true nature of unconscious reality—is not unlike Western consumer "Buddhist" conception of liberation as a "going with the flow."[119] This liberation is an idealized liberation—an infinite resistance, a continuous deterritorialization, a permanent revolution that seems to be, by definition, non-concrete.[120] Deleuze's affirmation, as well, comes off as abstract—as Hart writes, his "joyous affirmation of the world" is the kind that "can be accomplished only upon the mountaintops, from an impossibly sublime perspective"; this affirmation is only the most general evaluation, such that, as Hallward writes, "preoccupation with the world as such, let alone a concern with the orderly representation of the things of the world, serves only to inhibit any such affirmation."[121] Contrariwise, to be true to the world as experienced, to make a judgment about such, can be a critique that is true to the world and yet seeks to change it—surely this is what it means to be a part of the world, to be involved in it. From this perspective, pure acceptance or affirmation would be a turn into renunciation—a white night in which all

113. Desmond, *God and the Between*, 221.

114. O'Regan, *Gnostic Return*, 151.

115. O'Regan, *Gnostic Return*, 138, 134.

116. Hallward, *Out of This World*, 33–34, 50.

117. Hallward, *Out of This World*, 57, 67.

118. Desmond, *God and the Between*, 223.

119. Justaert, "Évaluation Théologique," 543–44.

120. Hart, *The Beauty of the Infinite*, 70; Justaert, "Évaluation Théologique," 536.

121. Hart, *The Beauty of the Infinite*, 70–71; Hallward, *Out of This World*, 6.

cows are white. An affirmation that absolves one of relation to the actual world (and of oneself as well)—a "dissipation of the actual," an "intensive disembodiment."[122]

Deleuze's immanent philosophical religiosity would "complete the human adventure by escaping it" through the invention of "forms of transformative subtraction or purification."[123] This philosophical religiosity is an austere renouncer path that is a strange asceticism or self-dissolution.[124] Justaert again draws parallels between Deleuze (and Spinoza behind him) with Western consumer Buddhism: a discovery of the very nature of reality, understanding the subject and consciousness as an illusion, an immanent vision of the world, and a denial of the world of representation.[125] Deleuze echoes Desmond's observation that Gnosticism can embrace both extreme asceticism and antinomic liberty, for in Deleuze, the more actively (freely, unconstrainedly) creative one is, the more spiritual one is—those that tend toward the virtual are the Deleuzian *pneumatachoi*.[126] The result, as René Girard commented upon the publication of *Anti-Oedipus*, is "appearances notwithstanding, a new form of particularly ethereal piety."[127]

The redemptive re-orientation toward dissolution, in the more specific context of the human, entails a redemption from the human as the task of the human—the gospel of Spinoza according to Deleuze.[128] This abandonment of the subject, of actors, is an abandonment of the active development of persons and a mysticism in which the self/soul is dispersed into a micropolitics that has nothing to say to individuals but to cease to be—"to depersonalize or counter-actualize themselves and thereby become an adequate channel for creation as such."[129] The result, Justaert concludes, is an "indifferent, noncommittal world-view" in that "Deleuze's philosophy of uncertainty, contingency and of ungrounded Being does not seem to offer

122. Hallward, *Out of This World*, 90.

123. Hallward, *Out of This World*, 20, 45.

124. Justaert, "Transcendence"; Hallward, *Out of This World*, 80; Balthasar, *Cosmic Liturgy*, 45. Hallward is apparently undecided as to whether Deleuze's philosophy can be described as ascetic (Hallward, *Out of This World*, 82, 86).

125. Justaert, "Évaluation Théologique," 542–43.

126. Desmond, *God and the Between*, 210; Hallward, *Out of This World*, 1. As Hallward writes: "All being is creative, we know, but it is unequally so. These material situations are governed by the lowest form of creativity, in which almost nothing happens—in other words, they are situations in which what happens tends to conform to predictable patterns of causation" (Hallward, *Out of This World*, 41).

127. Quoted in Dosse, *Intersecting Lives*, 213.

128. Hallward, *Out of This World*, 3, 64, 80.

129. Justaert, "Évaluation Théologique," 538–39; Hallward, *Out of This World*, 93.

much of an answer to the question of how to act."[130] In rejecting "all forms of moral valuation or strategic judgment" and preferring an, at best, untenable "anti-normative" view of justice, the subject, the actor, is paralyzed.[131] For the Deleuzian preference for the minority, for example, ends up being arbitrary.[132] While Anthony Paul Smith reasserts that "immanence does not name a flight from this world, but calls forth powers from this world so that we may believe in this world and act in it, not under the illusion that we are its masters, but as custodians tending to the machines of the universe,"[133] we are left with the pointed question of just who this "we" is. One cannot graft responsibility and ethical agency (not to mention something that looks a lot like a Christian understanding of stewardship) onto an immanent frame that would see, at the very least, a kind of ethical imperative in the dissolution of the illusion of agents with subjective consciousness that can be reasonably responsible for anything.[134] Smith himself recognizes something like this in a more recent essay observing that Deleuze and Guattari's thought "appears also to lack a mechanism by which to select the best organization of power other than vague suggestions at cautious experimentation."[135] It is difficult to escape the thought that the theorist, as Pickstock writes, "is simply the spectator of fated conflicts—between territorial politicisms and presidents, on the one hand, and deterritorialising terrorists and mavericks, on the other."[136]

With his emphasis on intensive, non-relational difference—virtual difference but no actual others (or selves for that matter)—Deleuze is left with little room for relationships between individuals, be they of conflict or solidarity. This rejection, in Hallward's terms, of "any viable theory of inter-individual relation" again leaves Deleuze "essentially indifferent to the politics of this world" and without any account of what could make any particular organization of power preferable to another.[137] He is left seeing

130. Justaert, "Transcendence."

131. Hallward, *Out of This World*, 163; Piloiu, "Anti-Juridical Utopia," 202; Milbank, "Immanence and Life," 17.

132. Piloiu, "Anti-Juridical Utopia," 224.

133. A. Smith, "Believing in this World," 109.

134. Hallward sees Deleuze's as "an account of the human and of the creatural more generally that both acknowledges its unreal or illusory status" (Hallward, *Out of This World*, 56).

135. A. Smith, "The Judgment of God and the Immeasurable," 81.

136. Pickstock, "Theology and Post-modernity," 77–78.

137. Hallward, *Out of This World*, 153–54, 162; A. Smith, "The Judgment of God and the Immeasurable," 72. "By 'relation' I mean a process that operates between two or more minimally discernible terms, in such a way as to condition or inflect (but not fully

political realities, human realities, like all realities, as little more than an unending "violent interplay between stasis and movement."[138] In Hart's judgment, this is due to the fact that Deleuze "fails to attend to the way in which difference concretely occurs" in actuality, dealing instead with an overly-idealized virtual pure difference.[139] It is thus, in Justaert's appraisal, that Deleuze's politics fails due to its lack of concrete political strength.[140]

Deleuzian spirituality as an ethical way of being is one of affirmation, but an *ideal* affirmation. In the *concrete* context, it is unclear what is to be affirmed in *actual* human life—the affirmation is in danger of being drowned in his nay-saying, an odd yea-saying. This, again, echoes the upside down and equivocal nature of Gnosticism—in particular, the world-affirming systematic deformation of the Valentinian narrative grammar.[141] There is little surprise that Deleuze is left with a tragic equivocity: seeking to affirm the world but, in the end, having the difficulty of believing in the world. Deleuze wants to affirm the world—"this," Hart writes, "is the first wisdom."[142] But there are two voices in Deleuze's thought: the Nietzschean, pagan, Dionysian voice that would affirm the world as it is and the Gnostic voice that would seek to escape it and so leave one without a world to be found to believe in. With the virtual as associated with what is to be affirmed and the actual with what is to be escaped, we are to escape what we are at pains to see as bad rather than innocent and to affirm what we are at pains to see as good. We are to affirm a life that is and yet is not this life. In so doing, are we affirming a world that does not exist?

Bibliography

Albert, Eliot. "Deleuze's Impersonal, Hylozoic Cosmology: The Expulsion of Theology." In *Deleuze and Religion*, edited by Mary Bryden, 184–96. London: Routledge, 2001.

Balthasar, Han Urs von. *Cosmic Liturgy: The Universe according to Maximus the Confessor.* Translated by Brian E. Daley. San Francisco: Ignatius, 2003.

---

to generate) the individuality of each term. A relation is only a relation in this sense if its terms retain some limited autonomy with respect to each other. A relation is only a relation if it is between terms that can be meaningfully discerned, even if the means of this discernment proceed at the very limit of indiscernment" (Hallward, *Out of This World*, 152).

138. Pickstock, "Theology and Post-modernity," 81.

139. Hart, *The Beauty of the Infinite*, 281.

140. Justaert, "Évaluation Théologique," 532.

141. Desmond, *God and the Between*, 219; O'Regan, *Gnostic Return*, 45.

142. Hart, *The Beauty of the Infinite*, 92.

Bonta, Mark. "Rhizome of Boehme and Deleuze: Esoteric Precursors of the God of Complexity." *SubStance* 39.1 (2010) 62–75.

Burrell, David. *Freedom and Creation in Three Traditions.* South Bend, IN: University of Notre Dame Press, 1993.

Clark, Tim. "A Whiteheadian Chaosmos: Process Philosophy from a Deleuzean Perspective." *Process Studies* 28.3–4 (1999) 179–94.

Crockett, Clayton. *Radical Political Theology: Religion and Politics After Liberalism.* New York: Columbia University Press, 2011.

Davies, Oliver. "Thinking Difference: A Comparative Study of Gilles Deleuze, Plotinus and Meister Eckhart." In *Deleuze and Religion,* edited by Mary Bryden, 76–86. London: Routledge, 2001.

Deleuze, Gilles (with Claire Parnet). *L'Abécédaire de Gilles Deleuze.* 3 DVDs. Montparnesse: Arte Video, 1997. English overview by Charles J. Stivale at http://www.langlab.wayne.edu/CStivale/D-G/ABC1.html (accessed 13 September, 2011.)

Deleuze, Gilles. *Bergsonism.* Translated by Barbara Habberjam and Hugh Tomlinson. Brooklyn: Zone, 1990.

———. *Difference and Repetition.* Translated by Paul Patton. New York: Columbia University Press, 1995.

Desmond, William. *Art, Origins, Otherness: Between Philosophy and Art.* Albany, NY: SUNY Press, 2003.

———. *Ethics and the Between.* Albany, NY: SUNY Press, 2001.

———. "From Under the Ground of the Cave: Schopenhauer and the Philosophy of the Dark Origin." In *A Companion to Schopenhauer,* edited by Bart Vandenabeele, 89–104. Blackwell Companions to Philosophy. Oxford: Wiley-Blackwell, 2012.

———. *God and the Between.* Oxford: Blackwell, 2008.

Dosse, François. *Gilles Deleuze & Félix Guattari: Intersecting Lives.* Translated by Deborah Glassman. New York: Columbia University Press, 2010.

Hallward, Peter. *Out of this World.* London: Verso, 2006.

Hart, David Bentley. *The Beauty of the Infinite: The Aesthetics of Christian Truth.* Grand Rapids: Eerdmans, 2003.

Justaert, Kristien. "Gilles Deleuze and the Transcendence of the Immanent." Unpublished essay (2011).

———. "Gilles Deleuze: Évaluation Théologique." *Laval Théologique et Philosophique* 65.3 (2009) 531–44.

Kaufman, Eleanor. "Klossowski, Deleuze, and Orthodoxy." *Diacritics* 35.1 (2005) 47–59.

Kerslake, Christian. "Hoëne Wronski and Francis Warrain." In *Deleuze's Philosophical Lineage,* edited by Graham Jones and Jon Roffe, 167–89. Edinburgh: Edinburgh University Press, 2009.

———. "The Somnambulist and the Hermaphrodite: Deleuze and Johann de Montereggio and Occultism" Culture Machine, InterZone, http://www.culturemachine.net/index.php/cm/article/viewArticle/243/225 (accessed August 11, 2011).

McCabe, Herbert. *God Matters.* London: Continuum, 1987.

———. *God Still Matters.* London: Continuum, 2002.

Milbank, John. "Immanence and Life." Stanton Lectures at Cambridge University, 26 January 2011.

————. "The Mystery of Reason." In *The Grandeur of Reason: Religion, Tradition and Universalism*, edited by Peter M. Candler Jr. and Conor Cunningham, 68–117. London: SCM, 2010.

————. "The Soul of Reciprocity (Part Two)." *Modern Theology* 17.4 (2001) 485–507.

————. *Theology and Social Theory*. 2nd ed. Oxford: Blackwell, 2006.

O'Regan, Cyril. *Gnostic Return in Modernity*. Albany, NY: SUNY Press, 2001.

Pickstock, Catherine. *After Writing: On the Liturgical Consummation of Philosophy*. Oxford: Blackwell, 1998.

————. "Theology and Post-modernity: An Exploration of the Origins of a New Alliance." In *New Directions In Philosophical Theology: Essays in Honour of Don Cupitt*, edited by Gavin Hyman, 67–84. Aldershot, UK: Ashgate, 2004.

Piloiu, Rares. "Gilles Deleuze's Concept of 'Immanence' as Anti-Juridical Utopia." *Soundings* 87.1–2 (2004) 201–29.

Sherman, Jacob Holsinger. "No Werewolves in Theology? Transcendence, Immanence, and Becoming-Divine in Gilles Deleuze." *Modern Theology* 25.1 (2009) 1–20.

Simpson, Christopher Ben. *Deleuze and Theology*. London: Bloomsbury, 2012.

————. *Religion, Metaphysics and the Postmodern: William Desmond and John D. Caputo*. Bloomington, IN: Indiana University Press, 2009.

Smith, Anthony Paul. "Believing in this World for this Making of Gods: Ecology of the Virtual and the Actual." *SubStance* 39.1 (2010) 103–14.

————. "Judgment of God and the Immeasurable: Political Theology and Organizations of Power," *Political Theology* 12.1 (2011) 69–86.

Smith, Daniel W. "The Doctrine of Univocity: Deleuze's Ontology of Immanence." In *Deleuze and Religion*, edited by Mary Bryden, 167–83. London: Routledge, 2001.

4

Poetry and the Exculpation of Flesh

JENNIFER NEWSOME MARTIN

"What's meaning but vanity? A word is a sound—
one of the handmaidens of the seraphim."

—Osip Mandelstam, no. 47, *Stone*

"And he answered and said unto them, I tell you that, if these
should hold their peace, the stones would immediately cry out."

—Luke 19:40

Cyril O'Regan is best known for works like *The Heterodox Hegel* (1994), *Gnostic Return in Modernity* (2001), *Gnostic Apocalypse: Jacob Boehme's Haunted Narrative* (2002), and *The Anatomy of Misremembering: Von Balthasar's Response to Philosophical Modernity, Volume I: Hegel* (2014) and the forthcoming *Anatomy* volumes on Heidegger, as well as numerous articles, essays, and book chapters that index his constitutively anti-Gnostic profile. Though readers may have seen and appreciated his original poetic epigraphs occasionally published with these academic books, they may be unaware that he is an accomplished poet with several lengthy collections of poems.[1] I will proceed by introducing one such collection as the primary text

---

1. The collections are entitled *Origen in Alexandria, Poems: Sacred and Profane*, and *The Companion of Theseus*. For a popular-level reflection on poetry, see O'Regan

for this essay. *The Companion of Theseus* is an unpublished, unfinished cycle of poetry composed while O'Regan was a graduate student at University College Dublin between 1975 and 1978 and redacted a decade later at St. John's Collegeville. Of the three intended parts of this work, only the first two are complete. The first part, *Withered Water*, has fourteen poems connected by seven interpolated choruses (see Appendix 1); the second part, *The Centaurs*, has eighteen poems with nine choruses (see Appendix 2).

I suggest that the poems, lovely in their own right, perform an anti-Gnosticism thematically if not methodologically resonant with the more discursive work, given their resolute emphasis on the un-romanticized flesh of bodies vulnerable to injury and contagion. These themes are recognizable from Irenaeus and Tertullian. Populating dialogical space alongside these patristic figures are modern interlocutors, who, with respect to the somatic, are as uncompromising as the latter. I will consider them in three categories: (1) the poetic (Osip Mandelstam and Anna Akhmatova), (2) the phenomenological (Maurice Merleau-Ponty), and (3) the psychoanalytic (Julia Kristeva), with the caveat that the implicit and explicit references O'Regan makes in a gestural mode massively exceed these three interlocutions. Indeed, the poem cycle can be read as a provisional map of the kinds of conversation partners that characterize the wide-angled nature of his work.[2]

O'Regan's decision to opt for the primacy of the somatic is enacted not only in the structure and content of the poems, but also in their performance; they deploy modes of expression that are neither interested in nor constrained by the genres or protocols of academic discourse. The poems in *The Companion of Theseus* represent—indeed *are*—a kind of primordial speech that is pre-rational and experiential, though certainly not irrational. I go on to identify a thematic correlation between flesh and writing, suggesting ultimately that the exigencies of flesh and language—as exposed

---

"Ambassadors of Divine Glory." For a treatment of Cyril as poet which prioritizes the *Origen in Alexandria* volume, see Astell, "O'Regan as Origen."

2. For example, in the poem "Voice," in *Withered Water*, Voëgelin and Jüng appear under the guises of the "beautiful Greek words" (20) of "periagoge" and "enantiodromia" (21) respectively. He gestures to Gaston Bachelard's notion of the Empedocles Complex and the ontology of fire in "Withered Water," which would burn the corpse so as to leave behind no possibility of commemoration: no body, no ash, no urn, no marker of any kind. Angelus Silesius' rose is evoked in the "whyless wheat" of the first few lines of the third chorus of part one (29). Both Jacob Boehme's *Signatura Rerum* (*The Signature of All Things*) and Jacques Derrida's "Signature Event Context" from *Limited, Inc.* get a nod when Perithous is speaking in "Eros" of the "pointer, a signature, / a dream vague and general" (1). Rilke is evoked everywhere, especially in the figuration of the angels as compromised by violence in "Even the Angels," as evidenced in the refrain: "The years are angels / And in the titanomachies / even the angels engage / in carnage" (7, 8, 9–10, 11); cf. O'Regan's explicit naming of Rilke in "Hunger" (48).

entities subject entirely to harm—unite body and text in a shared economy of vulnerability that evokes without explicitly invoking the wounded Word/flesh of Christ.[3]

Structure and Allusions

The poems in *The Companion of Theseus* oscillate between the two spaces of the mythological and the modern, bound and/or interrupted by a set of choruses, an arrangement that indicates that the structure is fixed and must be read in the given order.[4] Moreover, biblical, classical, Zen Buddhist, and other mythological (including Norse, Sumerian, Egyptian, and Babylonian) symbolic economies populate the same semiotic field of the poem cycle, inhabiting geographical spaces as varied as ancient Greece, Egypt, Mesopotamia, and modern Dublin. References to Greek myth, however, are the most prominent by far. It is especially the titular story of Theseus and his hapless companion, Perithous, king of the Lapiths and husband of Hippodamia, which shapes the poetic cycle and gives it its name. Despite the fact that Nestor invokes Perithous in Book I of the *Iliad* as one of several examples of past heroism, "of champions among men of earth, who fought / with champions, with wild things of the mountains, / great centaurs whom they broke and overpowered,"[5] in O'Regan's poem Perithous is styled not as a hero but as an anti-hero, his unhappy, humiliating fate being to have his buttocks fused eternally to the stone Chairs of Forgetfulness (*Lethe*) after a botched attempt to abduct Persephone from Hades.[6]

3. This close association of language and flesh has a long theological and philosophical history, especially from within the Johannine corpus ("And the Word was made flesh, and dwelt among us" (John 1:14)). More modern philosophical examples might include works like Nancy, *Corpus*; recent secondary sources might include works like Rivera, *Poetics of the Flesh*, which includes a chapter on Tertullian; MacKendrick, *Word Made Skin*; Henry, *Incarnation*; Ricoeur, *Oneself as Another*; Merleau-Ponty, *The Prose of the World*; Falque, *God*, especially the section "Language of the Flesh and Flesh of Language," 168–79.

4. This mythological-modern alternative structure seems to bear the mark of poet and novelist John Fowles, who composed quite a number of his poems while living in Greece, as well, perhaps, as W. H. Auden's classic "The Shield of Achilles," where the stanzas of the poem vacillate between the bleak space of modern warfare and the disillusioned gaze of the goddess Thetis upon the titular shield, which represents quite a tragic departure from the victorious tone of Book XVII of Homer's *Iliad*.

5. Cf. Book I, lines 311–17 of Homer, *The Iliad*, 14.

6. Some versions have serpents bind the legs and feet of Perithous and Theseus, while others prioritize the soldering of stone and flesh. Theseus is rescued by Hercules, but Perithous is left behind. See Virgil's *Aeneid*, Book 6, 393 for mention of Perithous as being punished for wanting the wife of a god (Hades). Also cf. Apollodorus, Library,

The characters that populate the first two poems include the Greek figures of Hippodameia, Perithous, Theseus, Thea, Hippolytus, Helen, Persephone (in "The Labyrinth") alongside the Hebrew figures of Belial, Moah, Edom, Ham, Japheth, Elam, Ishmael, and Keturah (in "Even the Angels"), but neither poetic space is hermetically sealed. "The Labyrinth," set within Daedalus's maze on Crete, includes O'Regan's retelling of the Centauromachy—which ensued after the Centaur guests became intoxicated at the wedding of Hippodameia and Perithous and attempted to abduct the bride.[7] The language reaches Homeric levels of carnage and violence (evoking implicitly Book IX of *The Odyssey*, which will be more explicitly referenced by the *relecture* of the Polyphemus myth in "Cannot Kill"):[8] "He / tore their heads gleefully / from their bodies, no God figuring / in their genealogy. Theseus / how the blood spurts, the flanks, / the hocks, the genitals, blood / matting the sour hair, again aping / inhabiting the precedent! / Once Heracles, now Perseus."[9] Though in this Greek mythological space, the lines that follow immediately—"I am now a limp / recall of the child's trust"— seem to conjure deliberately if obscurely the biblical figure of Jacob. (The Johannine resonance of the "I am" construction also seems unmistakable).[10] The character of Jacob appears (albeit cryptically) here not with the gravity of a biblical patriarch but precisely in his capacity for being wounded, as detailed in the Genesis 32 account in which the mysterious angel "struck Jacob's hip at its socket, so that Jacob's socket was dislocated as he wrestled with him" (Gen 32:26). The interruption in the lines between "limp" and "recall," where the language hesitates, cracked open by the line break, suggests the absolute identity of speaker with limp ("I am now a limp"). There is an infinite difference, of course, between *being* a limp and *having* one.[11]

2.5.12 and Apollodorus, *Epitome* e.1.24 [24].

7. See Ovid's *Metamorphoses* Bk XII, 210–44.

8. In particular, I have in mind when Poseidon's son Polyphemous announces that the Kyklopês are lawless and indifferent to the gods ("We Kyklopês / care not a whistle for your thundering Zeus / or all the gods in bliss; we have more force by far" (lines 298–300), directly before devouring Odysseus' companions in a grisly show of excessive violence: "Neither reply nor pity came from him, / but in one stride he clutched at my companions / and caught two in his hands like squirming puppies / to beat their brains out, spattering the floor. / Then he dismembered them and made his meal, / gaping and crunching like a mountain lion— / everything: innards, flesh, and marrow bones" (lines 312–18).

9. "The Labyrinth," 5.

10. Cf. "I Am," in *Withered Water*, 26–27, and certain lines in "Blackhall Street" which also reference the "I am" sayings of John: "I am said. / I am thought" (36); "John, I am the same. / I am the same wound. / I am the same stain / on the same meat" (37).

11. Jacob is also named unambiguously in the next poem, "Even the Angels" ("In

It is arguable that Jacob as wrestler is at the same time both himself and a stand-in for Theseus, thus further intermingling Greek and Hebrew/biblical space. In Greek myth, Cercyon (literally, "boar's tail") would stand in the roads of Eleusis and incite those who passed to engage in a brawl against their will. In these combats, Cercyon was always the victor, murdering the passer-by with his brute strength, until he challenged Theseus, who employed the theretofore unknown technique of wrestling in order to lift him up and throw him to his death. As Jacob wrestles (and is—ambiguously—victorious over) probable divinity in Genesis 32, so too is Theseus associated closely with the sport of wrestling in his defeat of Cercyon the Wrestler, a foe to whom the poems often recur, especially in the repetition of Perithous's lament, "I, Perithous, cannot kill / Cercyon, the tail of my own past."[12]

"Labyrinth" and "Cannot Kill," though separated by "Even the Angels" and the first few choruses, are unified not only by their shared Homeric references but also by this set of exactly repeated lines in the voice of Perithous that signals the story of Theseus's defeat of Cercyon. This recursive feature is not merely a matter of repeating content, but also surfaces thematically in a range of non-identical repetitions of the dense symbol of the open or broken circle (variously punctuated with images of a coil or spiral and usually affiliated with notions of story, history, and time). Whereas complete circles might indicate wholeness, totality, or perfection, in *The Companion of Theseus*, the open or disjunctive circle predominates. The Homeric references to the *Iliad* and the *Odyssey* populate a Plotinian matrix of going-out and return that approximates a circle but does not close it, especially since all that was lost during the course of the narrative is not restored (Odysseus' dead companions, the memory of the suitors, and so on).[13] For the character of Perithous in particular, there are no longer any beginnings or endings; he spirals futilely, waiting for a resolution that will never come: "And my years waited / for Theseus' enterprise / and the immensities / unable to waive . . . Grief was mimicry / engraving itself . . . a drought turning upon itself / somewhere / a drought turning upon itself / nowhere" ("The Labyrinth," 1–3). The poems in *The Centaurs* repeat and darken the image

---

the years of Ishmael / Hagar felt cheated / by the Lord and a son / pretended to be Jacob" (9)), and he reappears again in "Hunger," "wrestling with the angel / from the water near / the sewerage pipes / to explain, how, why / this lameness and limp to the world, / this twisted tendon of torn thigh / this ligature of loin / this leg swiveling in the socket / unable to connect, this walking / out of proper motion" (48–49).

12. Cf. "Cannot Kill," 13, 15 and "Labyrinth," 5–6.

13. For discussion of the "open circle," particularly in Bulgakov's *Master and Margarita* and in *Doctor Zhivago*, cf. Bethea, *Shape of Apocalypse*, 184–85, 266, 270.

by a shade in their more unequivocal association of the broken circle with the inevitabilities of time and history. In "Boy-King," for example, the image of the circle in the first part of the poem dissolves by its denouement: "The perennial dies. The year / is circular as a woman, / as fate, as once upon a time. / / Theseus looked into the boy's / eyes and saw his own face. / He looked into his eyes / and saw fate's squeeze. / Theseus looked to the ground / traced a circle breaking" (42). An apocalyptic seventh chorus heralds the end of history, evoking the alchemical symbol of the Ouroboros: "With me the world ends. / The scroll tired of stretching / suddenly retreats, collapses / to coil. Impossible sunsets / blot out. Noon reveals invisible / ink. / The grey fog of morning / swallows itself." The ninth chorus is similarly rueful as it invites the Hindu notion of *kundalini*, the serpentine primal energy coiled at the base of the spine: "Men are no different than / their erased dates. / / Who can stop the sobbing / of spent water, the bleak / kundalini uncoiling? Houdini / would not escape it" (54).

Flesh and Language

If there is one central theme to these poems, it is the vulnerability of human flesh and language to vicissitude and indignity. Both word and flesh are exposed not only to the *possibility* of harm but to its manifest inevitability. Being "flesh" in the economy of O'Regan's poems is a condition that is pre-rational, highly susceptible, and often coupled with failures of language. With respect to the first point, in the poem "Cannot Kill," Perithous describes the experience of dangerous passage by Cerberus as "my flesh a tympanum / vibrating the three gullets / of the dog's despair." That the flesh is a tympanum—an antique Greek hand-drum used in the Dionysian rites—is noteworthy: flesh is not the lyre or even the tambourine of the Romantic aesthetic, neither delicate nor requiring particular skill but sounded upon rather by crude, visceral, and inexact thrumming. The tympanum, like flesh, is pre-rational; it cannot be controlled by or made subject to the intellect, for what plays upon it is not the rational faculties but passion and appetite. Secondly, "flesh" in these poems is not romanticized, transfigured, deified, or made phantom or angelic. It is always already passing away. When Perithous descends into Hades in O'Regan's "Withered Water," he meditates upon the finality and bodily reality of death: "and I thought of Thanatos / in thinking of myself / for even the unthings of beginning / and end end in a body / and death's vacant body / gathers the end ashes and bones / from the last to the first place" (25). In "Chorus 3," we "plunge, dredging deeper / into the phlegm we are" (*Withered Water*, 30; cf. Chorus

4, in which "We are napkins wiping / the phlegm body, disposing / it"). In "Do Not," ill and dying bodies are "decomposing as protein" (34, 35). This inclination to concreteness gives "flesh" the heaviness and density of bladders, gullets, digestion, blood, phlegm, gall, injury, pleurisy, bones; it is of the earth, ordinary, frail, sometimes foolish, and deeply vulnerable to wounds, disease, and violence unto death.

Third, in the poems these exigencies of the flesh are connected with failures of breath, lungs, and air, all synecdoche for language itself. The fact that language is vulnerable (and furthermore *makes* vulnerable) is certainly clear from the poems' explicit themes. O'Regan signals the vulnerability of language, however, not only through content, but also at the sound and rhythm level of the words employed. In "Boy-King," for instance, he abruptly switches mythic fields from Greek to Sumerian after a set of ellipses that interrupt the page. Here he invokes the Sumerian deity Amaushumgalanna, and along with the voicing of this lengthy name comes an escalation of the vulnerability index: the name itself tempts division into syllables. We observe an analogous phenomenon in the first chorus of *The Centaurs* with reference to "ululation," itself not only another word that invites syllabic partition, but also an expenditure of breath inseparable from the embodied parts of tongue and uvula: "The voice ululates. The darkness / shines. Something is added / in the telling to make the story / rise. Moments, the voice hesitates / towards light but Truth is / beyond and is calling / will not stop calling / like / is" (7). The aggressive line-breaks in "Voice" amplify the tendency of O'Regan's language to mime the wound of fragmentation as isolated words become disconnected from meaningful context, standing exposed as bare, solitary selves. When read aloud, the punctuated line-breaks get translated to hesitations in which the reader must take a breath.

In the explicit content of the poems, however, the function of mouths, throats, lungs, and breath miscarries spectacularly, even as the poems themselves are manifestly efficacious. The mouth in "Even the Angels" is reduced only to a soliloquizing "blue sentry"; it is a "noiseless / blue mouth / gone / looking for a voice" (8–9). In "Riverbed," the speaker "will not speak again / My throat will be a purse / Hanseled with stale echoes / of stale half-questions" (38). "Do Not" implores: "Forgive my Dominic Savio face," referencing the young saint who died at fourteen from pleurisy, a sickness that takes root deep in the lungs and chest cavity and impedes breathing. "Chorus 5" says of death that it "had but one speech / the monotone origin / crackled behind accidental dialects, / the energetic silence / the lungs wished to speak / but the throat denied" (42). "Lie" both opens and closes this way: "In the night's failed lungs / a cough and breath chews / the darkness" (44). Even O'Regan's graphic setting of the descent into Hades to retrieve Persephone—itself a seeming re-performance of Dante's *Inferno*—utterly chokes the reader. Hades is described as a place where "the air failed," "where the wind stopped / and I became dependent / on my stale hand to brush / the flies, puncture and freshen / the air" (2).

O'Regan implies and performs a correlation between the susceptibilities of flesh and language. Here, the mixed metaphors (grammatical, bodily) are intentional and powerfully close the gap between word and body. In "Eros," the "hidden syntax, the interval, / the bitter enjambments of chaos / blood out in hoarse flesh" (4). In "Voice," "the nib / sinks / deep / push / lateral / from sinew to sinew." A similar formulation appears in "Blackhall Street," perhaps the tonal and thematic center of the collection: "and her mother / entered like an old broken / nib looking for some world / to be her inkwell" (34). Indeed, in "Blackhall Street," the vicissitudes of language, flesh, house, and memory are all devastatingly exposed as vulnerable to ruin, decline, demolition, and to being degenerated into syllables, letters, organs, nonsense, skin, mis-remembering, rubble, brick, and stone. The symbol of the house, as bearing witness to and internalizing its losses, is personified: it is "an old world, an old ache / taking sick" with a "slate kerchief / of memories or obsessions" (33).[14] In a gesture to the mythological space of the Greeks even in this poem's context of modern Dublin, O'Regan's lines—"Windows are continually replaced eyes / in a body of replaced cells. / None of her is the same / as the heirloom she pictures" (33)—evoke the philosophical puzzle of the ship of Theseus, which considers how to maintain stable identity through time, history, and flux. The theme of death becomes almost commonplace in a litany of one of this poem's speakers, a mother suffering from memory loss and senility ("Pat is dead," "Frank is dead," "They all leave me" (35)), but habituated all the same to loss as she is "silent and speaking, / speaking and silent, alternatively" (35). Indeed, the focus on speech and language in this poem reaches a level of attention and self-consciousness that is exceptional even in a set of poems already highly attuned to their operation.

Back in the Greek mythological space, we see the flesh and language of Perithous lapidify all at once. In "If Only," O'Regan closely correlates the dissolution of Perithous's flesh with the inaccessibility of speech as flesh unites with stone: "I was the stone's cartilage / shaping a movement / as if it would spasm / beyond its definition / I was a stone compressing / to an opaque mouth / the dark beak cry / of the night-jar shredding / in flint" (31–32). He

14. The poem "Deliverance" interestingly correlates the dilapidated house with the dilapidated body. The wallpaper that is stripped is "flesh-colored"; some shreds are stubborn, uncompliant to the sharp trowel's bidding. But "the knife is unable to prevent / the past's interrupted swelling / under the paper of flowers / the thick texture of the root, / the invisible profile, the shamed eczema / of the other side" (16).

continues a few lines later: "And I remember thinking if only / if only my face would soften to flesh / my skull throw up a crop of terse / ornament, my leg flex / I might find here among the twin / plots of reeds and asphodels / the anodyne of the spurge plant // I plunge into my bone / following the coils / looking for the syllable // that fell from my eyes / in some hermetic chamber / but some part of the library / holds the sentence / holds the syllable" (32). Similarly, in "Eros," the abandoned Perithous laments: "I saw my cogent face / break into pebbles, oracular / syllables of incompetence, / my torso granulate / into high relief, eyes / empty and conform / to a uniform grey. Theseus also but Theseus left" (2).

The Wounded Word

That O'Regan's poetry correlates the finitude and transitory nature of both flesh and language thematically and performatively suggests that it is oriented fundamentally, though never pedantically, to the Wounded Word of Christ. In "Not" (which corresponds thematically with "Do Not," especially with its images of illness, the incorrigible stain, and the ineffective poultice), the connection among flesh, language, and the person of Christ is gestural but striking: "We were there recording his interested / smile as John who loved him / as a brother told me / the warm marrow fled / from things he touched, and there / when Anthony spoke of the humid / flesh of language / with its proud / carrion smell" (41). But the sixth Chorus of Withered Water leans in altogether to the Christological, biblical, and Eucharistic themes of the wounded Word: "Communion frail flayed flesh fail / The words. 'Lamb of God / who takest away . . .' / The monstrance, / the censer, the fear the wafer / would blood the teeth. / Yet we must go out / if He is to come in" (51). These lines, echoing the Johannine figuration of John the Baptist in John 3:30, are made more pronounced in the final lines of the poem: "self-abandoning decrease / an increase in God / or imagination" (52). The apprehension that "the wafer / would blood the teeth" marks the poetic apogee of Word-made-flesh with the saturated presence of divinity—still bearing a linguistic character—enfleshed in the host.

Christ (*qui tollis peccata mundi*) is he who, as the poet of Second Isaiah pronounces, is "acquainted with infirmity" (Isa 53:3); "Surely," the author continues with the assurance of one who knows, "he has borne our infirmities and carried our diseases" (53:4). It is this real corporeality which Christ possessed precisely as his own, marked by fragility, and subject to disease and physical ailments, that is indeed the staggering truth of the incarnation. Tertullian's *De carne Christi* enunciates this "mineness" perceptible through the felt experience of being one's own as decisive for distinguishing between the flesh (*caro*) of Christ and the body (*Leib*), which are connected but not exactly identical. "Flesh" indicates radical proximity and the capacity for the body to perceive itself as perceiving. In Emmanuel Falque's magnificent gloss on *De carne Christi*, "the proximity of the body to oneself (*sibi proximam*), or in other words the impossibility of unstitching that which ties me to my skin, is precisely what makes it flesh."[15] Marsyas notwithstanding, no separation is possible.

Furthermore, when Word becomes flesh, counterintuitively that which is primordially verbal stumbles to silence. The life of Christ is bookended by two immense silences: the holy silence of Advent in which Christ the Word waited mutely in the womb of the Virgin and the great silence of his death and descent into Sheol. "Today," the ancient Holy Saturday homily reads, "there is a great silence over the earth, a great silence, and stillness, a great silence because the King sleeps; the earth was in terror and was still, because God slept in the flesh and raised up those who were sleeping from the ages. God has died in the flesh, and the underworld has trembled." This kenotic dissolution recalls what Hans Urs von Balthasar has called the "midpoint" between Word and Flesh, where Word becomes "not-word" in its entry into the silence of the womb and the silence of death and *Sheol*.[16] For Balthasar, the finitude of genuine human experience is posed against the horizon of death that is the foreclosure of speech, where "human utterance ends once for all, and what was spoken as word in the course of the mortal life, whether significant or insignificant, is in any case bound to the form of temporality and thus to transitoriness, and thereby inescapably to futility."[17] Nonetheless, this is the frail flesh upon which everything depends, this frail flesh which must bear "everything that is to be disclosed."[18] In this sense, then, though womb and burial are apophatic realities, it is manifestly true that "only the flesh speaks here."[19] The descent into the poetic space of Hades and perhaps

15. Falque, *God*, 156. Merleau-Ponty, with whom Falque is in dialogue, distinguishes body and flesh on similar grounds, locating the "flesh" in a liminal space between body and idea. In his chapter "The Intertwining—The Chiasm," Merleau-Ponty associates the concept of flesh with the "generality of the Sensible in itself." He goes on to say that "the flesh is not matter, is not mind, is not substance. To designate it, we should need the old term 'element,' in the sense it was used to speak of water, air, earth, and fire, that is, in the sense of a *general thing*, midway between the spatiotemporal individual and the idea, a sort of incarnate principle that brings a style of being wherever there is a fragment of being" (Merleau-Ponty, *Visible and the Invisible*, 139).

16. Balthasar, *Glory*, 7:142.

17. Balthasar, *Glory*, 7:143.

18. Balthasar, *Glory*, 7:143.

19. Falque, *God*, 164; cf. Balthasar, *Glory*, 7, 142–47.

even into the dense, sometimes impenetrable warrens of O'Regan's language mirrors this Christological descent where only the flesh can speak.[20]

Interlocutions: Patristic and Modern

O'Regan's consistent poetic assertion of the corporeal suggests that Irenaeus (and Tertullian with him) are among the patristic forebears invoked anonymously in the poems insofar as they privilege the flesh over and against positions that would attenuate it by diminution, demonization, or even a too hasty deification.[21] His emphasis on flesh suggests that the work as a whole could be considered a poetic recapitulation of the anti-Gnosticism of Tertullian, whose *De carne Christi* presents the fleshly body of Christ in terms similarly un-romantic and even comic in a concerted effort to denounce the various dilutions and attenuations of the flesh among his Gnostic and Marcionite opponents.[22] Tertullian describes the human being as "this clod formed in the womb among the refuse, this man coming into the world by the passageway of the shameful organs, this man nourished in the milieu of ridiculous caresses."[23] Tertullian continues and extrapolates the suggestive metaphor between flesh ("clod") and the earth, going as far as to correlate the body of Christ directly with physical landscape:

> muscles [*musculos*] similar to mounds of dirt, bones [*ossa*] similar to rocks and even hillocks and gravel, the interlacing of nerves [*nervorum tenaces conexus*] like forking roots, the branching network of veins [*venarum ramosos*] like winding streams, the downy fuzz [*lanuguines*] like moss, hair [*conum*]

---

20. Cf. O'Regan's reference to the image of the walls as "thin as a wren's bone," in Dylan Thomas' poem "Vision and Prayer," in which he sees compounded "the extremity of vulnerability, solidarity, and something like the mystery of vicariousness . . . the defaced one who on the cross was and is and will forever be that form for me and for others of love broken and shared." (O'Regan, "Ambassadors of Divine Glory," 30).

21. For a fascinating phenomenological treatment of both figures alongside Augustine, John Scotus Erigena, Meister Eckhart, Bonaventure, Origen, Aquinas, and John Duns Scotus, see Falque, *God*.

22. Cf. Hans Urs von Balthasar on Irenaeus and Tertullian as being "close to the earth and the world of the senses," in Balthasar, *Glory*, 2:79 and 1:401; referenced in Falque, *God*, 117. Falque goes on to discuss Tertullian's particular oppositions to spiritual / pneumatic flesh (Valentinus), soul-flesh / flesh-soul (Western Valentinians), Sidereal Flesh (Apelles), which involves a flesh-taking not from the body of ordinary humanity, but from "the stars and superior substances of the world" (150); and the spectral flesh/mirage of flesh (Marcion), 146–52.

23. Tertullian, *De Carne Christi*, IV, 3, p. 223; quoted in Falque, *God*, 153.

like grass, and the hidden treasure of marrow [*medullarum in abdito thesauros*] like ores of the flesh [*ut metalla carnis*].[24]

The Companion of Theseus is a complicated text in dialogue with numerous other poets. Of this great cloud of witnesses, I will emphasize only two: the Russian Acmeists Anna Akhmatova (1889–1966) and Osip Mandelstam (1891–1938).[25] Perithous—who does not rescue and is himself not rescued—is a humiliated anti-hero utterly farcical, quixotic, and failed. O'Regan's is not a poetic narrative that capitulates to Greek hero worship; there is no apotheosis of the hero but in its place brutal realism and antic dark comedy. In "Lie," Perithous laments "our buttocks / our buttocks / in their stone prisons. / I lied to make worthwhile, / to be a tragedian / not a buffoon . . ." (44), but the lies to that end are inadequate. I read this as a sly reference to Anna Akhmatova's *Poem Without a Hero: A Triptych* (1940–1962),[26] the title of which is probably itself a poetic response to the opening lines of Lord Byron's unfinished satirical poem *Don Juan* ("I want a

24. Tertullian, *De Carne Christi*, IX, 3, p. 253; quoted in Falque, *God*, 155. Tertullian's correlations of flesh and earth here suggest an unexpected resonance with post-war Polish poet Zbigniew Herbert (1924–98). In particular, Tertullian's invocation of flesh as like hillocks and mountains evokes Herbert's "Apollo and Marsyas," a poetic narration of Apollo tortuously flaying Marsyas of his skin. Like O'Regan's poetry in *The Companion of Theseus*—which mentions this episode in the poem "Cannot Kill" (13)—Herbert annexes the often grotesque power of Greek mythology to great effect while maintaining unambiguously the somatic impulse. The language is viscerally exact. As Marsyas is flayed alive, he "relates / the inexhaustible wealth / of his body / bald mountains of liver / white ravines of aliment / rustling forests of lung / sweet hillocks of muscle / joints bile blood and shudders / the wintry wind of bone / over the salt of memory." O'Regan's "Withered Water" likewise gestures to correlations between flesh and landscape: Perithous and Theseus make their descent into Hades, "having passed the sinus / between the hills, and seen / a space of land barren / and muscular as a heart" (23). And in an explicit recurrence to the themes of "Withered Water" in "Riverbed," the speaker of the poem says: "You asked me not to see, / the wounded gonads of the trees, the deserts in the early grass, the withered waters" (38).

25. Acmeism was formed around the personage of poet Nikolay Gumilev as a critical response to the Russian Symbolist poets (among whom numbered, most prominently, Alexander Blok and Andrey Bely), unified largely in their resistance to the symbolist's insistence upon the poetry effecting contact with other worlds. According to one commentator, "images were to be concrete and sharply realized and the statement of poems rigorously logical. Their strength . . . was to come from contact with the earth" (Introduction to Mandelstam, *Osip Mandelstam: Selected Poems*, viii–ix). Note, however, that Mandelstam himself had a rather idiosyncratic view of the movement, understanding this "logic" less rationalistically and more intuitively, what Brown calls the "purely verbal logic of inner association" (ix) where the poetry was "deliberately blurred and impressionistic" [v]. These characteristics are certainly repeated in O'Regan's own poetry, which likewise features intuitive verbal or sound parallels quite apart from content.

26. Akhmatova, *Complete Poems*, 541–91.

hero: an uncommon want, / When every year and month sends forth a new one, / Till, after cloying the gazettes with cant, / The age discovers he is not the true one"),[27] though he knew well that none would be forthcoming.[28] To compound the sense of continuity in our litany of farcical anti-heroes, Akhmatova employs a markedly sinister line from Mozart's *Don Giovanni* as the poem's first epigraph: *Di rider finirai / Pria dell'aurora*, that is, "You will stop laughing before dawn," words spoken by the statue of the Commendatore to Don Giovanni—another notable anti-hero—in order to foretell his being dragged into hell. This gallows humor, occupying the thin places between jocularity and tragedy, consistently punctuates *The Companion of Theseus*.

Mandelstam is perhaps more overtly present: indeed, in "Voice," O'Regan invokes Mandelstam by his first name, like an incantation or even a kind of prayer: "black as anthracite / indefinite as slack, extinguished / sparks panicked in his goings / and his comings smouldered / smokily in relief. Sinking / they raised the monstrance, / the gold weakening to tin, / corrugated to wound // the nib / scrapes / below // whatever / it / leans / one side / Osip / listening / the wisdom / music / the shoulder" (18–19). Mandelstam's earliest book of poetry, *Stone* (1913), makes abundant use of biblical imagery (cf. the Joseph cycle in no. 54) alongside references to Homer (nos. 62, 78). His *Tristia* collection alludes often to Greek epic and mythic literature: for example, no. 82 mentions Phaedra, Hippolytus, Theseus; no. 89 seemingly overlays St. Petersburg with Hades, invoking Persephone as its queen; no. 92 evokes a kind of nostalgia and loss similar to what we find in Auden's "Shield of Achilles" in its retrospective consideration of now empty and silent rooms that Penelope and Odysseus used to occupy.[29] Like O'Regan's, Mandelstam's poems are decisively of the flesh and the earth, sometimes darkly and even violently. For example, in no. 135, "The Age," in *Poems* (1928), Mandelstam writes, "Blood the maker gushes / from the throats of the things of earth / and flings onto a beach like a burning fish / a hot sand of sea-bones, / and down from the high bird-net, / out of the wet blocks of sky / it pours, pours, heedlessly / over your death-wound" (44). In no. 266, "To the German Language," there is also an association between language and the body: "Long before I dared to be born / I was a letter of the alphabet, a verse like a vine, / I was the book that you all see in dreams" (65).

27. Byron, *Don Juan*.

28. See Notes to "Poem Without a Hero," in Akhmatova, *Complete Poems*. 838.

29. Also cf. no. 112 (Psyche and Persephone); no. 113 (Antigone); no. 114 (Melpomene, Eurydice); no. 116 (Persephone); no. 119 (Troy, Priam).

Second, the fact that the poems in this cycle are so thoroughgoingly anti-dualist in their decision for the flesh over against or before the rational suggests that O'Regan's early poetry was in conversation with Maurice Merleau-Ponty. The first and most obvious connection is the avowal of the chiastic body and the refusal to capitulate to dualisms.[30] For Merleau-Ponty there is so close an identity between body and self that there can be no detachment of thinking subject from object. "*I am my body*," Merleau-Ponty writes, "at least wholly to the extent that I possess experience, and yet at the same time my body is at it were a 'natural' subject, a provisional sketch of my total being. Thus, experience of one's own body runs counter to the reflective procedure which detaches subject and object from each other, and which gives us only the thought about the body, or the body as an idea, and not the experience of the body or the body in reality."[31] The somatic impulse of the poems represents the same kind of decision for the priority of bodily experience.

The next point of contact is in their figurations of language. O'Regan and Merleau-Ponty insist in different ways that the phenomenon of language cannot be abstracted from physically embodied experience. "Language," Merleau-Ponty observes, is "a contraction of the throat, a sibilant emission of air between the tongue and teeth, a certain way of bringing the body into play suddenly allows itself to be invested with a *figurative significance* which is conveyed outside us."[32] More importantly, language cannot be subsumed entirely under the jurisdiction of the rational but is something more primal. Merleau-Ponty discusses, for instance, "first-hand" or "primal" speech, which is "that of the child uttering its first word, of the lover revealing his feelings, of the 'first man who spoke,' or of the writer and philosopher who reawaken primordial experience anterior to all traditions."[33] The idea is that speech/naming/denomination does not "translate ready-made thought, but accomplishes it,"[34] as in the phenomenon when a writer proceeds with her sentences only intuitively, through a glass darkly and not in full control: she can only recognize the "right" word or image when it is given, but it

30. Merleau-Ponty describes the phenomenon of one person's hands touching each other: the possibility of a reversal in sensing oneself as both touched and touching indicates the simultaneity of the self as both subject and object, "the body as sensible and the body as sentient . . . a being of two leaves, from one side a thing among things and otherwise what sees them and touches them" (Merleau-Ponty, *Visible and the Invisible*, 137).

31. Merleau-Ponty, *Phenomenology of Perception*, 231; italics added.

32. Merleau-Ponty, *Phenomenology of Perception*, 225.

33. Merleau-Ponty, *Phenomenology of Perception*, 208n.5.

34. Merleau-Ponty, *Phenomenology of Perception*, 207.

cannot be conceptually thought beforehand. Furthermore, Merleau-Ponty identifies in words the capacity to signify simultaneously conceptually and existentially. He writes:

> spoken or written words carry a top coating of meaning which sticks to them and which presents the thought as a style, an affective value, a piece of existential mimicry, rather than as a conceptual statement. We find here, beneath the conceptual meaning of the words, an existential meaning which is not only rendered by them, but which inhabits them, and is inseparable from them. . . . This power of expression is well known in the arts, for example in music. The musical meaning of a sonata is inseparable from the sounds which are its vehicle.[35]

Words, before they signify their intended content, express a mysterious affective value, even at the level of sound; they "sing" the world.[36] Certainly in O'Regan's poems the opacity of the language asserts itself as a primordially linguistic, emotional, or rhythmic phenomenon before it is or becomes—if it ever does—a conceptual or discursive one. Throughout, the poet maximizes the musicality of words with adroit, startling rhymes and half-rhymes like "remora . . . amphora" ("Labyrinth," 2); "acrobatically . . . idiopathy" ("Not," 40); "prehends . . . distends" ("Hunger," 47); and "peritonitis . . . meniscus" ("Hunger," 49). The poems are decidedly non-didactic; there is no message that can be abstracted from the language itself.

Finally, the rationale for suggesting Julia Kristeva (particularly her "Stabat Mater") as a possible interlocutor with *The Companion of Theseus* is two-fold.[37] First, the split pagination of "Stabat Mater" between the objective analytical discourse *about* the mother and the embodied, subjective experiences *of* the mother is maximally suggestive not only of both the mythological/modern structure of the poems and the vulnerabilities of language/text to disjunctive forces, but more persuasively, I think, of O'Regan's own split self as both poet and theologian. Second, in both Kristeva's essay and in O'Regan's poems there is an association without consummate identification of women and women's physical experience with the earth, the body, and the primal, pre-intellectual language of WORD FLESH, which is the condition of the possibility for exposure, vulnerability, and, consummately, love. Both the prioritization of these themes and the (thick, dense, in-articulable, untranslatable) deployment of language conspire to destabilize the hegemony of intellect alone as a means of coming to know both self and world.

---

35. Merleau-Ponty, *Phenomenology of Perception*, 212.

36. Merleau-Ponty, *Phenomenology of Perception*, 217.

37. Kristeva, "Stabat Mater."

The first point has got to do with the formal structure of "Stabat Mater." On the page, the text is presented sometimes in one column and sometimes two, with Kristeva's more discursive reflections on the history of the symbol and person of the Virgin Mary—the Mother *par excellence*—sharing a space with the first-person, highly subjective narrative of bodily and personal experience of a mother *by* a mother. Thus, the textual page—and the subject herself—are split. The question then becomes one of characterizing the relationship between the two selves or modes of expression; that is, are they related in a mode of mere juxtaposition, antagonism, or a symphonic dialogue or duet? Bringing sustained attention to O'Regan's poems may well provoke the same question: how ought the relation between the logocentric/discursive/philosophical of most of the published material and the lyrical/poetic/primal space of the unpublished poetry be characterized? If we imaginatively reconfigure O'Regan's whole body of work—philosophy, theology, literary criticism, and poetry—according to the space of the left-handed and the right-handed "columns," it is not a case, I would argue, of the left hand not knowing what the right hand is doing (Matt 6:3). Rather, much like the mythological and modern spaces of the poems in *Companion of Theseus*, the "two selves" of poet and academic remain always in contact. It turns out that the full corpus of his work is corporeal, anti-Gnostic; thematically, the poems are anti-Gnostic because they do not shy away from the flesh and the body and the embodied self. More than this, the performance of writing this kind of poetry is not just *about* the flesh but more importantly *from* the flesh. This fleshiness of poetic words makes them vulnerable, as flesh is vulnerable.

With respect to the second point, the poetry tends in certain respects to follow the literary tradition of correlating earth, physicality, women, and primal expression. In "Eros," for instance, Perithous thinks longingly of Persephone that she would "fatten him in expression, / weigh him in her earth, / her hands soothe him, face console him" (2). Likewise, in "The Centaurs," Mother Earth is connected with stereotypically feminized occupations like spinning and braiding as well as fleshiness (12–15). It is important to observe, however, that O'Regan does not fall prey to Kristeva's critique of constructions that suggest the feminine trucks exclusively in "the imprecise . . . with impulses, perhaps with primary processes."[38] The immediacy of the experience of the body—any body, and in the economy of the poem especially the male body of Perithous—and the "tellurian" (to quote from his poem "Ether and Angel") is valued more highly than experience "distant as a dry star I have / been the ineffable one of Dionysius, / the Attic simple of

---

38. Quoted in Edelstein, "Metaphor."

Moses Maimonides who said "I am" / is the faceless, the nameless, // beyond
anger, beyond mercy, // who does not come or go / or sensually intuit the
galaxies / with eye or ear, of whom / nothing tellurian, taste or touch / can
be said" (48).

Both O'Regan's poems and Kristeva's "Stabat Mater" aim toward primal expression before or beneath the words that codify it. Kristeva writes:

> Words are always too remote, too abstract to capture the
> subterranean swarm of seconds, insinuating themselves into
> unimaginable places. . . . Flash on the unnameable, woven of
> abstractions to be torn apart. Let a body finally venture out of its
> shelter, expose itself in meaning beneath a veil of words. WORD
> FLESH. From one to the other, eternally, fragmented visions,
> metaphors of the invisible."[39]

This primal experience, too, for both Kristeva and O'Regan, is first if not
always one of vulnerability to suffering, pain, the wound. In her insistence
upon the exigent bodily realities of pregnancy, birth, and caring for a new-
born child, Kristeva never allows the flesh of the body to be made secondary
to academic or discursive concerns. Moreover, for Kristeva, bodily fluids
like tears, blood, and breastmilk function as "metaphors of non-language,
of a 'semiotic' that does not coincide with linguistic communication. . . . [T]
hey reestablish the nonverbal and appear as a signifying modality closer
to the so-called primary processes."[40] Importantly, love, an "unfurling of
anguish" from which "no one is spared"[41] appears at this precise moment
and site: "When the possibilities of communication are swept away," she
writes, "the last remaining rampart against death is the subtle spectrum of
auditory, tactile, and visual memories that precede language and reemerge
in its absence."[42] Flesh, then, is not dumb; it communicates in spite of (or
perhaps because of) its materiality.[43]

---

39. Kristeva, "Stabat Mater," 134.

40. Kristeva, "Stabat Mater," 143.

41. Kristeva, "Stabat Mater," 145. Cf. the closing, elliptical lines of O'Regan's haunting poem "I Am," which follow visceral recollections of boyhood anguish: "Walk. Even
one's limbs / will not permit persuasion, / doodling in uncertain earth. / love breaks
upward / like a pistol crack and . . . ."

42. Kristeva, "Stabat Mater," 145.

43. Cf. Merleau-Ponty, Visible and the Invisible, 135: "the thickness of flesh between the seer and the thing . . . is not an obstacle between them, it is their means of
communication."

Conclusion/Choruses & Confession(s)

As previously noted, the poems in *The Companion of Theseus* follow a strict pattern, with the alternating spaces of mythological and modern interspersed by choruses. While the choruses might give the reader an impression of respite, the appearance of surfacing aboveground for air, these are *only* impressions and appearances. Rather, as in the mythical labyrinth of Daedalus and the fetid air of Hades and the derelict houses of Dublin into which readers are plunged and in which they have no choice but to wander, in his poems (as O'Regan said to me once in passing) "there are no doors." On my reading, this comment suggests that there is no possibility of genuine escape either from language or from bodies, even or especially since both present as a phenomenology of pure bodily and linguistic exposure which we must freely confess.

The interruptive breaks provided by the choruses are collisions and liminal spaces, intersections and textual folds between "myth" and "reality" that complicate not only the poetic text but also the apparent Cartesian disjunction between body and soul. Bodies become sites upon which wounds and sentences (grammatical, juridical) are inscribed without either foreknowledge or permission. This is something akin, perhaps, to the fate of the uncomprehending Condemned man in Kafka's story "In the Penal Colony," whose punishment was inscribed directly into his skin by the Harrow's needles. When it comes to light that the Condemned does not know his own sentence, nor even the nature of his crime, nor the language of those who are determining and executing the penalty, the Officer explains to the Traveler, "It would be useless to give him that information. He experiences it on his own body."[44] After six hours of the torture, he explains, though the meaning of the bloodied script carved into the body will be difficult if not impossible to decipher by reading, "our man deciphers it with his wounds."[45]

Many but not all of the choruses and some of the poems proper gesture thematically to the trope of confession. The first in-breaking of the chorus in *Withered Water* signals the significance of the theme, announcing pointedly, "I want to confess. / Do not draw the curtain, / Look at my face, mumble / Ritual words in distraction" (12). Chorus 7 repeats language from "The First Serpent," in which Horus Unnofer—a figure from Egyptian mythology— "wants to talk / to his father, the great beast / still stalking the living, / the eyebones emptying of their eyes / He wishes to confess" (57; cf. the repetition in Chorus 7: "winter teeth chewing / the menue of pain / talking he

44. Kafka, *In the Penal Colony*, 5.

45. Kafka, *In the Penal Colony*, 10.

cannot speak // he wishes to confess" (59)). The practice of confession in the poems, however, is not to confess some *thing*; it is, as the fourth chorus indicates, to confess *ourselves*, but to confess ourselves with no interest in absolution. The speaker of the poem says that we are "prepared to confess / ourselves secondary eddic sweat / from the obsolete Nordic God" (37).

Confession becomes a mode of self-reflection that unveils radical susceptibility: to confess flesh is to *be*—not exactly to *have*—sweat, phlegm, scars, wounds, infirmities, finitude, Jacob's limp. To confess is to say what has happened to me, to read aloud the litany of the "mineness" of my flesh upon which wounds are inscribed and for which I bear no genuine responsibility. Bodily and linguistic circumscription and their attendant susceptibilities to being ravaged are conditions for which it is impossible to make reparation. The poems thus seem to require their speakers to confess not with aspiration to beatitude, but more nearly to confess like the virtuous pagans in the ante-chambers of Dante's Limbo who have no defect other than being born before Christ, punished as inculpable with nothing but to "have no hope and yet [to] live in longing."[46] Giorgio Agamben characterizes the denizens of Limbo as "like letters with no addressee."[47] More interesting for our purposes, however, is his explicit comparison of souls in Limbo to the Condemned Man in Kafka's story—who, by the end of the narrative, has escaped (with the antics of dark comedy) from the fatal apparatus meant to execute him. Like the Condemned, Agamben writes that the beings of Limbo "have left the world of guilt and justice behind them: The light that rains down on them is that irreparable light of the dawn following the *novissima dies* of judgment. But the life that begins on earth after the last day is simply human life."[48]

There is something rather like Agamben's restriction to the immanent frame within the poetic world of *The Companion of Theseus* as well as a kind of reveling in the merely natural ends and means of poetry itself. Poetry is a kind of language that functions more like flesh than like thought: before it is a thought, Mandelstam tells us, "a word is a sound."[49] Poetry's rhythmic, aural, visual, affective, and formal capacities speak not to the intellect but immediately to and from the flesh. In poetry, language *is* flesh. In the third appearance of the chorus in *The Centaurs,* the speakers detail the impossibility of speech, where "the voice [is] in an odd quarter, / in a spare room,

46. Alighieri, *Inferno*, Canto IV.42.

47. Agamben, *The Coming Community*, 6. I am grateful to Jay Martin for providing this reference.

48. Agamben, *The Coming Community*, 6–7.

49. Mandelstam, "no. 47," from *Stone* in *Selected Poems*, 5.

outside narrative," where the voice is "a kind of theft / for which we are not yet punished. // An abrupt act of violence. // A kind of embezzlement" (21). Despite these impediments, "still," they say, "we want to speak" (21). What they say is telling:

> We open as epilogue to lesion.
> Understanding comes later with the truth
> of the inevitable falsification. *A poem speaks*
> *even when an architectonic is made*
> *of more subtle failures.* Memory speaks,
> amplifies to decibels of compulsive noise
> the inaudible secretion of connection,
> the unwinding of the spider's web
> before closed eyes. Wound
> is the conifer in a deciduous life.
>
> We want to remember.
> Cuts cauterize and broken clay vessels
> Caulk. Progress is a matter of hygiene.
>
> We heal into another wound.
> We heal into a cleaner wound" (21–22; italics added)

To speak, to confess, to remember is salutary but not miraculous. Might we then hope that poetic language (WORD-FLESH) is the impossible, improbable salve for the wounds sustained and inscribed in our bodies, for a language that falters, for a flesh turned to stone? ("A poem speaks / even when.") The impossible confession and the entirely naturalized absolution might well play out in the space of the word-flesh of poetry. I once heard O'Regan define forgiveness as "that infinitesimal distance between language and phenomenon."[50] That he has deployed persistently beautiful, dense, exact, gorgeously rendered language in *The Companion of Theseus* to name the wounds presences them in the memory but also creates the distance of absence. Insofar as their representation is more beautiful than the actual phenomenon of wounds inflicted, the language performs a kind of absolution (however constrained) in response to the confession of our (inscribed, hardly rescued) selves. To forgive and to be forgiven in this way is not to divest altogether from the wound but—far more modestly—to heal into another, cleaner one. Poetic language is not a re-inscription of violence but simultaneously its portrayal and its exculpation. And it is not improbable that in the descent into this Hades of broken and breaking word we might well find the One gone before us into a most vulnerable silence.

---

50. Cyril O'Regan, personal conversation.

Appendix

Structure of *The Companion of Theseus*

§

Part One, *Withered Water*

"The Labyrinth"
"Even the Angels"

CHORUS 1

"Cannot Kill"
"Voice"

CHORUS 2

"Withered Water"
"I Am"

CHORUS 3

"If Only"
"Do Not"

CHORUS 4

"Riverbed"
"Not"

CHORUS 5

"Lie"
"Hunger"

CHORUS 6

"Like Myth"
"The First Serpent"

CHORUS 7

§

Part Two, *The Centaurs*

"Eros"
"The Most"

CHORUS 1

"Telling"
"Spilling"

CHORUS 2

"The Centaurs"
"Deliverance"

CHORUS 3

"Sea"
"River"

CHORUS 4

"Origins"
"Creosote"

CHORUS 5

"Chameleons"
"Blackhall Street"

CHORUS 6

"Boy-King"
"Alchemy"

CHORUS 7

"Alphabet"
"Ether and Angel"

CHORUS 8

"Eleusis"
"The Second Time"

CHORUS 9

Bibliography

Alighieri, Dante. *Inferno*. Translated by Allen Mandelbaum. New York: Bantam Dell, 1980.

Agamben, Giorgio. *The Coming Community*. Translated by Michael Hardt. Minneapolis: University of Minnesota Press, 2009.

Akhmatova, Anna. *The Complete Poems of Anna Akhmatova*. Translated by Judith Hemschemeyer and edited by Roberta Reeder. Boston: Zephyr, 2000.

Astell, Ann. "O'Regan as Origen in Alexandria." In *An Apocalypse of Love: Essays in Honor of Cyril O'Regan*, edited by Jennifer Newsome Martin and Anthony Sciglitano, 164–82. New York: Crossroads, 2018.

Balthasar, Hans Urs von. *The Glory of the Lord*. 7 vols. San Francisco: Ignatius, 1982–90.

Bethea, David M. *The Shape of Apocalypse in Modern Russian Fiction*. Princeton, NJ: Princeton University Press, 1989.

Brown, Clarence, and W. S. Merwin, trans. *Osip Mandelstam: Selected Poems*. New York: Atheneum, 1974.

Byron, Gordon. *Don Juan: In Sixteen Cantos, with Notes by Lord Byron*. Halifax: Milner and Sowerby, 1837. Accessed at https://www.gutenberg.org/files/21700/21700–h/21700–h.htm.

Crownfield, David, ed. *Body/Text in Julia Kristeva: Religion, Women, and Psychoanalysis*. Albany, NY: SUNY Press, 1992.

Falque, Emmanuel. *God, the Flesh, and the Other: From Irenaeus to Duns Scotus*. Translated by William Christian Hackett. Evanston, IL: Northwestern University Press, 2015.

Henry, Michel. *Incarnation: A Philosophy of Flesh*. Translated by Karl Hefty. Evanston, IL: Northwestern University Press, 2015.

Homer. *The Iliad*. Translated by Robert Fitzgerald. New York: Farrar, Straus and Giroux, 2004.

Kafka, Franz. *In the Penal Colony*. CreateSpace, 2014.

Kristeva, Julia. "Stabat Mater." Translated by Arthur Goldhammer. *Poetics Today* 6.1/2 (1985) 133–52.

MacKendrick, Karmen. *Word Made Skin: Figuring Language at the Surface of Flesh*. New York: Fordham University Press, 2004.

Merleau-Ponty, Maurice. *Phenomenology of Perception*. Translated by Colin Smith. London: Routledge, 2002.

———. *The Prose of the World*. Translated by John O'Neill. Evanston, IL: Northwestern University Press, 1973.

———. *The Visible and the Invisible*. Edited by Claude Lefort and translated by Alphonso Lingis. Evanston, IL: Northwestern University Press, 1968.

Nancy, Jean-Luc. *Corpus*. Translated by Richard A. Rand. New York: Fordham University Press, 2008.

O'Regan, Cyril. "Ambassadors of Divine Glory." *Reflections: A Magazine of Theological and Ethical Inquiry from Yale Divinity School*, Spring 2015, 29–30.

Ricoeur, Paul. *Oneself as Another*. Translated by Kathleen Blamey. Chicago: University of Chicago Press, 1995.

Rivera, Mayra. *Poetics of the Flesh*. Durham, NC: Duke University Press, 2015.

APOCALYPSE AND THE LAND
OF COUNTERFEITS

5

The Apocalypse of the Modern Soul

Cyril O'Regan's Reading
of Hans Urs von Balthasar

D. C. SCHINDLER
The John Paul II Institute
Washington, DC

Hans Urs von Balthasar opens his first major publication, *The Apocalypse of the German Soul* (= *Apokalypse*), with the following powerful lines: "Apo-kalypsis means unveiling, which means in turn the same thing as making manifest [Offenbarung]: namely, *revelatio*. But it is the external that lies open; the internal remains veiled. This internal reality is the soul."[1] He goes on to explain, in the introduction, what we might call his methodological principles for this very unusual work, principles that place him outside any of the customary disciplinary boundaries. Although his understanding of the nature of his work was still somewhat raw in this first text and in need of maturation, it is nevertheless true that, as he said elsewhere, the beginning

---

1. Balthasar, *Apokalypse*, 1:3. The first two volumes of this book were initially composed in 1928–29—and so just as Heidegger was beginning to promote a notion of truth as "unconcealment" more basically than as correctness—but were set aside for the sake of his dissertation (completed in 1930), and then thoroughly reworked into three larger volumes, published, finally, between 1933 and 1935. See the account by Alois M. Haas, ibid., xxv.

is determinative for everything that follows:[2] Balthasar certainly deepened and expanded his point of origin, but in fact his work always sprung from this unique inter-disciplinary "space," which has proven to be a decisive mark of his thought, and a point of difficulty for more conventional theologians. Balthasar receives Christianity, not simply as *something* revealed, but as *revelation*.

Given that it is distinctively characteristic of his work, however, one might be surprised at how little attention has been given to the peculiarity of Balthasar's way of approaching God's revelation in the reception of his theology, apart from incidental remarks on Balthasar's penchant for literature, or his interest in the saints as theological sources. It is one of Cyril O'Regan's great achievements to have foregrounded Balthasar's "style" specifically as a theological theme.[3] His branding of Balthasar as a paradigmatically "apocalyptic" theologian may seem, on first hearing, a rather eccentric appellation, but O'Regan shows, quite compellingly, not only that the term captures what is distinctive in Balthasar's approach, but that it in fact gives expression to the very substance of his thought, which is what determines that approach. Even more, O'Regan shows that Balthasar's apocalyptic is not a mere idiosyncrasy but represents instead an essentially Christian way of receiving and interpreting Christian faith. In making this essentially Christian character clear, finally, O'Regan brings to light (apo-kalypsis) the specifically Gnostic counterfeits to Christianity that populate the modern (and postmodern) era, as various abstractions of content from the concreteness of revelation. While "apocalyptic theology" may appear to be largely a "sideshow" in the contemporary scene, O'Regan makes a strong case, in his interpretation of Hans Urs von Balthasar, that all genuine Christian theology is ultimately apocalyptic, properly understood; he thus discovers a key that helps bring to light, not just the distinctiveness of Balthasar, but in fact the profound unity of the great Christian tradition, in all of its irreducible diversity.

In the following essay, we will first very briefly present Balthasar's own articulation of his approach in *Apokalypse*, attempting to set into relief the uniqueness of his methodological principles. Then we will distill at greater length some of the basic features of Balthasar's "style" such as O'Regan interprets it, above all in his most recent work *The Anatomy of Misremembering*.

2. Balthasar, *Seeing the Form*, 17.

3. Balthasar uses the term "theological style" to indicate much more than rhetorical idiom. Instead, the term means the fundamental way that a thinker approaches the truth, the fundamental "ethos" or character of his thought, which is inseparable from its content. Balthasar uses this term to characterize the "object" of his monographs on the great aesthetic thinkers in the Western tradition, found in volumes 2 and 3 of the English translation of *The Glory of the Lord*.

It will become clear how O'Regan's characterizing of Balthasar as "apocalyptic" allows us to see an essential continuity between the early and later work, which might otherwise remain obscure. Catching sight of this continuity not only sheds light on the nature of Balthasar's first trilogy, but at the same time it deepens our appreciation of his later work, especially the way in which it presents a fidelity to Christ that opens to a *catholic* vision of the whole of reality. Finally, we will see how Balthasar's distinctive "style" sets into uncommonly sharp relief the shortcomings of the great modern pretension to such a "catholic" vision in G. W. F. Hegel. O'Regan doubtless will never be surpassed in the sophistication and breadth of his locating of Balthasar in terms of intellectual history, assessing the predecessors, rivals, and heirs of both Balthasar and his interlocutors. We will not pass judgment on any of this—which would lie quite beyond our competence—but will aim instead to distill the basic features of Balthasar's "theological style," as O'Regan has brought it to light.

I

Balthasar explains at the outset of *Apokalypse* that his unusual formulation, "apocalypse of the soul," is "simply a concrete way of saying 'eschatology.'"[4] What he means by this term is the traditional branch of theology concerned with the "eschaton," the "last things:" heaven and hell, man's ultimate destination, final judgment, the nature of the "visio beatifica," and so forth. But when Balthasar says his expression represents a "concrete" interpretation of the last things, there is much more going on here than a question of rhetorical presentation. As he goes on to explain, his approach in this book differs from traditional eschatology in a number of important respects. First of all, he means "eschatology" not only in its specifically religious sense, but also in a more general sense. While the word is typically used to indicate the study of representations of heaven and hell, the church's doctrine concerning the afterworld, and the like, one may also interpret the word etymologically, and consider its sense, so to speak, "from below." In this case, Balthasar explains, it indicates a study of what is ultimate, the most fundamental ground, the furthest horizon, the highest reference point, of *meaning* simply. It is this sense that governs Balthasar's approach in this book. Now, in the etymological sense of the word, we may say that there is a certain "eschaton" in every academic discipline, which grounds that discipline in its distinctiveness and so defines its limits. But all of these "relative eschata," as Balthasar puts it, point to what is "ultimate and absolute, just as every eschatology points

4. Balthasar, *Apokalypse*, 3.

back to a Logos of the eternal eschaton."[5] It may seem, at first, that ultimate meaning would be the business of philosophy, whose object, after all, is "being qua being," *extra qua non*, and this judgment would in a certain respect be valid. But Balthasar proposes that there is a more proper approach to ultimate meaning, which in some sense coincides with philosophy, but not completely, and it is this approach that he adopts: "If we understand eschatology as 'apocalypse of the soul,' or in other words as a penetrating through to the most concrete reality of all . . . then such an eschatology will use philosophy as a means, without thus surrendering the other two realms that aim in a privileged way at the unveiling of the concrete: theology, as discourse concerning the absolutely unique God, who addresses himself only to *this* man, not to 'essence' [*Wesen*] or 'existence' [*Existenz*]—and art, insofar as it, too, has as its sole theme to show forth what is most universal precisely in the unrepeatable moment."[6]

Note that Balthasar envisions, here, a kind of "meta-discipline," which configures itself in the triad of philosophy, theology, and art (clearly invoking Hegel's articulation of absolute spirit as art, religion, and philosophy: more on this anon).[7] As we will see, one of the significant ways he deepens this point of origin as his thought matures is, most basically, to recognize that theology is not just a discourse that may be juxtaposed with the others, relative to a meta-discourse, but is rather *itself* the meta-discourse, which comprehends the others in a certain sense, but only as simultaneously liberating them into their own absolute integrity. Already in this early work, however, Balthasar reveals a concern not to render any of these finally obsolete, as Hegel could not avoid doing himself. Without getting into the details of Balthasar's difference from Hegel just yet, the principal point we wish to highlight here is the emphasis Balthasar lays on the "allekonkreteste Wirklichkeit."[8] It is just this that prevents him from identifying eschatol-

5. Balthasar, *Apokalypse*, 4.

6. Balthasar, *Apokalypse*, 4.

7. "It follows from this that philosophy, theology, and art, in their talk about the eschaton, do not conduct a direct discourse; instead, they point and 'signify' ['meinen']. It is only with such pointing that we concern ourselves here, when we address these three forms of spirit's activity. We therefore do not wish to present our own spiritual activity as either philosophical, theological, or literary, in the strict sense of those words" (Balthasar, *Apokalypse*, 7).

8. It bears remarking that the particular way Balthasar emphasizes concreteness and the uniqueness of the individual in this early text betrays a certain nominalistic flavor, though never without significant counterbalancing thrusts. This flavor may be traced back above all to the primary place that phenomenology had in his first writings (due perhaps above all to the deep influence of Erich Przywara at this early stage of his thinking). That "flavor" was radically subsumed into the richer sense of being that

ogy *simply* with metaphysics.[9] In contrast to a certain "Platonizing" trend one can detect in the church fathers (concerning which Balthasar remains acutely vigilant from the beginning to the end of this thinking), a trend that absolutizes abstract essences and so casts a shadow over the particularity of the flesh and the material world in general, Balthasar insists that the "really real reality" is *concrete*.[10] In other words, it is neither an abstract essence, which eclipses individuality, nor is it uniqueness and particularity taken likewise in an abstract sense, which would come at the expense of universality. Instead, "really real reality" is both particularity and universality at once: *con-cretum*. A properly eschatological eschatology must begin and end with the "*allekonkreteste Wirklichkeit*," the "*concretissimum*."

The nature of reality in its concreteness demands a method, or an approach, that would seek to do justice to all the diverse aspects it holds in tension. At this point, Balthasar returns to his phrase, "apocalypse of the soul," and highlights the significance of his choice of the word "soul," as opposed to "spirit" or "mind" (*Geist*). He means by it man in his most concrete and ultimate reality, not as a mere object of psychology or philosophy, he explains, but rather in the sense indicated by the expression, "to save souls."[11] The "apo-" in his phrase signifies a "movement or a process," while the "logic" (of "eschatology," presumably[12]), refers to the fact that what *occurs* in this process is a time-transcending logos: we are speaking of an "event of meaning," so to speak, which takes place in man's innermost being. What Balthasar is aiming at, in other words, is the dramatic event of man's taking a position, in his heart of hearts, as it were, concerning what is ultimate, and

---

Balthasar received through the interchange with his two friends, Siewerth and Ulrich. It is not only the deepening of his *theological* vision, with the help of Henri de Lubac and Adrienne von Speyr, but also the deepening of his philosophical vision through these two Thomists that he succeeded in overcoming the traces of dualisms in this early work.

9. It would be very interesting to compare Balthasar's aim in *Apokalypse* to that of Heidegger in *Being and Time*. Heidegger, too, seeks to get to the origin of truth, so to speak, and does so through an analysis specifically of Dasein, the only being for whom being is a question. This analysis of Dasein's particular way of being, *In-der-Welt-sein*, represents what he calls a "fundamental ontology." Balthasar also seeks to disclose the meaning of the whole through an analysis of the human being that aims more radically than the usual disciplines are capable of doing. But his is an "unveiling of the soul," and rather than present a general analysis, as Heidegger does, he proceeds specifically by way of a thoughtful discernment of actual figures in modern and contemporary history.

10. Note O'Regan's very bold proposal that we consider Balthasar the "first Irenaeus": O'Regan, *Misremembering*, 296.

11. Balthasar, *Apokalypse*, 4.

12. One wonders whether there was a mistake, here, since the root "logos" does not appear in "apocalypsis," which is the word he is actually discussing (while it does appear, of course, in "eschatology"), but in any event the point he intends to make is clear.

thereby placing himself under judgment. Balthasar undertakes this project in *Apokalypse* by exploring the work of some of the landmark figures of German culture—the poets, the dramatists, the philosophers, and (to a lesser extent) the theologians. He clarifies that, in his exploration of the "doctrine of ultimate disposition,"[13] he is interested not in the subjectivity of the individuals as such, but in what they reveal about the meaning of history and the fate of humanity, though this larger meaning can never be isolated from the specific fate of German culture, or indeed from the specific fate of the individuals who most fruitfully generated that culture. Again, to absolutize the concrete means to refuse to separate the universal from the particular.

We will consider two final points in this brief presentation of Balthasar's early method, both of which concern the centrality of the *image* in his study.[14] First, he explains, in contrast to concepts, a proper image exhibits a complex relation to time; it manages to hold in tension the "already" and the "not-yet" aspects of concrete existence. Images are often a focus of traditional eschatology, especially in the version that compares cultural interpretations. But one may also explore the imagery that a single individual produces in his wrestling with his own individual fate and the meaning of the age in which he lives. Such a meaning, and such a fate, cannot be adequately presented simply as an idea, in the sense of a finished concept, because destiny is eminently historical, it is a meaning that is being decided, and the decision involves a complex web of relations, with decisions both future and past, as well as an eternal judgment. According to Balthasar, this concrete meaning can be grasped and expressed only in images, symbols, and stories, or in other words, in the medium of "mythos." There is an essential drama in this "mythos": as a truly transcendent end, the eschaton cannot help but bear on the individual *here and now*,[15] in a manner that requires his taking a position. If it were simply a matter of the "after"-world, a sphere of existence that lies simply in a period that follows history (i.e., comes temporally after it), the eschaton would be ultimate only in a superficial, reductively temporal sense. The eschaton is in some sense

---

13. Balthasar, *Apokalypse*, 5.

14. Balthasar goes on in the introduction to lay out the plan of his three volumes, and then finally to spell out more specifically the difference between the particular interpretation of eschatology he is offering in this work and that of other recent thinkers (Troeltsch, Althaus, Hoffman, Traub, Barth, and so forth).

15. "The soul is guided by the 'last things,' about which she has knowledge *now* and which direct her *now* as if these things were already her innermost truth, drawing her onto her path to her final destiny. But because her apocalypse has *not yet* come to pass, because she stands before herself as before a door that remains closed, she can grasp the logos of her eschaton only as something veiled," Balthasar, *Apokalypse*, 6.

"now," even as it remains nevertheless "last." It is the image that is best able to respect the complexity of this paradox.

Second, and related to this, the image holds together the delicate interplay of veiling and unveiling in the matter of ultimate meaning; it is able effectively to lay meaning bare, to communicate intelligible content, without surrendering the mystery that is inseparable from genuine ultimacy: "[a]ll directly rational utterances concerning the 'ultimate' are impossible for an essentially hidden *concrete* being. Such utterances can only touch on a general and abstract truth, an objectivity that at best can be, in turn, itself a 'mythos' for that which is concretely yet to come."[16] Balthasar is not denying here the indispensable place of propositional language and conceptual expression, and even goes on to emphasize in a footnote that he does not intend in the least to downplay the permanent validity of the *objective* dimension of truth.[17] Nevertheless, as the book's opening words already hint, he is insisting here that the innermost soul of the world that he is seeking to unveil can only be indicated or "meant" [*meinen*] rather than directly displayed. To be sure, *all* language is in some sense figurative, at least insofar as it intends anything beyond immediate sense experience,[18] but this general truth about language becomes increasingly significant the more fundamental the discourse. For what concerns Balthasar in *Apokalypse* specifically, the imaginative basis of language means that one may not privilege, in a one-sided way, the "logical" discourse of philosophy over the "poetic" discourse of poetry, the "literal" over the "figurative." It is indispensable to give conceptual expression to what we understand; language is not a veil that *hides* reality, but serves instead to make it *present*, to give us access to it. We will see below that this insistence on *integrating* the discursive with the intuitive is one of the features that distinguishes Balthasar from so many other "apocalyptic" thinkers. At the same time, this real access to things that language offers does not exhaust the depth of reality, but only makes that mystery more evident, the deeper we go, as it were. If Balthasar reads poets and dramatists as much as philosophers and theologians, it is because he recognizes all of them as trying in their distinctive ways to give expression to ultimate meaning.

16. Balthasar, *Apokalypse*, 6–7.

17. Balthasar, *Apokalypse*, 7n1.

18. Nietzsche famously made this claim in his 1873 essay, "On Truth and Lie in an Extra-Moral Sense," in Nietzsche, *The Portable Nietzsche*, 42–47, but it is acknowledged more generally. On the figurative character of language, and, related to this, the permanent validity of myth, see C. S. Lewis, "Meditation in a Woodshed," and "Myth Became Fact," in *God in the Dock*, 230–34 and 54–60.

In short, if reality is con-crete, so too is the image that conveys it, which holds together in a complex, unified whole the particular and the universal, the immanent and the transcendent, the already and the not yet, openness and closure, and revelation and hiddenness. It thus represents, itself, a medium fitting for a Christian thinker, one who contemplates not just the Word, but the Word made flesh, the eternal Logos in the material of historical existence. We will see how Balthasar, as his intellectual and ecclesial mission comes into greater focus, never abandons this unique starting point.

II

Those familiar with Balthasar's mature work typically find his first trilogy strange, evoking a spirit quite foreign to that expressed, for example, in the late trilogy that is rightly considered his *Meisterwerk*, namely, the *Glory of the Lord*, the *Theo-Drama*, and the *Theo-Logic*, which Balthasar completed only at the end of his life. It is not insignificant that Balthasar left to his archives the instruction to allow translation of the early trilogy only after a substantial amount of the later work was already available. The explicit notion of apocalypse as the unveiling of the individual soul, the very principle of that first trilogy, is scarcely to be found in his mature writings. As we mentioned at the outset, however, Cyril O'Regan deserves much credit for setting into relief a fundamental dimension in Balthasar's mature thought that stands in continuity with this initial principle, all the while deepening and, it must be said, correcting it.[19] Certain inadequacies in Balthasar's original formulation of his "style" become especially evident in the light of his later work. First of all, there are some grounds for suggesting that the notion of "apo-kalypsis" that Balthasar elaborates in *Apokalypse* betrays a certain tension, if not an outright contradiction: precisely as a general method, it seems to represent a universal, formal (and so relatively abstract) principle of concreteness.[20] The formality of this principle, however, gets relativized in the later works. As O'Regan shows, "apokalypse" becomes in Balthasar's mature thought inseparable from *the* "Apokalypse," which means biblical revelation as a whole, but most specifically, of course, its culminating book:

19. O'Regan acknowledges that "apocalyptic" is often used pejoratively in Balthasar, but he argues, against the surface evidence, that the *substance* of apocalyptic remains fundamental, and indeed the center: O'Regan, *Misremembering*, 178–79.

20. This is not to say that Balthasar in fact merely applies this principle in an extrinsic fashion to the various contents of German literary history as a mere formal methodological principle; in fact, his reading of these figures is quite rich and nuanced.

For Balthasar, authentic, that is, biblically saturated Christianity is defined by "Apocalypsis," a disclosure to a contemplator who is precisely not a spectator, who rather is radically involved in a seeing that finally is more an acceptance of being seen than a seeing which commands reality as it commends itself. In this sense, for Balthasar, . . . John and Paul are regulative. Of course, this view of Christianity as the definitive form of divine disclosure, is not the issue of a single statement of scripture, but the fruit of a proper exegesis of the Gospels as they find their center of gravity and integration in the Gospel of John.[21]

The Gospel of John, moreover, ultimately needs to be read in relation to John's Book of Revelation, as O'Regan points out repeatedly.[22] In addition to the closer connection to scripture, we see here another fundamental shift from the early work: what is disclosed in the unveiling is no longer primarily the individual soul, but *God*, though of course God's disclosure, which demands a response and thus initiates a "drama," inevitably entails *also* the disclosure of the individual soul.[23] But the centrality of concreteness remains, and in fact deepens: the event of the disclosure of ultimate meaning proves to be, not only a matter of the personal history of individuals, but originally a singular event in world history, namely, the coming of Christ, his passion, death, and resurrection, and the unfolding of the meaning of this event in the Holy Spirit. Scripture is not mythology, philosophy, or theology; it is first of all the presentation of this real event, not as positivistic history, to be sure, but in the densely meaning-ful medium of symbol and narrative. As we will explain in more detail in the third section, the concreteness of revelation becomes a basic criterion for Balthasar's judgment of other forms of thought: any attempt to make "apocalyptic" an abstract principle—whether it be the formalism of a mere literary genre, such as we find in some of the Old Testament prophets, or especially in many of the post-Christian thinkers of modernity—is to be criticized.

It is crucial to note, straightaway, that to insist on rooting apocalypse in the particularity of Christ as attested to in scripture is not at all to deny

21. O'Regan, *Misremembering*, 87.

22. See, for example, O'Regan, *Misremembering*, 377, 388. As Balthasar puts it in his introduction to Adrienne von Speyr's commentary on this book, "if one can even speak seriously of [apocalyptic as] a 'literary genre,' [John's Revelation] is the analogatum princeps." Von Speyr's, *Apokalypse*, 7.

23. To be sure, Balthasar also acknowledges this fact, but reverses the emphasis. In comparing Balthasar in the first trilogy to the later one, we have something analogous to Heidegger's "Kehre," which moved from a focus on Dasein to Sein, even while acknowledging their inseparability in both "phases" (which is why some claim there is no real shift). There is no need, however, to exaggerate the comparison.

that "apokalypsis" has an analogous extension beyond God's self-manifestation in Christ;[24] nevertheless, this extension must be recognized precisely as
analogous, and so as generated by and, for that reason, intrinsically related
to this singular reality. It is precisely O'Regan's bringing to light the meaning
of "apocalyptic" in Balthasar's mature thought that allows us to see another
fundamental deficiency in Balthasar's trilogy, which we alluded to at the
outset: there is a connection between his initial view of apokalypsis as a general principle, detached from God's self-revelation in Christ, and his grop-
ing for a meta-discipline beyond art, philosophy, *and* theology. Balthasar
eventually comes to see the universal scope, and—as we will explain further
below—the radical *gift* character of Christ himself and his mission, which
implies both that theology is not one discipline juxtaposed to all the others,
but the "queen of the sciences," as the tradition puts it.[25] At the same time,
and for the same reason, the *privileging* of theology in this particular sense
does not render the other primary realms of philosophy and art merely
penultimate; instead, they turn out to bear a certain co-responsibility for
the whole. Thus, for Balthasar—in contrast to Barth, one may observe—a
radical Christocentrism, if it is genuine and true, demands just the sort of
recollection of the broad tradition, the sort of loving engagement with the
great figures in art, literature, and philosophy, that we find, for example, in
the crucially important volumes 4 and 5 of *The Glory of the Lord*.[26]

If there were no analogy in the sense of the *generosity* of God's self-disclosure in Christ, theology would be nothing but a re-reading of scripture,
and perhaps above all, the apocalyptic texts of Paul and John. We discover
such a radical restriction of view, for example, in Ernst Käsemann, whose
programmatic statement that "apocalyptic was the mother of all Christian
theology"[27] might initially sound like what O'Regan is ascribing to Balthasar,
and in Käsemann's student Louis Martyn, who has come to represent a

24. In the early works, such as the Barth book (*The Theology of Karl Barth*, 1992;
originally 1951), and *The Theology of History* (1994; originally published in 1959), there
remain palpable traces of a kind of formalism, connected with the nominalistic flavor
we mentioned above, but this fades as his thought progresses.

25. It is worth noting that O'Regan recognizes Bonaventure's importance to
Balthasar more than most commentators. As he shows, Bonaventure is important to
Balthasar because of his Christocentrism and the place of theology in the hierarchy of
the disciplines that this Christocentrism implies, and also because of the significance of
his notion of "expressio."

26. The English translation has more divisions than the original German volumes:
volumes 4 and 5, *The Realm of Metaphysics in Antiquity and in the Modern Age* are
volume III/1, parts 1 and 2 in German.

27. From Ernst Käsemann, "The Beginnings of Christian Theology," in *New Testament Questions of Today*, 102. See Aarde, "Matthew and Apocalypticism."

prominent voice in contemporary "apocalyptic theology."[28] According to this line of theology, which is one of the contemporary heirs of "dialectical theology," apocalyptic is essentially *interruptive*. God's self-revelation is not the presentation of some objective content that may be subjectively appropriated, dogmatically formulated, conceptually articulated, and so forth, but is meant to stop man so to speak in his tracks, to denounce the actual state of things and to call to conversion. In this respect, what is significant in Paul's Letter to the Galatians, for instance, is not so much what he says as it is the *act* of preaching itself: preaching is essentially intervention. O'Regan is especially helpful in showing how, in contrast to all of this, which he would call "minimally eidetic apocalyptic," Balthasar's apocalyptic is "maximally eidetic," meaning it is a disclosure that contains conceptually available theological content. The word "eidetic," which O'Regan draws from Balthasar himself,[29] most immediately evokes the phenomenology of Husserl,[30] but has its roots in Greek philosophy (Plato's *eidos*, or form), and above all in, of course, scripture itself: *eidos* means in the first place "vision."

Let us explore this point further, because it brings us to what is in our opinion one of O'Regan's genuine contributions. Against the backdrop of what we have just said regarding the deepening of the meaning of concreteness, we may see the articulation of the three parts of Balthasar's mature trilogy as a recapitulation of the "method" he proposed in *Apokalypse*, now from a perspective that is simultaneously more ample (catholic) and more Christ-centered. To put it in O'Regan's terminology, the very structure of the trilogy is an expression of a "maximally eidetic apocalypse." Balthasar begins his trilogy with an elaboration of the principles of a "theological aesthetics:" "Schau der Gestalt," or in other words, "seeing"—vision!—"the form." This form is ultimately the form of Christ, but, as Balthasar explains, one who is unable to see form in general will be unable to see the form of Christ, or more specifically unable to see that Christ presents a *form*. At the same time, the more properly one sees Christ the more adequately one may come to see reality in its own integrity and fullness. We see here a recollection of the indispensable primacy Balthasar gave to the *image* in *Apokalypse*, but, while in that early work, this importance was due above all to the (subjective) incapacity to articulate what is ultimate in a direct, rational way, here it is due to the absolute primacy of God, as revealed in Christ. God is not *first* an object of our thought, or indeed of our imaginative powers, however adequate or

---

28. Martyn, *Galatians*.

29. O'Regan, *Misremembering*, 376.

30 As O'Regan shows, Husserl's importance for Balthasar on this point lies in the priority of the object Husserl means to recognize in intentionality.

inadequate these prove to be; nor is he *first* a response to the question our desires and aspirations put to him. Instead, God *first* sovereignly displays himself: glory. As the Eastern church has seen so well, the incarnation, before it is a deed that remediates sin, is an *epiphany*. For this reason, O'Regan says, with beautiful succinctness, "*Christianity is first and foremost a matter of vision* that envelops as well as inspires all understanding."[31]

We will come back to the second part of this statement below, but we must first recognize the importance of making vision primary. This does not imply that God is simply the object of our sight, the prey, as it were, of the "lust of the eyes." Instead, vision is a response to God's absolute firstness. As O'Regan explains, "Christian perception or seeing is correlative to the meaning or form that is its object, rather than meaning or form being the objective correlate of perception or vision."[32] A crucial implication of the priority of the object, or better of the self-revealing God, is that it remains, precisely in being seen, *more* than the vision. Precisely because of its symbolic nature, O'Regan points out that the Book of Revelation makes this aspect especially evident: "The text could not make it more clear that vision is always a seeing of what exceeds the prospects of vision and that the symbols deployed are inadequate to what they aim to disclose."[33] For Balthasar, the lesson of Revelation is that the eidetic and the apophatic necessarily go together;[34] this point recapitulates the principle he presented in *Apokalypse*. What is seen is thus not *merely* seen, or in other words, vision goes beyond the simple surface; this means that the intellect, which penetrates through the surface to the mysterious interior (intus-legere), is necessarily involved in the perception. But the intellect is involved first precisely *in the perception*, which means that the disclosure never simply reduces to a universal intelligible content. Instead, the *Gestalt* one sees is perfectly con-crete; the symbol, the meaningful image that is seen, is so to speak an all-at-once synthesis of an infinite, and so inexhaustible, wealth of meaning: a diversity-in-unity. As O'Regan put it in the passage quoted earlier, vision envelops and inspires understanding. Christianity, to say it again in somewhat different words, is not a proposition, or even a rich collection of propositions, but is "first and foremost a vision" because it is a response to the infinitely mysterious form that is Christ, conveyed in the narrative of the Gospels and the symbolic of

---

31. O'Regan, *Misremembering*, 42 (italics added).

32. O'Regan, *Misremembering*, 375.

33. O'Regan, *Misremembering*, 276–77.

34 O'Regan's interpretation of Balthasar is especially strong in his recognition of this point. See, e.g., O'Regan, *Misremembering*, 122.

Revelation. It is more than the visible that shows itself, and so it is more than the eye that sees; instead, vision involves a response of the whole person.

Because of the Christian form's laying hold of the whole person, vision never degenerates into mere spectacle: the seer is taken up into the meaning, the form turns out to be a deed, which prompts free action as part of the "Theo-Drama." On this score, once again, the Book of Revelation proves to be essential:

> Revelation is the biblical text that effects the link between aesthetics and dramatics that all subsequent theology aspires to (*TD4*, 54). It offers as stage heaven and earth (*TD4*, 22–6, 48), time in its vastest extension and intensivity as parenthesis within eternity (*TD4*, 49), the disclosure of the Lamb who, as nothing less than the pivot upon which the world turns (*TD4*, 62–3), is its alpha and omega (*TD4*, 44), and who if he evokes adoration, also provokes rebellion.[35]

One cannot remain a detached observer, but must decide and act, and because this action always remains subordinate to the objectivity of the form, one's action necessarily comes under judgment.[36] At the same time, and ultimately for the very same reason, the most essential action turns out to be liturgical, the action of praise and thanksgiving (or, to use the beautiful French phrase, *l'action de grace*). It is not at all an accident that, as Balthasar himself puts it, "the simultaneity of liturgy and judgment is perhaps the most all-pervading leitmotif of the *Book of Revelation*."[37] What is presented, after all, is not a static image, simply to be contemplated, but both "symbol and story" at once, and, indeed, the story itself is not a simple closed narrative, but exhibits both closure and openness simultaneously. As we will explain further below, the "surplus" of meaning generously *given* in the absolute disclosure of the Christian form means that the story has an "open-ended" quality, a "yet-to-be-determined" sense that nevertheless coincides with an absolute completeness and coming to rest: "In this way we can grasp something of the paradox of the *Book of Revelation*: the Lamb can appear as the ultimate Victor and the Lord of all history, while at the same time he is depicted as riding out to do battle and to do slaughter (19:11ff)."[38]

---

35. O'Regan, *Misremembering*, 388.

36 Balthasar's notion of drama thus differs on this point from the interpretation of Francesca Murphy, who makes the action *itself* the final determinant of meaning and so compromises the time-transcending character of truth that is essential for genuine drama, at least as Balthasar understands it. See Murphy, "Is Liberalism a Heresy?"

37. Balthasar, *Theo-Drama 4*, 36, cited in O'Regan, *Misremembering*, 390.

38. Balthasar, *Theo-Drama 4*, 21; O'Regan also refers to ibid., 18 and 51.

This simultaneity explains one of the themes that O'Regan presents with exceptional clarity in the *Anatomy of Misremembering*, namely,
Balthasar's privileging of drama in Hegel's triad of lyric, drama, and epic,
in contrast to Hegel's ultimate settling, for his part, on epic, in spite of his
apparent celebration of drama. As O'Regan persuasively demonstrates,
Hegel elevates drama specifically in the sphere of *art*, but this sphere is itself
ultimately overtaken by religion, and finally—definitively—by philosophy.
In epic, the story is told from the perspective of an external narrator, who
is able to survey the whole, and give it the form he wants from a position of
relative safety, as it were. He is not involved; the action of the story makes no
particular claim on him.[39] In drama, by contrast, the story is not recounted
from a distance, nor is it meant simply to be read (or heard). Instead, a
drama is played out, and the actual performance is a kind of incarnation
of a logos, which inevitably integrates elements of the novelty of historical
existence into given meaning. The very same play can have a significantly
different meaning in different contexts, depending on the actors, the direc-
tor, the conditions of the performance, and even the quality of the audience.
As O'Regan is absolutely right to point out in contrast to the many critics
who fail to see this crucial point, drama does not require, in order to be
dramatic, some uncertainty, a *lack* of closure or completeness, or absence
of overarching form.[40] As we just explained, the decisive point for Balthasar
is precisely the *simultaneity* of openness and closure, which implies that the
novelty and freedom in drama would be weakened in the absence of such
closure. Apocalyptic in its authentic sense entails drama; in its inauthentic
sense, such as we find it in Hegel and other major figures in modernity,
apocalyptic tends toward the merely "epical": a capacity to grasp the ultimate meaning in a univocal fashion, not as something that comprehends
one (which *demands* drama), but which one comprehends, in the sense that
one is able to fit it wholly inside one's particular intelligence. In this case, the
ultimate meaning is something to which one can give a finite form, subject

39. O'Regan avoids all of the typical oversimplifications of Hegel on this point, and
passes judgment with significant nuance, but with no less clarity. Hegel is one of the
great discoverers of the principle of drama; it is just that his fundamental presupposi-
tions cannot sustain his insight on this point.

40. This point is frequently missed in discussions of theological drama: see, e.g.,
Quash, "Drama and the Ends of Modernity," in Gardner et al., *Balthasar at the End of
Modernity* and Kilby, *A (Very) Critical Introduction*. These studies judge that Balthasar
compromises drama because of his insistence on completeness or wholeness, but the
assumption behind this charge is that drama is exclusively a matter of open-endedness.
O'Regan is very clear that this represents a misunderstanding of Balthasar: O'Regan,
Misremembering, 388. See our own criticisms of this assumption: Schindler, *Dramatic
Structure of Truth*, 17–25; and Schindler, "A Very Critical Response."

to manipulation, and able to be appropriated conceptually. O'Regan shows, at great length, that there is a connection between inauthentic apocalyptic and Gnosticism.

Finally, the engagement with the form that has disclosed itself results in understanding, but specifically in a concrete and intimate way that remains open to what is ever greater. The very point of Balthasar's *Theo-Logic* is to articulate a sense of truth that affirms the finite without excluding the infinite and affirms the infinite without absorbing the finite. The grasp of such truth is therefore always ordered to contemplation, worship, and praise above all. As Hegel saw, the absolutizing of "ratio" in modernity makes a specifically finite form of understanding most basic, but this is not of course adequate to truly *ultimate* meaning. In aiming at Absolute Knowledge, beyond the finite form, however, Hegel may be said to "backslide into the Enlightenment," as O'Regan puts it.[41] On the other hand, if one seeks to avoid rationalistic collapse, it is not sufficient simply to close reason to the ultimate and settle for ethics or kerygma, for example.[42] Instead, ratio needs to be given its proper place inside of a dynamic of knowing that moves beyond itself and precisely thus comes to its proper fulfillment.[43] It is, O'Regan insightfully argues, precisely a recovery of a proper sense of apocalyptic that allows us to do this. At the core of apocalyptic, as we have seen, is "symbol and story." This moving image, which one sees in being seen, is not a *veil* over truth, but rather, as we suggested earlier, its superabundant disclosure, a communication to reason that transcends reason, not by excluding it, but by including it—*all* of it, in its complete integrity, essential necessities, logical clarity, and so forth—and surpassing it in what remains ever-greater. O'Regan brings out what is perhaps one of the most distinctive aspects of Balthasar's theology, which sets him far apart from the general drift of postmodern thought on this score: for Balthasar, the proper response to rationalism is not apophaticism, which can lead to intellectual free fall if it is untethered from anything positive, but excessive self-disclosure.[44] This super-abundance of meaning lies at the core of apocalyptic vision. The image is a positive manifestation that remains both thinkable and "in excess of thought."[45]

It is important to see the connection between the primacy of image, as Balthasar understands it, and his privileging of "kata-logy," which is meaning that descends from above, over "analogy," which is reason's ascent to

41. O'Regan, *Misremembering*, 109.
42. O'Regan, *Misremembering*, 375.
43. O'Regan, *Misremembering*, 134.
44. O'Regan, *Misremembering*, 38.
45. O'Regan, *Misremembering*, 400.

what exceeds it.[46] The latter emphasizes the apophatic precisely because reason herein makes *itself* the measure, and so acknowledges what transcends it most basically as negative. In "kata-logy," reason *receives* its measure from what transcends it, which necessarily precedes reason in a positive sense, and so begins with its own manifestation: apo-kalypsis. Apocalyptic is therefore, on the one hand, the proper response to Hegel's "panopticism,"[47] but on the other hand it remains a *seeing*—or to use O'Regan's term, drawn from Balthasar, it remains "eidetic."

O'Regan makes one of his most significant contributions to the reception of Balthasar, no doubt, in his careful distinguishing of Balthasar from other postmodern apocalyptic thinkers who are equally critical, explicitly or implicitly, of Hegelian absolute knowledge. For example, O'Regan presents Walter Benjamin as taking a position at the end of the spectrum opposite to Hegelianism, adopting what can be called a "non-eidetic apocalyptic." O'Regan brilliantly shows that the difference between Benjamin and Balthasar stands out, obliquely but no less starkly, when one compares their respective privileging of German *Trauerspiel* and Spanish Baroque drama, at the core of which lies a difference in the interpretation of symbol, in comparison to allegory: "The concern for both [Balthasar and Benjamin] is the issue of truth, and more specifically, whether meaning or its interruption is the more basic requirement."[48] O'Regan refers repeatedly to the expression Balthasar uses to describe Benjamin's thought: "lightning flashes." The essence of *allegory* is to point *away* (*allos*) to ultimate meaning, which is utterly other, absent, discontinuous with what is given. In this regard, truth comes to bear on experience only in the explosive instant, and can be read only post hoc, negatively, in the disruption it has caused in its wake. *Symbol*, by contrast, implies meaning's being actually present, here and now, though without exhausting itself, so to speak, on the surface. In the first case, we have revelation as sheer event, a condemnation of the present that points to the eschaton beyond, and in the second we have revelation as glorious self-manifestation (*Herrlichkeit*), which is also a deed initiating a free response (Theo-Drama), and one that finally communicates meaning, but a meaning that, in its closure, is always open for more (Theo-logic). The vision of God in the Apocalypse, while truly vision, is

> just the opposite of spectacle; in Revelation, as much as the Gospel of John, the Lamb calls forth a response in human beings to

46. O'Regan, *Misremembering*, 398. The priority of "katalogy," it should be noted, does not exclude analogy, but actually entails it.

47. O'Regan, *Misremembering*, 178.

48. O'Regan, *Misremembering*, 470.

pattern their existence on the self-giving illustrated by the Lamb in all their actions, practices, and forms of life. In Balthasar's articulation of a paschal theology, the Trinity provides the ultimate horizon, the ultimate "stage," for all human action, and is the subject as well as object of worship.[49]

It is just for this reason—the real communication of meaning from above, rather than mere disruption—that apocalyptic is, for Balthasar, not just a formal principle but a matter of *substance*.[50] The Book of Revelation is not just an example of a general type. Instead, the essence of the Apocalypse is the revelation of the trinitarian God in Christ, in a way that includes the whole of history without undermining the drama and novelty implied in freedom.[51] O'Regan's presentation of Balthasar's apocalyptic, in contrast to Hegel's, culminates quite insightfully in the concept of "traditio," which proves to be the key, both to the unity of Balthasar's theological vision and to his critique of modernity.[52] There is a profound connection between traditio and apokalypsis, and that connection may be identified as perfect, self-giving, gratuitous *love*. Apokalypsis is a revelation, a showing forth; if this showing forth is truly generous, it is not a mere show, a flat appearance, but a *giving* of the self, a "handing over": traditio. It is this generosity, in fact, that underlies the distinction between symbol, as Balthasar interprets it (rather than Hegel[53]), and allegory, because this generosity is what enables the "real presence" of what discloses itself. At the same time, the gratuity of this presence is the opposite of the mere filling of a need (even if it entails a special kind of need itself), which is why the giver is not *lost* in the gift, but transcends it "gloriously," even in his presence within it. This is also why the revelation does not eliminate the mystery, but precisely intensifies it with the actual communication.

Moreover, the gratuity at the heart of apokalypsis is at the same time what liberates the freedom of the revelation's recipient—Mary, the church, the believers with the church, and so forth. The disclosure, in other words, does not simply *end* history, with a "literal" prediction of its outcome (Gnostic apocalyptic), but discloses its essential meaning in a dramatic manner that keeps the destiny open, and so in a way that precisely includes the—likewise gratuitous—freedom of the response. As Balthasar puts it, the Book

49. O'Regan, *Misremembering*, 43.

50. This theme is expounded in chapter two in O'Regan, *Misremembering*, 117–81.

51. See O'Regan, *Misremembering*, 383.

52. O'Regan, *Misremembering*, 256.

53. O'Regan, *Misremembering*, 130ff.

of Revelation contains the *whole* of history,[54] but as we said, it "contains" that history precisely in an open, affirming, and inclusive manner. O'Regan explains that, "[t]ogether with the Gospel of John, which itself functions in *Theo-Drama* 5 as a diagnostic tool for apocalyptic and Valentinian narratives in modern and contemporary forms of thought, Revelation articulates the theodramatic conspectus of existence (*TD4*, 45) that is the opposite of the epical figurations of messianic apocalyptic and Valentinian apocalypse."[55] The key is image as actually and generously disclosive. While the Book of Revelation takes up images from the Old Testament, it does not simply repeat them according to the abstract demands of the genre. Instead, these images are "reborn":

> [T]hese reborn images remain images: they remind believers that the prophetic content of the evangelical words and deeds of Jesus and the apostles open up dimensions that Christian faith can never change into complacent possession.[56]

This is why there is a "reciprocity" of sorts between Revelation and John's Gospel, at the climax of which, of course, is the passion, death, and resurrection of the Son: the event of the sacrifice is the fullness of time, God's definitive self-revelation, and so the end of history; the Book of Revelation is the unveiling of the symbolic depth of this event, the disclosure of its infinitely generous capaciousness for the movement of history, to which it does not stand indifferent, as one discrete point *in* time next to others, but as comprehending all of time and so able to give the *whole* of it the Christian form. Without the cross, Revelation would be a mythological shell, an instance of a type, communicating a "universal" meaning that can be abstracted from history; without Revelation, the cross would be—or at least would be interpreted as—a singular historical event and not a revelation of the meaning of the whole.[57] The reciprocity between John's Gospel and his Revelation is itself a manifestation of gratuitous love.

God can only reveal himself as love, and do so lovingly, because he is already perfect love in himself. Tradition is not just the history of the church; it is more fundamentally Christ's "handing himself over" on the cross. But this, too, is a disclosure (*apokalypsis*) of what we might call the "Ur-traditio," which is Balthasar's bold interpretation of the Son's procession from the Father in the Trinity. O'Regan rightly speaks of the "necessarily

54 See Balthasar, *Theo-Drama 4*, 44.

55. O'Regan, *Misremembering*, 386.

56. Balthasar, *Theo-Drama 4*, 47, cited in O'Regan *Misremembering*, 387.

57 This is the basis of O'Regan's important distinction between a theology that is cross-focused and one that is cross-contracted: O'Regan, *Misremembering*, 188.

trinitarian horizon of tradition."[58] The Father "hands over" the divine nature, his Godhood, to the Son. Understood by analogy to the gratuity we have been discussing, and guided by the church's dogma, we can see that the Father gives the whole of the divine substance *perfectly*, without holding back the slightest trace, but at the very same time without ceasing to possess it himself. Here we have the "absolute" instance of the "excessive self-revelation" we have seen characterize image as symbol in general. The cross, as Balthasar is well-known to have affirmed, is the Son's revelation of the love that *is* God, a disclosure of the Father's most original love and the "traditio" it implies. In a striking passage cited by O'Regan, worth quoting at length insofar as it arguably represents the key to Balthasar's apocalyptic, which will distinguish him definitively from Hegel, Balthasar explains:

> The motif of tradition, "handing on," beginning in God and extending to the creation through him who is "the beginning of God's creation" (3:14), will prove to be a fundamental theme of the theo-drama, constant through all acts. Traditio begins within God (as the doctrine of the Trinity formulates it), and this prevents God's self-giving to the world from being interpreted mythologically: God is not swallowed up by the world. It is not through this self-giving that God becomes a lover—he already is a lover. And this same traditio, this same self-giving within the Godhead, also means that God does not merely hover above the world as the *hen* of philosophy, as the *noesis noeseos*: rather, the divine self-giving becomes the prototype and archetype of his self-giving to the world and all the traditio that follows from it.[59]

As the passage makes clear, just as the Father is not "spent" in the begetting of the Son, God is not exhausted in his self-manifestation in the event of redemption. O'Regan casts a compelling light on how, for Balthasar, the "economic" truly can be *in some sense* the immanent Trinity, but without simply reducing the latter to the former. The absolute gratuity at the core is what distinguishes Balthasar from Rahner on this score. God is involved in the world but remains absolutely transcendent to the world; he reveals himself perfectly, without exhausting himself; he contains the whole without eliminating its free otherness; he conveys his inner life, without reducing it to a univocal, finite form. In all of this, Balthasar distinguishes himself from the apocalypse in its Gnostic form—the form it takes in modernity.

---

58. O'Regan, *Misremembering*, 298

59. Balthasar, *Theo-Drama 4*, 52–53, cited in O'Regan, *Misremembering*, 256.

III

O'Regan affirms, quite provocatively, that Revelation is "regulative for a theology that transcends modernity."[60] On its face, such a claim seems not only unappealing—for a theology centered on the Book of Revelation would seem ipso facto marginal at best—but in fact simply implausible. One of the characteristics of *modern* thought, at least in some of its significant manifestations, is a preoccupation with apocalyptic: a fascination with the sensational and the violent, a return to superstition, an obsession with power, an unfettered curiosity, a desire to glimpse secret outcomes, an effort to control through knowledge, and so forth. But once one has entered into the depths of O'Regan's reading of Balthasar, one begins to see the great wisdom of this judgment. A truly apocalyptic theology is one that gives an absolute priority to the *concretissimum* of God's self-revelation, such as it has been received and communicated in scripture, above all in the Gospels read in relation to Revelation. But because this revelation, as gratuitous love, is at the same time a liberation of history, the reception of revelation will not bypass, but will essentially include, the gathering of representative figures who have seen the glory of God in nature, history, and being, those who have had a vision of the form of Christ and grappled with their own fate, to be sure, but only as part of the fate of man more generally, and have given this grappling an objective form, whether in their lives taken as a meaning-ful disclosure of the whole (metaphysics of the saints) or directly in their artistic, literary, philosophical, and theological work. In other words, only a false apocalyptic is merely interruptive, bursting into the givenness of real-ity in sheer discontinuity and so having as its content only the overturning of all content. A genuine apocalyptic does not compromise discontinuity, the ever-greater difference of God in his ultimate transcendence, but recog-nizes that this transcendence also implies a genuine immanence, a generous *abiding* in the world and the form this abiding receives in the work of poets and philosophers. In Balthasar's gathering of figures, we see a recapitulation of what may have seemed otherwise an eccentric methodology in his first work, now taken up as a kind of essential Christian mode, a Catholic theol-ogy *par excellence*. An astonishing implication of this deepening is that one cannot separate one's relation to these representative figures simply from one's own relation to God in faith. To be a believer is to enter into the great tradition that unfolds from the church, but also necessarily exceeds her vis-ible boundaries. Another of O'Regan's great achievements is to have seen

60. O'Regan, *Misremembering*, 378.

the connection between tradition and apocalyptic, and indeed between all of this and genuine Christian existence simpliciter.

It is in light of this point that we can understand the gravity of the judgment of modernity that O'Regan presents with such exquisite nuance above all in *The Anatomy of Misremembering*. As he puts it in the opening pages of the book, "modernity is bedeviled by a pervasive, deep, and aggressive form of forgetfulness."[61] Forgetfulness might seem initially a minor infraction, an innocent mistake, of the mind rather than of the will. But in light of what we have seen, it becomes apparent that what is at stake in this forgetfulness is in fact the very heart of Christian revelation. A "rupture" with tradition, which is exactly what *defines* modernity,[62] is a rejection of the gift that has been "handed over" (*traditio*). It is a disruption, in other words, of the inner "logic," or perhaps better, inner "form," of Christianity itself. If the unfolding of the reception of revelation in history—centrally, but never exclusively, the history of the church—is genuinely analogous to the manifestation of divine love on the cross, and this manifestation is itself the "perfect image," so to speak, of the inner-trinitarian life of God himself, then the radical forgetfulness of tradition is a perversion of the nature of God—not in itself, of course, but in our reception of God in faith (and indeed in the culture born of that faith).[63] Indeed, if the Spirit's role is the "exegesis" of God's self-revelation in Christ in history,[64] then there is some warrant for suggesting that the rupture with tradition that specifically characterizes modernity is a paradigm of the "sin against the Holy Spirit"(Mark 3:28–30). In this respect, modernity is radically anti-Christian, even when it presents itself as a defender of Christianity in a new guise.

One of the implications of modernity's rupture with tradition is its natural tendency to absolutize itself, and this occurs in spite of, or indeed arguably *because* of, what it protests is its discovery of modesty or epistemic humility, in contrast to the presumption of, for example, medieval thought. If modernity detaches itself from tradition, it is no longer part of a more

61. O'Regan, *Misremembering*, 11.

62. O'Regan, *Misremembering*, 4. Not everything new and contemporary is "modern" in the technical sense, but only that which understands itself as having broken with the past. On all of this, see Spaemann's succinct presentation of modernity, its essential form and its implications: Spaemann, "The End of Modernity?" in Spaemann, *Philosophical Essays*, 211–29.

63 Our reception of God, of course, cannot simply be separated from God in himself, which is simply another way of saying that there is an intrinsic relation between the economic and immanent Trinity, even in their necessary distinction from each other. It is for this reason that the revelation of God's inner nature takes the form of the cross and resurrection in the fallen world.

64. Balthasar, *Theo-Logic*, 13–16.

encompassing whole, but now becomes itself, by necessity, a standard by which to measure itself and everything else: "the only game in which it is willing to participate is one in which it is player, referee, and rules committee."[65] As a result, modernity presents a form that is a perversion of the Christian form that we have been describing, i.e., the form Balthasar had attempted to convey through the creative recollection of scripture and tradition that he sought in his own theology. This perversion of form has anthropological implications. As O'Regan explains, the "lightness of being" that results from modernity's forgetfulness "involves the reduction of human being to the three-dimensionalities of calculative rationality, hedonism, or heroic virtue."[66] The three features that come to light in this "apocalypse of the modern soul" may be read as corruptions, so to speak, of the three dimensions Balthasar displays in his trilogy: in contrast to the revelation of God's glory in the theological aesthetics, which inspires "vision" and "rapture," we have "hedonism," immediacy, and direct gratification; in contrast to the dramatic action of the will's yielding to God's supreme sacrificial deed, we have "heroic virtue," the will's display of its own invincible power; and in contrast to the contemplative vision that bears fruit in understanding, we have "calculative rationality," the empty formality of thinking instrumentalized to nonrational purposes. In all of this, we have the undermining of not only the content of Christian revelation, but simultaneously of the form from which the content is ultimately inseparable.

While the contrast between Christianity and modernity may seem obvious, there is a subtler expression of modernity that presents a form far closer to the Christian one, at least in appearance. This subtler form appears in the great modern critics of modernity, from among which O'Regan insightfully singles out Hegel and Heidegger, for these thinkers intend, each in his own distinctive way, precisely to overcome the forgetfulness of modernity, but to do so *otherwise* than through the recollection of the Christian tradition *as* Christian and *as* tradition. In assessing these attempts, O'Regan's work proves itself a kind of apokalypsis in its own right. A central feature of apokalypsis is discernment, which in the present epoch is perhaps even more urgent than in the past, insofar as the betrayal of Christianity can take an ostensibly Christian form. As O'Regan puts it,

---

65. O'Regan, *Misremembering*, 3. Fundamentally in agreement with O'Regan's assessment here, Spaemann argues that if modernity's contributions are to be affirmed and preserved, they must be re-connected, so to speak, with their roots in the greater tradition, which is to say that modernity must be interpreted against itself: see Spaemann, *Philosophical Essays*, 212.

66. O'Regan, *Misremembering*, 12–13.

This is one of the main reasons why Revelation is so important: as it outlines the apocalyptic dimensions of decision, it also announces the apocalyptic dimensions of unveiling forms of thought difficult to tell apart. The telling has to and will occur; the stakes are in the post-Enlightenment period too high. Perhaps Revelation declares a general truth: the stakes are always too high not to intervene, not to unveil and tell apart, not to effect a judgment that is in significant part eschatological. After all the sifting and discerning, what is required is a vision that burns away accident.[67]

Because this task is more delicate, and at the same time more fruitful, since a more precise and careful discernment of an imitator bring out all the more intensely the distinctiveness of the reality, O'Regan devotes his attention above all to Balthasar's assessment of Hegel and Heidegger. We are yet waiting for the engagement with Heidegger, which is soon to appear, but we may close our essay here with a brief description of the *Auseinandersetzung* O'Regan stages between Balthasar and Hegel, whom O'Regan presents as decisively modern, but a "first among equals,"[68] who is more dangerous than the rest, precisely because he is significantly more adequate.[69]

Balthasar appreciates Hegel because he affirmed the central importance of the very features we have seen to be indispensable to a Catholic vision:

> Balthasar valorizes Hegel's dramatically colored view of the divine, his Johannine rendering of Christ as defined by the glory of the cross, and his determination that the Trinity is the encompassing as well as synoptic symbol of Christianity. The affinity is formal in that Balthasar affirms Hegel's understanding of the disclosive power of artistic, philosophical and religious discourse, and his triangulation of these discourses, and thinks that any relevant theology will have to work within a horizon of understanding that acknowledges the necessity of the intermediation of Christian and theological discourses with other kinds of discourse.[70]

The essential difference between the two, however, ultimately comes down to the absence of *love* in Hegel, which we saw lies at the origin of

---

67. O'Regan, *Misremembering*, 370.

68. O'Regan, *Misremembering*, 320.

69. See O'Regan, *Misremembering*, 104.

70. O'Regan, *Misremembering*, 36.

genuine apo-kalypsis and Christian *traditio*.[71] Thus, the divine kenosis is not a "figure of gift" for Hegel,[72] but rather of need-driven eros.[73] To summarize the implications in short order: God's involvement in history thus becomes, for Hegel, a radical dependence on it, which in turn implies the elimination of any difference between the immanent and economic Trinity, and so between God's creation of the world and the Father's begetting of the Son. Moreover, the absence of gratuity means both that history is deprived of its freedom, and even more profoundly that God surrenders his mystery in his self-revelation. In other words, God becomes perfectly accessible in his disclosure, as it were, which means that his manifestation to the senses (art) and to representative imagination (religion) finally demands the definitive appropriation in thought (philosophy). God, in "giving" himself, conspires in his own overcoming.[74] For all of the drama that Hegel sought to discover in the divine life, which he opened up through the great contribution of his recollection of the Trinity,[75] he cannot avoid finally culminating, as we have seen, in the definitive "pastness" of epic, and finally in the absolute stasis of thought thinking itself.[76] "Misremembering" is thus the "counterfeit double" of *traditio*;[77] it is a recovery of the forms of the past, not as the inexhaustibly creative communication of a gift made once and for all in the *concretissimum* of the cross, but as provisional signs of an abstract universal meaning.[78] It is thus apocalyptic in the mode of secret, definitive disclosure to the elite knowers (gnosis) rather than as the "open mystery" of

71 Hegel notoriously explains that the goal of his philosophy—and indeed of human thought in general—is to "lay aside the title '*love* of knowing' and be *actual* knowing": paragraph 5 of the preface to *The Phenomenology of Spirit*, 3.

72. O'Regan, *Misremembering*, 259; cf., ibid., 341.

73. O'Regan, *Misremembering*, 160–61.

74. In a certain respect, this is precisely what the cross represents. But, as O'Regan shows, God remains present in this sacrifice, which remains transcendent precisely because of its gratuity. The Eucharist is, so to speak, the extension of this presence in history. Hegel's rejection of the Catholic practice of adoration as absurd—the Eucharist, he says, is meant to be *consumed*, and so appropriated into one's subjectivity (or better: into the subjectivity of the community), rather than simply "stared at"—is a telling sign of just what is missing in his thought.

75. See O'Regan, *Misremembering*, 36.

76. Hegel famously concludes his *Encyclopedia* by citing without comment Aristotle's description of God as the pure actuality of self-thinking thought: this is the absolute toward which all else in Hegel's philosophy tends.

77. The expression "counterfeit double" comes from William Desmond: see Desmond, *Hegel's God*.

78 O'Regan offers a fascinating critique of Hegel's reduction of the event of Christ to the formal principle of the concrete universal: see, e.g., O'Regan, *Misremembering*, 185–97; 260.

vision inviting free response, judgment, and liturgical praise.[79] This vision, as we have said, remains open even in its definitiveness, because the image that generates it remains ever new, not simply repeated, but "reborn." (Such a rebirth can occur only in the living church.) As O'Regan puts it, "even if Christianity casts a critical eye on the new, and inquires whether its newness is shadow or substance, Christianity is not the classicist dream of the contained past and its limited forms. For Christianity never affirms the old as the old, but only the old as the new, the ever new."[80] The infinite generosity of God's self-revelation is why there is no end to its possible renewals, which is why we recollect Christ only by at the same time recollecting those who have handed him on: "These interpreters do not simply pass on (*traditio*), but in and through interpretation reveal new facets of the phenomenon of Christ and thus 'give back' (*reditio*). This giving back is what makes the tradition ever new."[81] If Balthasar shows a certain "reluctance to condemn" or exclude from the tradition,[82] it is because of his conviction regarding the generosity of God's self-disclosure. Tradition is not a single melodic line, such as we find in Hegel's history of philosophy and philosophy of history, but is a *sym-phonia*, a glorious whole that reveals itself precisely in the interplay between irreducibly unique and yet representative figures, each serving successively, not to replace, but to amplify the others.[83]

What is at stake, here, is not only the revelation of Christ, but the determination of the fate of individual figures in and with the fate of the whole: the "apocalypse of the soul" that Balthasar pursued in the beginning remains a goal through to the end. According to the early approach, sketched somewhat crudely at first, but deepened as Balthasar saw it comprehended and liberated by the form of Christ, individual thinkers present an image, which is both a complete statement of a vision and a freely-affirmed open-ended invitation to freedom. In recollecting these figures, we co-operate in a limited, no doubt, but very real sense in their ultimate meaning. Balthasar's admittedly quite controversial "hope for universal salvation," whatever one

79 See O'Regan, *Misremembering*, 378, 390.

80. O'Regan, *Misremembering*, 10. This statement requires some significant qualification: Christianity *also* affirms the old as the old, insofar as it gives a certain priority precisely to what it receives, i.e., what is "already" there. The point is that it does not affirm the old exclusively as the old, but always also as the new. The text that O'Regan refers to here, from Augustine, *Confessions* X, displays both: "ever ancient, ever new."

81. O'Regan, *Misremembering*, 135.

82. O'Regan, *Misremembering*, 333–34.

83. Balthasar thus presents a "pantheon" of figures, from different epochs and nations, rather than a series of actors serving a single plot line, as in Hegel. The theme of a non-leveling unity in diversity is a regular one for Balthasar: see Balthasar, *Truth is Symphonic*.

might ultimately make of it, cannot properly be understood outside of the task of *traditio*. One might look at Balthasar's interpretation of these figures as a spiritual exercise in the Ignatian sense: Balthasar, the priest, helps the individual discern and decide (*unterscheiden* and *entscheiden*); in so doing, the individual is able to lay bare his innermost being (apocalypse of the soul), as it were, making a confession that invites a judgment, certainly, but a redeeming one. In this respect, Balthasar's theology is a Christian mission, a genuine expression of and humble participation in the work of Christ, who called his disciples to extend the Christian form, as it were, to the ends of the earth, and through the whole of history. We might see O'Regan's reception of Balthasar, insofar as it is a "remembering" that amplifies, as a creative repetition of the same mission.

Bibliography

Aarde, Andries van. "Matthew and Apocalypticism as the 'Mother of Christian Theology': Ernst Käsemann Revisited." *HTS Teologiese Studies/Theological Studies* 58 (2009) 118–42.

Balthasar, Hans Urs von. *Apokalypse der deutschen Seele: Studien zu einer Lehre von letzten Haltungen.* 3 vols. 2nd ed. Freiburg: Johannes Verlag Einsiedeln, 1998.

————. *Glory of the Lord, Vol. 1: Seeing the Form.* San Francisco: Ignatius, 1982.

————. *Theo-Drama: Theological Dramatic Theory, Vol. 1: Prolegomena.* San Francisco: Ignatius, 1989.

————. *Theo-Logic: Theological Logical Theory.* San Francisco: Ignatius, 2004.

————. *Truth Is Symphonic: Aspects of Christian Pluralism.* San Francisco: Ignatius, 1987.

Desmond, William. *Hegel's God: A Counterfeit Double?* Burlington, VT: Ashgate, 2003.

Gardner, Lucy, et al. *Balthasar at the End of Modernity.* Edinburgh: T. & T. Clark, 1999.

Käsemann, Ernst. *New Testament Questions of Today.* London: SCM, 1969.

Kilby, Karen. "A Very Critical Response to Karen Kilby: On Failing to See the Form." *Radical Orthodoxy: Theology, Philosophy, Politics* 3.1 (2015) 68–87.

Lewis, C. S. *God in the Dock.* Grand Rapids: Eerdmans, 1970.

Martyn, Louis. *Galatians.* Anchor Yale Bible Commentaries. New Haven: Yale University Press, 2004.

Murphy, Francesca. "Is Liberalism a Heresy?" *First Things*, June 2016; https://www.firstthings.com/article/2016/06/is-liberalism-a-heresy. Accessed 28 October 2019.

Nietzsche, Friedrich. *The Portable Nietzsche.* Translated by Walter Kaufmann. New York: Penguin, 1954.

O'Regan, Cyril. *Anatomy of Misremembering: Von Balthasar's Response to Philosophical Modernity. Vol. 1: Hegel.* Chestnut Ridge, NY: Crossroad, 2014.

Schindler, D. C. *The Dramatic Structure of Truth.* New York: Fordham University Press, 2004.

Spaemann, Robert. *A Robert Spaemann Reader: Philosophical Essays on Nature, God, and the Human Person.* Oxford: Oxford University Press, 2015.

Speyr, Adrienne von. *Apokalypse: Betrachtungen über die geheime Offenbarung.* Freiburg: Johannes Verlag Einsiedeln, 1950.

6

Metaphysics and Apocalypse

Apocalyptic Motifs in the Late Work of Erich Przywara

JOHN BETZ

University of Notre Dame

Metaphysics and apocalypse bear such different connotations as to be near opposites. The former recalls the origins of Greek philosophy and the pre-Socratic search for *archai*, for the beginnings and principles of things; the latter, Hebraic in spirit, reminds us of the prophetic visions of Ezekiel and Daniel, the apocalyptic communities of the Second Temple period, and, above all, the Apocalypse of John. The former conveys a sense of cosmic order and completion, as with the *kyklophoria* of Aristotle, which reflects the order of thought, of divine reason, cycling eternally and peacefully in itself (*noesis noeseos*); the latter, inherently temporal, signifies an interruption from outside the established order, which shakes the certainties of a given age to their foundations, indeed, the violent overthrow of the old and the advent of something new. Whereas the former connotes (ontically) eternal structure and stability, the latter connotes temporal instability and conflict; whereas the former connotes (noetically) luminous clarity and a corresponding insight into first principles, the latter connotes a darkness brooding over unfathomable depths and an anxious waiting for a new light to dawn. It is exceedingly rare, therefore, to find a thinker who appreciates both styles of thought, and rarer still to find a thinker who attempts to unite both metaphysics and apocalypse into a single vision of reality—into what we might call an *apocalyptic metaphysics.* Yet this seemingly impossible aspiration is precisely what we find in the remarkable twentieth-century Jesuit Erich Przywara.[1]

Certainly, Przywara is better known for his contributions to philosophical and theological metaphysics, above all, for his magnum opus, *Analogia Entis* (1932), which after any first reading would seem to belie the foregoing claim. Indeed, up to this point there is little in Przywara's writings that would suggest the kind of apocalyptic concerns that one finds in his protégé, Hans Urs von Balthasar, whose thought was engaged with apocalyptic themes from the start, and who remained to the end, as Cyril O'Regan like none other has shown, a thoroughly apocalyptic thinker.[2] In the years leading up to the Second World War, however, and especially during it, Przywara's own thought takes a decidedly apocalyptic turn—as one sees in *Crucis Mysterium* (1939) and other works that were written during the war, but for various reasons could not be published until after it, including *Hölderlin* (1948), *Vier Predigten über das Abendland* (1948), and *Alter und Neuer Bund* (1956).[3]

Given the aforementioned contrast in style and content between metaphysical and apocalyptic discourses, one might reasonably expect that such a turn would have entailed a break with Przywara's earlier work, or at least some revision of his earlier concerns. For apocalyptic would seem to entail the "crisis" of metaphysics—indeed, a judgment upon it—precisely in the way that for Karl Barth divine revelation makes naught of philosophical preconceptions like so many clay vessels shattered by a rod of iron (Rev 2:27). Strikingly, however, Przywara's apocalyptic turn entailed nothing of the kind—even though his idiom now sounds more Barthian. There was never a turn away from metaphysics, and he never rejected any of his earlier work. On the contrary, the metaphysical grammar he laid out in *Analogia Entis* remains intact to the end, which raises the question of how metaphysics and apocalyptic can be related—as they are in Przywara—and, if so, then in what form.

---

1. For the most important attempt to date to think with Przywara and Balthasar about how these two discourses might be combined into an "analogical-apocalyptic metaphysics," which unites the metaphysics of the *analogia entis* with a pleromatic apocalyptic theology in the spirit of Cyril O'Regan, see Gonzales, *Reimagining the Analogia Entis.*

2. See Cyril O'Regan, *Misremembering.*

3. Przywara, *Crucis Mysterium*; Przywara, *Vier Predigten*; Przywara, *Alter und Neuer Bund.* The text of *Vier Predigten* was included as the first chapter of *Alter und Neuer Bund.*

My goal in pursuing the question of apocalyptic in Przywara is accordingly twofold. On the one hand, it is to broaden and enrich our perspective on Przywara as a thinker capable of a variety of modes of thought—ranging from philosophical metaphysics to literary, biblical, and cultural criticism to prophetic and apocalyptic discourse—and as a man of his time who lived through the horrors of the Second World War and wrestled with the existential questions it inevitably posed to the intellectuals of his generation. On the other hand, it is to show how the apocalyptic elements of his later thought are integrated into his understanding of the *analogia entis*, or put differently, how Przywara's metaphysics is fundamentally open to apocalyptic—as though nothing less could satisfy it.

While a complete account of apocalyptic in Przywara would include his readings of Hölderlin, which are of interest chiefly for their emphasis upon the Johannine elements in the German poet (vis-a-vis Heidegger who made nothing of them), in the following I will focus on two of the foregoing works, *Crucis Mysterium* and *Four Sermons*, each of which reveals Przywara's understanding of apocalyptic in a distinct mode—whether his focus be the confrontation between Christ and Anti-Christ (Nietzsche) or the prophetic words of scripture as they might apply to the apparent end of Christendom after the Reformation and the apparent end of a once Christian Europe on the eve of its apocalyptic ruin.

1. Ignatius and Nietzsche: Or "the Christian and the Anti-Christ"

The last of Przywara's works to be published before the war, *Crucis Mysterium: Das christliche Heute* (1939), occupies a unique place in his oeuvre, marking the threshold between his early and his late work, which becomes increasingly somber and apocalyptic as the war goes on. Formally speaking, it is also something of an oddity, being an amalgam of such sundry and seemingly unrelated figures and topics as Nietzsche, Ignatius, Thomas, liturgical renewal, Carmelite mysticism, the Sacred Heart devotion, Mariology, and the mysteries of marriage, suffering, and death. It is not obvious, therefore, that it belongs in the category of apocalyptic literature. Nevertheless, it is a fair indicator of Przywara's growing apocalyptic concerns. This is most evident from the first part, which bears the title, "The Christian and the Anti-Christ" [*Christ und Anti-Christ*], and which Przywara stylizes as a confrontation between Ignatius of Loyola (and Aquinas) and Nietzsche. It is also indicated, though less obviously, by the title, which is taken from the *Vexilla regis*[4] (and bears a reminder that Christ is the true king and the true leader of German Christians), and the subtitle, which signals that the mystery of the cross is the prophetic word Przywara wants to speak "today" in view of impending national and international disaster. Accordingly, he begins the work, with the following admonition:

> *In nomine Jesu.* Thus begins the introit for the liturgy on the Wednesday of Holy Week. We have lost our name; we have lost our vocation; we have nothing but this *one* name as our only name and our only vocation: Jesus, which is to say: redeemed by God. Our *one* name is our *one* vocation: to cooperate with Him, the Redeemer, in the *one* work of redemption. Thus we enter into the *one* Passion.[5]

The message is clear: in Przywara's view, Christian Europe, or what is left of it, has lost is way; insofar as it is still Christian, however, it must be prepared to follow Christ in his passion. Accordingly, against this foreboding backdrop, the work may be read as Przywara's clarion call for Christians to return to Christ and to cooperate in the one work of redemption. And for Przywara, as a literary and cultural critic, part of this work meant confronting the spirit of the age with discernment, knowing how to distinguish the spirit of Christ from that of Anti-Christ, figured in this case in the differences between Ignatius and Nietzsche.

Among the more salient aspects of Przywara's comparison is how generously he cites passages from Nietzsche, attempting to identify what is most compelling about him—so close to the truth—but also, therefore, most tragic. Above all he picks up on the theme of the Übermensch and those passages in which Nietzsche speaks of human greatness in terms of self-transcendence, indeed, even of self-forgetfulness and self-expenditure—precisely the kind of tropes that mimic a Christian understanding of holiness through ever greater self-emptying and love.[6] As Przywara

---

4. *Vexilla regis prodeunt / fulget crucis mysterium, / quo carne carnis conditor / suspensus est patibulo.* [The banners of the King are led forth in procession, shining with the mystery of the cross, where the Creator of flesh is himself suspended by the crossbar in the flesh.]

5. Przywara, *Crucis Mysterium*, 13.

6. Thus Przywara notes (*Crucis Mysterium*, 22) that the *Übermensch* is not only "superior to himself"—*über* in the sense of above," as in the "Über" of the noble, aristocratic soul—but also *über* in the sense of "beyond" himself, e.g., beyond the vanity attached to creation and resignation. Thus, as Przywara reads it, the *Über* in *Übermensch* carries the connotation of "above" as well as "beyond." All of which makes the *Übermensch* for Przywara a mythical ersatz for the transcendent God signified by the *analogia entis*, who is "above-and-beyond" creation.

observes, for Nietzsche, "The genuine greatness of man is that 'he expends himself' and 'does not seek to save himself' and 'forgets himself.' . . . To make oneself superfluous—that is the glory of all the great ones."[7] Indeed, he observes, for Nietzsche, "True humanity consists not in safety, but in self-abandonment," citing the famous passage in which Nietzsche says, "'Believe me! The mystery of reaping the greatest fruitfulness and pleasure from existence is: to live dangerously. Build your cities next to Vesuvius! Send your ships into uncharted seas! Live at war with those like you and with yourselves!'"[8] In fact, so much does Nietzsche see "the essence of man in being 'ever beyond himself' [*je über hinaus*] that the man who would cling to himself becomes a source of 'ridicule or a painful embarrassment.'"[9]

Accordingly, Przywara sees Nietzsche's longing for a humanity that is more than human as an implicit longing for a divine humanity [*eine Gott-Form des Menschen*]—a humanity that is divinely independent and ever struggling to be "superior to itself."[10] And for Przywara this emphasis on greatness through struggle puts Nietzsche into surprisingly close proximity to Ignatius and the *magis*—the *Jeweils-mehr*—that characterizes the spirituality of his order.[11] Indeed, Przywara observes, Nietzsche suggests the comparison himself: "While popular Greek pedagogy stipulates that every endowment be developed through struggle, our contemporary pedagogues have no greater fear than the unleashing of so-called ambition . . . with the exception of the Jesuits, who are of the same mind as the ancients and may therefore be regarded as the most effective pedagogues of our time."[12] The contest between Nietzsche and Christianity is thus, more specifically, a contest between Nietzsche and that order that he finds most attractive ("live at war with those like you"). As Nietzsche admits to Peter Gast on October 5, 1879, "honestly," compared to Ignatius, "I am no longer able to say anything respectful about Luther."[13] And the similarity to Ignatius (and to Christ) goes so far that, for Nietzsche, the "heroic man" is willing not only to struggle, but even to sacrifice himself, being indifferent to personal happiness, even ascending out of "hells" with a greater measure of "the blessedness of

7. Przywara, *Crucis Mysterium*, 19–20.

8. Przywara, *Crucis Mysterium*, 24f.

9. Przywara, *Crucis Mysterium*, 20.

10. Przywara, *Crucis Mysterium*, 22.

11. Przywara, *Crucis Mysterium*, 38: "Der Nietzsche-Mensch des Je-über-hinaus ist deutlicher Anruf an den ignatianischen Menschen des Jeweils-mehr (más) im Je-mehr-heraus-aus-sich-selbst (Exerc. Nr. 189)."

12. Przywara, *Crucis Mysterium*, 23.

13. Przywara, *Crucis Mysterium*, 38.

love."[14] Indeed, there is even the theme of new life through death: "You must want to burn away in your own flame—else how are you to become new if you have not been burned to ashes!"[15]

Of course, Przywara is well aware that these similarities only go so far, and that Nietzsche presents his *Übermensch* in the spirit of Dionysus precisely in order to contrast him with Christ, indeed, to present him as an alternative to him. What is so striking, however, about Przywara's account, and what makes Nietzsche a genuine harbinger of Anti-Christ, is precisely how closely the antitype (the counterfeit) resembles the original, and how asymptotically close Nietzsche comes to the kind of saint he seems most to have admired—so much so that, after all other existential possibilities have been excluded, Nietzsche himself recognizes only two paths, viz., that of the saint and that of the tragic artist.[16] And even here the similarities are so great as to conceal the differences between them:

> The "aristocratic radicalism" of Nietzsche's Übermensch stands eye-to-eye with certain personal traits of St. Ignatius: the "wanderer" corresponds to the "pilgrim" (as Ignatius calls himself) and the fundamental detachment of the Jesuit (for the sake of being a pure instrument); the "dancer," to the Ignatian requirement of always having a "joyful countenance,"[17] indeed, the requirement "that one should laugh" (as Ignatius says to his novices: *volo te ridere, mi fili*); and "the solitary in the midst of the flame," to that most authentically Ignatian characteristic of being sent "to set the world on fire" (*ite, incendite mundum*) in strictly "solitary disposal to God alone" (*solus soli Deo vacare*) ... for the sake of "the service of the Divine Majesty."[18]

Przywara then adduces a series of themes from the "Principle and Foundation" of the *Spiritual Exercises* that bring out the, so to speak, "ever greater dissimilarity" (*maior dissimilitudo*) between them—the saint and the tragic artist—in the midst of every similarity, "however great" (*tanta similitudo*). Firstly, over against the "dancing," "childlike" freedom that Nietzsche presents as his "ideal" and that he seeks to establish by means of the

14. Przywara, *Crucis Mysterium*, 32.

15. Przywara, *Crucis Mysterium*, 32.

16. Przywara, *Crucis Mysterium*, 27.

17. Przywara, *Crucis Mysterium*, 39. *Regulas de la Modestia*, nr. 5: *"Todo el rostro muestre antes alegria que tristeza . . .";* *Facies universa laetitiam potius prae se ferat quam maestitiam*. See *Monumenta Ignatiana ex autographis vel ex antiquioribus exemplis collecta* (Roma: Borgo S. Spirito, 1934), 519, 521.

18. Przywara, *Crucis Mysterium*, 39f.

myth of the eternal return,[19] Przywara poses genuine Ignatian indifference, which is free of the illusion of possessing in one's own right the kind of freedom Nietzsche seeks but which makes one free in the service of God, who is freedom itself. Secondly, over against the strict Apollonian discipline that forms the Dionysian, he poses the "unconditional obedience" of the saint; and over against Nietzsche's "heroic atheism," the saint who "goes forth from himself," from all that belongs to him, seeking "nothing except the greater praise and glory of God our Lord."[20] But what if Nietzsche's atheistic heroism looks more heroic than that of the saint since, doing without the solace of a divine comforter, it seeks to forge meaning in the naked absence of it—alone before the void?

For Przywara this is the real nub of the debate—"the mystery of this Nothingness." And so, in response to Nietzsche he adduces a third interpretation of the *Exercises,* which underscores the difference between a general service of the sacred and a service of redemption in the Cross, which, unlike the former, has the appearance of service to the Greatness of God's Nothingness. Indeed, inasmuch as it stands in service to the Word of the Cross, such service has the appearance of serving a "scandal" and "folly," so that once again a parallel emerges between the service of the saint and Nietzsche's "hero and fool" [*Held und Naar*].[21] And Przywara is perfectly willing to contest Nietzsche on this ground:

> Since Nietzsche appeals to "Dionysus against the Crucified," but does not make an issue of martyrdom, a proper response must begin with the "meaning" of the "Crucified." And since Nietzsche identifies the "Crucified" with the "curse of life" and the "Dionysian" with the "promise of life," one must respond to his appeal not only with the true Christian promise of "eternal life," but also by explicitly disclosing that it is a promise of "life in the curse," through which and into which we are redeemed: since Christ "became a curse" (Gal. 3:13), so that we "might be accursed for the sake of [our] brothers" (Rom. 9:3), and "bear the disgrace" with him "outside of the city gates" (Heb. 13:12–13), and in this way become "participants of the divine nature" (Phil. 2:1–11; 2 Pet. 1:4). Whereas Nietzsche in truth fled from the "curse" of his actual life into the dreamy intoxication of the Dionysian and saw the "world . . . transfigured" in the moment his despair turned inevitably into madness, authentic Christianity is the undeceived suffering of the "curse," so that in the

19. Przywara, *Crucis Mysterium*, 31.

20. Przywara, *Crucis Mysterium*, 42f. Nr. 189.

21. Przywara, *Crucis Mysterium*, 45.

suffering of these "birth pangs" the "freedom of the children of God" might become manifest (Rom. 7–8).[22]

For Przywara, therefore, it is actually the disciple of Christ who enters into the world in all its reality and suffering, while Nietzsche, for all his life-affirming rhetoric, flees from it and from the reality of the cross into his own dreamy mythology. Indeed, as Przywara sees it, Nietzsche's refusal of the Crucified is at the end of the day not really about life-affirmation at all, but rather about the pride of a Luciferian *non serviam*. And so, to underscore the difference between the disciple of Christ and the disciple of Anti-Christ, he invites the reader to consider the dynamic *magis* in Ignatius's "third kind of humility": "[In order to imitate and be in reality *more* like Christ our Lord,] I desire and choose poverty with the poor Christ *more* than riches; to be disgraced with Christ *more* than to be honored; and I long to be accounted as worthless and a fool for Christ *more* than to be esteemed as wise and prudent in this world"[23]—this being, in the language of the constitutions, the "service uniform of Christ."[24] As Przywara sees it, the dynamic self-transcendence of Nietzsche's Übermensch, who remains tragically cramped in himself, is hereby overcome, being eclipsed by and delivered into the dynamic comparative—the *magis*—of ever greater service rendered to the infinite, i.e., ever greater God.[25] For the dynamism of the infinite God, which "calls the dynamism proper to human beings upward ever anew [*je neu aufgerufen*], tempers it within its genuinely human limits and thereby liberates it," as the minimalist equilibrium of the "no more than" is broken through by the "more than."[26] In this way "the proper sense of Nietzsche's frenzied reeling between the ever-higher [*Je-immer-höher*] and the ever-deeper [*Je-immer-tiefer*] is both grasped and overcome."[27]

Given Przywara's prior metaphysical commitment to the *analogia entis*, we can hardly be surprised that it should at some level enter into his response to Nietzsche. What is more noticeable now, however, having just

22. Przywara, *Crucis Mysterium*, 45f. Among other citations, Przywara refers here to Nietzsche's letter to Peter Gast (4 January 1889).

23. Przywara, *Crucis Mysterium*, 46. Nr. 167. Puhl's translation modified to draw out Przywara's emphasis on the *magis*—the *"jeweils mehr."*

24. Przywara, *Crucis Mysterium*, 46f. Mon. Ign. III, 2; 84ff. In short, following Ignatius, one should choose "whatever leads *more* to the goal for which we are made" (ibid., 47).

25. Przywara, *Crucis Mysterium*, 47: "The innermost condition of the 'ever more' is the Augustinian correlation between endless searching and the infinite God: the 'ever greater searching' because God is the *Deus semper maior."*

26. Przywara, *Crucis Mysterium*, 47.

27. Przywara, *Crucis Mysterium*, 47f.

completed his three-volume commentary on the *Exercises*, is that he gives the analogy of being a decidedly Ignatian twist. Certainly, for Przywara the Ignatian *magis* is grounded in the Augustinian *Deus semper maior*,[28] and in Augustine's understanding of the restless dynamic of human nature as an analogy of the infinite God—as one deep calling to another (*abyssus abyssum invocat*). The difference, however, is that Augustine's ever renewed searching (*ut inventus quaeratur, immensus est*)[29] is transformed into ever greater service of the Divine Majesty. For it is only thus that created being genuinely *corresponds* to the Creator and that the analogy of being is fulfilled. Indeed, for the creature, such is its only ontologically appropriate response. But, for Przywara, what this concretely means is ever greater conformity to Christ as the true measure of human greatness: "For the ever greater greatness of God is revealed precisely in the mystery of redemption, in which he empties himself ever more (Phil. 2:7), and in that he 'ascends ever higher' as the one who 'descends ever lower' (Eph. 4:9f.)."[30] Accordingly, what this means for the human being, whom both Przywara and Nietzsche recognize as a self-transcending being, is that human transcendence [*das Je-über-hinaus des Menschen*] is achieved "*to the extent* that one descends ever more with Christ, who descends ever more deeply, in 'service' to the ever greater God."[31] In this way, Przywara avers, by means of this Christological anthropology, which he takes to be the only authentic anthropology, "the glittering demonism of [Nietzsche's] magical pride and magical humility is overcome."[32]

For Przywara the rest of the *Exercises* only underscore these differences. In conclusion, though, and naturally enough given the terms of the debate declared by Nietzsche between "Christ and Anti-Christ," he draws our attention to the "Two Standards," which "answers to the most deceptive element in Nietzsche's 'heroic atheism,'" namely, his "'heroic going without God.'" Over against this most deceptive type of heroism, Ignatius presents the follower of Christ as one who is

> abandoned with the self-abandoning God to the point of becoming nothing with the God who made himself nothing (Phil. 2:7). "Heroic atheism" is hereby unmasked not only as a faint copy of the actual mystery of redemption, but as a flight from it,

---

28. Augustine, *In Ps.* LXII, xvi.

29. Augustine, *In Jo. Tract.* LXIII, i.: "*Ut inveniendus quaeratur, occultus est; ut inventus quaeratur, immensus est. Unde alibi dicitur, "Quaerite faciem ejus semper."*

30. Przywara, *Crucis Mysterium*, 48.

31. Przywara, *Crucis Mysterium*, 48. My emphasis.

32. Przywara, *Crucis Mysterium*, 48.

such that the mystery of redemption is evacuated of its heroism
and flight is made into something heroic.[33]

The "definitive" answer to Nietzsche, however, arises from the final exercise in love from the Third Week in which we are asked to consider "how the divinity hides itself" (Nr. 196), and which leads from the contemplation of Christ's suffering to an analogous self-offering—in the night of God's apparent absence—in the *sume et suscipe*. For Przywara, accordingly, it is here that we see the full measure of man on brilliant display: veiled in the mystery of the cross (*fulget crucis mysterium*), in which the apparent horror of the Son's abandonment by the Father is revealed to be the "flaming and flowing of divine 'love.'"[34] For such is the manner in which God goes forth from himself in the mystery of creation: going forth to the very end of redemption in order to draw all things back to himself: "It is the Areopagitic-Thomistic procession of God from himself for the sake of the restoration of all things to himself in the creation and perfection of the creature (*De div. nom.* IV, 14; *De ver.* Q. 24, a. 4 corp.)—the *one* reality of which Nietzsche's 'eternal return' is a dream."[35]

2. Four Sermons on the West

In early November 1943, Przywara delivered a series of sermons in the Ludwigskirche in Munich that were published after the war by Johannes Verlag, the publishing house of his protégé and friend, Hans Urs von Balthasar, under the title *Vier Predigten über das Abendland*. The publication also included a preface by Balthasar in which he situates these sermons in their apocalyptic context:

> Erich Przywara gave these talks when Germany was in apocalyptic flames and Munich was burning down, increasingly buried beneath the rubble. In such circumstances he held out to the end as one who provided comfort, admonishment, and assistance until his own strength and health collapsed. It can be of no surprise to us, therefore, that the horrors of these times should be reflected here at the level of thought—in a contemplation of the collapse of centuries of ideals . . . .[36]

---

33. Przywara, *Crucis Mysterium*, 48.
34. Przywara, *Crucis Mysterium*, 48.
35. Przywara, *Crucis Mysterium*, 51. Trans.: *Nach-Traum*.
36. Przywara, *Vier Predigten*, 7.

Indeed, according to Balthasar, what we find in these wartime sermons is a picture of reality seen through the flames—an "apocalyptic metaphysics" (*Enthüllungsmetaphysik*) that penetrates past all foregrounds and unsparingly discloses the abysses gaping in the background.[37]

At the same time, however, Balthasar suggests that Przywara's perspective in these sermons is limited by an inverse proportion, since the more it penetrates into the backgrounds the more it ignores the foregrounds.[38] He also expresses his concern about the dialectical direction he thinks Przywara's thought had taken in recent years, suggesting that even "the master of the *analogia entis*" had succumbed to Lutheran dialectics, and that his eschatology had taken a corresponding intra-historical turn.[39] From such comments it is clear that Balthasar had some reservations about these sermons and, as their publisher, wanted to distance himself from them—presumably, to judge from their content, because he thought that they were *too* apocalyptic, to the point of undermining the stability of the institutional church.

Reservations notwithstanding, however, Balthasar concludes that Przywara's sermons "retain their relevance to westerners today":

> They are an urgent and necessary warning that the earthquakes that have temporarily subsided could resume at any time with greater force; that, while a part of Europe is amusing itself in its prosperity, other parts have experienced no such intermission. . . . One does not get the impression that, three years after the collapse, today's Christians and Catholics are especially aware of the depth of the gaping abyss.[40]

And so, thinking of the future of the church, he concludes: "Few have a clearer vocation to advise, to clarify, to illuminate and, even if they cannot join in the planning themselves, train those who would do so for their mission, than Erich Przywara."[41] All of which makes these sermons of particular interest—more incidentally, for what they might reveal about the differences between the student and his teacher; more generally and importantly,

---

37. Przywara, *Vier Predigten*, 7.

38. For example, he suggests that Przywara's view of Protestantism and Russian Orthodoxy are out of date, having been superseded by the events of the past five years, and in general that these sermons are products of their time and place.

39. For his part, Przywara was (not unreasonably) offended by Balthasar's introduction, whose publication caused a temporary rift in their friendship. See Lochbrunner, *Hans Urs von Balthasar*, 62ff.

40. Przywara, *Vier Predigten*, 8.

41. Przywara, *Vier Predigten*, 8.

for what relevance they might still have for thinking about the current state and future of Christianity in the western world. Indeed, in this last respect, one could argue, being prophetic words addressed by a prominent Catholic theologian to a Christian culture on the brink of collapse, they bear an almost timeless quality—like the words of Augustine in view of the end of Christendom with the fall of Rome in 410, but now at a time of even greater, heretofore unthinkable devastation.

So, what is the gist of the sermons? Among those who heard them was Gerda Walther, the quondam Marxist and erstwhile student of Husserl,[42] who was sufficiently inspired by them to become Catholic. In her autobiography she offers the following account of their scope and critical standpoint:[43]

> Father Przywara went back to the time of the Reformation, and to the idealism and the materialism of the nineteenth century: increasingly left to itself, conceived as "evil" and rejected as "sinful," "the world" became increasingly independent of the divine and the spiritual, until in defiance it finally opposed itself to them. Names like Hegel, Bakunin, and Nietzsche were mentioned. . . . Finally, a new philosopher [came along] who posited the human being into the void, into the midst of nothing, into the abyss of nothingness, out of which the human being now had to "posit" and shape the world as a demiurge. No name was mentioned—surely out of consideration of the lurking Gestapo who were ready to record everything. Whom could Przywara have meant? It could only have been Heidegger. "That is Satanic," the preacher continued. The atheists proclaimed "the death of God." What collapsed, however, was only a false concept of God, the arrogance of humanity, and the world of its making which has now been reduced to rubble.[44]

42. In the end, however, Walther completed her dissertation in Munich under Alexander Pfänder.

43. Walther, *Zum anderen Ufer*, 630: "They had already begun," she says, "by the time I could orient myself in the church, which according to regulations had to be kept dark on account of the airstrikes. No lights could be lit, and so the speaker was not standing at the pulpit as I had expected. But then I heard a rather high-pitched voice and followed it. On the side of the church a short man with short hair and a noticeably high brow was standing in front of a covered lamp that was hanging down from above near the altar of St. Joseph. Curtains had been put up that made it into an enclosed little room, almost like a tent. The audience sat on the benches around the speaker. As I later learned all the sermons were recorded by stenographers and countless copies were distributed throughout [Germany]."

44. Walther, *Zum anderen Ufer*, 630f.

The positive core of these sermons, however, is the prophetic testimony of scripture that in the midst of the collapse of historical civilizations—whether that of ancient Israel, or the *sacrum imperium* of the Middle Ages, or the modern Christian West—God is brooding over the darkness with words of comfort: "*Ecce nova facio omnia*—Behold, I make all things new."[45] We first see these words, Przywara notes, in Isaiah 43:19, in the context of Israel's apparent abandonment to its enemies and the dissolution of the Old Covenant. We see it again in Paul's words to the Corinthians: "*vetera transierunt, ecce, nova facta sunt omnia*"—"everything old has passed away; behold, everything has been made new."[46] And we see it, finally, at the conclusion of scripture in the (so to speak) apocalypse of apocalypses, the Apocalypse of John, which speaks of the end of all things and of the passing away of the old heaven and the old earth. Indeed, it is then, when the whole creation is in the flames of the fire of God's wrath, that the joyful song erupts of the dawning of God himself who is the light of the new heaven and the new earth: God himself as the new sun and the new temple and the new paradise.[47] Such is the theme that Przywara then elaborates in his four sermons entitled, respectively, "The Man of the West," "Old and New Reformation," "Old and New Church," and "Old and New God," each of which I will treat in corresponding order.

2.1. The Man of the West

Przywara's first sermon concerns the end of western humanism, which is to say, more precisely, the end of the Greco-Roman image of the human being as a "mean." As he observes,

> Greco-Roman antiquity speaks of the human being as a mean: according to Plato, the human being is a bound rhythm; according to Aristotle, the human being is a formative middle, the man of *schola et disciplina,* as Latin-Roman tradition has it. This notion then enters Roman-German tradition by way of the concept of the "*Mâsze,*" and of the "measured" human being [*des Maßes*]. Finally, European modernity is conceived in terms of the human being of humanity. That is the compass of the human being of the West. And we stand under the harrowing impression that

---

45. Rev 21:5.

46. 2 Cor 5:17.

47. Przywara, *Vier Predigten*, 10.

this human being is collapsing. And we ask ourselves, what does this mean?[48]

Przywara's answer to this question is bound up with his contention that the ideal humanity of the West was in some sense always a fiction, an ideal construct threatened on all sides by real infinities. In geographical terms, for instance, Plato's conception of the human being as a "bound rhythm" was always threatened by the unbounded infinity—the *apeiron*—of the East; and something similar is true of Aristotle, notwithstanding his masterful attempt to gain control of reality by means of thought, i.e., by grounding it in thought thinking itself. So, too, politically: just as the *imperium Romanum* was unable to maintain its *ordo* in the face of the unmasterable reality of eastern peoples, the *sacrum imperium* was constantly threatened from the East in the form of Islam. Accordingly, by the time this ideal appears in the quattrocento the man of the Renaissance does not belong any longer to a self-contained *ordo* of the West, but stands alone, as it were, in a monstrously infinite cosmos. As Pascal would famously say, speaking precisely as a modern man after the discoveries of Copernicus and Galileo, "*Le silence eternel des ces espaces infinis m'effraie*."[49]

In due course, therefore, Przywara observes, a new conception of man emerges as one who does not know how to master reality or time, and therefore lives only in the moment:

> The past has slipped away from him like one infinity, the future stretches before him like another, neither of which he can measure or calculate; and so he stands alone. . . . He is no longer the man of a definite yesterday; he is no longer the man of a predictable tomorrow; he is the man of a pure today, the man of the moment, ever renewed.[50]

What then, if anything, does Christianity have to say to modern man in this new situation? Does it indicate an apocalyptic end or an apocalyptic beginning? According to Przywara, the Christian faith indicates that it is both an end and a beginning:

> It is a collapsing, but it is the collapsing of an idol—the idol of humanity that thought it could control and subdue the cosmic powers. It is the collapsing of a godlike man [*eines gotthaften Menschen*]. It is the birth . . . of the Christian man; for at the center of our Christian faith stands the word: *anthropos kainos*, the

---

48. Przywara, *Vier Predigten*, 11f.

49. Pascal, *Pensées*, S 233/L 201.

50. Przywara, *Vier Predigten*, 13.

new man, the man who is ever new. Such is the deeper mystery, the mystery the liturgy imparts to us—to be sure, ever anew for deaf ears—at Christmas and Easter: *Repelle vetustatem humanam, affer novitatem tuam!* . . . The authentically Christian man is thus the new man. And this new man is the man who exists from God alone.

The godlike man, for Przywara, is the man who would make himself like God.[51] The new man, by contrast, the *genuinely* godlike man, is the one who does *not* confuse himself with God, but humbles himself before him—the man who not only recognizes that he is decidedly *not* God (such is the fundamental point of Przywara's metaphysics of analogy), but who completely gives up his own pretensions and claims to righteousness, his own attempts to control his life and the rest of the world by the power of his own will, and follows the God-man into his own humanity.

Accordingly, following Christ, the new man does not grasp after Divinity,[52] but following the Word of God empties himself of all claims to it.[53] Such, Przywara avers, is God's eternal Word to a prideful humanity: "The God who alone is infinite, who alone is the power and the righteousness, becomes *Deus descendens* and *Deus exinanitus*—the God who abases himself, who empties himself, and who makes himself as nothing," citing Ephesians 4: "'*Qui descendit, ipse est qui ascendit.*' The one who descends is the one who ascends."[54] As the *eternal* Word, however, the Word was not spoken once in the past (*Deus dixit*) and destined to fade away; it is not shut up in time, but resonates as an eternal novelty through the ages. For "this Jesus Christ is the one who is ever descending and ever ascending anew, is Christ yesterday and today and in all eternity."[55] Being ever new, the Word of God is thus set against the oldness—the *vetustas*—of every proud age that would fortify itself against it, refusing to be changed by the God who makes all things new. Put positively, following Augustine, Przywara's point is that one should live not in the past, as though God were the past, nor in the future, as though God were the future, but in the freedom of the Moment that God is: "Man is now called to live alone in the freedom of the occasional lightning flash of the grace of God, which breaks through when God so pleases. . . . St. Augustine says that God is Today. God is not the past,

---

51. Gen 3.
52. Gen 3:7.
53. Phil 2:6f.
54. Przywara, *Vier Predigten*, 14.
55. Przywara, *Vier Predigten*, 14.

nor is he the future. Rather, being the fullness of Now and Today, he is the Moment Itself."[56]

In view of such language it is easy to see why Balthasar was concerned that Przywara, "the master of the *analogia entis*," might have fallen victim to the Lutheran dialectics the analogy of being was (in part) intended to overcome. For if God is identified with a dialectical moment it would seem to make the Christian tradition qua tradition *eo ipso* suspect—and clinging to tradition, conceivably, a clinging to nothing but the vain traditions of men.[57] All of which raises the question as to whether Przywara's understanding of analogy has mutated into dialectic, as Balthasar seems to have thought, or whether it has deepened into what we might call a "dialectical analogy," which remains Thomistic in its basic orientation, but at the same time does justice to the voluntarism in the late Augustine, which leads via Scotus and Ockham to Luther and Calvin. By the same token, it raises pertinent questions as to what such formulations might mean for Przywara's ecclesiology, and whether it has changed with respect to earlier works such as his 1929 essay, "Das katholische Kirchenprinzip," which was written in view of Barth and intended to address what he took to be problems with Barth's excessively *dialectical* ecclesiology.[58]

Here, too, however, the profounder question is whether Przywara's ecclesiology has changed or whether it has deepened—more precisely, whether it has become radical in the sense of revolutionary, or whether it has become radical in the positive sense of getting to the *radix*, the root—and hence to that "dearest freshness deep down"—of things. For his part, it is clear that Przywara does not think that he has abandoned his early thought, much less Catholic tradition. Rather, he thinks that he is going deeper, attempting to establish the church on its proper basis—not in a static past for tradition's sake, nor in the future of our own making, but in the Word of God who in

---

56. Przywara, *Vier Predigten*, 14.

57. Cf. Matt 15:9; Mark 7:8–13.

58. We cannot yet answer such questions adequately, however. At the very least, we would have to disambiguate the senses of old at play here. For practicing the "old" tradition (ecclesial or otherwise) without hearing the Word, or worse, practicing tradition as an excuse not to hear it, is one thing; understanding tradition as the bearer of the novelty of the Word, who through divine tradition is ever breaking through the old patterns of sin and making all things new, is quite another. For now we can simply note that Przywara takes himself to be following Augustine—which certainly does put him into qualified proximity to Luther—and that his positive point is that the *anthropos kainos*, the new man, lives neither as a conservative in the past, nor as a liberal in the utopia of some imagined future, but in the grace of God in the moment, indeed, in the God who is the moment itself, precisely in the spirit of Kierkegaard's doctrine of contemporaneity with Christ.

the grace of the moment—not here nor there[59]—makes all things new. As he puts it in a passage that deserves to be quoted *in extenso*:

> This is the Christian foundation [*diesem Grundchristlichen*] for all Christian constructions hitherto, and for which the inalienable tradition of the Christian West has coined the terms *Corpus Christi, Civitas Dei, Imperium Sacrum, Theios Kosmos*: the body of Christ, the city of God, a holy kingdom, a divine cosmos. These four terms encompass the mystery of the incarnation— since in God's incarnation it was not just the one human body of Jesus Christ that became the body of God, but the whole body of humanity that became the body of Christ, its one head; hence the whole of humanity is formed into a city, a city of this God, and so into an *imperium divinum*, a kingdom of God, which extends not only to the whole of humanity, but to the entire cosmos, which is included by way of the sacramental mystery not only of the bread and the wine, but of all the sacramentals, the entire cosmos, which according to the letter to the Colossians, has its substance in Christ, and, according to the Greek fathers, has on this account become a divine cosmos.—Without question, this is the immensely grand edifice that stands at the heart of the Christian West. Indeed, the Christian tradition is summarized in these four words, which at the same time capture the full extent of the greatness of western man: that it was entrusted to him to protect this edifice as a holy inheritance: the Church as the body of Christ, humanity as the body of Christ, humanity as a city of God, the world as the cosmos of Christ.[60]

In light of this passage we see in what sense Przywara is radical—obviously, not in the sense that he rejects Catholic tradition. On the contrary, this is the sacred inheritance of the West, which the West was called to preserve.

But, for Przywara, this same tradition is also radically relativized from its revolutionary root for the sake of which alone it exists: namely, for the sake of the renewal of humanity—the creation of the new man—in Christ. Such is the radical presupposition of all this tradition and the revolutionary message it bears: the gospel of "the *anthropos kainos*."[61] Nor should this surprise us. For, as Przywara reminds us, "the New Covenant . . . commenced precisely with a divine revolution, an upheaval so great that the veil of the temple was torn, the graves were opened, and the earth quaked," indeed, such that the Lord spoke of "hatred between father and mother, children

---

59. Luke 17:21.
60. Przywara, *Vier Predigten*, 15.
61. Przywara, *Vier Predigten*, 15.

and parents."[62] The danger, accordingly, is that the very tradition that is meant to carry on this revolution can at times, due to its own ossification and petrification—its own *self*-importance—get in the way of it. In short, instead of revealing the gospel, it can willy-nilly conceal it. All of which leads Przywara into the following radical, even paradoxical, apocalyptic reflection:

> This revolution, which demands that the rigidity and self-asser-
> tion of the old become new, is the basis of the Christian tradi-
> tion. Therefore, God does not merely allow it; on the contrary,
> it is part of his most Christian providence that in the history
> of the Church, the history of Christendom, the history of the
> Christian West, the history of Christian Europe, he continually
> allows a given Christian formation to collapse—allowing the
> body of Christ to become an *"ecclesia dilacerata"*; allowing the
> *Civitas Dei* to become secularized and worldly, torn apart in a
> life-or-death battle between Christian peoples who maul each
> other to the last drop of blood; allowing the very *imperium sa-*
> *crum*, which he intended his holy Church, his Christendom, his
> city of God to become, to be torn and shred apart in a life-and-
> death battle between worldly empires; and, allowing, finally, in
> a *"providentia christianissima,"* the cosmos he consecrated in
> sacraments, in the water of baptism, in the bread and wine of the
> Eucharist, in the chrism of confirmation, priestly ordination,
> and last rites, and in countless sacramentals and consecrations,
> to fall to pieces as if it were nothing but a hell of unleashed ele-
> ments, hellish waters, hellish fires, a hellish sulfur, nothing but a
> Satanic chemistry of unbound elements.

And yet, Przywara contends, precisely when we might be wont to de-spair over the course of history and the *lacrimae rerum*, wondering how God could allow hell to be unleashed on earth, "None of this signals a failure on God's part." Rather, it points to the words of Christ, *"Ecce, nova facio om-nia,"* signaling that a Christian tradition that had become arrogant, a body of Christ that had become haughty and rigid, a holy kingdom and divine cosmos that had become old, must pass again through the fire of God, who is a 'consuming fire': *'Deus noster ignis consumens est.'*[63] Przywara's message, then, is one of dreadful discipline, but also of hope that in and through such times of darkness and destruction God is renewing all things: "Now more than ever it is the hour of proclamation over the West; the shadows of the Spirit of God, the Creator Spirit, are hovering over it . . . *'spiritus*

62. Przywara, *Vier Predigten*, 15. Luke 14:26.
63. Przywara, *Vier Predigten*, 16. Heb 12:29.

obumbrabit tibi, the Spirit of God [will] overshadow you, O Christian West."
And so Przywara concludes his first sermon with the prayer, "'Send forth
your Spirit, and everything will be new.' Everything will be new as this one
Christ and Lord, in whom God, the eternally new God, became man and
becomes it ever anew. Send forth your Spirit, and let us become a new, more
radiant West, *Christus omnia in omnibus!* Amen."[64]

2.2. The Old and New Reformation

Having introduced his theme, in his second sermon Przywara takes us back
to what he calls "the central event in the history of the West," the "so-called
Reformation." And it is easy to see why, for his own apocalyptic message
would seem very close to it in spirit. Indeed, in light of his first sermon
one could get the impression that he has essentially become a Protestant, as
though he were pitting the revolutionary novelty of the gospel against the
antiquity and substance of the church, which is entrusted with this message
and called to proclaim it. But, as sympathetic as Przywara is with Luther's
emphasis on the God of grace and his desire for the reform of the church, if
indeed *ecclesia semper reformanda*—this being the objective correlate, as it
were, of *"ecce, nova facio omnia"*—he is equally clear that he thinks Luther
went too far:

> Luther wanted nothing but reform. He goes beyond tradition,
> pushing to the absolute. The result is not reformation within the
> church, but reformation *as* the church, and so in place of the
> church—to the point of becoming a sheer protest against every
> order and development. The Reformation thus became the ar-
> chetypal revolution—the *Ur-Revolution.* This lay in the essence
> of the old Reformation as it broke out in Luther.

And, for Przywara, we continue to see the problematic effects of its doctrines
today under the sign of "the new Reformation," specifically, its doctrines of
"sin alone," "conscience alone," "word alone," and "Christ alone." This is not
to say that Przywara did not appreciate what was to be appreciated in these
doctrines: he was far too Catholic and thus generous in his sensibility not to
recognize what good there was in them. The problem, however, Przywara
avers, was that the Reformation mutated from a corrective into a negation—
into a Protestant "No," reminiscent of the diction of Barth.

Accordingly, beginning with the Reformation's doctrine of sin, Przywara readily admits that this was a necessary correction for a church that is

always in danger of forgetting this presupposition and *sui securus,* under the pretense of its own holiness, essentially positing itself in the place of God as a pure participation in God. But this same doctrine, taken to the point of the Calvinist doctrine of total depravity, led to a negation of creation: "The world is evil and abandoned to evil, abandoned to a fundamental worldliness, a world without God."[65] So, too, its doctrine of the conscience and its emphasis on the interior faith of the believer was a necessary correction for a church that is always in danger of replacing the religious immediacy between God and the soul with its own sacred hierarchy, such that "the living God appears bound to the official hierarchy of a heavenly and earthly court, and the living human being is objectified as an official within a curial hierarchy."[66] But here again, Przywara avers, the Reformation goes too far, leading to the negation of all visible forms and all visible authority and thus willy-nilly to the affirmation of "the sectarianism of purely autonomous intuition."[67]

So, too, with its doctrine of *verbum solum,* the Reformation was a positive correction to a church that is always in danger of treating the "words of spirit and life" as something secondary to the fleshly and thing-like nature of the sacraments. But, Przywara observes, this led not only to an absolute spirituality disconnected from all materiality, but also down the road to an absolute intellectualism, whereby human understanding becomes the measure of all things, indeed, as for Heidegger, is the essence of things. Thus, Przywara avers, following the logic of the Reformation we are eventually led to a purely literary account of things: "to a world of words in place of a world of things," or, as we might put it today, to Derrida's grammatological world without substance, without living presence, without any final significance.[68] Accordingly, when the Word of God, in whom all things are united, is no longer heard in human words, we no longer have any solutions, but instead the absolutizing of "dialectic," of problems and *aporiae,* of the "conflict of interpretations." And so Przywara concludes, with Heidegger clearly in mind, that whereas Christianity begins with God, the Word, this beginning has now been parodied, secularized into the word *as* God—into "verbal idolatry and verbal magic."[69]

Finally, regarding the Reformation's doctrine of *solus Christus,* Przywara is happy to celebrate the centrality of Christ, and even to affirm that

---

65. Przywara, *Vier Predigten,* 21.

66. Przywara, *Vier Predigten,* 23.

67. Przywara, *Vier Predigten,* 23.

68. Przywara, *Vier Predigten,* 25.

69. Przywara, *Vier Predigten,* 26.

"theology and anthropology are concrete *only* as Christology."[70] Indeed, with the Reformers he lyrically confesses his faith in the One who says "I am the good shepherd," "I am the bread of life," "I am the resurrection and the life"; who in Paul's summary judgment "unites all things in heaven and on earth" (Eph 1:10), indeed, all things above the heavens and under the earth, so that he might "fill all things" (Eph 4:9–10), so that "all life, in all its stages and transformations, might be a single life shared with him and in him, conceived with him, born with him, lived with him, worked with him, crucified with him, died with him, buried with him, resurrected with him, ascended with him, and seated with him at the right hand of God, the Father—'Christ, my life'" (Phil 1:21); and who in the final apocalypse identifies himself as "the Alpha and the Omega, the first and the last, the beginning and the end (Rev 22:13). All of this is utterly affirmed, so much so that Przywara can see in the Lutheran *solus Christus* a genuine renaissance of the Augustinian doctrine "through Christ, in Christ, and to Christ, i.e., through Christ as man to Christ as God"; and can see all of this confirmed by the church itself and the great, concluding liturgical Amen: *per Christum Dominum nostrum*—as pertains to all human prayer to God, and all the grace of God to men.[71]

What is more, drawing parallels to the reforms of Bernard, Francis, and Ignatius, all of whom emphasized a "living walk with Christ," Przywara can see in this doctrine of the Reformers a corrective for a church whose hierarchy is ever in danger of becoming worldly, of becoming a "corporate Church" [*Korporation Kirche*], a juridical institution like any other:

> Either it becomes one-sidedly theo-logical and theo-centric, [i.e., other worldly], forgetting that God conceived of his creation only in Christ (Jn 1, Col. 1:15–20). Or it becomes one-sidedly ecclesio-logical and ecclesio-centric, forgetting that, precisely as the church, it is the living "body of Christ" and thus not a human institution that rests in itself, but only and solely from its sovereign head, a head who is, more profoundly, "Christ in us" (Rom. 8:10; 2 Cor. 13:5).[72]

But precisely here, Przywara contends, with regard to its noblest of doctrines, the Reformation is increasingly perverted into a Protestant "No." In its very origins Christ becomes the *iustitia formalis* of the human being. What is at issue is neither the nature of God, nor the nature of Christ, nor even the inner nature of the human being, but only his or her justification—and

---

70. Przywara, *Vier Predigten*, 26.

71. Przywara, *Vier Predigten*, 27.

72. Przywara, *Vier Predigten*, 27f.

even then it is about neither the righteousness of God, nor the righteousness of man, but solely the righteousness of Christ, in whom the righteousness of God becomes the formal righteousness of man. All of which, in Przywara's view, led to unforeseeable negative consequences:

> Here the terrible foundation was laid, whose final consequences were inexorably and relentlessly worked out over the next centuries: the identity of God and man in Christ. To be sure, during the historical Reformation, the name for this identity was Christ. But inasmuch as Christ is living, strictly speaking, only as the "righteousness of Christ," and the Church, on the other hand, is rejected as the continuation of Christ's living authority, here already we begin to see, however unintended and unconsciously, a [mutation] of Christ into the divine form of man himself [*Gottform des Menschen*]. Dispossessed of his divinity, God in Christ becomes the form of humanity, while the human being in Christ, dispossessed of his humanity [i.e., his creaturely status], becomes the bearer of this form. The German idealism of the nineteenth century was therefore utterly consistent when it dissolved the historical Christ into the inner messianism of the human being as such—into that messianic humanity, whose formula was provided by Hegel and Humboldt (and bears an uncanny affinity to the collective messianism that is the only messianism recognized by post-Christian Judaism). And then— all that is left is for Nietzsche to utter the terrible words that he speaks throughout his entire, genuinely anti-Christian gospel, whose prophetic fulfillment we are witnessing today: that man himself is the only Christ in the world. Thus, as an eerie consequence, Christ devolves into anti-Christ: the God-man becomes a man-God.[73]

The historical conclusion of the Reformation is thus, in Przywara's view, at once ironic and tragic, for the movement that in its zealous origins was all about God in Christ, and about the individual's direct relationship with God, without sacramental mediation, ends up giving birth to a world without God:[74] "The world has become 'just the world' [*nur Welt*]: in an extreme autonomy of purely worldly culture, purely worldly ethics, purely worldly politics, and purely worldly science."[75] More precisely, in Przywara's view, the Reformation has led to a world that in the name of its autonomy—corroborated by a metaphysics of pure finitude (in Heidegger and Hartmann)—has

73. Przywara, *Vier Predigten*, 28.

74. See Brad Gregory's monumental study, *The Unintended Reformation*.

75. Przywara, *Vier Predigten*, 30.

de facto dethroned God and installed itself in his place, not contenting itself to be created, but wanting to be the Creator.[76]

Of course, as Przywara points out, in one of his most apocalyptic passages, Heidegger's world of pure finitude, or in the post-modern language of Deleuze, the world of pure immanence, is in fact no such thing; on the contrary, such philosophies have unsealed the abyss and turned the world into an open theater of evil—the very thing the Reformers were wont to see in it:

> It is the world that, in Nietzsche's anti-Christian pathos and Bakunin's eastern ecstasies, openly professes "the fruitfulness of evil," "the power of evil and lies," "the palingenetic power of destruction"—whose fulfillment we see today in the fire and flames that have broken out over us. The Reformers' demonizing of the world is finally working itself out to its logical conclusion. For the fanatic, ecstatic "will to evil" properly defines the Satanic. In this hour the spectral shape of something limitless and absolute is spiriting about, which either sucks the life out of you [*vor dem man ent-markt hinsinkt*] or turns one into a completely servile instrument, indeed, a medium. Our world of smoke and flames, which has now been reduced to burning ash, is a dark reflection of the one who wanted to "make himself like the Most High" [Isa 12:14], who as Luci-fer, the light-bearer, wanted to be God, the Light, himself, but only to ape the Absolute as a de-natured, stuffed-up dark fire and fiery darkness.[77]

The Reformation's darkly prophetic utterances concerning the nature of sin, of *peccatum solum*, of total depravity, and its denial of every *analogia entis* and all natural theology, hence of any natural traces of the Logos in the world the Logos made (John 1:3), is thus realized: "The 'sin alone' of the Reformation has become a dread reality: the world is indeed now, to all appearances, nothing but the accursed world of sin and death and hell."[78] And something similar is true, Przywara thinks, of the other doctrines of the Reformation—*conscientia sola, verbum solum*, etc.—each of which has ushered the West into an apocalyptic situation: "The old Reformation, which

---

76. Cf. Przywara, *Vier Predigten*, 35: "Such precisely is the dream of modernity from its origin: the absolutely creative man assuming the place of God, the Creator, and thus in a special way, in place of God, the Word, through whom all things were made (Jn 1:3). The magic of a godlike humanity, from positively creative magic to the magic of . . . creative destruction—that is the Satanism, and the final consequence of the Reformation . . . as we have seen."

77. Przywara, *Vier Predigten*, 31.

78. Przywara, *Vier Predigten*, 31.

once stood at the center of the West, is now, as the new Reformation, the most acute sign of its final crisis [*End-Krise*]."[79]

Take, for instance, the doctrine of "conscience alone," which is the only place to stand once the external world, the visible authority of the church, and all enduring order have been demonized:

> Pure interiority, pure intuition, the pure moment of pure insight, all the pure dynamism that broke out in these ways is now concentrated in the very thing that constitutes the essence of hell . . . in the absolute spontaneity of the individual I [*des Ich*] in the lightning flash of the arbitrary moment. God alone is the "I am who I am" (Ex. 3:14). It is therefore properly Satanic if the creature wants to be this "I," unbound by a visible external world, by a visible authority, by a visible order. To be sure, it is the lightning flash of the moment, but it is the destructive lightning flash of Satan. God alone is *Actus purus*, the infinite moment in himself. The creature that wants to be this kind of flashy reality [*blitzhaft Aktuale*] is thus, like Satan and in Satan, a spewing forth of fireworks, of the "smoke and fire" of his hell.[80]

And the matter is similar, Przywara thinks, with the Reformation's doctrine of *verbum solum* and its corresponding denigration of the sacramental mediation of material reality. For inasmuch as it exclusively emphasized the creative power of the Word, it willy-nilly paved the way for the creative power of human words, no longer analogically related to the Word, to shape the world into a phantasmagoria of conjured realities disconnected from the nature of things: "The Satanism of the 'I' leads intrinsically the Satanism of the magical Word."[81]

But precisely here, in the midst of the "however great" of this Satanic power, Przywara looks deeper into the metaphysical background in which Christ, the "ever greater" Word of God is "making all things new."[82] For the crisis that the old Reformation inadvertently brought about also bears within it the matrix, the divine possibility, of something new. To be sure, "up until this very hour the old Reformation has taken its rejection of the substance of the West to an extreme." Nevertheless, Przywara avers, "it is more profoundly the hour of a genuinely new Reformation, for in the midst of

---

79. Przywara, *Vier Predigten*, 29.

80. Przywara, *Vier Predigten*, 32.

81. Przywara, *Vier Predigten*, 33.

82. Cf. Przywara, *Vier Predigten*, 31. As Przywara inimitably puts it in an attempt to translate Paul (Rom 5:20): where the curse of sin is "overflowing" [*überströmend*], it-self is flooded over [*über-überströmt*] by the even more immeasurable blessing of grace.

. . . these flames, the Reformation and the church are being led back to one another, not by means of human negotiations and human compromises, but solely by him who says, in the midst of most extreme decrepitude, 'Behold, I make all things new.'"[83] Specifically, he suggests that the old Reformation is beginning to wake up to the call to return to the church, and that the church is beginning to recognize and recover as its own various aspects of the Reformation: "The camp of the Reformation is awakening to Catholicism, and the Catholic camp is awakening to the primal Christian elements of the Reformation."[84] And, once again, he sees all of this taking place right when one would least expect it, amid "the dread shadows of this Satanic culmination" of the Reformation: "the ever-greater God is at work, leading Reformation invisibility and Catholic visibility, Reformation interiority and Catholic authority, Reformation dynamism and Catholic order, back to one another."[85]

In view of the foregoing we can now see how, for Przywara, metaphysics and apocalypse intersect (and do so, centrally, in the Cross), as unrelated as they might on the face of it seem: in that the ever greater, ever more majestic God of the *analogia entis,* who apart from his historical apocalypse would remain an abstraction, is manifest in full color, paradoxically, *in* the darkness of the drama of salvation—specifically, *in* the apparent nothingness of the hiddenness and humility of a handmaid (Luke 1:48), in the apparent weakness, defeat, and ignominious end of the Cross, and analogously *in* the apparent nothingness of the destruction and subsequent marginalization—to the point of risible irrelevance—of a paradoxically "universal" church in a post-Christian world; moreover, in such a way that one apocalypse, namely, the revelation of the abyss of Satan (cf. Rev 2:24), is outstripped by the deeper abyss of God's creative love, in keeping with Paul's dictum that "where sin abounds, grace abounds all the more" (Rom 5:20). As Przywara strikingly puts it, "Precisely at this point when everything

---

83. Przywara, *Vier Predigten,* 29.

84. Przywara, *Vier Predigten,* 30. For example, Przywara suggests that the Catholic Church has come to a deeper appreciation of its own presupposition, its own sinfulness and need for conversion, its need for the repentance of the poor tax collector; conversely, he suggests, the (churches of) the Reformation are beginning to see that the presupposition of sin, made absolute, into "sin alone," makes any kingdom of God impossible, and that the presupposition of the world's sin has to pass over into the kingdom of God, and thus into the church as a substantial presence in this world. To be sure, Przywara says, the kingdom of God cannot be in us if we are not completely converted (meta-noeite) from the pride of the self-righteous to the humility of poor sinners. Equally, however, this conversion cannot be genuine unless it is at the same time a conversion and return to the kingdom of God.

85. Przywara, *Vier Predigten,* 32.

seems to be at stake, in the midst of outright opposition between Christ and Anti-Christ—precisely here, in the midst of the darkness of the apparent end of the Christian West, the light of the most joyous morning of a unified Christianity [*eines einigen 'Christus Heute'*] is beginning to break forth, that unity in Christ, the Lord, the unity of the 'one shepherd and the one flock' in which the church and the Reformation alike rejoice." And so he concludes his second sermon, reflecting in hope on the novelty that "the one Christ, our Lord, is leading his flock back together in the midst of the hollowing of hell in the midst of a world without God."[86]

2.3. The Old and New Church

For Przywara, what applies to the church vis-a-vis the Reformation also applies to intra-mural conflicts within the Catholic Church, specifically, between the "old Church," by which he means the church leading up to and including the Counter-Reformation, and what he calls *die junge Kirche*—the recent or contemporary church. For here, too, he thinks that out of these tensions and conflicts God is creating something new: a "new Church."

But let us first specify the contest as Przywara sees it: whereas the "old Church" is characterized by a "metaphysical Catholicism" along the lines of the *ordo universi* of Aquinas and by a "cultural-engagement Catholicism" in the spirit of Ignatius, the desideratum of the "contemporary Church" is a "purely religious Catholicism." As such, it is interested neither in the inward-looking church of tradition, which is ensconced in its own order, viz., the church of the Middle Ages, nor in the apologetically minded church of the *Kulturkampfzeit,* which defined the church of the nineteenth century.[87] The contemporary church wants to be measured neither by the church's intellectual tradition, nor by its cultural life, much less by its power, but solely by the fruitfulness of its inner religious life. Accordingly, it has no interest in purely rational, intellectual, ethical, or cultural forms of Catholicism, preferring cultural poverty to cultural recognition, and powerlessness to power; indeed, so much so that it would prefer to be an "*ecclesia in loco deserto,*" a church "suspended in empty space" along with a "God of poverty and powerlessness."[88] Likewise, Przywara thinks, the "contemporary Church" tends to emphasize the uniformity of the liturgy over against the diversity of private devotion, organic membership in the *corpus Christi mysticum* over against the hierarchical authority of the *Rechtskirche,* and

---

86. Przywara, *Vier Predigten,* 36.

87. Przywara, *Vier Predigten,* 40.

88. Przywara, *Vier Predigten,* 39.

in general a vibrant pneumatic-Christocentric Christianity over against a tired institutional Christianity that has lost touch with its vital center in the "living Christ."

Without question Przywara finds much to appreciate in these contemporary movements. Indeed, at their best they represent a genuine recovery of vital elements of the ancient faith, as Przywara is likewise able to appreciate in the case of Luther, particularly his recovery of the Pauline and patristic teaching of the marvelous exchange (*commercium admirabile*) that is effected by faith in Christ between a holy God and sinful humanity. Nevertheless, he thinks that the "contemporary Church" is in danger of missing what is needed in this hour—not a reactionary return with the Reformation to what is old, whether to the patristic period or to a reconstructed *Urchristentum,* but rather attention to what God is doing now. Consequently, he suggests that the "contemporary Church" not make facile attempts to re-pristinate past ecclesial forms, as though these could be transferred without further ado into the present, but that it have the courage to face up to the contemporary crisis of the church and endure the night of the apparent end of Christendom:

> The renewal that the contemporary Church seeks can come about at first only by standing unflinchingly in the void, the nothingness, in which we currently find ourselves . . . [and] by waiting to hear the creative Word of God, "Let it be renewed," that God is speaking in this hour. It is not even the time to sketch out a particular program, standpoint, or perspective; rather, the immensity of this hour is that it is a void, whose positive sense God alone knows. To be young is to stand face-to-face with the God, who wants to make all things new in his holy Church.[89]

Such is Przywara's counsel for the "contemporary Church" in what he saw as the hour of crisis for the church at large: that it wait in the dark like Samuel and listen attentively for God's Word before running ahead with any particular program or any repristination of older ecclesial forms, "for God is not the God of a fixed program, not the God of *Urchristentum,* not the God of the early Middle Ages, not the God of the Baroque, not the God of

---

89. Przywara, *Vier Predigten,* 39. On the face of it, this passage sounds almost like a transcription into Christian terms of Heidegger's 1929 lecture "What is Metaphysics?" But he consistently repudiates Heidegger's ontological nihilism here and elsewhere as a perversion of the gospel, as a counterfeit of Christian apophaticism, kenoticism, and the waiting in the dark of the saints—who have nothing left to hold on to—for the advent of Christ. In other words, it is Heidegger who is borrowing from Christianity and translating it into the idiom of his own philosophy, and not Przywara who is translating Heidegger into Christian terms.

modernity, not the God of an old or a contemporary Church, but God now, today," who wants to make all things new.[90]

At the same time, while Przywara believes that the contemporary church is called to enter into the novelty of God's creative work in the present, for him this does not entail a rejection of the old church and its sacred deposit. On the contrary, the more open the contemporary church is to an encounter with Christ in the present, the more it is called to appreciate the "greater maturity" of the old church, which knew not to limit Christ to the moment of a personal encounter or to the liturgy or to the tabernacle, but to see his reign extended to daily life and to the uttermost ends of the earth—to the end of a sacred cosmos, *theios kosmos,* in which God in Christ is "all in all":

> For if we really believe in this God for his own sake, then we cannot help but believe in him as 'God all in all.' And if this is so, then this God is not a God of the sacristy and the tabernacle and the church alone, but the God of life, the God of the public, the God of the understanding, the God of the will, the God of culture, the God even of forms of the state.[91]

In sum, the "new Church," Przywara suggests, will be the church born out of the "contemporary Church" once it finds its way back to the old church— once, upon discovering the "living Christ" in the present, it rediscovers the universality of his body, the catholicity of the church, and so manages to unite subjective contemporaneity with Christ (the best of the Reformation) with the objective sacramentality of a genuine Catholic universality.

2.4. The Old and the New God

Thus far, Przywara's sermons have been apocalyptic in the sense that in the midst of potential despair over the fate of Christendom—over, indeed, its apparent end—they have sought to disclose something new that God is bringing about in the midst of the old. In his final sermon, however, he is even more apocalyptic in that the crisis of faith is not simply a crisis of Christendom (will it survive?), but now a crisis of faith in God as such:

> Is God even there? For it would seem that we stand before a silent God, before a God who has died, or even before the God [whose goodness even] St. Paul questioned, crying out in the middle of his letter to the Romans from the bottom of his heart,

90. Przywara, *Vier Predigten,* 42.
91. Przywara, *Vier Predigten,* 42.

"Numquid iniquitas apud Deum"? "Is God unjust?" (Rom. 9:14)
Or if we translate *iniquitas* still more pointedly: Is God evil? This
is what is at issue in this decisive hour of the West.[92]

The context of Paul's burning question in Romans is, of course, the
brewing strife between Jewish and gentile Christians and, more generally,
between Jews and Christians, which Przywara elsewhere calls the *Ur-Riss*,
the "original rift," in the economy of salvation. Is God, then, Przywara
rhetorically asks, the *Ur-Grund* of this horrendous development—the *Ur-
Grund* of the *Ur-Riss*—as though God himself were a God of dialectical self-
contradiction? If so, one might think him unjust, as Paul himself admits.
And over time, Przywara observes, instead of the economy of salvation unambiguously testifying to divine providence, much less to a divine logic, the
vexing questions only increase—after Rome was twice destroyed, and with
it all hopes of a cultured Christian empire, causing Augustine and Gregory
the Great to raise similarly vexing questions about a God who could incom-
prehensibly allow an entire Christian civilization to fall to pieces. Indeed,
in the end, Przywara observes, even Luther came to despair as he saw Satan
everywhere at work, undoing what he thought he had done to restore the
church. Paul's burning question thus arises again, but now with greater ur-
gency. In Przywara's words, "Who is this God who allows his own body, the
Church, to be torn to pieces, who apparently allows his kingdom of love and
glory to become a kingdom of Satan?"

And what about today—after the diabolism of the throwing into
confusion of a once Christian world? In the twentieth century, Przywara
continues, the "noble atheism" of the nineteenth century has given way to
a "Satanic contra-theism"—to an open hatred for God. But this is not the
worst of it. For, Przywara avers, the worst aspect of the contemporary situation is that

> [t]his despair over God, this rebellion against God, lives on in
> Christians themselves, however unconsciously or concealed or
> bravely and heroically resisted it may be, such that we ask our-
> selves: "Where is God? Does God even exist? And if he does,
> how can I bear him?" That is the background to our question
> concerning God, yesterday and today. It is the hour in which Ni-
> etzsche's blasphemous saying would seem to be fulfilled: "God
> is dead."

Such, in Przywara's view, was the extremity of the situation in November
1943: not only had Christendom been destroyed—after the Reformation

---

92. Przywara, *Vier Predigten*, 46.

and the religious wars of the seventeenth century, and now after the most horrific wars to date of supposedly Christian nations—but faith in the God who guaranteed it as well. "God" himself had become unbelievable.

And yet, just when the darkness could not seem darker, in the apocalyptic hour of the West, Przywara sees a light shining in it, an apocalypse *strictu senso* of God himself:

> But it is [also] the hour in which, to a greater and more powerful degree, the words of the second letter to the Corinthians are fulfilled: "God who called light out of darkness, has himself appeared" (2 Cor. 4:6)—[the hour, that is, of] God's death and God's resurrection. A God has died, and a God has risen. It is only by passing through this dying of a God and through this rising of a God that, thrown to our knees, we can reverently, silently begin to intimate what God actually is.[93]

For the God of the West who died, Przywara strikingly goes on to explain (in a manner reminiscent of Pascal), was never anything but an idol in the first place, being in one way or another a "God" we could calculate or comprehend, whether as the capstone of a realist or as the Absolute of an idealist system of philosophy. That is to say, for Przywara, the supposed death of God is in reality only a twilight of the gods—a *Götzendämmerung*. But as such, understood in its positive core, this twilight of the gods, this "death of God," is also the condition for the apocalypse of the one and only God:

> Have we Christians not again and again reckoned with a God with whom one can reckon, whom we almost imagine to see with our eyes? Have we ever really believed in the God of the Old and New Testament—the God who appeared to Moses in the burning bush and on the fiery mountain, the God before whom Job sank to his knees, whom he was compelled to confess to be incomprehensible, surpassing every measure of wisdom and justice? Have we ever really believed in the God who stands at the center of St. Paul's letter to the Romans: "O the depth and the wisdom and knowledge of God; how unsearchable are his judgments and how inscrutable his ways" (Rom. 11:33). Have we ever really believed in the God proclaimed by St. Augustine: *"Si comprehendis non est Deus"*? ["If you comprehend, it is not God."] And have we ever believed in the God proclaimed by Thomas Aquinas: *"Deus tamquam ignotus"*—the God who is known as unknown, but as such the real God, the God of unfathomable power, unfathomable glory, and unfathomable love?

93. Przywara, *Vier Predigten*, 46.

For us, therefore, the hour is that of Job, moreover, the hour that
asks us to have faith in God as the Church confessed him to be
at the [First] Vatican Council: "God, who is ineffably sublime,
beyond everything . . . that can be conceived." It is the hour of
the twilight of the gods, and the hour of the dawning of the true
God. It is the twilight of the God we have duped ourselves into
believing, and whose image has now been broken. It is not God
who is dead, but an idol that is dead and broken. The one, true,
and living God now wishes to reveal himself to us. It is the hour
of a theophany, of the appearing of God as he is.[94]

And who is this God? As Przywara has already indicated by reference to
Paul, it is none other than the same inscrutable and incomprehensible God
who called light out of darkness "who has shone in our hearts to enlighten
us with the knowledge of the glory of God in the face of Jesus Christ" (2 Cor
4:6).[95] Which leaves us only one final task, namely, in this light to clarify
the twilight of the theological idols that Przywara thinks have seen their
day of judgment—after which the connection between metaphysics and
apocalypse will also be apparent; or, put differently, we will see what kind of
metaphysics is able to withstand, as the fitting creaturely preparation for, the
apocalypse of God in Jesus Christ.

Of the theological idols Przywara has two chief types in mind, each of
which has its roots in an idolatrous one-sided absolutization of one aspect
of the real distinction between essence and existence. On the one hand, he
has in mind any metaphysics for which God functions essentially as the
foundation and guarantor of a particular cultural order. This, he says, is the
"God" of the ancient world: "This God was in the best case the idol of an
unshakable order that was deemed to be indispensable. . . . God functioned
for us in the way that Immanuel Kant described him: as the guarantor of a
human and cultural order. He was there . . . for the sake of order. And he
suffered the fate of this order because he was bound to it."[96] But this danger
was also present, Przywara suggests, in the *Summae* of the Middle Ages, inasmuch as they threatened to confuse God with the cosmic order, a danger
that was realized when, in the course of modern philosophy, the sacral order was eventually replaced by, and essentially identified with, the political
order: "In the end German and European philosophy knew no other God
than this sacral order, [understood as] the order of forms of law and political constitutions. This was the God in which humanity believed after it had

94. Przywara, *Vier Predigten*, 48.
95. Przywara, *Vier Predigten*, 56.
96. Przywara, *Vier Predigten*, 48.

renounced Christ and his Church: 'order' as such, without knowing that this order was a secularized Christianity."[97]

By the *fin de siècle*, however, Przywara observes, what remained of the idolatry of antiquity gave way to a more honest variety, which no longer put any credence in an objectively existing order, much less in an objectively existing holy order, but recognized all order to be, at the end of the day, a human construct, the product of the human being as *homo demiourgos*. In this respect Przywara naturally speaks of Kant and his faith in the transcendental project qua world project, but in Przywara's view (which bears comparison to Adorno's) Kant is at the end of the day only a precursor, a bridge to Nietzsche and Heidegger. Though Heidegger goes unnamed, it is nevertheless obvious who Przywara means when he refers to a prominent "philosopher of our day" who has taken modern unbelief to its logical conclusion: "For now the *homo demiourgos* faces the void and projects himself into it, in order Satanically, as it were, to shape it into a godlike [*gotthaften*] world. We have now witnessed the most horrific collapse of this [project]. For the *homo demiourgos*, who would make himself divine, has now been exposed as the man of destruction."[98] Such is Przywara's apocalyptic judgment with regard to the early Heidegger, who ironically represents the logical conclusion of the onto-theological tradition to which he later objected: the "God" that has died is not God, but a humanity that idolatrously made itself into God.[99]

But, according to Przywara, all of this is the fate of only one of the metaphysical idols—the fate of the metaphysics of an "ideal order," which begins with God (as the principle of order both in antiquity and in the *sacrum imperium* of the Middle Ages) and ends with humanity (as the only principle of order in a world that is essentially meaningless). The other metaphysical idol, which is exposed in this apocalyptic hour, is the kind of metaphysics that arises out of late-medieval nominalism and finds its paramount expression in the theologies of the Reformation: not the "old" God of a static *order*, who can be described in substantive terms, but the "new" God of a dynamic *movement*, who can be described only adverbially in terms of the suddenness—the ἐξαίφνης—of an inscrutable sovereign judgment. This "God"—a distinctly modern God, the apotheosis of pure, unadulterated freedom—is so little bound to a fixed order that he is not even bound to his own goodness, being a God who makes judgments and gives grace, as

---

97. Przywara, *Vier Predigten*, 49.
98. Przywara, *Vier Predigten*, 49.
99. Przywara, *Vier Predigten*, 49.

it were, arbitrarily. Such, Przywara points out, is Luther's God in his "most powerful" work, *De servo arbitrio.*

On the one hand, Przywara finds something to appreciate in this "new" concept of God, namely, a genuine intuition of the divine Majesty. For God appears here, independently of any creation or order, in terms of a sovereign will, which is epitomized by a "holy judgment" and a "holy love." What is more, Przywara sees in this "new" God, a genuine retrieval of the God who, for Augustine and Aquinas, is neither the God of an ancient past nor the God of an anticipated future, but the God who is an eternal "today"—*hodie.* Indeed, he can see in the Reformer's concept of God a certain corrective to the God of the sacred order of the Middle Ages, as we have already seen from a previous sermon. On the other hand, he is sensible of the destructive potential lurking in this new concept of God, which harbors a protest not only against the "static order" of the medieval church, but against all determinate order—ultimately unleashing, however unwittingly, an "unbounded dynamic" that "eternalized" the catastrophe in which the Middle Ages went up in flames, and with it every prospect of a body of Christ, a "*Civitas Dei,*" an *Imperium Sacrum,* and a divine cosmos.[100]

In the end, therefore, inasmuch as it radically undermines divine intentions, viz., that God be not only incarnate in Christ, but through his body, the church, "all in all" (1 Cor 15:28), the "new" God (the voluntarist's God of a dynamic existentialism) turns out to be just as much an idol as the "old" God (the rationalist's God of a static essentialism), which it replaced: "Not only is the God of order an idol; the God of movement is also an idol, and both idolatries, which mutually determine one another, belong to the past."[101] But, Przywara goes on to say, the twilight of these conceptual idols, the static as well as the dynamic image of God, is also a grace. For precisely in the midst of their collapse and not after it—grace being the very cause of their collapse—God is appearing as he is: "We do not recognize the darkness for what it really is until the light has dawned, illuminating it, judging it, and extinguishing it."[102] But then who is the real God whose apocalypse is also a judgment upon these "gods" of the past, the "god" of "absolute order" and the "god" of "absolute movement"?

The real God, as he would appear to us *today* is, firstly, Przywara says, "the God of the fire of judgment and love—the God of fire inasmuch as he is in himself the inextinguishable burning [fire] of life and glory," and as such "the judgment upon all creaturely idolatries."[103] This much, Przywara

100. Przywara, *Vier Predigten,* 51.
101. Przywara, *Vier Predigten,* 52.
102. Przywara, *Vier Predigten,* 53.
103. Przywara, *Vier Predigten,* 53.

suggests, the Reformation got right, inasmuch as it echoed the verdicts of the prophets against the complacencies of the priesthood. "But," he goes on to say, "this in itself is not yet the [full] reality," for "the tragedy of the Reformation is that it believed at bottom in the God of judgment and not in the God of love, when in reality the God of judgment is already the God of love."[104] For "his fire is a saving [*heimholendes*] fire; it is the fire that burns in order to burn us into itself [*hineinzubrennen in sich*]."[105] In other words, Przywara thinks, the theologies of the Reformation (epitomized by Luther or Calvin) ultimately halved the mystery of God, separating the sovereignty of the divine will (in which they presumed to locate God's glory) from the divine nature as love (manifested in Christ). The result was willy-nilly the fabrication of an idol comparable to human freedom, but divorced from any (essentially good) nature and extended to infinity—an idol whose "glory" is identified not so much with God's love in Christ as with the sovereign exercise of the power arbitrarily to condemn. This "God," too, therefore, the "God" of the Reformation, was destined for judgment:

> Before the God who alone is God—*Deus solus*—and who is incomparable with creaturely analogies, all the idols that result from confusing God with order or movement, with an absolute stasis or an absolute dynamic, are shattered. . . . He is the fire of judgment upon the absolutization of order and the absolutization of movement, but precisely as such the God of love, who is above all and before all: God alone is love.[106]

For Przywara, then, God is neither the absolutization of static order nor the absolutization of dynamic movement, neither the absolutization of unchanging essence nor the absolutization of ever-changing existence; in short, he is neither the God of the *sacrum imperium* nor the God of the Reformation, neither the God of Parmenides nor the God of Heraclitus. Rather, he is the God of *love*, who ever again confounds the ideologues of (traditional) order and (revolutionary) movement, who would posit one or the other as absolute, by wondrously manifesting the glorious unity—indeed identity—of order and movement, essence and existence, the fire of love and the fire of judgment, in the cross of Christ:

> To use the sharp words of St. Paul, order and movement, stasis and dynamis, amount [in and of themselves] to an "*evacuatio crucis*"; they posit an ideal order or an ideal movement in

104. Przywara, *Vier Predigten*, 53.
105. Przywara, *Vier Predigten*, 53.
106. Przywara, *Vier Predigten*, 53f.

opposition to the crossbeams of the Cross, thereby emptying the Cross into a mistaken and deceptive idealism. But in its true sense the Cross is nothing other than the manifestation [*Aufgehen*] of glory: "The Son of man must be lifted up on the Cross in order to draw all to himself." And the Cross is itself the exaltation. From the Cross resound the seven words of the Lord as the creative words of the new creation, of the new heaven and the new earth, and so the Cross is the glory: "*fulget crucis mysterium*," the mystery of the Cross as the fulguration of glory.[107]

Here, then, for Przywara, is the God in whom we are to believe: the God who has appeared in the Cross, "which is at once a *scandalum* and *excessus*," a stumbling block, but also the site of glorious excess.

Finally, the apocalypse of this hour is an apocalypse of the Holy Spirit, and so, just as Przywara sees in God's apocalypse the revelation of the unity of the fire of judgment and love expressed in the scandal of the glory of the Cross, now he speaks of the spiritual fire of fullness and emptiness—of "God as the 'pleroma,' 'the fullness of all in all,' but a fullness that is fulfilled only when it has become nothing [*zum Nichts geworden ist*]." In this connection Przywara alludes to Christ's cleansing of the temple as an image of the cleansing fire of the Spirit, and to the pure in heart, in whom God flows as infinite fullness. Thus, however painful, the apocalyptic fire of judgment, for individuals or for nations, is ultimately good news: judgment is not for the sake of judgment, whether of individuals or nations, but for the sake of the edification of the whole of creation as a cosmic dwelling of God's Spirit. What is absolute therefore, Przywara now reiterates, but with greater justification in view of the real end, is neither the idolatry of a static order "that refuses to become nothing, seeking instead to be in itself a perpetual completion" (by which he means a Catholic traditionalism that idolizes the *sacrum imperium*), nor the kind of specifically modern idolatry that "Satanically confuses God with a dynamic judgment and seeks to capture the living God in the formula of a creaturely movement" (by which he means the Reformation), but rather "God all in all" (1 Cor 15:28).[108] For as the idols are broken in his apocalypse,

107. Przywara, *Vier Predigten*, 54. There is, one suspects, a double entendre here in the word "Aufgehen," since it can mean both going up or rising, as in the dawning of the sun, as well as a being used up without remainder, felicitously uniting the Christological sense of a going up as a going down.

108. Although it is a general typology and as such subject to any number of qualifications, Przywara's critique of the religion of the Middle Ages (with its tendency to idolize the political order of the *sacrum imperium*) and of the religion of the Reformation (with its idolatrous celebration of divine judgment as the *ne plus ultra*) bears countless implications, indicting *eo ipso* the idolization of any religious or political order or any

God arises as the *teleiosis*—the end and seal [of all things]—in the Holy Spirit: God as the Creator Spirit, who hovers over the nothingness [*dem Nichts*] of the beginning and brings about the plenitude of heaven and earth; God as the Creator Spirit, who hovers over the nothingness of the collapsing old covenant and brings about the fullness of the new covenant: Christ all in all; God as the Creator Spirit, who hovers now especially over the nothingness of the Christian West, which we intensely feel, in order that a Christian world of unanticipated fullness, extending over every part of the earth, might arise: a truly cosmic God who is "all in all."[109]

Such is Przywara's message in this apocalyptic hour, which remains, perhaps, our hour today. In the twilight of the idols of antiquity (including the Middle Ages) and modernity, he hopes we can begin to appreciate what God really means. For then, and then alone, we might be ready to talk about a new order, which is grounded entirely in God's will, and a new movement, which is a being moved entirely by God [*Durchwogtsein ganz von Gott her*], immersed in and moved along by the flowing of the divine sea. In other words, Przywara thinks, we need to understand order and movement anew—not in isolation but together—entirely from God: "For orders may come and movements may come, but none is more adventitious [*kommender*], none is more worthy of hope [*erhoffter*], none more worthy of belief and love, than when room has been made in purified souls for the true God."[110] And so he concludes his sermons with hope in

a new world that this God might bestow on us, with a sense that the earthquake that is now shaking us is a Pentecostal earthquake, and in a new substance of the Christian West—that it might now become the yeast of the whole world: that the Christian West might now become in truth an *"instrumentum redemptionis,"* an instrument of redemption, precisely when in what would appear to be its final hour. For in death we are redeemed, by his death Christ redeemed us, the sacrifice of the mass is a mystery of death; in death the Church is Co-redemptrix of humanity with Christ. And if the West is now also worthy of dying, then it is also worthy of its Good Friday, and one can already hear the sounds of the Easter bells of an Easter morning of the whole world, in which the resurrected body of Christ will be resurrected with its Head, the resurrected *Civitas Dei*, the

religious or political movement.

109. Przywara, *Vier Predigten*, 55.

110. Przywara, *Vier Predigten*, 56.

resurrected cosmic [*sacrum*] *imperium*, the resurrected divine cosmos. Then we will bend the knee before the God . . . who is God yesterday, today, and in all eternity, who "called light out of darkness who has shone in our hearts to enlighten us with the knowledge of the glory of God in the face of Jesus Christ" (2 Cor. 4:6).[111]

Conclusion: An Apocalyptic Metaphysics

What then, finally, is the relationship between metaphysics and apocalypse? It is not that the latter is judged by the former; it is rather that the former is judged by the latter, and along with it all metaphysical idols that would absolutize one or another aspect of creaturely being, be it reason or freedom, order or movement, essence or existence. But does this spell the end of metaphysics? No, it simply delimits the metaphysical possibilities to a metaphysics that is open to revelation and capable of being informed by it. Which leaves in the end only one kind of metaphysics, namely, the kind of metaphysics to which Przywara unwaveringly subscribed: an analogical metaphysics of reason and freedom, order and movement, being and becoming, essence and existence, with each pair pointing inexorably beyond itself to the ever-greater God who is their inscrutable identity, *Eternal Life*, and who appears in his apocalypse—in the fire of judgment and love, and in the seeming nothingness that is really everything, and in the apparent obscurity that is really the light of the world—in the face of Jesus Christ. Thus, just when all looks dark over the West, and even God himself seems absent, eliciting widespread atheism and unbelief, Przywara concludes his sermons with a word of hope in this apparently final hour: "'*Fiat lux Deus!*' Let there be light, the light that God himself is. Amen."

Bibliography

Gonzales, Philip. *Reimagining the Analogia Entis: The Future of Erich Przywara's Christian Vision*. Grand Rapids: Eerdmans, 2019.

Gregory, Brad. *The Unintended Reformation: How a Religious Revolution Secularized Society*. Cambridge, MA: Belknap, 2015.

Lochbrunner, Manfred. *Hans Urs von Balthasar und seine Theologenkollegen*. Würzburg: Echter, 2009.

O'Regan, Cyril. *Anatomy of Misremembering: Von Balthasar's Response to Philosophical Modernity. Volume 1: Hegel*. Chestnut Ridge, NY: Crossroad, 2014.

111. Przywara, *Vier Predigten*, 56.

Przywara, Erich. *Alter und Neuer Bund: Theologie der Stunde*. Vienna: Herold, 1956.
———. *Crucis Mysterium: Das Christliche Heute*. Paderborn: Schöningh, 1939.
———. *Vier Predigten über das Abendland*. Einsiedeln: Johannes, 1948.
Walther, Gerda. *Zum anderen Ufer: Vom Marxismus und Atheismus zum Christentum*. Remagen: Reichl, 1960.

7

The Heart's Spectacular Silence
Time and Memory in Paul Ricoeur and Cyril O'Regan

CAITLIN SMITH GILSON

"It is fearful how God randomly scatters the living, and how very far."

—Friedrich Hölderlin, "Patmos"[1]

"Truth predicts the eclipse of truth, and in that eclipse it condemns man."

—Jack Clemo, "On the Death of Karl Barth"[2]

On an unremarked and unremarkable speck of land, washed by sunlight on water, and bruised by shadow at night, the words of St. John's Book of Revelation came to be. Everything remarkable begins in the incredible,[3] in the Patmos of the soul, unblemished either by time or memory, in order to

1. Hölderlin, "Patmos," in *Poems*, 42.

2. Clemo, "On the Death of Karl Barth," in Davie, *Christian Verse*, 291.

3. Cf. Augustine, *City of God*, 22.5: "It is incredible that Christ should have risen in His flesh and, with His flesh, have ascended into heaven; it is incredible that the world should have believed a thing so incredible; it is incredible that men so rude and lowly, so few and unaccomplished, should have convinced the world, including men of learning, of something so incredible and have convinced men so conclusively."

be the bearer of time and memory. This is that "irony of eternal things," that "predestined intuition," that "contentment in finitude" of which Santayana spoke[4] but which he could never decipher, and which Cyril O'Regan and Paul Ricoeur have sought to meditate on, elucidate, and clarify. The enigma of Being does not block understanding but rather provokes it.[5]

The Patmos Soul: Abiding by the Origin

A comparison of the spaces of convergence between Cyril O'Regan and Paul Ricoeur would fail from the outset if it sought a merely topographical harmony, not because of a lack of solid convergence but because the source of union would have been bypassed, overlooked in favor of a confined ratiocination of effects, ideas, and concepts. What unites and yet differentiates them is their consistent adherence to the beginning, remaining always within the Christ-event as the exegesis of their work unfolds.[6] And it is why they possess the ability to withstand and overcome the substitutional forms of meaning that evoke, while degrading, the Christian impetus.[7] Their work codifies the uneasy reality that truth predicts the eclipse of truth, and that in that eclipse none can escape its eviction. Only the truth that incarnates meaning can survive. This originary endeavor is not a mere historico-chronological beginning, but the beginning of the moment beyond history when everything in history is taken up and apocalyptically shaped by an

---

4. Santayana, *Soliloquies*, 2–3.

5. Ricoeur, *Freud and Philosophy*, 18.

6. Balthasar, *Razing the Bastions*, 34–35: "To honor the tradition does not excuse one from the obligation of beginning everything from the beginning each time, not with Augustine or Thomas or Newman, but with Christ. And the greatest figures of Christian salvation history are honored only by the one who does today what they did then, or what they would have done if they had lived today. The cross-check is quickly done, and it shows the tremendous impoverishment, not only in spirit and life, but also quite existentially: in thoughts and points of view, themes and ideas, where people are content to understand tradition as the handing-on of readymade results. Boredom manifests itself at once, and the neatest systematics fails to convince, remains of little consequence. The little groups of those who have come to an understanding with one another and cultivate what they take to be the tradition become more and more esoteric, foreign to the world, and more and more misunderstood, although they do not condescend to take notice of their alienation. And one day the storm that blows the dried-up branch away can no longer be delayed, and this collapse will not be great, because what collapses had been a hollow shell for a very long time."

7. O'Regan, *Theology and the Spaces of Apocalyptic*, 106: "Revelation represents the continuation of the prophetic tradition rather than its overcoming[;] . . . if apocalyptic is a legitimate Christian discourse, then it is taken up within the Christian theological tradition, which re-expresses it within the ambit of interpretation."

end that is sensuous, abysmal, immemorial, and inescapable, even and especially as it is denied.

Evidence of their shared mindful beginning resides in the fact that
their meditations proceed as Christ proceeds: into the All, the particular, the
myriad, the meandering, the restless, the deadly, the salvific.[8] As such, both
acknowledge that rare *chorismos*—breaking point, gap, *differance*—inherent in the startling, revelatory forms of meditation. Abiding by the Christo-
eschaton involves a beginning that not only can never be exhausted, but
also converts all meditations from an empirical reflection to those shaped
by that beginning in its *hereness*; and yet because it has always happened,
because the mystery refuses temporal reduction in order to be disclosive, it
has never merely "occurred."[9] This is the chase into language which defines
wisdom as surely as it eludes capture. This is the love that is authentically
self-intoxicating because it begins in the immanent alterity of the True and
the Beautiful. Both Ricoeur and O'Regan understand the natureless-nature
of this immemorially entrenched starting point, and a tracing of their work
invites us into that Patmos of the soul where revelation is stamped and en-
graved. The danger of such a drive to remember and reenact the beginning
requires precision, rigor, clarity, and endurance. The same sensuousness
that draws one to the Christ-event triggers the imitative and overtly sensuous Gnostic heterodoxies,[10] which, among other things, reduce revelation to
the philosophical faith of a Jaspers[11] and into the imaginative register of, for
example, a Valentinus or a Jacob Boehme.[12]

8. See in particular Ricoeur's passion narratives, which dwell on the limits of the se-
miotics of narrative to express adequately the plurivocity of the Christ-event. Ricoeur,
Figuring the Sacred,189–90.

9. This indeed is why Hegel permeates all post-modern theological movements and
why his specter precedes even himself historically. And it is why, for example, someone
like Voegelin is wary of the Pauline vision of the resurrected, because the Christo-
eschaton's temporalizing non-temporality appears too encompassing, too dramatic for
its own good, so much so that history cannot emancipate itself from the movement of
Christ. Cf. Voegelin, *The Ecumenic Age*, ch. 5. History cannot indeed emancipate itself
from Christ, the incarnation secures this reality while the Trinity secures it beyond
time. Thus, to call a thinker originary, indeed genuinely apocalyptic, means that he or
she has understood how historical thinking is as much ahistorical as it is in time. This
requires that any programmatic tracing returns us to the origins in a way Heidegger
suspected but could never accept.

10. Cf. Gilson, "The Dilution of the Agonic Need: Jaspers and Voegelin," in *The
Philosophical Question of Christ*, 102–6.

11. Cf. Jaspers, *Philosophic Faith and Revelation*.

12. For a larger, more detailed discussion of this inversion of theological categories
of revelation, Cf. O'Regan, *Gnostic Apocalypse*.

This unity within the beginning-which-endures-and-transforms also differentiates O'Regan's and Ricoeur's enterprises, because true unity is always *chorismos*; it casts the thinker into the region of the unrepeatable so as to witness the remarkably unremarked, to trace the minutiae as the brilliance of the divine. What holds true is that both think Christ in the revelatory way of the beginning and moreover achieve this in the presence of the abandonment and disillusion of the post-modern context. Both navigate the error as well as the creeping wisdom of the ancient Gnostic soul endlessly merging with the ghost in the machine to form the techno-Gnosticism anticipated by Hegel, where the absolutism of ego promises its unfettered end in a secular apocalypse:

> It is precisely the similarity of Hegelian apocalypse to the genuine biblical form that makes Hegel a dangerous thinker for Christianity. Hegel does not forget, he misremembers. The misremembering is structural and displays itself in the way in which the biblical narrative is subjected to torque in which the meaning of each and every episode of the drama of love, creation, incarnation, redemption, sanctification, and eschaton are changed, and other practices and forms of life substituted for determinately Christian ones. Hegel generates a *doppelgänger* that recalls only to distort what the common tradition has felt to be the community reading and reception of scripture.[13]

And with Ricoeur:

> All that is lacking is the speculative dimension announced by Novalis, proclaiming that "history produces itself." Hegel's text on "Reason in History" crowns this conceptual epic. It is under the aegis of the dialectic of the objective spirit that the pact between the rational and the real is sealed, the pact that is said to be an expression of the highest idea of philosophy. At the same time, a certain distance is taken with respect to the ordinary historical discipline, which is reproached for dwelling in the house of the dead. In this, we must recognize our debt to Hegel for his critique of the abstract idea of a world that is no longer the power of life carried by the Spirit into the heart of the present. Something is announced here that will find a vehement outcome in Nietzsche's praise of life, and also in Heidegger's opposition between the having-been of the authentic past and the elapsed past that escapes our grasp. But neither can we allow to pass in silence, under the cover of Hegelian philosophy (in this, heir to the antitheological orientation of the Enlightenment

13. O'Regan, *Misremembering*, 516.

thinkers rather than to the Romantics), the birth of secular religion resulting from the equation between history and reason.
History *is* the development of spirit at the heart of humanity. . . .
It is by virtue of this kinship, and this substitution, that the idealist philosophy of history was able to rise above simple causal
analyses, integrate multiple temporalities, open itself to the future, or better, open a new future, and in this way reinterpret the
ancient *topos* of history, teacher of life, following the promises of
redemption spilling out upon humanity to come by the French
Revolution, the mother of all ruptures.[14]

Differentiating those substitute forms of apocalypse from Christ's, and then
clarifying redemption as it endures, are the essential gifts and forms of unity
between Ricoeur and O'Regan.

We will attempt to proceed from the rigor of their thinking, each
born from the incredible wisdom of Patmos. For the Patmos soul, the act of
knowledge involves an apex in turmoil, a culmination that requires, indeed
demands, a pushing past the limits of recognition, and into the thicket of
non-being: "We need to know what is the time (*kairos*) in which we live. It
is already the hour to awaken. . . . The night is almost over, and the dawn of
the day draws near."[15] This is the place where meaning can become ecstatic
and numinous because it has learned to wait, and by waiting it has stretched
into the manifold forms of memory which—while most dangerous, because
sensuously clinging to all and nothing—is where true wisdom and true harmony reside. Thus, to set out what is meant by remembering, recollection,
forgetting, amnesia, misremembering, and remembering *again*, but for the
first time, we will set out to accompany Ricoeur and O'Regan into the uncreated annihilatory basis of all incredibly credible meaning.

If the incredible guides the credible by the two-fold power of the
promise of a raised nature but also with its oft-ignored and always unseemly
incredulity, then it can be claimed that the rare greats of Christianity never
tread far from the underbelly of Being. Their forms of assent which cause in
us a vertiginous awe begin in, and never leave, a caressing of that original
incredulity. And while a Christian can mouth the words that the figure of
Christ gains and never loses, when up against the scathing heartache of a
Nietzsche or an Ivan Karamazov, it takes those who have lain with the incredulity to take hold of how much has actually been gained. Those fearful of a
bedfellow like Hegel either ignore or mount the usual rejection or find everything conveniently reduced into some form of sublation or another. This

14. Ricoeur, *Memory, History and Forgetting*, 300–301.
15. Rom 13:11–12 (DV).

refusal to confront the ruthless incredulity is not a strange image peculiar to stranger prisoners[16] but the common denominator in much of Christian philosophy. Not only unable to comprehend the monstrous symbiosis at work between the Hegelian architectonic and the Christian, we become unwilling to kneel before the spectacle and see its Beauty: to "test everything; and hold fast what is good [*kalon*]."[17]

Hegel & the Apocalyptic Actors

No one Evangelist would have sufficed
To tell us of the pains of Jesus Christ,
Nor does each tell it as the others do;
Nevertheless, what each has said is true . . .[18]

Absolute testimony . . . in concrete singularity gives a caution to the truth without which its authority remains in suspense. Testimony, each time singular, confers the sanction of reality on ideas, ideals, and modes of being that the symbol depicts and discovers for us only as our most personal possibilities.[19]

Christ is the always impossible, freely given, and utterly necessary reality, and it is this origin that O'Regan and Ricoeur never leave, and it is why their thinking can be termed *active* and *acting*. Speculative thinking—as exemplified in Hegel—bonds itself to the reciprocity of the idea to the point of a gradual and then sudden disavowal of the extramental reality as disclosive. As ideational, it is oddly unable to achieve immateriality,[20] becoming more or less an advocate for materialism and rationalism. But thinking which acts upon, in, and guided by the origin which precedes all pattern in order *to be* the pattern, requires a different expression. Thinking

16. Cf. Plato, *The Republic*, 515a in *Plato: Complete Works*.
17. 1 Thess 5:21
18. Chaucer, *The Canterbury Tales*, 184.
19. Ricoeur, *Essays on Biblical Interpretation*, 122.
20. St. Thomas Aquinas, *Summa Theologiae*, I, 84, 2, resp.

out the spaces of apocalyptic[21] is more closely an *action*,[22] an achieving of event-fullness in likening power to the Christ-event itself. This thoughtful *acting-in-the-Christ-event* sounds a commonplace truism for any scholarship in Christian theology. But it is a rare and exotic meditation. It is the question Ricoeur consistently asked: "How is the will affected in its most intimate desire by the representation of this [Christological] model, this archetype of a humanity agreeable to God, which the believer calls the Son of God?"[23] And it is the fulcrum gift of the *Anatomy of Misremembering* that reveals the coalescing specter of Hegelian pneumatic displacement as lacking "the essential conditions that make drama possible: dialogue between two personal centers of freedom (divine and human)."[24] To remain imbedded within the Christ-presence is precisely what constitutes the apocalyptic *activity* of O'Regan and Ricoeur and it irrevocably differentiates them from Hegel. They remain within the presence, even and especially as this Event hurtles outward into regions of Hegelian post-modernity and through the shades of a Gnostic substitutional apocalyptic.

Differentiating the Hegelian move from the apocalyptic adherence to the Christ-event requires recovering several footholds within the revelatory spaces to which we belong:

21. Cf. O'Regan *Theology and the Spaces of Apocalyptic*, 26: "When it comes to forms of apocalyptic, instead of speaking of types, which tends to repress rather than exhibit the plurality of apocalyptic discourses, I prefer the metaphorics of space. Here 'space' is better understood in terms of mechanics than geometry: it indicates fields of force that attract some discourses and repel others. A space of apocalyptic suggests a constellation of discourses that bear close family resemblances to each other." O'Regan's shedding of "types" in favor of "spaces" is such an example of thinking recovering its more primal engagement as *act*. This differentiation also attests to the failure to unite and differentiate key meanings and thinkers on primal ground, more often than not confining them to the phenomenal and apparential. The patois of an "interdisciplinary" approach has been thrown around so indiscriminately that it has become anemic at one end of the spectrum and pernicious at the other. It attempts to unite that which should already be united and ignores what cannot be unified precisely because it cannot touch the distinctions, having *already* misunderstood the nature of union. By ignoring the region of unity—the primordial *zuhandenheit*—such failed approaches connect ideas and meaning in the superficiality that Heidegger knew to be nothing more than ontically designated presences-at-hand. The *chorismos* of meaning becomes the vortex of onticity.

22. Cf. Pegis, *Introduction to St. Thomas Aquinas*, xxiv, for a companion sentiment: "Modern man indeed became a thinker only after he had ruined himself as a knower." See also, Leahy, *Beyond Sovereignty*, 23–24.

23. Ricoeur, *The Conflict of Interpretations*, 345.

24. O'Regan, *Misremembering*, 522–23.

1. Recovering the temporality of the Christ-event. This is critical to distinguishing those surrogate forms of apocalyptic thinking from those that truly abide by the origin; this indeed requires understanding the crucial distinction between historicism and historical meaning.[25]

2. Revealing how Hegel's monophysitism is a symptom of pernicious adjustments to the Christ-event through an altering of both its temporality and its memory.[26] Hegelian Christianity attempts to subsume and re-appropriate what Ricoeur called Christ's "antinomic anthropology"[27] While the God-Man unites the two natures without abolishing the distinction, Hegel's unity is a conflation enabling the finite to be the sole intelligibility of infinite meaning, because it *is* infinite meaning.[28]

3. Reviving the memorial meaning attached to apocalyptic temporality. This temporality makes a plaything of memory as Ricoeur and O'Regan have imagined. By plaything, we do not mean something flippant but rather meaning as stable *because* it is in play, something that exhausts the imagination so as to be at the origins of the *sacred*. We are reminded here of Platonic sense of *sacra*,[29] originating in the

---

25. Cf. Taylor, *The Faith of a Moralist*, II, 14; Taylor, *The Problem of Conduct*, 428.

26. O'Regan, *Misremembering*, 194: "In any event, at no point in principle or in fact does Hegel support a Chalcedonian view of Christ. Rather, his Christology is thoroughly monophysite with the 'from above' aspect matching seamlessly with the 'from below': Christ is the divine precisely *as* human, the human precisely *as* the divine. But this implies, as already suggested, the replacement of the properly morphological understanding of Kenosis by an essentialist form, and inscribes Christology in a completion dynamic in which Christ is reduced to being an instrument of divine self-realization. To accuse Hegel of monophysitism seems quite odd in a situation in which Balthasar also accuses Hegel of evacuating Christology altogether by reducing Christ to a function of 'otherness' equally served by the world of nature and finite spirit. Balthasar, however, believes that Christological evacuation and monophysitism are two sides of the same coin. Given the dialectical nature of Hegel's thought, one can focus on either the compromise to the finite or the infinite effected in making the finite a function of the infinite." This is, indeed, why historicism and absolutism can be married in the Hegelian *Geist*.

27. Ricoeur, *Figuring the Sacred*, 206.

28. Severed from its hypostatic identity as antinomic, as uniting what consciousness cannot unite, the God-Man is then reoriented in consciousness as a reductively monophysitic entity. In this devolution, the Christology does what it cannot and should not do: it puts into an ideational sequence a teleological blueprint from nature to a perfection man can craft with his own powers, all the while rendering Christ irrelevant. This is Hegel's error, and it is found oddly hidden beneath much of speculative theology.

29. Cf. Plato, *Laws*, VII 803 in *Plato: Complete Works*.

seriousness of play, as much as play can only be enacted by what is designated as the space of the sacred.[30]

The tempting tendency to separate Christ from the implications of the God-Man is not only a question of a deleterious suppression of one of the two natures, but a programmatic dissimilation of revelation from the incommunicable, the spiritual from the ethical. More than that, it is a separation from the very meaning of temporality as it is impressed upon each being. It is also the darkest and most abysmal power of all secular appetite, for it is historicism having misplaced history as a series of past events and thus condemned all actors to that past which has no meaning other than what the present gives it, which can have no meaning other than impermanence. Christ may be permitted as a figure *in* time as God is *out* of time, but neither is the figuring of incarnate meaning, for the incarnation as a summing up, as an *apokálypsis*, is rendered impossible, for nothing can be disclosive except the ego in Hegel's sense. For O'Regan, nuancing Balthasar, the prime failure of Gnosticism is its pandemic inability to recognize Christ as the God-Man:

> [T]his failure is accompanied by an arrogant presumption of knowing that can safely by-pass the straightforward deliverances of scripture and tradition. Indeed, the presumption authorizes tendentious interpretations of the biblical narrative that run just the opposite direction to the community interpretation and the community's rules for interpretation. Balthasar records with approval Irenaeus' objections to the Gnostic separation of the demiurge from the unknowable transcendent divine and the separation of Christ from the law-giver of Genesis, and affirms Irenaeus' energetic defense of the biblical God as being both mysterious and creative, at once a God of justice and love. . . . Crucial to any defense against historical Gnosticism, or its return in modernity, is a dramatic Christology of the kind elaborated by Irenaeus. As the divine-human who suffers and dies on our behalf, and who expresses God's love, Christ is the center of the drama of salvation history. Indeed, Christ represents the "summing up" or *anakephalaiosis* of all history.[31]

Gnosticism finds its new domain in Hegel, who then remakes what it could not originally incorporate—that *anakephalaiosis* of all history. The Christ-event is intoxicatingly misremembered in Hegel's triadically directed dialectic that carries out a sublation into the Spirit, which is itself non-emancipated from existence. Existence is the totality of the Spirit

30. Cf. Huizinga, *Homo Ludens*.

31. O'Regan, *Misremembering*, 83–84.

which first manifested itself imperfectly in the finite as symbolic and out-ward. The *Geist*, therefore, does not call forth another Other outside the finite but reveals, in the sublation of the thesis and antithesis, that the finite *is* the non-emancipated Absolute. There can be no contrary but the active contrariety of the *Geist*, which has no Other because it is consciousness in the totality of itself. It is "pure" in the modern sense. This is historicism with all its claims of finitude and limitation merging with the absolutisms that disregard the finite as but manifestations of an ideational whole.[32] When the Christ-event is read this way, Christ is but a vacant particular as much as he is an elusive absolute. His particularity and absolutivity have been trans-ferred into the non-contrariety of the *Geist*, thus rendering Christ nothing more than nothing. This is not a forgetting of Christ but a misremembering of his nature so as to enable existence to act as if it can bypass or manage the implications.[33] But for those faithful to the true apocalyptic summing-up,

---

32. Ricoeur, echoing Louis Mink, speaks of this conflating of time and eternity as the very exegesis of all comprehension. Such a form of comprehension is a prime refer-ence to our fall *into* knowledge and *away* from meaning, as well as being part of the *natural* hierarchical claims of all knowledge and action. This is thus suggestive of both the utter nearness of the Hegelian project to genuine apocalyptic Christianity as well as its ruthless difference. Cf. Ricoeur, *Time and Narrative*, 1:159–60: "Comprehension in the broad sense presents one fundamental feature that has important implications for the narrative mode of comprehension. All comprehension, as Mink declares, has an ideal aim, even if it is unattainable, of comprehending the world as a *totality*. To put it another way, this goal is unattainable because it would amount to divine comprehen-sion; yet it is significant because 'the human project is to take God's place.' This sudden intrusion of a theological theme is in no way marginal. The alleged ultimate goal of the three modes of comprehension proceeds from a transposition of Boethius's definition of 'God's knowledge of the world as a *totum simul*, in which the successive movements of all time are copresent in a single perception, as a landscape of events.'"

33. O'Regan's recognition of the abandonment of the Christ presence, not as a for-getting but as a misremembering, can be seen in the arguments surrounding even and especially abortion. Christ's presence requires, indeed demands, a subordination of all things to his presence as *anakephalaiosis*. This "summing up" is the prime metaphysical undercurrent of the scandal of the incarnation and the meta-temporal dictate of its es-chatology as understood in the Pauline vision of the resurrected. The creeping modern variants of Gnosticism can be seen in the debates over life precisely because what is lost is the fact that all ethical questions must be subordinated to the presence as spiritual, as creative and incommunicable. Indeed, when abortion became an *ethical* problem the arguments for life were deeply infirmed precisely because *how* it is to be an advocacy for life functioned on a misremembering. By originating only or primarily as an ethical problem—and with the pernicious Gnostic strain of reference to God but a one aimed more so at deviation and bypass—the questions over life bogged down into biological, scientific, and legal statutes which, again, can only pay lip-service to Christ. By begin-ning the argument for life in the ethical, the ethical realm is improperly emancipated from its subordination to the spiritual dimension of Christ and then pressed to argue for a totality of meaning which it cannot possess. Pro-life advocacy sought for an eerily

the Event becomes what it always was, and thus evolves. While refusing to
be anything other, it thus precedes every evolution.

> The immemorial past in some way underlies the present of
> revelation, and if I may put it this way, the future of the expecta-
> tion of the kingdom, rather than being before the present of the
> one and the future of the other. We move beyond all narrative
> linearity; or if we can still speak of narration, this would be a
> narration that will have broken with all chronology. As for the
> present of revelation, the today of the jubilation of the lover and
> the beloved, the today of the commandment "Love me," is not a
> present that passes, merely serving as a transition between the
> future of expectation and the past of memory.[34]

O'Regan and Ricoeur are apocalyptic *actors*, not only because, as in
O'Regan, there is a programmatic tracing of the kenomatic and pleromatic
apocalyptic strands,[35] but because their thought is always and actively
mindful of the beyond-history sensuousness of the Christ-presence. Any
misstep within this apocalyptically immemorial ground has the making of
historicism or absolutism or, most critically, the historicist absolutism of
Hegel, altogether becoming the interlocked temporal manifestations of all
Gnostic movement. The "sensuous representation of the Absolute itself"[36] is,
for Hegel, "handicapped by its abstract and unyielding Catholic principle"[37]
which prevents the faithful from recognizing that the real power of the
Christian *mythos* is in its being an expression of the synthetic inwardness of
the *Geist*. The Christ-event's true handicap seduces the human person into
redirecting that inwardness of consciousness onto a distracted and erotic
form of the antithesis where the Absolute as truly Other is an emancipatory
power *bringing out* a perfection in us that we ourselves cannot cultivate. The
moment we recognize Christ to be *the* expression of the Absolute, distinct
from any Hegelian immanentized mediation of the Absolute as historical
consciousness, Hegel's project has failed.

> Hegel's own emphasis is upon the work of Christ rather than
> his person, an emphasis that makes Hegel impatient with the
> ontological modes of Christological discourse. In a move that

---

similar Hegelian program to absolutize its points precisely because it had deviated from
the only absolute that can be concrete, particular, and creative: the only mystery to
invoke clarity.

34. Ricoeur, *Figuring the Sacred*, 103.

35. O'Regan, *Theology and the Spaces Apocalyptic*, 15–60.

36. Hegel, *On Art, Religion, and the History of Philosophy*, 103.

37. Hegel, *The Philosophy of Fine Art*, 272.

smacks more of the early than of the later Luther, and not at all of Lutheran orthodoxy, Hegel shows a particular impatience with the two nature/one person classical and conciliar view of Christ. Hegel is as clear in ["The Spirit of Christianity and Its Fate"], as he will be in *PS*, that the historical Jesus must be surpassed in the Christ of faith, the Christ that is appropriated in Spirit.[38]

Christ intrudes on historical thought, gets in its way, and while for Hegel, he must accordingly be reduced, absorbed, ignored, or rejected,[39] for the true apocalyptic *actor*, this intrusion is the only meaning worthy of life: it is a holy non-sequitur reminding us of the inescapability of the origin. Everything written begins and ends with him but *does not* add up to him—this is the true insight of the *anakephalaiosis*, the summing up of the all into Christ.

One cannot step outside of the Triune Christ-event, for any mistaken sense of exiting the presence misses it altogether and ushers in, pervasively and suddenly, an almost metaleptic identification of Christianity: the infirmed idea of Christ spoken "outside" the presence, which can never be done, creates an alter-reality, a whole nuanced lineage, dark and deep, further infirming the Christianity in which it dwells. The human existent has the natural tendency to separate from the world in order to gain the requisite distance for a knowing and recollective *point de vantage*. Some of this is from its nature as a reasoning being, which requires the step back out of the metaxic flux. Yet this step back, acted out in a fallen world, perverts the order of the authentic step back insofar as it conditions the soul to believe it can only be a step outside the world that captures the eternal. But it only "captures" the vacant "now" and never the *hereness*. Thus, we are enticed by our nature to step back in order to know and love, while our condition sterilizes that knowledge and infirms our love by placing us in a deontological void where only aseity leads us, masquerading as alterity. The step back is required and yet it cannot be genuine if it affirms the general, individual, and ideational over, above, and prior to the specific, personal, and incarnate, for then neither is present and only convention remains, and that only for an historical while. If we are primordially the other before we are reflexively "I"—because our selfhood is bound up in our constitution as the other of the uncreated—then the step back is not directed by our status as *ego* but as *other*. When the noetic distance is actualized under the misconstrued priority of ego over *otherness*, it places us outside the world and disengages

---

38. O'Regan, *The Heterodox Hegel*, 191.

39. Cf. Gilson, *The Philosophical Question of Christ*, xi–xxvi.

us from immediacy because it attempts to make what is secondary—the
I—have the *Actus* of the primary. And this was Hegel's error.[40] Ricoeur in-
terrogatively lifts the veil:

> But under what condition is this other not just a reduplication of
> myself—another myself, an alter ego—but genuinely an other,
> other than myself? In this regard, the reflexivity from which
> self-esteem proceeds remains abstract, in the sense that it does
> not mark the difference between me and you.[41]

And because the I is dependent on our original and continuing union in
our contact with the uncreated which renders us its other, when we make
the ego primary we reinvest that dependency on things that cannot assimilate us. And this is the underlying metaphysics of the Gnostic error.[42] We
make the world dead and inert and in doing so we mute the obediential
potency of our open natures as entheotic, indeed engodded, as the central
metaphysical meaning of the Christ-event. This is the Hegelian apocalyptic
as deicidal, homicidal, suicidal, genocidal, and regicidal, precisely because
it has severed contact with the ground that assimilates the self and makes
it reflexively personal. And because this impersonal self cannot assimilate
itself as person, the deicidal, suicidal ego, in its heartrendingly rabid search
for personhood, attempts to have itself communicated by and through the
things of the world that have not the *Actus* to assimilate and constitute it
as person. Because lesser than the human soul, each is emptied of its con-
natural intelligibility. Not only is the intelligibility of the sensible world dismissed by this inverted priority, but the reflexive self is either destroyed or
indefinitely suspended. It becomes, in a word, a self without other, peering
outward, needing something to assimilate it and, finding nothing, closing
in on itself, destroying its own self-presence. The ruins of its open nature
reside in the graveyard of the world of ontical ladders. This ego does not
lie buried. It resurrects and soon plays a caricature game mimicking its lost
nature, assuming the roles of I and Other and, most perniciously, I and God.

Gnosticism, whether historicist or absolutist, or whether it crystallizes
in the unity of the two, is not simply a pinpointing of features, as O'Regan
flawlessly sets out.[43] Instead, it is an investigation into this primordial misstep where, because we cannot actually step outside of the Christ-event, this
undermining is always entrenched within. Any recovery from this misstep

40. Cf. Gilson, *Immediacy and Meaning*, 114–22.

41. Ricoeur, *Oneself as Another*, 181.

42. Cf. O'Regan, *The Gnostic Return in Modernity*, 242.

43. Cf. O'Regan, *Gnostic Apocalypse*.

is not only an isolation of problematic features but a relentless widening of vision to take in the movements where thought attempts to step outside the presence.

Acknowledging that we cannot step outside the Event cannot itself become a misremembering of the "remaining-within"—as being swept along the historicist tide. This stance is accentuated in Ricoeur's meditations on the meaning of testimony as a synonym for revelation in Christ. He who sees Christ sees with the eyes that originate the *apokalypsis*; he who hears Christ hears with the ears that enable the revelation. The witness is particular because particularized in Christ whom he witnesses, but what is witnessed is so inseparable from the Event—for the testimony is the revelation—that the absolute has truly become the meaning of the particular. This is the serious play of Christ's immemorial temporality, and it is what Hegel desires to sublate—a memorial act that is not merely a past event but an enactment of the absolute:

> Revelation 1:2 speaks of the testimony, "*marturia*," of Jesus Christ as a synonym for "revelation," *apokalupsis* of Jesus Christ. . . . The *exegesis* of God and the *testimony* of the Son are the same thing. . . . The notion of the eyewitness is thus profoundly overthrown by the dual theme of Christ—a faithful witness—and of testimony—testimony to the light. The two themes, moreover, are linked in that Christ, a faithful witness, has himself come "to render testimony." This is what the Johannine Christ declares before Pilate: "You say that I am a king. For this I was born, and for this I have come into the world, to bear witness to the truth." This *marturia ton ergon* on the part of Christ himself, makes testimony that is given to him not testimony to an idea, to an a-temporal *logos*, but to an incarnate person.[44]

The Hegelian dialectic is a meticulous reenactment of Christ's temporal presence. The lines of the play have been memorized without pause or hesitation, the stages have been carefully arranged so as to advance the dialogue and the event, appropriate costumes and embellishments decorate the narrative, but Hegel is unable to possess the meaning. Upon the stage of reenactment, Hegel has achieved only its evacuation. The very act of setting the stage, those embellishments carried over in the furthering of the dialectic, betrays in advance the possibility of such a possession—namely, of the *Geist* becoming revelatory in time.

Genuine apocalyptic meaning is *revelatory* precisely because it understands that each is called to witness for the first time what has occurred

---

44. Ricoeur, *Essays on Biblical Interpretation*, 137.

and is always occurring. The Event is both encompassing and immemorial, always the preceding cause even as it appears as the effect. God's uncreated cognition knows our actions "in advance" *because* they are acted out on his Being. But this is no process theology, because created action always occurs on the uncreated. This is why the unrepeatability of the historical fact resolves itself in the repeatability of the liturgical act; the *imitatio* of the priest resolves itself in the *repetitio* of the Mass.[45] Apocalyptic thinking—remaining within the Christ-event—also means that temporality is not solely in time, but in him as the preceding cause that enables mediation. With Ricoeur, recalling Augustine:

> Chronology—or chronography—does not have just one contrary, the a-chronology of laws or models, its true contrary is temporality itself. Indeed, it was necessary to confess what is other than time in order to be in a position to give full justice to human temporality and to propose not to abolish it but to probe deeper into it, to hierarchize it, and to unfold its following levels of temporalization that are less "distended" and more and more "held firmly," *non secundum distentionem sed secundum intentionem.*[46]

45. Cf. Cantalamessa, O.F.M. Cap, homily: "On the Cross, he defeated the ancient enemy. Our swords—exclaims Saint John Chrysostom—were not bloodied, we were not in agony, we were not wounded, we did not even see the battle and yet we obtain the victory. His was the fight, ours the crown. And because we are also the conquerors, let us imitate what soldiers do in such cases: with joyful voices let us exalt the victory, let us intone hymns of praise to the Lord! It is not possible to explain better the meaning of the liturgy we are celebrating. However, is what we are doing itself an image, a representation of a reality of the past, or is it the reality itself? It is both things! We–said Saint Augustine to the people—know and believe with very certain faith that Christ died only once for us. . . . You know perfectly that all that happened only once, and yet the solemnity renews it periodically. . . . Historical truth and liturgical solemnity are not opposed to one another, as if the second is fallacious and the first alone corresponds to the truth. In fact, of what history says occurred only once in reality, the solemnity repeatedly renews the celebration in the hearts of the faithful. The liturgy 'renews' the event: how many discussions have taken place for the past five centuries on the meaning of this word, especially when it is applied to the sacrifice of the Cross and to the Mass! Paul VI used a verb that could smooth the way to an ecumenical agreement on such an argument: the verb 'to represent,' understood in the strong sense of re-presenting, namely to render what happened again present and operative."

46. Ricoeur, *Time and Narrative*, 30. Additionally, the distinction here is not between the cosmological/cyclical temporality of the "pre-historical" compact societies on the one hand, and the Augustinian linearly directed movement of history on the other. I would argue in fact, with Ricoeur, that the ancient cyclical eternal return symbolization has far more in common with the Augustinian/Christian unrepeatability than either one has with the positivist linear successiveness or the Hegelian/historicist cyclical progressivity found in modernity.

When we act in time we act, in a way, from eternity, from our participation in the uncreated immediacy of Being, giving genuine gravitas to our
acts. True apocalyptic *acting* understands that to step outside the Event is
to cease genuine thinking in favor of some form of suppressive absolutism,
and remaining within would amount to the same misremembering if it is
conceived as a perspectival historicism. The apocalyptic *actor* also knows
that attempting to straddle both the *step-outside* and the *remaining-within*,
from the basis of consciousness, irreverent of consciousness *of*, carries a peculiar sensuousness blindingly near to Hegel. The way in which Christianity
straddles the within and the beyond—the memorial and immemorial—and
without trespassing its originary intelligibility, is frightful and often unap-
proached precisely because Hegel seizes upon a shared metaphysical under-
pinning. His radical monophysitism has cannibalized the impossible unity
that the God-Man offers between the memorial and the immemorial, the
particular and the universal, the finite and the infinite, the temporal and the
eternal. But, of course, Hegel has actively misremembered that only a God-
Man can unite these things because they *cannot* become *idea* but only the
incarnate activity one in Being with Christ. Hegel's nearness cannot simply
be discarded because, for the genuine apocalyptic *actor*, it has risen from the
very ground of all Christological movement.

> Since Hegel's best known theodicy assertions occur in the con-
> text of his reflection on history, it is natural to locate Hegel's
> thought in the context of previous salvation history models. But
> if the canvas is extended beyond that of history, and Hegelian
> ontotheology as a whole is taken into consideration, then the
> nature of Hegel's theodicy commitment is seen to be more com-
> plex. When Hegel makes a theodicy appeal . . . he seems to be
> speaking not simply of the divine march through history but of
> the encompassing narrative of the revelation of the divine with-
> in which the Christological moment is decisive. Too often Hegel
> scholars focus on Hegelian theodicy as reducible to his view of
> divine providence (*Vorsehung*), ignoring both metaphysical and
> quasi-metaphysical justifications which are there in Hegelian
> texts, plus the inclusive narrative frame within which historical
> activity is inserted.[47]

Hegel's monophysitism renders the Christ-event as testimony to the
Absolute rather than the absolute as subordinated to Christ. Man masks and
infirms the divine nature because, for the Hegelian, metaphysics can only
function in reason and not in revelation. In a ground where reason stands

---

47. O'Regan, *The Heterodox Hegel*, 446.

alienated from revelation, the human *pathos* can stand alienated from divine reality. Hegel misappropriates Christ's kenotic ardor as a sign of one of the stages to the Absolute and not as the Absolute itself, not as the terminus of the *Geist*.[48] Christ is the immemorial *eschaton* through which all events find their meaning. In order to appropriate such a reality into sublated and purely philosophical language, one has to step outside the event—*per impossible*—and suppress the apophatic criterion of immemoriality, effectively having it reduced to a product of consciousness:

> Hegel's Trinitarian eschatology is, of course, only one of many Christian counterfeits in history. . . . [It is as] systematic as it is captivating. Hegel is the most dangerous of friends, since he is convinced that, if only ultimately, knowledge is a match for all the dimensions of the divine-world relationship and their why. Moreover, at the level of subtext at least, the pivot of Hegel's thought is the cross as the Trinity provides the infinite dimensions. Hegel, however, overcomes the symbolic matrix of Christianity, deletes its apophatic element, alters the meaning of Christ, and provides an analysis of Trinity that not only dismisses any separation between ontological and economic Trinity, but also discounts a hypostatic interpretation of triunity, and insists that the trinitarian divine is one of self-becoming and self-development.[49]

Apocalyptic Temporality: Becoming God's Plaything

> God alone is worthy of supreme seriousness, but man is made God's plaything, and that is the best part of him. Therefore, every man and woman should live life accordingly, and play the noblest games, and be of another mind from what they are at present. For they deem war a serious thing, though in war there is neither play nor culture worthy the name, which are the things we deem most serious. Hence all must live in peace as well as they possibly can. What, then, is the right way of living? Life must be lived as play, playing certain games, making sacrifices, singing and dancing, and then a man will be able to

---

48. Cf. O'Regan, *The Heterodox Hegel*, 220–21: "Hegel's view [is] that the human *is* the alienated form of the divine and that suffering and death are nothing but the extreme of such alienation. Kenosis, here, consists not in a relative but an *absolute* masking of the divine, even if Hegel suggests that this masking itself is not fully definitive of the divine."

49. O'Regan, *Theology and the Spaces Apocalyptic*, 49.

propitiate the gods, and defend himself against his enemies, and win in the contest.[50]

It is certainly a lot to be an apocalyptic *actor*, to recognize the entrenched missteps, never to step outside the event and yet remain within the Event in a way unlike any other human maintenance. Beckett said it best:

> It's a lot to expect of one creature . . . that he should first behave as if he were not, then as if he were, before being admitted to that peace where he neither is, nor is not, and where the language dies that permits of such expressions.[51]

This temporality—this *acting* on the horizon between time and eternity[52]— has certainly made a plaything of memory and identity, exhausting consciousness so as to be the bearer of the sacred. This *confinium* makes the Christ-event present to us as much as absent, renders all confirmation a risk, and enables all risk to rest on an enduring and elusive form of certainty. In concert with O'Regan:

> Now, for Balthasar, it must be granted that this God does not appear always to be an effective presence in our individual lives or to be manifest in what James Joyce refers to in *Finnegans Wake* as the "nightmare of history." . . . [H]ope lies in the cross, in God's presence in Christ on Holy Saturday in which Christ identifies with the dead. The presence is real if mysterious and grounds us in our journey towards the eschaton.[53]

One can recognize the tension between the absent-and-present God in its surrogate forms in the Hegelian informed *Monstrosity of Christ*[54] in which Žižek defends and attempts to resurrect the "God is dead" theological movement most notably envisioned by Thomas Altizer in the mid to late 60s. Altizer's landmark *The Gospel of Christian Atheism*,[55] which, among other things, posits that God Himself died as Christ died on the

---

50. Plato, *Laws* VII 803.

51. Beckett, "The Unnamable," in *Three Novels*, 328.

52. Cf. St. Thomas Aquinas, *Summa Contra Gentiles*, II, 80; III, 61; II, 68: Man, by virtue of his intellectual soul stands on the borderline, "the horizon or confinium between eternity and time." St. Thomas stresses this point throughout his works emphasizing that the soul is shown to hold the highest spot in embodiment and the lowest in the spiritual life. See also St. Thomas Aquinas, *Disputed Questions on Truth*, X, 8 *resp.*

53. O'Regan, *Misremembering*, 453.

54. Žižek, "The Fear of Four Words: A Modest Plea for the Hegelian Reading of Christianity," in Milbank and Žižek, *The Monstrosity of Christ*, 24–109.

55. Altizer, *The Gospel of Christian Atheism*.

Cross, proceeds to evacuate the transcendence of God, replacing it with an evolutionary secularized community of believers embracing a Holy Spirit not dissimilar to the *Geist*. This death of God and subsequent transition from a transcendent God to an evolving immanence of Spirit works within a monophysitic identification that suppresses the divinity in favor of the humanity and, by doing so, suppresses the infinite in favor of the finite, the presence in favor of the absence, so that this suppressive mold can be situated in the communion of individuals who revolt, who stand apart embodied and purified by this theology of absence. Ricoeur, in his series of lectures on Job,[56] approaches, in sheer proximity, that post-Hegelian faith, but does so only to affirm the vantage or space of the apocalyptic *actor*.[57] This "death" of the ethical and providential God does, for Ricoeur, enable a transition to a new view of the faith while also being one that cycles within the liturgical movement, a "tragic faith beyond any assurance or protection."[58] The death of God for Ricoeur does not signal the evisceration of his transcendence but is the path to its recovery, for again we are on the horizon between time and eternity, which always and heartbreakingly involves appearance always open to disappearance; the presence becomes as much the absence. Job is the exemplar of a convergence of the post-Hegelian forms of faith advocated by the death of God proponents while also retaining the providential faith that cannot step outside the presence, as such a death not only portends but demands. Job embodies the genuine apocalyptic faith because this faith does not shy away from the limit, the point of breaking, in a way Hegel rightly understood. But unlike Hegel, Ricoeur sees Job as the exemplar *because* he lets himself be worn down by the faith rather than conceive—as Altizer and Žižek do—the breaking point as identical to a noetic or epistemological end, a death in the form of cessation and not in the form of the *eschaton*. This faith

> would be a faith that wanders in the darkness, in a "new night
> of understanding" to use the language of the mystics—before a

56. Cf. Ricoeur "The Reaffirmation of the Tragic," in *Symbolism of Evil*, 310–26. See also Ricoeur, "Religion, Atheism and Faith," in *Conflict of Interpretations*, 440–67.

57. In articulating an appropriate theodicy in confrontation to a real filiation with the Hegelian move which must be resisted, Ricoeur does advocate for a Kantian view, not incompatible with the martyrological ethics of Edward Schillebeeckx. See Schillebeeckx, *Christ*, especially, "Suffering for Others: The Future of a Better World," and "The Gospel of Suffering for Others," 211–27. Cf. O'Regan, *The Heterodox Hegel*, 453: "Kant is of the opinion that the experiential attitude of authentic theodicy is embodied by Job. The contrast between 'in spite of' and 'because of' is borrowed essentially from Paul Ricoeur who takes the side of Job and Kant against Hegel concerning the possibility of an authentic theodicy."

58. Ricoeur, "The Reaffirmation of the Tragic," 440.

God who has not the attributes of "providence." This God does not protect me but delivers me up to the dangers of a life worthy of being called human. Is not this God the Crucified, the dying God, the God whose weakness alone may help me? The new night of the understanding is a night for our desire as much as for our fear, a night for our longing for a protective father. Beyond this night, and only beyond it, will be recovered the true meaning of the God of consolation, the God of the Resurrection, the Pantocrator of Byzantine and Romanesque image.[59]

The glory of theology resides in its failure, this attempt to approach what is absent, to be mindful of this apocalyptic presence that evokes absence *because* it evokes hope. We are, through time and memory, God's playthings, and to accept that, as Job did, returns us to the Patmos soul, to those "words of love that tunnel through the heart's spectacular silence towards a morning of fierce light."[60] Tunnelling through that spectacular silence towards a fierce light implies both the need for night as much as our exhaustion from the light. The apocalyptic *actor* knows that the true stability, the genuine endurance learned from the Christ-event, is that life is in play, that the *eschaton* cannot be situated and meted out in a vulgar teleology of clear-and-distinct ideas or an overarching spirit of consciousness. The *presence* of the Christ-event is equally presence and absence, and when the presence overwhelms, the absence beckons. To be an apocalyptic *actor* involves a thinking that stays close to Christ not in name only but in *act*, in the way in which we are God's playthings and in the way in which memory needs the curtain to fall . . . at least for a time:

> In our rhythm of earthly life we tire of light. We are glad when the day ends, when the play ends; and ecstasy is too much pain.
>
> We are children quickly tired: children who are up in the night and fall asleep as the rocket is fired; and the day is long for work or play.
>
> We tire of distraction or concentration, we sleep and are glad to sleep.
>
> Controlled by the rhythm of blood and the day and the night and the seasons.
>
> And we must extinguish the candle, put out the light and relight it;
>
> Forever must quench, forever relight the flame.

59. Ricoeur, "The Reaffirmation of the Tragic," 460.

60. O'Regan, "Requiem," in *Misremembering*, v.

> Therefore, we thank Thee for our little light, that is dappled
> with shadow.[61]

The genuine noetic retreat, which alone unveils our genuine *apocalyptic* personhood, is a sacral immersion into the un-remarked minuteness of the world. It is thus not a stoic distance or dismissal of the world in favor of ideological vacancies, but a return to the thicket of creativity. Any movement to God commencing from the misconceived notion of the I as prior removes God and replaces him with idolatry. To move towards God requires a step back from God which is only completed when we step into the world and resurrect within us a love for the unstripped immediacy of the Christ-event, within the little things in relation to ourselves. And if God is innermost to Being[62] in its full play, the step-back from God is a step-into God, into the Christ-event. And it is in this serious play that recollection *recalls* the event not as past but as present and operative, when the memorial recedes from the immemorial, and when what is forgotten is remembered again for the first time:

> It is to memory that the sense of orientation in the passage of
> time is linked; orientation in two senses, from the past to the
> future, by a push from behind, so to speak, following the arrow
> of time and change, but also from the future towards the past,
> following the inverse movement of transit from expectation to-
> ward memory, across the living present.[63]

This is the *anamnesis* that Plato more than suspected,[64] and what the apocalyptic *actor* has substantialized. And it is the true convergence of time and memory in Ricoeur and O'Regan.

> The power of time is great. One perhaps does not notice it in
> time, because time slyly steals a little bit away at a time. Perhaps
> one will get to know this clearly for the first time in eternity
> when one is required to look back again and around to see what
> one has managed to get together with the help of time and forty

---

61. Eliot, "The Rock," in *Collected Poems*, 170–71.

62. St. Thomas Aquinas, *ST* I, 8, 1 *resp.*

63. Ricoeur, *Memory, History, Forgetting*, 97.

64. Cf. Plato, *Phaedo* 96a–c. See also Nancy, *The Birth to Presence*, 169: "That is why philosophy has known (accepting it or not, which is another matter) that it could not be anything other than a 'return to the things themselves,' and that it must not cease coming back, and bringing itself back, to this return. Ever since Plato's anamnesis, it has been a question of nothing else: the truth, the gravity of the *on*, of the thing insofar as it *is*, beyond all *toiouton* (this or thatness). And that, very clearly, is why anamnesis must memorialize the immemorial, the immemorable."

years. Yes, time has a dangerous power; in time it is so easy to make a beginning again and thereby forget where one left off. Even when one begins to read a very big book and does not completely trust his memory, he puts in a bookmark. But, O, with respect to his whole life, how often one forgets to put in a marker in order to be able to find his place![65]

Bibliography

Altizer, Thomas J. J. *The Gospel of Christian Atheism.* Aurora, CO: Davies, 2002.

St. Augustine. *City of God.* Edited by Vernon J. Bourke. New York: Image, 1958.

Balthasar, Hans Urs von. *Razing the Bastions.* San Francisco: Ignatius, 1993.

Beckett, Samuel. *Three Novels: Molloy, Malone Dies, The Unnamable.* Edited by Laura Lindgren. New York: Grove, 2009.

Cantalamessa, Raniero, O.F.M. Cap. Homily, St Peter's Basilica, Good Friday, 2012.

Chaucer, Geoffrey. *The Canterbury Tales.* Translated by Nevill Coghill. London: Penguin, 1951.

Davie, Donald, ed., *The New Oxford Book of Christian Verse.* Oxford: Oxford University Press, 1981.

Eliot, T. S. *T. S. Eliot: Collected Poems, 1909–1962.* Orlando, FL: Harcourt, 1991.

Gilson, Caitlin Smith. *Immediacy and Meaning: J. K. Huysmans and the Immemorial Origin of Metaphysics.* New York: Bloomsbury, 2017.

———. *The Philosophical Question of Christ.* New York: Bloomsbury, 2013.

Hegel, G. W. F. *On Art, Religion, and the History of Philosophy.* Translated by E. S. Haldane. New York: Harper & Row, 1970.

———. *The Philosophy of Fine Art.* Translated by F. P. B. Osmaston, London: Bell & Sons, 1920.

Hölderlin, Friedrich. *Poems of Friedrich Hölderlin.* Translated by James Mitchell. San Francisco: Ithuriel's Spear, 2004.

Huizinga, Johan. *Homo Ludens: A Study of the Play Element in Culture.* Translated by R. F. C. Hull. London: Routledge & Kegan Paul, 1949.

Jaspers, Karl. *Philosophic Faith and Revelation.* Translated by E. B. Ashton. New York: Harper & Row, 1967.

Kierkegaard, Søren. *Works of Love.* Translated by Howard Hong and Edna Hong. New York: Harper, 2009.

Leahy, D. G. *Beyond Sovereignty.* Aurora, CO: Davies, 2010.

Nancy, Jean-Luc. *The Birth to Presence.* Stanford, CA: Stanford University Press, 1993.

O'Regan, Cyril. *The Anatomy of Misremembering.* New York: Crossroad, 2014.

———. *Gnostic Apocalypse: Jacob Boehme's Haunted Narrative.* Albany, NY: SUNY Press, 2002.

———. *The Gnostic Return in Modernity.* Albany, NY: SUNY Press, 2001.

———. *The Heterodox Hegel.* Albany, NY: SUNY Press, 1994.

———. *Theology and the Spaces of Apocalyptic.* Milwaukee, WI: Marquette University Press, 2009.

---

65. Kierkegaard, *Works of Love,* 325.

Pegis, A. C. *Introduction to St. Thomas Aquinas*. New York: Modern Library, 1948.

Plato. *Complete Works*. Edited by J. M. Cooper. Indianapolis, IN: Hackett, 1997.

Ricoeur, Paul. *The Conflict of Interpretations*. Edited by Don Ihde. Evanston, IL: Northwestern University Press, 1974.

———. *Essays on Biblical Interpretation*. Edited by Lewis Mudge. Philadelphia: Fortress, 1980.

———. *Figuring the Sacred*. Translated by David Pellauer. Minneapolis, MN: Fortress, 1995.

———. *Freud and Philosophy: An Essay on Interpretation*. Translated by Denis Savage. New Haven, CT: Yale University Press, 1970.

———. *Memory, History and Forgetting*. Translated by Kathleen Blamey and David Pellauer. Chicago: University of Chicago Press, 2004.

———. *Oneself as Another*. Translated by Kathleen Blamey. Chicago: University of Chicago Press, 1992.

———. *The Symbolism of Evil*. Translated by Emerson Buchanan. New York: Harper & Row, 1967.

———. *Time and Narrative, Vol. 1*. Translated by Kathleen McLaughlin and David Pellauer. Chicago: University of Chicago Press, 1984.

Santayana, George. *Soliloquies in England and Later Soliloquies*. Ann Arbor, MI: University of Michigan Press, 1967.

Schillebeeckx, Edward. *The Collected Works of Edward Shillebeeckx Vol. VII: Christ, The Christian Experience in the Modern World*. New York: Bloomsbury, 2015.

Taylor, A. E. *The Faith of a Moralist Series I & II*. London: Macmillan, 1931.

———. *The Problem of Conduct: A Study in the Phenomenology of Ethics*. Toronto: University of Toronto Press, 1901.

Thomas Aquinas. *Disputed Questions on Truth*. Translated by Robert W. Mulligan. Chicago: Regnery, 1952.

———. *Summa Contra Gentiles*. Translated by James F. Anderson. South Bend, IN: University of Notre Dame Press, 1992.

———. *Summa Theologiae*. Edited by Thomas Gilby. New York: Cambridge University Press, 1967.

Voegelin, Eric. *Order and History, Vol. 4: The Ecumenic Age*. Baton Rouge, LA: LSU Press, 1974.

Žižek, Slavoj, and Milbank, John. *The Monstrosity of Christ: Paradox or Dialectic?* Edited by Creston Davis. Cambridge: MIT Press, 2011.

AUSEINANDERSETZUNG

8

Geist's Kaleidoscope

Some Questions for Cyril O'Regan

DAVID BENTLEY HART

I

Sometimes a thwarted journey leads to a better destination. I confess that, when I agreed to contribute to this volume, my sights were set upon a very particular expanse of terrain, which I intended to explore for rare fauna and unnamed flora with almost theatrical diligence; but then I found that two other authors had furtively preceded me, and had wantonly carried away all the choicest specimens before I had ever set out. So I have chosen to abandon that territory entirely, and all its adjacent fields, fens, and forests, and to make for higher elevations instead, simply to take in the wider lay of the land and to enjoy the view—which is, as it happens, an extremely bracing one. I have immense admiration for Cyril O'Regan, both as a scholar and as a person, and enormous sympathy for his project as a whole. I admire especially his obviously tireless commitment to the hard labor of memory, of *anamnesis,* which for Christian thought is a sacred vocation. And I feel an affinity for his work—both intellectual and temperamental—that is far more than mere polite curiosity or general approbation. I tend to think that his larger philosophical and theological vision and mine coincide to an extraordinarily great degree; and, even where we might disagree in certain of our conclusions, we certainly seem to concur as regards which issues are most important, and how they should be addressed. He is one of that very small set of scholars by whom I am always willing to be informed or persuaded without any of the sullen resentment I would normally harbor towards someone who had the temerity to tell me something interesting that I did not already know or to prompt me to think thoughts not of my own devising. It would, in fact, be very easy (if also perhaps a little self-serving) just to offer a testimonial here and then to switch off the lights on the way out of the room. But encomiasts are obliged to speak in generalities, and I have a deeper, much more particular interest in O'Regan's work. That same affinity that draws me to his thought makes it also an occasion for thinking through a number of the intellectual intuitions I believe I share with him, and so for posing a few questions aloud that have been quietly incubating in my mind for some time now—perhaps as much in regard to myself as to him, and perhaps in the hope that he can provide certain answers that still elude me.

The first of those questions is the broadest: What really happened? That is to say, I am wholly prepared to agree with O'Regan (and William Desmond) that something occurred in the course of modern Western thought that created what might be called a "false double" or violent inversion or "misremembering" or counterfeit of the Christian story, at least as it had to that point been generally understood.[1] I agree also that this phantom simulacrum or reverse image of what is normally regarded as orthodoxy remains haunted by—but also has come to haunt our understanding of—traditional Christian thought. And, like O'Regan, I see this conceptual revolution as having assumed an almost archetypal purity and compendiousness in Hegel's system. I assume, moreover, that we are in agreement that, speaking purely formally, this reverse image of the more traditional narrative introduces into the Christian story certain offenses, both metaphysical and moral, that had been largely absent before: metaphysical, that is, insofar as this newer version of the Christian story appears to lack much of the logical and conceptual coherence of the more classical models of the transcendent and the created; moral, in that it quite monstrously imports the violence of nature and history into the eternal identity of the divine, and thereby grants that violence an eternal validity and necessity. Where, however, I demur somewhat from O'Regan's view of things is that I do not regard it as correct to think of these developments as the "return" of something called "Gnosticism" (not even as a general name for a kind of narrative grammar). In fact, I think this is a category error, and perhaps a kind of

---

1. See, for instance, O'Regan, *Heterodox Hegel*; O'Regan, *Gnostic Return*; O'Regan, *Misremembering*; Desmond, *Hegel's God*.

false memory in its own right, hiding a somewhat more troubling tale from view—though, to be fair, it is not an error of O'Regan's invention. Much of our modern understanding of those late antique systems of thought and devotion that we now (rather injudiciously, I think) collectively designate as "Gnosticism," was shaped by a number of scholars (many of them German, such as Neander and Baur) who chose to read those traditions through the violet-tinted spectacles of German idealism.[2] The result, to my mind, was the invention of a historical fiction, a bizarre theological chimaera so anachronistic in its alleged tenets and tendencies as to be utterly preposterous. Nothing of the sort could ever have actually existed in the late antique world, and even before the discoveries at Nag Hammadi we had more than sufficient evidence that nothing of the sort ever had. And yet, in the secondary scholarly literature, it has enjoyed many generations of rude vitality. I will dilate on this below, however. Here I will simply say that I do not believe that there has been a "Gnostic return in modernity." Or, rather, I do, but only in the sense that I believe that a dimension of religious discourse and thought that we might call "Gnostic" is always arising anew in Christian history, but only because it has always been an integral aspect of aboriginal Christianity: a certain spiritual suspicion or agitation or disquiet, typically latent but also frequently resurgent, intrinsic to the very substance of the gospel in its first, apocalyptic proclamation. And I think that this dimension must necessarily persist so long as any trace of original Christianity remains alive within Christian tradition, and that its ultimate disappearance would be also the final eclipse of the Christian kerygma. Far from nurturing and sheltering a spectral recrudescence of the ancient Gnostic systems, I would argue, Hegel's system is (along with all its most salient precursors and sequels, whether Jakob Boehme's mystical theology or the systematic theology of many more recent Lutheran thinkers) an attempt to accomplish exactly the opposite: the final exorcism of a vital spiritual presence within Christian thought, typically suppressed or forgotten, but perennially active

2. It is a tragedy of academic history that the modern study of ancient Gnosticism—and with it the utterly fanciful concept of Gnosticism as a kind of precocious speculative precursor of the most daring of modern German philosophical schools— was inaugurated by Johann August Neander's *Genetische Entwicklung der vornehmsten gnostischen Systeme* (1818), Jacques Matter's *Histoire critique du Gnosticisme et de son influence sur les sectes religieuses et philosophiques des six premiers siècles de 1ère chrétienne* (1828), and (most disastrously of all) Ferdinand Christian Baur's immense and immensely confused *Die christliche Gnosis, oder die Religionsphilosophie in ihrer geschichtlichen Entwicklung* (1835). The last of these volumes exercised so baleful an influence over subsequent scholarship that its wild conjectures and patent misrepresentations remained somehow part of the canonical understanding of "Gnosticism" well into the last century, and can still be discerned (if only faintly) even in the works of scholars who should have long been disabused of its errors.

and even occasionally enlivening. As for the true genealogy of modernity's "false double" of the Christian story, conversely, I think it nothing more than a grim but probably inevitable—even, I would argue, somehow natural—metastasis of certain elements unique to what we normally take to be Christian orthodoxy.

On the one hand, all of this may amount to no more than a difference between two differing historical reconstructions of a single phenomenon regarding which, in all its specific concrete details, there is otherwise more or less perfect agreement. On the other hand, however, historical memory is precisely what is probably most at issue here. Much of the special and truly absorbing brilliance of O'Regan's work lies in his recognition that, to a very large extent, the great drama of modern philosophy's struggle for the past is also a war for the future. Every age, of course, seeks to remember the immemorial, and to invent a past by which to make sense of the present, and to make it easier both to conjecture about and to determine what the future will bring. But usually this desire has expressed itself in myths or in heroic fables about times and persons only vaguely recalled. Only in modernity did it become the driving force of an ideological struggle as well. The Renaissance is perhaps the inaugural phase of this change; those of the period and (more particularly) of later generations who refused to see the philosophical and artistic achievements of the fifteenth and sixteenth centuries as having in any way naturally evolved from the culture of the high Middle Ages, and who preferred to speak instead of the rebirth of an ancient wisdom out of the darkness of mediaeval forgetfulness, were engaged at one and the same time in the invention of a classical past (based in part on reality, in part on a hermetic fantasy) and in the willful forgetting of a much more immediate past. More radical still was the later mythology of Enlightenment, and the quaint delusion it cultivated that the modern period was in the process of wholly abandoning the obscurantisms and barbarisms of an inherently defective past, and of generating an entirely new order of values for itself out of the now liberated operations of pure rationality. But Hegel's ambitions far exceeded those of his predecessors in this labor of fabulous recollection and willful oblivion; he was not content simply to take leave of a fictional past in pursuit of a fantastic future, but aspired to a complete revision of all historical memory, in order to subsume all that had come and gone, without remainder, into his majestic epic of *Geist*. It is therefore quite understandable that O'Regan has devoted so much of his work over the years to an engagement with Hegel's project. And it makes perfect sense as well that he is now every bit as much engaged with Heidegger's. The two projects are, at the last, two versions of the same imperial aspiration, the same diegetic quest to conquer all the territories of human thought and to bring them under the canopy of a single inescapable total narrative that, in essence, renders all further philosophy otiose. Hegel's version is a magnificent late Christian contrapuntal composition, played out through all the major and minor scales; Heidegger's transposes the melody into the harmonically minimalist, more purely evocative, more plaintive modal keys of a receding and largely forgotten pagan prehistory. But both tellings of the tale—the Concept's continuous historical diremption and sublation into *Geist*, the epochal "sending" of Being in a process of disclosure-as-dissemblance—undertake the recovery of the past as a total revision of memory, reducing the whole of history to a necessary sequence of rational or fateful moments that culminates in—or that is finally "healed" by—a speculative project resolving all the contradictions of the past. In either version of the tale, moreover, Christian thought is assigned a vital but in most respects obsolete role: either that of the illuminating but still inchoate mythic premonition of a wisdom yet to be realized as explicit reflective knowledge, or that of one of the most crucial and catastrophic episodes in the history of metaphysics, deeply complicit in Western thought's "oblivion of Being" and its ever more explicitly nihilistic destiny. Hegel's clairvoyant recollection of the whole of history and penetration into the inner mysteries of its intrinsic logic, Heidegger's vatic intimations of the hidden figure of Being moving like a colossal, shapeless shadow behind the veils of history—in either case, theology appears in the tale as an essentially infantile discourse, capable of disclosing its truth only retrospectively, once childish things have been put away, when religion has been superseded by a philosophy come of age and doctrine can now be plundered of its hidden speculative treasures at leisure. In either case, theology's place has indeed been usurped by its own double or phantom.

So, then, my second question is this: How did this really happen?

II

It was the peculiar genius of Hegel—the secret of his system's power not only to encompass every antinomy of reason but also to say anything and its opposite with equal emphasis—to recognize that every structure of ideas can be approached purely as an assemblage of binary oppositions, organized into a kind of speculative mechanism made up of interlocking and oscillating inversions. And it was his peculiar accomplishment to translate this insight into a massive feat of philosophical engineering, a conceptual machine so immensely comprehensive and yet so finely calibrated that he never needed suffer the least anxiety that it would not continue operating in perpetuity. Where else, after all, have the worlds of Heracleitus and Parmenides existed together in such exquisite equilibrium, each not merely complementing but also repeating and implying and requiring the other? What other philosopher ever produced so replete and total a vision of reality in both its abstract and its concrete dimensions, its necessities and its contingencies, or one containing so limitless a range of potential configurations, or one so capable of accommodating even the most seemingly enormous revolutions in thought and meaning without in the least endangering its imperturbable stability? There could scarcely be a more misleading claim than Kierkegaard's canard that Hegel had erected a magnificent palace of ideas but was forced to live in a hovel outside. In fact, Hegel's palace was a triumph not only of architectonic inspiration, but of sorcery. It could magically transport all thought and experience into itself while never providing any means of egress. And there really is no escape for those trapped within its walls, even when they imagine they have slipped the sorcerer's bonds. Even the most thoroughgoing rejection of the system can be recuperated into the system again, as a negation or polarity already comprised within its logic. The whole structure consists in nothing but polarities, reciprocal negations, each containing its opposite as an only seemingly dormant force within itself, and as the inner secret of its own intelligibility. Again, the best metaphor is that of a machine, a dynamo in perpetual motion, generating endlessly new patterns within itself—a machine whose design, moreover, is held together and set in action by a simple spring of vertical contraction. From at least the time of Plato, pre-modern Western thought had presumed something like a necessary μεταξύτης or interval between the transcendent and the immanent, the absolute and the conditional, a kind of ontological and analogical median at once uniting and dividing the there above and the here below, and by its very fixity preserving them in their distinct positions in a single hierarchy of relations. But Hegel discovered that the collapse of that interval could produce something truly astonishing, and that this could be accomplished by only the slightest revision of reason's expectations. In place of that interval, he realized, one need imagine only a kind of crystal line of division running through the middle of every discrete antithesis, the horizon of a specular and speculative chiasmus, like the surface of one of the mirrors in a kaleidoscope; and, just as in a kaleidoscope, it requires only the smallest adjustment of the relative positions of the poles—the smallest movement of rotation from above to below—to initiate a gorgeous, fluid, thoroughly precise, but also infinitely variable spectacle of countless reversals and reflections and reconfigurations.

Nor need there be anything at all regular or static about the way in which those transformations occur. The various oppositions composing the picture need not change in synchrony with one another. Some polarities might be entirely reversed while others remain more or less as they were. We see this, certainly, in the dazzling variety of ways in which Hegel's system was received by parties of every persuasion. Theological models of the Trinity influenced by the system, for instance, could invert the traditional opposition between eternity and time while at the same time leaving that between spirit and matter largely unchanged; Marxists, by contrast, were willing to invert both, but not to disturb that between rational truth and vulgar opinion; for certain Hegelians of revolutionary disposition, metaphysical and social hierarchies must be overturned, but not necessarily all the moral ones; for certain Hegelians of a reactionary disposition, both must in the end be restored to their original places, even if only at the end of a long historical odyssey; and so on. The system as a whole constitutes a kind of ontological palindrome, albeit in three dimensions: it can be read from left to right or right to left, but also backwards or forwards, as well as *de haut en bas* (so to speak) or *e terris ad astra*. Each of its interlocking binaries can oscillate one way or the other largely independently of all the rest: necessity and contingency, order and chaos, identity and difference, unity and plurality, personality and impersonality, rational autonomy and historical destiny, the universal and the particular, being and becoming, existence and nothingness, infinity and totality, mind and mechanism, Classical and Romantic, and so on. And the system in its entirety, depending on the angle from which it is viewed, is susceptible of every possible characterization or interpretation: disembodied abstraction or radical empiricism, mystification or disenchantment, absolute idealism or dialectical materialism, Mandarin detachment or bourgeois conformity, historical essentialism or essential historicism, a "totalizing metaphysics" or the ultimate "deconstruction of metaphysics," and so on and so on. As long as the system of binaries is preserved, the relative ascendancy of one pole or the other within any of them is a matter of no consequence. All remains integrated and luminous and rational throughout. Even whether one regards the system as a whole as either "true" or "false" somehow does not matter. The system says everything and nothing at once, and everything as nothing; and therein lies its invincible genius.

Whatever one's opinion of his system, however, I think it fair to say that Hegel—probably inadvertently—discovered a genuine law of spontaneous development in philosophy. This kaleidoscope rotates under its own momentum and requires no adventitious force to turn it. And what seem like great peripeties and innovations and subversions in the course of philosophical history are quite likely nothing of the sort, but only automatic expressions of that law. Most intellectual revolutions are really only natural evolutions, most violent convulsions just the predictable effects of inertia, most apostasies merely the fully ripened fruit of orthodoxies. More often than not, it is all a matter of fashion. Any system of ideas, after all, can come in time to feel like a spiritual prison rather than a home, simply because a system is necessarily shaped as much by its disjunctions as by its connections. It requires walls no less than paths, deep trenches no less than elevated causeways, and countless locked doors ranged all along its open corridors. For this very reason, no system can endure indefinitely, though practically any can enjoy periodic revival: even the richest and most ingenious comes at last to seem not merely trite, but also a kind of captivity of the imagination, an edifice composed of arbitrary and barren conceptual conventions, long ago evacuated of intellectual vitality. Inevitably there must come that reflective moment when the rational soul ventures out beyond the grounds, turns to survey the estate from a distance, and sees it for the first time set off against a much larger landscape. And, just as inevitably, a certain fatigue or restive curiosity prompts the mind idly to wonder what the scene would look like turned upside down, or peered at through the wrong end of a telescope, or captured in a mirror, or perhaps in a photographic negative. And thus, the kaleidoscope turns. What in all likelihood follows is not, of course, a total desertion of the past, because absolute vagrancy in a boundless wilderness is a far more terrifying prospect than mere confinement in a bounded but still reasonably spacious estate. Rather, there comes a kind of *Wiederkehr des Verdrängten*, a return of the repressed, by which the hidden negation that every philosophical principle conceals within itself breaks forth, demanding to be affirmed in its own right, and then strives to assume a dominant station in the hierarchy of truths. What has been determines what is to come, as the negated becomes the posited and the principle that once prevailed becomes a repressed memory. Deleuze is sired by Plato, but resentfully denies his paternity. This, at any rate, is the one law that I think Hegel did genuinely discover: that the ultimate cause of most philosophical revolutions is, simply enough, boredom.

Why, though, dwell on these things here? As I say, I am very much in agreement with O'Regan regarding the "false double" of Christianity created by the Hegelian system, for all the metaphysical and moral reasons mentioned above, and for many other reasons as well. Above all else, I lament the disappearance in Hegel's thought of that vital analogical interval between the transcendent and the immanent, and the reversal of ontological reasoning this interval precipitates. The moment the classical understanding of the immanent Trinity's expression in the economic is supplanted by the notion that the economic Trinity actually somehow constitutes the immanent in its eternal identity, the nature of God becomes war rather than peace, or war as much as peace, and war as the necessary foundation of peace. In the system, the abstract form of a high trinitarian ontology may remain—God's paternal depth manifesting and knowing itself in the generation of the Logos and returning to itself in the rational and joyful satiety of Spirit—but the open space of grace has disappeared, and with it the innocence of God. The Hegelian divine is one whose nature is not simply expressed upon the Cross, but also fashioned through the probative negation of crucifixion as such, as well as through every other form of conflict arising out of the contradictions and limitations of finitude, and therefore one in which that violence is necessarily—tragically, comically, ironically—eternalized by its sublation into *Geist*. I am in agreement with O'Regan as well that the story of *Geist* is also a ghost story, a narrative haunted by the recalcitrant specter of the older tale it has attempted to absorb into itself. Where I depart from him is in the matter of genealogy (or, perhaps I should say, pathology). Even then, I do not want to give the impression that this is a simple issue, or that O'Regan speaks of a "Gnostic return" in modernity without nuance, hesitation, or considerable attention to fine details. Still, I find the language problematic. To my mind, what achieves its fullest expression in Hegel's reading of the Christian story is not the return of anything properly called "Gnosticism." It is, rather, as I have suggested already, the long attempt not merely to suppress, but completely to eradicate, a certain "Gnostic dimension" within Christian self-understanding and imagination; and its inevitable result is both an excluded middle and an extreme—yet still predictable—formulation of Christian terms no longer restrained by any analogical reservations. Hegelianism, I would argue, is one exceedingly pure specimen of what remains of a certain stream of "orthodoxy" when it has been wholly purged of "Gnostic" irony. Or so, at least, it seems provocatively interesting to assert.

My third question for O'Regan, then, is: Should perhaps the very concept of a "Gnostic return" in modernity be reconsidered, or at least severely qualified?

III

As a critical category for understanding early Christian history, the very term "Gnosticism" has become increasingly suspect in recent years, and for good reason. I am not yet ready myself to relinquish it altogether, but only because I take it to be a convenient designation for a pervasive intonation within early Christianity (including a great deal of the New Testament) that assumed exaggerated and often mythopoetically garish forms in the spiritual communities we traditionally call "Gnostic," and that had analogous expressions in almost all the spiritual systems of its time and place, Jewish, Christian, pagan, Orphic, or what have you. It was a pervasive reality of the whole imaginative and spiritual continuum in which what we now forcibly isolate in our collective memory as the one true orthodox form of early Christianity was itself firmly situated. But this real, historically identifiable "Gnosticism" has been so deeply distorted in much modern scholarship that the word has become for us today almost a cipher, carelessly associated with a system of belief that would have been unthinkable before the early modern period. And it is only in this misrepresented and fanciful form that early Gnostic thought—say, that of the Valentinians, the Basilideans, or the Sethians, to take the most elaborate and astonishing examples—could be mistaken for a prefiguration or hidden wellspring of such things as Boehme's theology or Hegel's system or the middle Schelling's metaphysics. In many scholars' minds, it is almost a banal truism that the Gnostic systems of late antiquity were built around one or another narrative of a divine fall, a cataclysm that somehow involved even God Most High, and asserted the emergence of evil or defect from God's own depths, all of which was then followed by a redemption that effected not only a restoration, but even an advance toward perfect fullness, within God himself. Supposedly, at the heart of these systems lay a tale of theogony, of God coming to himself at the far end of a refining process of tragic loss and comic rescue. This is simply false. It is a relic of a now thoroughly discredited historical narrative. And that narrative was based upon a misunderstanding of the very concept of the "divine" in late antiquity, and of its immense diversity of connotations, and upon a failure to grasp the utterly inviolable distinction that was preserved in all the late antique systems of spiritual salvation—the "Gnostic" no less than any of the others—between the realm of the inaccessible Father, or "God" as specified by the definite article (ὁ θεός), or the One, or what have you, and the created or emanated "divine," or celestial, or supercelestial, or "aeonian" realm. There were definitely schools and sects that spoke of a fall within the heavenly plenum, the πλήρωμα, and many told the tale of Sophia's departure from that fullness as a result of her mad desire to know the Father in himself. But the πλήρωμα is not God, nor is it part of God in his transcendent nature, nor is the identity of God properly speaking involved either in its fall or in its redemption.[3] God is beyond both the cosmos

3. The habit of superimposing German idealism upon ancient Gnostic beliefs is so deeply imbrued in the secondary literature that even as fine a historian of antiquity as Giovanni Filoramo feels free to speak vaguely of a Gnostic concept of "theogony" germane not only to the "divine" powers but somehow to God Most High, and to assert in general that for Gnostic thought the action by which the eternal God emanates or puts forth the various aeons and hypostases constituting the heavenly πλήρωμα is

and the heavenly orders, fallen and unfallen alike; he is the always more encompassing reality that holds all other things in itself, even the highest cosmic sphere, beyond the reach of any other reality; in him all things live and move and have their being, but he does not dwell in or among them, or take his own life or movement or being from their histories in return.[4]

also a kind of becoming or advance in self-knowledge on God's part: "This process of emanation, of the progressive issue of the divine substance, by means of which God manifests to himself the totality of his infinite potentialities, is a process of enrichment, but also of impoverishment. Indeed, only by the concrete manifestation of the complex articulation of his potential nature can God truly know himself." Filoramo, *History of Gnosticism*, 59. His only citations in support of this extravagant claim, of course, are from secondary sources, none of which in turn grounds the claim in any of the original texts. Moreover, quite without noticing the contradiction, Filoramo then goes on to provide several quotations and epitomes taken from the ancient sources that demonstrate quite the opposite to be the case.

4. If anything, ancient "Gnostic" literature emphasizes the remoteness of God from every cosmic or even heavenly process to a more extreme degree than did most later "orthodox" writers. Perfectly typical, for example, is the description of the true God in the epistolary treatise *Eugnostos the Blessed*, which tells us that God in himself is eternally beyond all principles and powers, dominions and subordinations, and is unknown to any creatures, untouched by any movements of becoming, by deficiencies, by dependences, by limits, or by anything else conditional—so much so that he is only improperly called "the Father of the All" and were better called "the Forefather," as he is the absolute and eternal ground of all real knowledge and the origin of all else (*Nag Hammadi Corpus* [*NHC*] III.71.13–18). Similarly, that compendium of Valentinian metaphysics and theology, *The Tripartite Tractate*, tells us that God the Father is absolute unity, alone and prior to all, the Forefather who is the source and root of the Son and all the aeons, but who is himself perfect, changeless, ungenerated and unending, nameless, the Good as such that is the source only of goodness and that is forever immune from every effect of evil, the One whose form and essence are beyond the reach of all other beings, and whose depths and greatness are unattainable to all but himself (*NHC* I.5.51.8–18; I.5.54.2–23). The Sethian doxologies found in *The Three Steles of Seth* describe God the Father—to whom the suppliant reciting the verses longs to ascend—as the unmoving and self-generated One (*NHC* VII.5.119.15–16), the unseen Father who is prior even to being and therefore non-being, from whom the secondary principle (Barbelo) eternally proceeds (*NHC* VII.5.121.20–122.8). According to Irenaeus, the Valentinian teacher Ptolemy described God in himself as prior to being, pre-primordial, ὁ βυθός the first cause of all, ungenerated, incomprehensible, abiding throughout the infinite ages in absolute stillness and serenity (Irenaeus, *Adversus haereses* [*AH*] I.1.1). Perhaps the fullest and most elaborate description of God's transcendence in "Gnostic" literature is the one found at the beginning of the Sethian masterpiece *Apocryphon of John*: God is the pure Monad, the Father of the πλήρωμα, beyond genesis and corruption, dwelling in immaculate light, into which no eye may gaze, superior to mere divinity, incapable of occupying any station inferior to anything, lacking absolutely nothing, "for he is an absolute fullness that has never become defective in any way in order to be made complete, but rather is forever perfect" [!], limitless, fathomless, measureless, eternal, ineffable, unnameable, pure, beyond every pollution, indeed beyond even perfection and beatitude and divinity, unquantifiable, uncreated, unthinkable, not an existent thing among other existent things but rather higher than

There are, it is true, texts that tell of this God generating creation through the ἔννοια, the "thinking" or "intellection," that is with him in the beginning,[5] just as Christian orthodoxy has always spoken of God the Father as creating through his λόγος in the beginning. There are texts also that speak of the Father knowing himself reflectively, either by seeing himself in himself, as his own mirror,[6] or in the luminous water of life that is his own eternal immaculate light,[7] just as later orthodox trinitarian theology will speak of the Father's λόγος as his own eternal self-knowing. But in none of these texts is there any hint that the Father enters into, suffers, or recovers from a divine fall or crisis "within the godhead," or that his creative or emanative self-manifestation is in any sense his discovery of his own inherent potencies.[8] Again, we must not confuse talk of the "divine" in late antiquity for a privileged discourse regarding only the truly transcendent God, or talk of the "divine realm" of the heavenly beings above as somehow other than creaturely. In fact, in all the spiritual systems of the time, the Father (or the One, or the Monad, or ὁ βυθός, or so forth) remains untouched by his creatures, even the most divine or angelic among them, and comes into relation with lower reality only indirectly, through a lesser intermediary, or

---

all beings, not sharing in the ages but rather beyond all times and ages, never divided, receiving nothing from beyond, gazing upon himself only within his perfect light, himself the source of all life, blessedness, gnosis, mercy, ransom, and grace, ever at peace, the head and strength of all the aeons, reflecting upon and knowing his image only in his own light, the luminous and pure wellspring of living water in which he dwells (*Berlin Gnostic Codex* [*BGC*] XXII.19–XXVI.15; *NHC* XI.2.25–4.19). This is not, one must emphasize (though one should not have to), a description of the Concept in its abstract plenitude logically prior to its realization as living knowledge in *Geist*, nor certainly a description of *Geist* as having been achieved by a process of divine emanation and reflection, nor yet a description of a realm of divine potentialities awaiting their emergence into, and reflective discovery through, actuality. It is an account of the one transcendent, fully actual, and eternally self-knowing God beyond all things, as affirmed in all the monotheisms—pagan, Jewish, Christian, "Gnostic"—of Graeco-Roman and Hellenistic Semitic late antiquity.

5. Irenaeus, *AH* I.1.1.

6. *The Wisdom of Jesus the Christ, BGC* XCI.4–7.

7. *The Apocryphon of John, BGC* XXVI.15.

8. Here, I earnestly believe, is where O'Regan's terminology, more than in any other aspect of his project, goes amiss, and where I would entreat him to reconsider and ultimately revise it, for the sake both of historical accuracy and of a better genealogy of the heterodoxy he has set out to expose. True, I hold Neander and Baur to blame, not O'Regan; but O'Regan is definitely mischaracterizing Valentinian speculation when he speaks of it as inhabiting or promoting a theogonic genre, or as telling the tale "of the becoming of the perfection of the divine," or as presenting a "paradox" in its account of the pleroma's revelation of God as unrevealed (O'Regan, *Gnostic Return*, 45, 138–48). On these matters, Valentinianism is no less "orthodox" than, say, the most recent edition of the Roman Catholic Catechism.

several lesser intermediaries: the Angel of Mighty Counsel, the λόγος, νοῦς, the hierarchy of pleromatic hypostases. In all these systems, as well, there is a tale to tell of a catastrophe in the heavenly or aeonian or pleromatic or "divine" places above: the fall of the rebel angels under the leadership of Semyâzâ or Samael, the fall of spirits through the aetherial spaces of the celestial spheres, the mutiny of the spiritual principalities and powers who preside over this world, the expulsion from Eden (often allegorized as a pre-temporal apostasy of spirits), the rupture of the pleromatic harmony, the truancy of Sophia; at the very least (in the case of Plotinian Neoplatonism), there is a kind of constant benignly tragic departure from simplicity that must be healed by a return to the noetic contemplation of the One. In every case, however, God in the proper sense remains immune to all becoming and all change, and innocent of every evil.

It seems to me best, then, to think of the "Gnostic" schools of the early Christian centuries as extreme expressions—bedizened with often tediously opulent mythologies, some perhaps only allegorical, many probably not—of a dualistic theological register that is already present, in perhaps a slightly more muted and qualified form, in the earliest Christian documents, and that is especially conspicuous in the Pauline corpus and in the fourth Gospel. As does much of the New Testament, the "Gnostic" narrative tells of a cosmic dispensation under the reign of the god of this aeon (2 Cor 4:4) or the Archon of this cosmos (John 14:30; Eph 2:2), and of spiritual beings hopelessly immured within heavenly spheres thronged by hostile archons and powers and principalities and daemons (Rom 8:3, 39; 1 Cor 10:20–21; 15:24; Eph 1:21; etc.), bound under and cursed by a law that was in fact ordained by lesser, merely angelic or archontic powers (Gal 3:10–11, 19–20). Into this prison of spirits, this darkness that knows nothing of the true light (John 1:5), a divine savior descends from the aeon above (John 3:31; 8:23; etc.), bringing with him a wisdom that has been hidden from before the ages (Rom 16:25–26; Gal 1:12; Eph 3:3–9; Col 1:26), a secret wisdom unknown even to "the archons of this cosmos" (1 Cor 2:7–8) that has the power to liberate fallen spirits (John 8:31–32, etc.). Now those blessed persons who possess "gnosis" (1 Cor 8:7; 13:2) constitute something of an exceptional company, "spiritual persons" (πνευματικοί), who enjoy a knowledge of the truth denied to the merely "psychical" (ψυχικοί) among us (1 Cor 14:36; Gal 6:1; Jude 19). By his triumph over the cosmic archons, moreover, this savior has opened a pathway through the planetary spheres, the encompassing heavens, the armies of the air and the potentates on high, so that now "neither death nor life nor angels nor Archons nor things present nor things imminent nor Powers nor height nor depth nor any other creature will be able to separate us from the love of God" (Rom 8:38–39). Where the so-called "Gnostic" systems seem clearly to depart from the more general narrative morphology is in their willingness to amplify the provisional or qualified dualism implicit in this vision of things into a complete ontological schism, such that creation is conceived of as having no natural relation to God at all, even in his eternal intentions. Not only is lower reality the work of a lesser or intermediary kind of divinity; it is wholly the product of an alienation from God. As a result, here in the land of unlikeness, below the turning spheres of the planetary heavens, all is governed by cosmic fate, εἱμαρμένη, rather than by divine providence; and, far from achieving his essence through creation, in time, by way of a fall and return, the true God is so far beyond the reach of cosmic eventuality that this world has no ontological relation to him at all, not even of the most tenuously analogical variety. In place, then, of the Platonic μεταξύτης between the transcendent and the immanent, and of the metaphysics of participation this permitted, these schools provided only a mediating mythology of absolute estrangement, a grand epic of exile and ruin followed by rescue and restoration. At least, so we are told by contemporary sources, and so their own literary remains largely seem to confirm. Still, throughout the whole of that tale, in every school, God—hidden forever in his hyperouranian and inaccessible light, infinitely removed from time and nature and history—is eternally the same. It is not his story. He has no story.

We are, I should add, as likely as not today to exaggerate just how great a departure from the "orthodox" narrative all of this constituted. A long tradition of platitudinous theology tells us that the "Gnostics" differed from the orthodox in their detestation of the flesh, while orthodox Christianity robustly affirmed the material world as God's good creation. But, of course, it is Paul—far more explicitly than any other early Christian writer whose works are still extant—who proclaims that "flesh and blood cannot inherit the Kingdom of God" (1 Cor 15:50) and who teaches that the "psychical body" composed of flesh and blood must be transformed into a body composed wholly of "spirit" in order to enter the Age to come and to bear the image of the "celestial man" (1 Cor 15:35–49). Of course, in general, modern Christians have so hazy an understanding of late antique conceptions of "spirit" and "soul," and are so likely to take as metaphorical language that Paul intends to be taken with the utmost physical literality, that it is almost impossible for them to locate Paul's language in the picture of reality it reflects. We are also told that the "Gnostics" differed radically from the "orthodox" in teaching that salvation comes through a secret knowledge imparted to the elect rather than through sacramental incorporation into the body of Christ, and perhaps there is some truth in this; but it is a difference of degree at most. All the historical evidence tells us that the "Gnostic" sects practiced saving mysteries—including baptisms, anointings, eucharists, even "extreme unctions"[9]—while Christians of every persuasion believed that they had received a saving "gnosis." Even Irenaeus did not arraign these schools for allegedly privileging knowledge over sacramental grace, or for trusting in saving knowledge in the abstract. He condemned them for promoting a "gnosis falsely so-called" in place of the "true gnosis" delivered to the apostles, and for inventing lavish and absurd myths. By the same token, the sins we might wish to attribute to Hegelianism from an orthodox perspective could not be more different in kind from those that can be legitimately laid at the feet of the ancient "Gnostics." One may be dismayed that Hegel turns the story of God's kenosis in Christ into the speculative tale of a divine reality both spilled out into the tragedy of history and perfected in itself through the fruitful negation of all historical particularity; but this is not a "Gnostic" subversion of the orthodox narrative. And, if one can fairly say that for Hegel the cross of Christ in its historical concreteness constitutes primarily a moment of dialectical disclosure, one that yields explicit and properly reflective knowledge of eternal truth only insofar as it taken as a symbol, negated in its particularity, evacuated of its historical accidents, and recuperated into speculative wisdom—though one has to make even this claim with a certain prudent hesitancy, given the system's extraordinary capacity for unresolved amphibologies—this is also to say precisely the opposite of what ancient Christian "Gnosticism" asserted. To a Valentinian of old, for instance, what the cross of Christ reveals may indeed be an eternal truth about the divine (and, of course, no orthodox Christian could demur from that), but the cross was also an entirely apocalyptic moment of disclosure, one that did not reveal anything at all about the rationality of history or the truth of the universal, but that instead disrupted the order of this aeon entirely, and exposed it as absolute falsehood, illusion, and captivity. And the one historical Christ was, for these same Valentinians, the sole and indispensable savior from this world in his very particularity, the one who alone was able by his divine power to penetrate the defenses of the heavenly powers, to enter their cosmos, to overthrow their reign over spiritual beings, and to set the captives free, the only possible mediator between this world and the Father; he was not a mere symbol of anything.[10] This event of revelation in Christ, moreover, did not contribute to God's self-awakening, or help to transform the implicit truth of the eternal Concept into the explicit

9. Irenaeus, for instance, mentions "Gnostics" anointing the dying with oil and perfumed water to aid them in their impending ascent through the spheres of the Archons: *AH* I.21.5.

10. This too Irenaeus confirms: *AH* I.2.1. See also *The Tripartite Tractate, NHC* I.5.65–66; *The Gospel of Truth, NHC* I.5.18.11—21.25.

living knowledge of *Geist*, but instead apprised the elect of the truth that this world has nothing whatsoever to do with the true God, and is no part of who he is or of who they are. Frankly, it is precisely this Gnostic moment or dimension of sullen suspicion and restless rebellion—this essentially dualistic intuition of the absolute vacuity of this world, of its inimical malice, its falsehood, and its final irredeemability—that is entirely absent from the Hegelian construal of the Christian narrative. Conversely, those aspects of the Hegelian system that are most necessarily constitutive of its revision of the Christian narrative are precisely the ones most conspicuously absent from the ancient "Gnostic" systems: a providential understanding of cosmic history, an ontological continuity between the divine and the created, and (perhaps above all) a certain metaphysics of the will.

In a sense, the most hideous characteristic of the Hegelian system is its unrelieved providential optimism. An absolute dualism, of course, is a very grim thing indeed; but a narrative monism unqualified by any hint of true Gnostic detachment, irony, sedition, or doubt—by any proper sense, that is, that the fashion of this world is horribly out of joint, that we are prisoners of delusion, that not every evil can be accounted for as part of divine necessity—turns out to be at least as monstrous. It leads to a theology so deliriously insensible to its own moral ambiguities that it can view nothing as pure privation, pure absence, ultimate evil. In some sense, it must affirm that even war is good, that the *Weltgeist* strides across the stage of history when the battle of Jena (or any other battle) is fought, that God comes to himself in the death of a child no less than in a gesture of love. It seems to me that in Hegel's thought a certain Protestant enthusiasm reaches a febrile pitch, a rapt delight in divine sovereignty so total that it sees even the devil as only one of God's innumerable masks. At a deeper level, however, this eminently reasonable and providential vision within the Hegelian system is sustained by the latent and paradoxical presence of something prior to and indomitable by all reason, a spontaneous power of becoming in some sense more original than the Concept itself. Here, definitely, the Schelling of the middle period was a more rigorous logician. Hegel, quite *contre cœur* no doubt, was necessarily obliged by his understanding of the great epic of *Geist* to presume, however obscurely, the reality of a kind of "striving" or purely voluntative impulse in the absolute even more primordial than rationality or identity, a kind of intentionality prior to its own rationale, because the final cause of *Geist* can reside nowhere but in *Geist* itself, as an end already achieved. In the system, however, with its collapse of the analogical interval between eternity and time, that finality is not available outside the drama of history and of the serial recuperation of finitude into reflective wisdom. This tacit metaphysical voluntarism—this quiet but persistent premise of some kind of original, as yet irrational spontaneity in the divine—certainly has no prefigurations in any of the ancient Gnosticisms. It can, of course, quite plausibly be traced back to Jakob Boehme. But Boehme was not any kind of "Gnostic," at least not if the word has any cogent meaning at all; he was a Lutheran. And, of course, Luther was no "Gnostic" either; he was a late mediaeval Augustinian.

Really, there is something oddly exhilarating about this particular rotation of the kaleidoscope, something sublime about the way in which the sheer brute historical momentum of a large but unstable idea can carry it onward through every possible transmutation until it arrives very nearly at its own opposite. There is, clandestinely implicit in Hegel's thought, something like a pure self-positing divine will, something on the order of Boehme's dark divine *Ungrund* or Schelling's realm of pure potency—the whole of Hegel's system presumes and depends upon it—but this, however bizarre a deformation it appears to us, is merely the product of a predictable process of unbroken development within the larger Christian doctrinal and theological tradition. It is the exaggeration and specular inversion of a divine voluntarism first fully enunciated in the late Middle Ages; and this voluntarism was itself the extreme expression—and millennial hypertrophy—of a story of divine freedom that entered the Christian narrative as early as the late Augustine's increasingly bleak and pitilessly morbid theology of predestination *ante praevisa merita*. The moment in which God was conceived as acting toward creatures in a way for which theology could adduce no real rationale other than the absolute and mysterious sovereignty of its exercise, the first ectoplasmic wisp of the specter of an essential arbitrariness within God was summoned up in the Christian imagination. It was inevitable that this would produce, in the fullness of time, a voluntarist understanding of rational freedom in the abstract as a kind of pure spontaneity of intention, expressed most perfectly precisely when expressed most arbitrarily. Taken to an extreme within theology, it produced a model of divine freedom in which the rationality of God's power lay simply in its utter liberty from any rational measure other than sovereignty as such. And, taken to a similar extreme as a metaphysics of *all* rational freedom, divine or creaturely, it produced a picture of the will as essentially a spontaneous and indeterminate impulse toward a purely elective end, an end that is "rational" solely because it somehow miraculously fulfills that more deeply "irrational" movement of volition. Hegel's *Geist* is born from this all but inevitable voluntarist turn in Western Christian thought, no less than is the undeniably evil God of Calvinism and Baroque Thomism. Again, these binary oppositions must eventually, as the kaleidoscope turns, shift from one pole to the other. The infinite God of absolute volition is inverted into infinite indeterminate volition becoming God. God willfully positing a history of predilective predestination as an act of omnipotent sovereignty is inverted into God sovereignly determining and "electing" himself in and through history. The trinitarian God choosing to save and to damn as an act of perfect libertarian freedom is inverted into a unitary divine source of being electing to become Trinity in and through the drama of salvation and damnation. None of it is "Gnostic." All of it is a particular trajectory within orthodox tradition succumbing to its own volatility.

And so, truth be told, to employ the word "Gnosticism" here, even if only to indicate a certain set of morphological resemblances between, say, Boehme's thought and that of Valentinus (for instance, a taste for mythopoeic exorbitances), has the unintended effect of conflating conceptual languages that are in fact opposites in their intentions and meanings.[11] Hegel and his kith were, of course, all too happy to associate their philosophical "discoveries" with aberrant or heterodox thinkers and sects of the Christian past, in the hope thereby of borrowing something of their hermetic and seditious glamor. But, in fact (and this is something of a surprising twist in the plot), this is itself part of the very project of "misremembering" that O'Regan has striven so sedulously to expose, but that here perhaps has caught even him in its trammels: the creation of a false Christian past, the myth of a suppressed speculative counter-history or shadow-tradition within Christian thought, a forgotten deeper or truer version of the story that has now supposedly been rediscovered, revived, and properly curated only in German idealist thought. In this way, a very particular and wholly modern "false double" of the gospel endued itself with a phantom pedigree, one of seemingly profound and majestically mysterious antiquity. Hegel, certainly, would have been delighted to invoke, say, Valentinus as a kind of exotic ornamental motif in his great recovery of the "true" Christian

---

11. Here, perhaps, is where O'Regan and I diverge most sharply in our genealogy (or maybe I should say our "phantasmatology") of this particular "false double." While, for him, Boehme constitutes "a highly plausible candidate for designating the alpha point of the genealogy of Gnostic return in modernity" (*Gnostic Return*, 9), to me something very much like the opposite seems to be the case: Boehme may represent a particular moment of inflection at a certain point within modern Christian thought, and even the "alpha point" of a new departure from "orthodoxy," but only because he represents one inevitable omega point in the development of a particular voluntarist strain in Western orthodox reflection, that exquisitely exact instant when a theological principle of remarkable consequence suddenly switched polarity, and allowed a hitherto negated possibility in Christian metaphysics to assume the status of a positive principle. And this was achieved precisely through the suppression of the last trace of a certain "Gnostic" suspicion, an unyielding refusal to grant the history of this world a determinative or probative ultimacy, or to see it as in any sense a true manifestation of the divine nature.

rationality. But, frankly, Valentinus is as out of place in the system as a Chinese dragon in a cuckoo-clock.

Which brings me to my fourth question: Is perhaps the story of a "Gnostic return in modernity" itself potentially an example of the very same "misremembering" that O'Regan elsewhere identifies with great precision, a false history that might too readily exculpate certain Christian orthodoxies of the part they played in the genesis of modernity and that sometimes hides the true genealogy behind a spectral double?

IV

Not that I am entirely certain that I know of any wholly satisfying definition of "orthodoxy" in the first place. Like O'Regan, I want to distinguish to whatever degree I can between the genuine Christian story (which I certainly believe can be told, if not necessarily *in unica voce*) and all of its many spectral inversions or caricatures or *Doppelgänger*. At the most mundane level, of course, this requires only meager powers of discernment; cultural "Christianity" at any given moment and in any given place produces countless warped parodies of the gospel. But the lines of demarcation become ever more sinuously involved, confusingly elliptical, and gallingly illegible the more intently one undertakes the serious hermeneutical and historical labor of separating an original "orthodoxy" out from the impossible historical welter of all its simulacra and counterfeits and ghosts. And those demarcations prove especially vague and fluid whenever one attempts, from the perspective of the present, to isolate which strains of Christian thought today fall within the boundaries of orthodox (or *reasonably* orthodox) belief and which do not. For the most part, we identify the former as those traditions (be they ever so diverse in detail or ecclesial affiliation) that incorporate certain cardinal principles of a larger theological or doctrinal grammar—say, certain aspects of Nicene and Chalcedonian dogma, a generally consistent notion of grace or sin or redemption, and so on—and the latter as those that, at some crucial doctrinal boundary, seem to us to go over the line. The one set includes all those denominations or schools with which ecumenical or intra-theological dialogue is possible; the other includes only forms of heresy in need of radical correction. But then, of course, all such distinctions, if they are indeed anything more than the parochial prejudices dominant at a particular place and time, presume both the veridicality of Christian memory and the possibility of a fully persuasive historical reconstruction of Christian belief from its origins. But neither memory nor historical reconstruction proves particularly solvent here. We can speak with dangerous confidence about the "true" Christian story, as distinct from all the "false" versions; but surely one of the lessons of theological history is that the "original" form of tradition is, as often as not, a final formal construct arrived at by a process of dialectical attrition and synthetic composition, one that simultaneously sums up and invents its own past, and that thereby retrospectively reduces all other variants of the tradition, no matter how ancient, to the status of perverse deviations. Thus, for the Hindu fundamentalist of today, the one true "divine" text of the *Ramayana* is the final high Sanskrit redaction produced for the Gupta court, whereas all the local, heteroclite, dialect versions of the epic or of the stories from which it arose, scattered so prodigally throughout the various linguistic clades of the subcontinent and Indo-China, are heretical corruptions. Theological history also teaches us, moreover, that the seemingly intrinsic unity of a dogmatic continuum is often much more credible when viewed from the present, as a *fait accompli*, since each of its various historical transitions seems to have been logically entailed in what preceded it. Viewed from the past forward, however, the sequence tends to look somewhat more fortuitous and spasmodic, and the final results perhaps more logically remote from their putative first causes than might have been had certain other possible paths of development not been foreclosed by dogmatic tradition.

I am not, incidentally, denying the reality of divine inspiration in the development of doctrine (though I would definitely deny that the distinction between the truly inspired and the perversely deviant is anything more than a judgment of faith that can never be fully verified historically or critically). I do not even presume that the past cannot really be determined "backwards," so to speak, in those magical moments in which a whole diverse ensemble of prior historical forces inexorably arrive at their true final cause, only to find that the full form of that endpoint had until then remained largely unanticipated. (One should not, after all, assume that time functions by a kind of mechanical causality.) Still, one has to wonder about how we have reached our present state. Much of what we today, at the end of two millennia of Christian thought, would consider more or less orthodox incorporates a huge number of elements—say, certain understandings of grace and nature, nature and supernature, flesh and spirit, the angelic and the demonic, redemption and justification, and so forth—that are not only different from, but also utterly irreconcilable with, what Paul believed had happened in Christ. At the same time, almost the entirety of the cosmology and the soteriology presumed by Paul as essential to understanding what Christ had accomplished—including a very particular theology of the hostile celestial powers, and of the shape of the cosmos, and of its relation to God's empyrean, and of the difference between psychical and spiritual

life, and of any number of other beliefs—is almost entirely absent from or
violently distorted in much of the most authoritative theological language
of later centuries. At least, so all the best historical and biblical scholarship
seems to tell us. Frankly, it would be of only very dubious historical validity to suggest that, say, Valentinus's understanding of salvation was more
remote from Paul's, in either shape or substance, than was Calvin's idiotic
theology of substitutionary atonement. In fact, it would be plainly false. And
it would be of still more dubious theological validity to claim that Hegel's
system is any more alien to the theology of the New Testament and of early
Christian metaphysics than is Baroque Thomism. In fact, in many respects
precisely the opposite is surely the case. Really, compared to the teachings
by which the early "Gnostic" or proto-Gnostic sects allegedly departed from
the beliefs of the apostolic age, much of that same Thomist tradition is far
more extravagantly heterodox. Certainly, at least, the somewhat puerile
dualisms of certain early Gnostic sects is no more repugnant to the Pauline
vision of things than is the far more horrifying voluntative monism of much
early modern Western theology. And only indifference to the religious and
speculative language of the first century would permit anyone to imagine
that Thomas or Luther or Calvin clearly practiced a faith any more consistent with Paul's beliefs than did, say, Marcion. And, as far as simple historical plausibility is concerned, how do we really convince ourselves that the
Jesus "remembered" by Hegel is any less fantastic—any less spectral—than
the Christ memorialized in the developed doctrine of the late patristic period? It may well be that, somewhere amid the vast, roiling, dazzling flood
and farrago of rival versions of the true Christian story, the one true original can be found and precisely delineated from all the simulacra and failed
drafts and haunting echoes. But, when one goes in search of it as an object
of either historical or genealogical judgment, one enters an endless hall of
mirrors, full of inverted figures, or inverted inversions of figures, and on
and on indefinitely, merging and separating and recombining—doubles
doubled and redoubled, ghosts and ghosts of ghosts, endless divergences
and convergences and reversals. If we are certain that the original really
exists, it is only because we are convinced that the entire spectacle must
have been produced by something real, particular, and complete in itself,
something that would be left standing even after all the mirrors had been
shattered, intact and distinctly visible among the shards of broken glass. But
perhaps we are instead really only gazing into a kaleidoscope, and the appearance of a single coherent and symmetrical pattern is merely an illusion,
a product of the intersection of multiple reflections of what in reality is only
a random, fragmentary, and constantly shifting collection of brightly-hued

and disconnected pieces. Inevitably, refuge from such doubts can be sought only in the presumed authority of received tradition.

It may be, however, that the very concept of theological tradition is incorrigibly equivocal. On the one hand, it is a notion that necessarily presumes the stable continuity of certain beliefs and practices that must be in some sense unalterable, preserved by the community they define, and certifying their own authority by that very changelessness. On the other, however, it must also be a name for the dynamic continuity of a living process of development, one that preserves the truth it proclaims precisely by allowing it to unfold into an incalculable variety of unpredictable new expressions. And both senses of the term are equally indispensable. Every living tradition derives its authority from some initiating moment of awakening or discovery that can never be forgotten or altered; and yet, no less essentially, that initial moment is validated only in and by the richness, capaciousness, and perdurability of the historical developments to which it continually gives rise. Thus the concept of tradition, if it is to have any function at all, must be invoked as a justification both for what has never changed and for everything that has—every cultural, social, religious, and intellectual reconfiguration serially assumed and serially abandoned over the course of generations. That means, though, it can serve as a justification for anything, a mystifying euphemism for whatever haphazardly happens to happen, or for that matter happens to fail to happen. Being simultaneously a principle both of immutability and of ceaseless transformation, it boasts an almost limitless plasticity. And this means also that its invocation is always attended by two equally disturbing possibilities: *either* there is no ultimate distinction between what is essential and what accidental in any given tradition (which would mean that the tradition has no inner rationale to speak of), *or* the difference between essence and accident is so easy to identify that most of the tradition's historical forms are nothing but convenient vehicles of cultural transmission that can be dispensed with altogether by true savants and *cognoscenti*. And historical scholarship is of only very limited value in deciding whether or not there really is a *Ding-an-sich* there or not, or how to isolate it from its ever-shifting epiphenomenal shapes. History provides us with the *event* of a tradition, in all its contingency and morphological variety, but not its essence; it records processes of both accumulation and attrition, of both retention and forgetting, but in so doing raises the portentous possibility that there is no discernible reason why some aspects of a tradition prove ephemeral and others perennial. Here, it would seem, only faith in the Holy Spirit and a certain patience with mystery can rescue the scrupulous Christian scholar from doubt. He or she absolutely must trust that the continuity of theological tradition is in some sense nourished by something that is never really visible—except perhaps indirectly, in the fluent succession of its historical accidents—to the eyes of disinterested scholarship: something by its very nature hidden behind the very cultural and intellectual forms to which it gives rise. Only the supposition of this truth silently abiding below the surface provides any explanation of both the tradition's persistence and its dynamism. Otherwise every historical transition could be interpreted only as a defeat. How one knows this truth, though, assuming one really can know it, lies outside most of the critical categories by which we try to judge the relative validity of this or that particular dogmatic or theological development—in something like "tacit knowledge," or an "illative sense," or the light of the spiritual senses. Unlike historical science, this kind of knowledge must involve some kind of understanding not only of the first "cause of motion" at a tradition's inception, but also of the final cause to which that motion corresponds, the "eschatological" consummation that is the tradition's whole rational meaning (ideally, in the case of Christian thought, this means a proleptic awareness of the divinization of creatures who are by nature meant to become gods in God). One can know that truth, then, not as any single discrete phenomenon appearing within religious experience, but rather only as the whole intentional horizon of belief, a sort of constant transcendental orientation of faith or reason that allows any religious phenomenon to appear in the first place, as both an intelligible form of, and an insufficient symbol for, a fullness ultimately lying beyond any historical expression.

Even formally defined dogmas are of only so much help here. Throughout Christian history, the formulations produced by doctrinal decisions have necessarily been of the most severely minimalist kind; and (as any good Hegelian knows) no thesis can be stated in such a way that its terms preclude radical—even radically contradictory—differences of interpretation. How many Lutheran systematic theologians of the twentieth century, for instance, found it possible to propose the most audacious revisions of trinitarian theology and Christology without for a moment wavering in their fidelity to the canonical language of Nicene and Chalcedonian orthodoxy? In truth, the very concept of doctrinal *definition* is an obscure one. Every dogmatic pronouncement of the church or churches over the centuries has been at once the concrescence of a great number of prior theological or devotional forces and also the inauguration of an entirely new sequence of evolutions, discords, speculative elaborations, and reformulations. A dogmatic definition forecloses the further unfolding of certain currents of the theological past precisely by opening entirely new streams of ungovernable future development. Nor does history provide us with quite the tidy and comforting narrative of doctrinal history that we might desire:

a story, that is, of a single dominant *consensus fidelium*, implicit in Christian confession from the first moment of the faith, smoothly and continuously crystallizing into ever more lucid and precise confessional propositions, all the while exposing opposing views as perverse novelties and heretical subversions. If anything, it tells us practically the reverse story, that of an often fitful invention of willfully ambiguous and hitherto unprecedented models of confession, successfully capturing something of the force of what preceded them, but only in the shape of synthetic formulations that also deeply altered much of the meaning of past beliefs and practices. In every instance, moreover, these innovations were obliged to claim the authority of the past solely for themselves, and therefore to rewrite the history they aspired to sum up in themselves. Dogmas arise out of rare moments of acute tension in the tradition's understanding of itself; and they can resolve the impasses these tensions create only insofar as a certain degree of calculating historical forgetfulness is cultivated around them, refashioning the past, purging it of the very complexities that made the new doctrinal formulation necessary in the first place. For a dogmatic definition to succeed, it is not enough that it supply us with an adequate answer; it must cause us to forget the original question. What we come to regard as "orthodoxy" and "heresy" are retrospective and (to be honest) transparently ideological constructions, and it is only natural that they should be. But, apart from faith in the ineffably cunning operations of the Holy Spirit, a Christian historian might be tempted to see nothing in the chronicle of official doctrine other than a continuous process of political crisis and historical revisionism. Nor can one simply repose one's confidence in the ecclesial continuity of Christian confession to dispel uncertainty here. Not that this is by any means an irrelevant thing; but, again, what truly persists in ecclesial evolution is something clearly visible, if at all, chiefly to the eyes of faith. Disinterested historical scholarship is more likely than not to see only the purely formal contiguity of various institutional forms over the centuries—structures of authority and privilege, words, repeated practices, and so forth—creating a relatively stable façade, behind which is hidden a ceaseless succession of immense conceptual, social, and ethical convulsions.

One can confirm this, in fact, by looking at the first and most consequential doctrinal definition of Christian tradition, that of the first Nicene Council. The Arian controversy was that crucial moment when a now politically enfranchised church for the first time officially *legislated* the proper content of the faith, and thereby demoted all incompatible forms of confession, however well-established or devout, to the status of damnable expressions of infidelity. As an historical judgment, of course, that was pure fiction. Arius was in many respects a profoundly conservative theologian;

certainly, in the context of Alexandrian theology, he was a more faithful representative of the most venerable schools of trinitarian thought than were the champions of the Nicene settlement. He may have been a somewhat unimaginative thinker, admittedly, but he was seeking to preserve, in what he took to be a logically cogent form, the "subordinationist" metaphysics that in his part of the Christian world had served for generations to describe the relation of heaven and earth in a single hierarchy of powers while preserving a sense of the absolute inaccessibility of God Most High. That the Father was absolutely hidden from the eyes of all other beings, and that he was known to creatures only through the subalternate and necessarily limited agency of his Logos, and that the Logos was by nature inferior to the Father, was nothing more to his mind than ancient apostolic orthodoxy. Even in insisting that the divine Son was a creature, he was not adopting an especially outlandish position. Many Christians had long believed that the Logos was merely the most exalted figure in the divine court, the Angel of Mighty Counsel, the heavenly high priest who served as the sole "priestly" mediator between the unseen Father and all other creatures. It was simply an unfortunate reality for Arius that he happened to live at a moment when too great a diversity of beliefs had become an intolerable reality for the institutional church. In the age of Constantine, doctrinal disagreement was a scandal not so much of theology as of imperial policy. And, as it happened, the Nicene party did have the better arguments. At least, their picture of things made sense of a larger range of shared Christian beliefs and spiritual expectations, and arguably provided a richer theology of the intimacy between God and his creatures in Christ. And theirs, it turned out over time, was the more coherent metaphysics. Still, the Arians and Semi-Arians were theological conservatives, not wild innovators; the Nicene party, by contrast, was advancing a conceptual and doctrinal vocabulary with only very contestable antecedents.[12] And such has always been the pattern (or something like it) of doctrinal development.

Again, I am not attempting to relativize away all Christian claims into a kind of inadjudicable equivalence. I, for instance, cordially loathe much of the Hegelian construal of Christian theological history. I think a great deal of it brilliant in a purely formal way, simply by virtue of having been dreamed up by a philosopher of colossally creative originality. I also, however, believe it morally abrasive, metaphysically vulgar, logically incoherent, and tediously fantastic. I believe that one can demonstrate in any number of ways—logically, morally, metaphysically, aesthetically, hermeneutically,

12. In English, the best and most insightful portrait of Arius and of the controversy he provoked is the one found in Williams, *Arius*.

historically, practically—that there are far better and more plausible and more persuasive and more spiritually liberating readings of the record. But I do not believe that this is something that can be argued in either a catechetical or a purely genealogical mode. I think that, to the degree any one of us possesses a clearer knowledge than any other not simply of the historical and textual facts of the Christian tradition, but also of the proper reading and interpretation of those facts, it is a knowledge inspired by a largely inexpressible and necessarily imprecise awareness of the eschatological horizon—the final cause—of the tradition, as vouchsafed by constant and various exposure to the event of revelation in Christ and formation in that revelation's attendant intellectual and moral virtues. Not being myself a saint, I cannot pretend to believe my sense of the truth in this matter particularly sound. And, for just this reason, I also cannot think of this matter in terms of a single correct original version of the tale and its many "false doubles," or of a verifiably correct memory of the tale as opposed to various forms of "misremembering." I think of the matter, rather, in terms of better and worse enunciations and interpretations within the unfolding historical effects of a revelation that, even in its very first annunciation, always had something of a polyphonic character about it. And to discern which is which, which authentic and which counterfeit, one must rely on any number of ancillary but indispensable intellectual resources, such as coherent metaphysical reasoning and (no less important) simple good taste. I say all of this not on account of some kind of moral tact or agnostic tentativeness on my part. I am altogether happy to denounce what I take to be abominably foolish readings of the tradition, and think it possible to adduce good reasons for doing so. But I also believe that fidelity to the wisdom of the tradition includes a willingness to recover aspects of its truth that have been lost in the contingencies of doctrinal history, by accidental association with streams of reflection that at one time or another were retroactively condemned as forms of apostasy or deviation, in some cases rather unfairly. After all, simply as a matter of critical probity, how can one definitively and impartially distinguish with finality between heretical distortions and legitimate developments of doctrine, when both have often departed with equal abruptness from what preceded them? What is the phantom reflection and what the true semblance of the tradition? Who enjoys the privilege of remembering "correctly?" Surely it would be little more than an evasion for the historian of ideas to invoke something like Newman's theory of doctrinal development (that grand exercise in tautologous reasoning). If all tradition, all "orthodoxy," is a tale at once of unbroken continuity and of constant novelty, and of a practice of pious recollection that is also a ruthless revision of the past, surely one must exercise a certain salutary diffidence here. What, for instance, might at first appear at any given moment to be the recrudescence of a heterodox school long ago consigned to the midden of deviant theologies might in fact be only—or, at the very least, *also*—a suppressed but ineradicable element of the tradition rising to the surface once more, perhaps in an unfortunately extreme form. Even if there has been some kind of Gnostic return in modernity, then, we might do well to ask what has really prompted it, and whether it might actually be the necessary resurgence of some aspect of the theological imagination whose long absence from Christian consciousness has left a vacancy that nothing else can fill.

Perhaps the best questions to ask of ourselves before even attempting to isolate the true transmission of the tradition from its errant imitations would be this: How has our own memory been constituted? What necessary moments of willful forgetfulness does it depend upon? But, then, if we ask these things in earnest, a potentially interminable historical aetiology and reconstruction has been inaugurated. And here yet another specter arises: the disturbing possibility that, within the record of the tradition, no final distinction between the one original true text and the many palimpsests obscuring it can be drawn, simply because the "original" itself is not a discrete, inert object; it is, rather, by its very nature, a dynamic process of change, one not only tolerating, but actually subsisting in, a series of accretions, suppressions, revisions, and renewals. Again, how can we know that the original is not itself only a phantom figure produced solely by the play of simulacra—a haunting absence that must occasionally be concealed by one or another doctrinal compromise, or a haunting ubiquity that perpetually refuses reduction to a single uniform manifestation? Perhaps, when all those opaque or diaphanous layers of historical contingency are stripped away, all that remains is an open question. Perhaps the odyssey back to the one true homeland of the faith is a fantasy, and Ithaca's headland will always lie somewhere just beyond an endlessly receding succession of jetties, bluffs, capes, chersoneses, and the occasional mirage. If nothing else, the one true great Hegelian discovery—the binary mechanisms of conceptual change, the kaleidoscopic flow of ceaseless inversion, the always vital and refractory latency of every principle in its own negation—suggests that this could prove to be the whole story at the last. Perhaps what we deem to be either orthodoxy or heterodoxy—anamnesis or "misremembering," the original or its ghostly double—is entirely determined by our relative appetites for the familiar or the exotic. I do not want to exaggerate my own skepticism on this issue, of course. Again, I believe there are a great many ways of negotiating the ambiguities of the tradition, and of distinguishing between better and worse expressions of its truths. But I do think that there are questions here that one may genuinely pose with regard to a project of historical reconstructions and analytical discriminations like O'Regan's (without for a moment denying its rigor, comprehensiveness, subtlety, or brilliance). At the very least, one might ask where so grand a project of recollection, and so tireless a labor of isolating the true version of the Christian story while exposing its counterfeits, can safely and convincingly come to a halt; one might justly wonder whether, once initiated, the entire enterprise might prove to be, just as a matter of logical consistency, an indefatigable and universal solvent, ultimately dispelling the entire insubstantial pageant, leaving not a rack behind.

So, then, my final question: Can O'Regan enunciate and fully elaborate a systematic set of principles and a clear method for discriminating, wholly in terms of his genealogical and historical project and without any leaps of faith, between the true Christian narrative and its false doubles? Though, really, Yeats phrased the matter far better:

> O chestnut tree, great-rooted blossomer,
> Are you the leaf, the blossom or the bole?
> O body swayed to music, O brightening glance,
> How can we know the dancer from the dance?

Bibliography

Desmond, William. *Hegel's God: A Counterfeit Double?* Aldershot, UK: Ashgate, 2003.

Filoramo, Giovanni. *A History of Gnosticism.* Oxford: Blackwell, 1992.

O'Regan, Cyril. *Anatomy of Misremembering: Von Balthasar's Response to Philosophical Modernity. Volume 1: Hegel.* New York: Crossroads, 2014.

———. *Gnostic Return in Modernity.* New York: SUNY Press, 2001.

———. *The Heterodox Hegel.* New York: SUNY Press, 1994.

Williams, Rowan. *Arius: Heresy and Tradition.* Rev. ed. Grand Rapids: Eerdmans, 2002.

9

Orthodoxy, Knowledge, and Freedom

JOHN MILBANK

1. O'Regan's Conflicted Balthasar

Cyril O'Regan's *The Anatomy of Misremembering* constitutes a profound breakthrough in Balthasar studies.[1] For it abandons the dominant exegetical mode of doxography in relation to the great Swiss Catholic theologian. For this mode, over-beguiled by the comprehensive weight of his written production, Balthasar tends to be regarded as the compiler of a new and authoritative modern *Summa*, offering a remarkably variegated yet substantially unified vision of immense originality.

While not altogether denying this perspective, O'Regan opens up a different one which exhibits Balthasar both as more conflicted and more in continuity with several existing modern traditions. Yet this renders him, one might argue, not less but more interesting and not less but more pivotal. It does, however, begin to suggest that one should regard his work not so much as an achieved monument, but rather as a site of crucially realized perplexities that remain for theology further to explore.

Thus, the most striking thing about the book is that O'Regan in effect, and to my mind correctly, suggests that Balthasar is paradoxically marked by the most suspicious of currents of thought that he is nonetheless the most constantly drawn to. These currents are four: Romanticism, Neoplatonism,

1. Cyril O'Regan, *Anatomy*.

Gnosticism and apocalyptic. One can I think add esotericism, to which O'Regan also pays some attention to.

This fivefold extreme tension—simultaneous fascination and revulsion in each case—is not, however, as O'Regan makes so abundantly clear, with endless telling detail, any sort of idiosyncrasy on Balthasar's part. To the contrary, in the longest possible perspective it is an incredibly serious and somewhat agonized engagement with the question of Christian theological identity and indeed Christian identity *tout court*. For Balthasar as a Catholic is committed to the essential need for intellectual and cultural mediation of the Word of God if it is in the first place to arrive. Thus, he is far from thinking that the cognitively and aesthetically formal expression of the gospel is extrinsic to its substance, much less the envisaging of the kind of spirituality or *mystique* that it entails. To the contrary, he is fully apprised of the fact that this expression begins in the Bible itself and that if, thereby, a tension arises, then it is already there in the scriptures, or more especially in the textual penumbra that surrounds them.

This tension therefore concerns the nature of orthodoxy and orthopraxis themselves: just what are the essential bounds of Christian belief, experience, and performance? Here Balthasar, like O'Regan himself, is haunted by the uneasy sense that what is false may be all too akin to what is true. For both theologians, the deepest danger arises not from the evident enemy—the village atheist so to speak—but rather from the simulated friend: the teller of the runes on the village outskirts, who may confusingly turn up at the Parish Mass from time to time. Again, for both thinkers this is one reason why apocalyptic is a central subject of perplexity: not only is it one of five genres to be treated with a merely cautious welcome, it also allegorizes their shared ambiguity in terms of the thematic of the *counterfeit double*, to use the phrase of O'Regan's ideological ally and fellow-Irishman, William Desmond. Alongside the images of the truth, apocalyptic literature offers us also parodic images of falsity, warning us of how they may beguile.

In a shorter historical perspective, it turns out, on O'Regan's exhaustive and illuminating analysis, that Balthasar is mostly just sustaining an anxiety that has been frequent, if not almost dominant in German Catholic thought, ever since the emergence of Schelling and Hegel. Already the Catholic Tübingen school engaged not just the thought of Schleiermacher, but also that of the speculative idealists. In particular, Franz Staudenmaier sought both to learn from and yet ultimately to criticize Hegel. In negative agreement with the Protestant theologian Ferdinand Christian Baur (as David Bentley Hart details in this volume), he saw in Hegel a recrudescence of ancient Gnosticism and Neoplatonism, and in consequence a certain falsification of the Christian trinitarian legacy: a subjection of God to a theogonic and pantheistic process of becoming, and to a necessitated and agonistic self-alienation. Perceptively, as Balthasar noted, he initially proffered the early medieval Eriugena as a more acceptably Neoplatonic antidote to Hegel, although he later came to worry that he too much exhibited the same necessitarian vices, rendering the Creator dependent on his connection with the creation. As O'Regan notes, Balthasar suggested that Maximus the Confessor would have been the better alternative.

And yet, O'Regan admirably brings to the fore the fact that Balthasar is not consistently at ease even with Maximus or Gregory of Nyssa, and still less with Dionysius. Any deep embrace of Neoplatonic elements seems for him to run the risk of over-embracing the speculative at the expense of faith, or the necessitated at the expense of freedom. Similarly, any engagement with Romantic aesthetics, even though this is absolutely central to Balthasar's own philosophical and theological enterprise, is always fraught with the danger of confusing glory with mere beauty and reducing the realm of religion to the realm of art. Again, even though Balthasar follows Sergei Bulgakov in making the Apocalypse of John absolutely pivotal for his own speculations (despite early Christian unease in some quarters about this text's canonicity), he nonetheless worries continuously that apocalyptic as a genre is excessively and too explicitly *eidetic*, too knowing about eternity and the final future, and too obsessed with blood and retribution, even though Balthasar sustains his own Johannine version of that emphasis. As to the esoteric, O'Regan does not shy away from the implausible degree to which Balthasar claims that Soloviev's immersion in this field is merely a vehicle for a more classical Christian spirituality, and he could have mentioned how the same gesture is made in relation to the modern Christian esotericist and sophiologist Valentin Tomberg.[2] In both cases, Balthasar evidences a considerable degree of knowledge of Hermeticism and magic that might appear suspicious to those inclined (perhaps wrongly) to be suspicious of such things. The Swiss theologian seems at once to wish to harvest for orthodoxy many more arcane insights and suggestions of deeper recesses of reserved mystical knowledge and yet also to draw back from any endorsement of their hinterland of magical and theurgic assumptions. But he must have well known that it is difficult to detach these assumptions from exactly that metaphysics of attributive analogy which he wishes strongly to endorse: in Proclus, from whom it ultimately derives, the linguistic affirmation of ineffable likeness is inherently bound up with the ontological affirmation of occult connection.

---

2. Balthasar, "Afterword," in Anonymous, *Meditations on the Tarot*, 659–65.

The esoteric is, of course, also profoundly linked both to *gnosis* and to apocalyptic, even though the latter are central to Christianity as such. It was declared in the patristic and medieval eras that, while prophecy ends with Christ in whom it is fulfilled, the apocalyptic genre survives this fulfilment, since it is concerned with a deeper contemplative insight into the eternal mysteries which that fulfilment opens up to us.[3] And as the end of time has begun to arrive with this fulfilment in Christ, such insight into the eternal is taken to coincide with an insight into temporal finality that is more than merely prophetic, because more suffused with a "Gnostic" sense of completion.

Yet, as O'Regan notes, Balthasar refuses to follow Soloviev and Berdaev in their esotericist exultation in the florid symbolism of earlier intertestamental apocalyptic, especially the books of 1 Enoch and 2 Esdras. I have already mentioned his other reasons for reserve in this respect. And yet even this reserve can only be the expression of a tension: naturally Balthasar is all too aware of the link of the crucial "Son of Man" apocalyptic passage in Matthew to a particular sequence in Enoch, and the way in which its more benign tempering of the latter's ferocity still sustains its apparently bloodcurdling threats.

What is more and supremely important, as well brought out by O'Regan, is the fact that Balthasar borrows many of his most distinctive theological themes from Sergei Bulgakov, in whom all the supposedly ambiguous elements we have considered so far are fully present: Romanticism, critical engagement with Hegel and Schelling, strongly Neoplatonic elements, centrality of apocalyptic, and decidedly esoteric and Gnostic borrowings. Once again, these dimensions, which Balthasar takes to be already tempered by Bulgakov, are further qualified by him, especially such that what in idealism may appear to be determined and impersonal process is now rendered an interpersonal drama between divine and human liberty.

Nevertheless, the Swiss theologian's focus on the emanation of divine glory is a somewhat muted version of the Russian theologian's concern with the divine Wisdom: *Herrlichkeit* is Sophia's paler sister. Likewise, his entire linkage of the Trinity with the passion, by insistence (and rightly, against the run of modern critical exegesis) on the continuity of Johannine Apocalypse with the Johannine Gospel, is borrowed from Bulgakov. The same is true—though ultimately after Nicholas of Cusa—of his Holy Saturday theology of Christ's atoning suffering in hell. More absent, one might add, from Balthasar is the theurgic dimension, which arguably links to his

3. See for example, Grosseste, *Cessation of the Laws*, 200.

playing down of liturgical synergism in favor of interactive cosmic drama. With Bulgakov there is surely more balance of the two.

This absence in Balthasar is linked to his crucial preference, as noted by O'Regan, for Plotinus over Proclus, on the debatable grounds of the greater speculative character of the latter.[4] This involves him in a certain playing-down of the Proclean element in Dionysius, Maximus, and Aquinas and an ignoring of the way in which cognitive shifts parallel to the Iamblichan and Proclean are made in relation to Plotinus by Gregory of Nyssa and Augustine.[5] This element and these shifts all involve a deepened attention to the cosmos, to the revelatory importance of liturgy, and to the grounding even of finite difference in ultimate mystical Unity. By anachronistically regarding such moves as tainted with later notes of idealism, pantheism, and left-handed occultism, Balthasar was somewhat failing to see (for all his contradictory celebration of "cosmic liturgy" in Maximus) how Christian theology does require an account of the ultimate value of the creation (including each and every one of its creatures) and the finite totality of the cosmos in relation to God himself. It is not enough merely to ascribe this to the divine will and the divine generosity, because this still leaves the created order as somewhat accidental and therefore lacking in irreplaceable significance, which contradicts its absolute conjoining to the eternal godhead in the case of the incarnation.

O'Regan also well delineates, and largely himself endorses, Balthasar's continued affirmation of trans-epochal continuities that were already claimed in the German nineteenth century (again see Hart's essay). Thus, Hegelianism is seen as a continuation of a return in modern times of Valentinian Gnosticism, inaugurated by Jacob Boehme. German idealism in general is regarded as being in continuity with antique Neoplatonism in terms of its ontological priority of the intellectual and its cosmic horizon for the divine. Eckhart, Cusa, and Ficino, never mind Bruno, are regarded as mediating links. Both the Gnostic and the Neoplatonic currents are regarded by Balthasar as inhibiting the freedom of God and as tarnishing the liberty of human beings. Above all, a late antique "Gnostic" distortion of Christianity is blamed for a confusion of divinely immanent logic with divinely contingent narrative, such that lapse and evil are introduced into the very godhead.

Following Eric Voegelin, in O'Regan's case, this lamentable ontological agonism is seen as inherently linked with an excessive speculative claim

---

4. Proclus is drier and more summary and less experiential in tone, but not necessarily more speculative.

5. See Jason B. Parnell's highly insightful monograph, *The Theurgic Turn*.

to know the absolute, and also with the heterodox eschatology of Joachim of Fiore. Certainly, in the writings of several nineteenth-century thinkers of disparate ideology, the Joachite "age of the spirit" beyond the "age of the Son" got secularized to support both progressivism and utopianism, as Henri de Lubac delineated.[6] In the case of Schelling and other German writers, this thematic was merged with the Behmenist dramatization and historicization of the Trinity itself. This merging gives us that combination of a historiography of three ages with a now historicized process of spiritual alienation and return, whose most famous exemplification lies in Marxism. However, this is a specifically nineteenth-century fusion. Even though there may possibly be Joachite images in Boehme, O'Regan has himself shown that in the seventeenth century these two heterodox trajectories did not, as yet, really overlap.[7] Joachim divided and periodized the hitherto unified economic action of the three persons *ad extra,* but sustained an orthodox account of the immanent Trinity; Boehme sustained an orthodox seven-age sacred historiography, but divided and agonized the immanent unity of the Trinity itself. As O'Regan details, for Boehme, unlike Joachim, the *whole* of salvation history belongs to the "third kingdom of the Spirit," since this is the realm and epoch of the necessary temporal healing of the eternal tension between divine Father and Son.[8] Yet despite his own observations, he too much tends to speak as if a later synthesis of these two diverse currents can be projected backwards.

2. The Question of Divine Freedom

In his essay in this volume, John Betz significantly shows how some of the tensions that O'Regan divulges in Balthasar are also manifest in the case of Erich Przywara, one of the most decisive influences on the Swiss theologian. As Betz discusses, in sermons preached during the war, the Polish-German Catholic philosopher seemed to qualify his analogical vision with a theology of crisis and dialectics more reminiscent of Barth, or of the British Dissenting theologian Peter Taylor Forsyth during World War I. Human measures in every sense have failed, Przywara now thunders, amidst the terrible ruins of the German cities. We must turn instead to the pure biblical self-disclosure of God.

Betz shows how, nonetheless, there is not a total rupture here: Przywara, like Balthasar and today O'Regan, continues to see that the problem

---

6. De Lubac, *Joachim de Flore.*

7. See de Lubac's cautious discussion in *Joachim de Flore,* 218–23.

8. O'Regan, *Gnostic Apocalypse,* 167–73.

inherited from nominalism and the Reformation is a false sundering of will from *logos*, and of grace from nature, such that the Protestant (and often also Baroque Catholic) insistence on an absolute divorce of will from reason, and of nature from grace, led to a dialectical inversion whereby a purely self-sufficient and fatally determined cosmos is seen as encompassing all of reality. All the same, Betz still considers that Przywara now thinks that late mediaeval and Protestant voluntarism provides a corrective to the danger that analogy will lose the priority of the katalogical or the top-downwards; thus, a pure reserve of incalculable divine will beyond analogical eminence must be sustained. Just this arguably incoherent combining of an analogical cosmos with a voluntarist exceptionalism is, one can add, constantly traceable in Balthasar also and is present in his tendency (which he shares with Ratzinger) to oscillate between Thomistic and Bonaventuran emphases.[9]

But the whole idea that the crucial mark of divine personal transcendence is the divine freedom is surely debatable. Indeed, it is in danger of falling into anthropomorphic idolatry by failing to see that if God is entirely simple and unified, then there cannot be for him, however incomprehensible this is for us, any division between freedom and necessity, or between willing and reasoning. Yet even at the human level, any absolute distinction is dubious, as the earlier Schelling showed in the case of the supreme liberty of art. And Thomas Pfau has described how a facultative division of reason and will is only a post-Scotist outcome that tends to lose the earlier sense (as reinstated by Cudworth and later Coleridge) that they are fused as a kind of probing desire, lured ultimately by the one supernatural end.[10] Conceived as such a mode of desire it becomes much harder to corral either the will or the reason as immanent, purely individual, and absolute. For now will is only will to the degree that it remotely intimates and recognizes the eternal Good; reason is only reason to the degree that it remotely longs and actively searches for a complete intelligence that is always more than its own. Just to the degree that the will and the reason involve each other, they also reveal their respective incompletions and excess over any finite self-containment.

This unifying eroticism should also warn us against the slight tendency of both O'Regan and Desmond to subscribe (in contrast to either Dionysius or Augustine) to a duality of *agape* and *eros*.[11] It can be insightful to read Gnosticism as a dark eroticism, yet the specifically modern (including the Hegelian) mode of claiming a full speculative access for the finite knowing subject is less rooted in a (vertical and horizontal) relational erotics, than in

9. See Milbank, *The Suspended Middle*, 69–84.

10. Pfau, *Minding the Modern*.

11. See for example, Desmond, *Being and the Between*.

a decisionistic self-positing and self-giving that results from a modern sense of the "absolute command" of will as choice and the "absolute command" of the one-way gift as a purely sacrificial gesture without any looked-for return of reciprocal affirmation of the specific and embodied personal self.

3. Hart versus O'Regan

These latter remarks can serve as a preface to a consideration of David Bentley Hart's response to O'Regan in this volume, which goes beyond the latter's concern with tensions in relation to everything "Gnostic," to a whole-sale querying of the very idea of "Gnostic return in modernity."[12]

The core of Hart's critique is very simple. Balthasar was simply repeating the fantasized back-projections made by nineteenth-century German scholarship of post-Kantian speculative idealism upon ancient "Gnosticism"—to such a degree, indeed, that the supposed unified reality of the latter is largely a result of these projections. Unfortunately, they were sustained till well into the twentieth century, and long past their international scholarly sell-by date, by the likes of such luminaries as Rudolf Bultmann, Hans Jonas, Eric Voegelin, and Hans Blumenberg. According to these projections (which one can note, now implicate Heidegger besides Hegel), "Gnosticism" involved inflated theosophical speculations about the inner reality of the divine and stories of divine rupture and fall with a coming to genuine divine selfhood achieved by his entering into the resulting realm of unlikeness.

But in reality, there was no single ancient "Gnosticism," rendering long debates about whether it was pre- or post-Christian largely redundant. There was rather a shared family affinity across different faiths and philosophies between recrudescent mythologies arising within the embrace of monotheism, all tending to focus on a negative view of the current cosmos, on the circumstances of its derivation through corrupted mediators, and on the possibilities of deliverance from its malignance at the hands of benign ones. The divine mystical secret as both lost and recoverable was not a cognitive, speculative one, but something inexpressible and ineffable, attainable only through ritual initiations recalling revelatory or oracular disclosures and its accompanying acts of trust, persuasion, or faith (*pistis*).

Nor, as Hart stresses, was any sort of Hegelian surpassing of ordinary religious devotion involved, even though there were recognized degrees of initiation—as, indeed with orthodox Christianity. God himself was not deemed to be in any way implicated in the fall, which affected only the *pleroma*. Free will was generally involved in this lapse, as with the corrupted

12. See O'Regan, *Gnostic Return.*

desire of Sophia to be equal to God in wisdom—showing that, if anything, as Hart says, a "Hegelian" mode of speculation would have been the supreme sin for the Gnostics. And by the same token, no sort of "divine becoming" was involved whatsoever.

Indeed, one can say that Hegel's excessive concern to affirm the necessity and ultimacy of the finite with respect to God is specifically a distortion of an *orthodox* emphasis, rather than anything deriving from doubtful hinterlands. After all, it is surely obvious that "theosophy," or the logical and narrated exploration of the inner life of God, is only really possible as a Christian trinitarian exposition.

Just for this reason, as O'Regan discusses, Staudenmaier rightly saw Eriugena as a more orthodox alternative to Hegelian elaborations. For Eriugena had realized that if the creation derives from God, who is entirely replete and is indeed "everything," then even from the divine point of view it has to have some sort of irreplaceable, absolute value. Although the finite lacks the positive lack which is the infinite, there must be something positively unique and uniquely valuable about this very absence. Thus, Eriugena suggested that the finite eternally realizes for God a definite and bounded knowledge of himself as "created God" lacking from his infinity, which as boundless and so undefined is, after Gregory of Nyssa, a kind of "unknowing" of himself. (In both thinkers this doctrine correlates with the idea of finite beatitude as infinite advance or *epectasis*—Eriugena and later Cusanus seek arguably to mediate between this view and Dionysian immediacy of final vision, as they do between infinite ontological unknowing and the Dionysian divine coincidence of the finite and the infinite, the bounded and the unbounded.)

This is not at all to say that Hart dissents from O'Regan's negative verdict upon Hegel and Schelling, nor from his search to disinter "misremembrances" or seductive doubles of the Christian truth. Altogether to the contrary, in either case. However, Hart wishes to offer a different genealogy and to locate the crucial counterfeit double elsewhere than in the Gnostic legacy—much less in the Neoplatonic, Romantic, apocalyptic, or esoteric ones. And it is at this point that one sees the point of greatest dissent between him and O'Regan, after Balthasar.

The seductive danger has never for Hart been the neglect of liberty in favor of knowledge, but if anything, the very opposite: an exaltation of an arbitrary divine liberty over a divine erotic wisdom (fusing freedom and understanding) in which we can confidently participate. The combination of the true doctrine of divine omnipotence with the false doctrine of eternal punishment for the reprobate encouraged from Augustine onwards the gradual emergence of a doctrine of inscrutable double predestination. Even though much of the "Gnostic" and analogical vision survived for a long time in the West, eventually and inevitably this residue (as with the doctrine of the divine *potentia absoluta* even in Aquinas) undermined this vision. A resulting theological voluntarism was eventually inverted as various doctrines of blind and arbitrary natural and human striving or ungrounded choosing.

Even in the case of Hegel it is this more dangerous—because more presumptively "orthodox"—double that is secretly at work. For, as Hart well argues, Schelling was correct to see that what initially drives an empty because negative and formal ontological-historical dialectical process is an ungrounded impulse towards divine self-assertion—a pure willing. Voluntarism here assumes the nihilistic form of the story of a "null" God who wills to be through all the sufferings and horrors of the finite to which he is essentially indifferent.

Hart goes on to perpend more general remarks against any over-complacent account of Christian doctrinal development. Much of the time indeed (as in the example of the Western trajectory just given) it is subject to "mechanical" dialectical inversions of a Hegelian kind, which, Žižek-like, are little more than the oscillations of fashion. Any "authentic" line of accumulation can only be identified by the eye of discerning faith (which Hart of course does not deny) and would be invisible to the cold gaze of the objective historian. What is more, not all breaks and ruptures are progressive, as John Henry Newman too much assumed: a formal truth of "Protestantism" is that there can indeed be fatal forgettings of older deposits, some of them biblical. The sophiological enterprise itself, which Balthasar somewhat echoes, is an attempt to do more justice to neglected biblical material concerning wisdom, the eschatology of the Spirit, and the Pauline teaching concerning the eternal Adam and the eternal humanity of Christ—which for Paul became also incarnate, along with the divine *Logos,* to which it was eternally conjoined.

It is in this spirit that Hart rightly says that we need additionally to reckon with the "Gnostic" dimension in John and Paul: their distinguishing of an originally and finally pneumatic body from a fallen "earthly" one; their negative view of the current daemonically-governed cosmos; their association of the Hebrew law with this at best ambivalent rule; their belief that Christ has broken through this threatening dimension to offer us again the cosmically-occluded divine secret and that he cleaves a way before us safely to ascend after him to God without prevention by threatening archontic and fallen angelic powers. Of course, Soloviev, Florensky, Bulgakov, and Tomberg had already commenced to try to make continued modern sense of this dimension.

How are we to assess Hart's critique? Is there no truth at all in the idea of a modern Gnostic return? I think that in general and in all the respects just mentioned he is undoubtedly right. Nevertheless, one might slightly qualify what he says in ways that he might well be quite happy with, but which also allow slightly more veracity to O'Regan (and Balthasar's) genealogy.

Everything here pivots about the figure of Jacob Boehme. As Hart says, it is in Boehme and not in ancient Gnosticism that one first discovers the thematics of an *agon* within the Godhead itself and a cosmic fall and historical repair of a Trinity for which immanent and economic dimensions are now perfectly fused. Once more, however, and long before Hegel, Hart would be right to say that the real hidden culprit here is voluntarism. For it is precisely Boehme's *Lutheranism* that causes him to bend a received Renaissance esoteric tradition in a wholly novel direction. Indeed, already Luther had come very near to ascribing to God the source of a now positive evil.[13] O'Regan himself argues in his book on Boehme, *Gnostic Apocalypse*, that while Boehme resisted on ethical grounds the Lutheran doctrines of predestination and imputed justification, he nonetheless still sought a way to understand Luther's attribution of both ontological anger and ontological mercy to God, by narrativizing these dual characteristics as inner divine struggle between the "fire" of Paternal resistance to manifestation and the "light" of the manifesting Son: a struggle between naturalized competing wills. After the Spirit has realized this manifestation as creation, the necessary fiery precondition of light becomes the positive possibility of evil. Given the ontological necessity for conflict, grounded in God himself, it is difficult, as O'Regan notes, to see how a source of evil in God is really denied here, since good and evil themselves have been derived from embattled "meta-physical" qualities and thereby relativized and compromised in their ethical nature. This concurs with O'Regan's highly insightful observation that Boehme's doctrine of evil is one example of a specifically modern and rationalizing theodicy.[14]

It remains nevertheless that the specific ideological idiom that is transmitted to the German idealists and some Romantics is a Lutheran inflexion of an esotericism with some Gnostic elements in the broadest sense, as advertised by Hart. This broad sense may not always include any notion that the world is outright evil (as in the case of the Gnostic Justin, as reported by Hippolytus of Rome) and indeed this is largely absent from Jewish and Islamic Gnostic modes. Nonetheless, one might argue that, in the case of the Lurianic Kabbalah, the pleromic lapse has become somewhat more

13. See Milbank, "Reformation 500: Any Cause for Celebration?"
14. O'Regan, *Gnostic Apocalypse*, 31–55.

automatic—a matter of the unbearable light of divinity that causes a "shattering of the vessels." Moreover, a conflation of the moments of creation and fall that *does* track back to Valentinianism and the like and *is* transmitted to Hegel and Schelling is here sustained. Both things pass through Boehme's specifically Lutheran refraction. To this extent O'Regan is importantly right.

But it should also here be noted that Boehme is the main developer and transmitter of a sophiology that seems to have its origins with another Lutheran eccentric, Paracelsus, whose theology was arguably more exotic than heterodox.[15] It is these specifically modern and Lutheran currents as also variously mediated by later "left Lutheran" figures like Oetinger and Hamann and other pietists that both Bulgakov and Balthasar are crucially sifting and adapting.

In general, one can say that Balthasar and O'Regan are by no means wrong to see one aspect of modern Titanism as originating in specifically modern and hubristic mutations of the magical and alchemical dimension that always hovered at the fringes of a Hermetic-Neoplatonic tradition, much deployed by orthodoxy itself during the Renaissance period.[16] Hart himself obliquely acknowledges this. At the same time, it is also true that during this epoch the main lines of this tradition were not usually so contaminated. Even if there are ambiguities in this respect with Ficino, he was not Bruno, just as Fludd was not Boehme, Comenius was not Campanella, and so forth.

Moreover, I think that Hart is right to indicate that this is a genealogical subplot. The main historical forgery is far more insidiously like the genuine coin. It is rather to do, as Hart says, with a voluntarism that can look like a hyper-piety and is intimately linked (as many scholars have now better established) with a turn to univocity, to knowledge by representation, conceptions of the divine causality as in rivalry with created causal factors and a new ontological priority of the possible over the actual.[17] One cannot even safely consign this shift to nominalism, because the way for that was prepared by Scotist univocity of Being and the way for that in turn by an "atomist" understanding of Platonic forms (as being the same in their infinite and finite instantiations) and a sharp division of rational possibility from will as "election" (rather than just a priority for the will) in Alexander of Hales and Bonaventure, much indebted to Ibn Sina and arguably rooted in a specifically Islamic negotiation of the relationship between philosophy

15. Milbank, "Reformation 500."

16. One can think here of the ecclesially mainline figure of Giles of Viterbo, close to Ficino and head of the Augustinian order at the time when Luther was one of its members.

17. See Milbank, *Beyond Secular Order*.

and the God of revelation.[18] In this way, a subtle deviation hovers near to orthodox writers and ideas from whom in other respects there is of course much positively to be learnt.

The same consideration applies to the Joachite perversion of apocalyptic. In associating this with the "Gnostic," without any supplied evidence, Voegelin, as already noted, was simply repeating a nineteenth-century synthesis. A more genuine historical association is with the same Franciscan current of theology just alluded to. While, indeed, only the Spiritual Franciscans adopted the full Joachite position, Joseph Ratzinger showed in his controversial doctrinal dissertation that even Bonaventure adopted a semi-Joachite position (which Ratzinger at that stage celebrated), according to which Francis was the Apocalypse-prophesied herald of a spiritualizing era of more direct interior and less socially mediated contact with God.[19] One can argue that this correlates with the somewhat Nestorian drift of Franciscan Christology, as does the increasing separation of reason and will with the Franciscan retreat from substantive relations as defining the persons of the Trinity, in favor of these two faculties as distinguishing the Son and Spirit. This very move in the longest possible perspective opens the way for a "Gnostic" tensional interplay between the different persons in the cases of Boehme and Hegel, which would be impossible on an Augustinian or a Thomistic view.

To add these details to Hart's genealogy of deviation in the West is implicitly to ask the imponderable question as to how far it is accounted for by the very long-term factor of belief in the eternity of hell (of course much shared, if more mutedly, with the East, where it can be linked with different, though not entirely different, deviations) and how far by the shorter-term shifts that I have just indicated. All one can suggest here is that the doctrine of everlasting punishment did not of itself automatically generate voluntarism (as perhaps Hart too much suggests); all the shorter term more complex and specific cultural and intellectual shifts were required (including perhaps the encounter with Islam). Nonetheless, Hart is right to argue that the implication of an arbitrary God always hovered latently in the background: when combined with the separately derived short-term mutations it emerged into the foreground.

If the counterfeit is not so much hovering outside the door as already well over the threshold—and almost from the outset—then one needs

18. See Milbank, "Afterword: The Dissolution of Divine Government: Gilson and the 'Scotus Story,'" in Gilson, *John Duns Scotus*, 538–76.

19. See Milbank, "'There's always one day which isn't the same as the day before': Il Cristianesimo e La Storia nelli Scritti di Charles Péguy," and Milbank, "The Franciscan Conundrum."

equivalently to reassess the hoverers. All those in the West who either explicitly or implicitly rejected the eternity of hell and affirmed *apocatastasis* were also the same thinkers who insisted, without hubris, but often in reaction against currents that coherently combine excessive rationalism with excessive voluntarism (Abelard already, for example), that theology, if deification is real, must involve some attempt remotely and imperfectly to think the divine viewpoint, however much this may involve the entertaining of analogical paradox. I am thinking for example of Eriugena, Eckhart, Julian of Norwich, and Cusanus. In each case one could argue that their orthodoxy is more hyperbolic than it is marginal or dubious.

But this involves a considerable corrective to Balthasar's perspective, which is arguably now rather dated in scholarly terms, just as his literary criticism tends somewhat to the Victorian in its approach. He preserved the distorted reading of the entire German Albertine tradition as if it simply foreshadowed much later Teutonic obsessions, which has now been challenged by Alain de Libera, Johannes Hoff, and others.[20] This is altogether to play down the fact that Hegelian hubris is not a perennial Neoplatonic temptation, but rather something that arises specifically only after the Kantian critique. Hegel's efforts to encompass all of knowledge had to be undertaken precisely in order to achieve a rationalist defeat of skepticism, while still accepting Kantian restrictions on our scope of metaphysical understanding. Thus, for Hegel it is necessary, in order for the infinite to be known, that it be fully accommodated within our finite bounds, and this is the real source of his cognitive boasting and speculative excess. The Behmenist permutation of the Gnostic here undergoes a specifically "critical" further alteration. And one can add that the Kantian position (as André de Muralt and Ludger Honnefelder have now shown) derives specifically from a univocalist, nominalist, and voluntarist scholastic inheritance.

Balthasar's entire tendency to unleash finally a voluntarist mental reserve stands in contrast to later exponents of the *nouvelle théologie* like Jean Trouillard or Claude Bruaire who insist that the creation is not just a contingently willed divine arrangement, but necessarily follows an order of both derivation and self-government that proceeds from the intellectual through the psychic to the material, in accordance with Neoplatonic emanation or *fluxus*. Both Augustine and Aquinas thought of the creation in exactly this way.

In more general terms, all this much accords with Hart's advised caution as to over-confident accounts of Christian continuity. We cannot so safely segregate even the "deviant" Gnostics as we would like to think: for

---

20. Libera, *Métaphysique et noétique*; Hoff, *Analogical Turn*.

example, someone like the Gnostic Justin. And is it not the Gnostics who first tended to promote a drama of condescending divine retrieval instead of the sedate Middle Platonic human-ascension theology of apologists like Justin Martyr?[21] Irenaeus did not just rebut the Valentinians, he also amended their parody by rethinking restorative mimetic descent as recapitulation within horizontal time. In a parallel fashion, one can regard orthodox doctrines of incarnation, for example as presented by Augustine in his *Enarrationes in Psalmos*, as the most extreme developments of the theurgic: God himself in human person and then human beings in the church as the body of this divine humanity must offer worship to God if anyone is to be saved.[22]

One could even argue that orthodoxy is also an extreme mode of "Gnosticism," insofar as it non-dualistically considers that the fall is an "impossible" impairment of the divine glory itself, paradoxically affecting the impassible heart of God, since the orthodox God is both indivisible and fully omnipresent, and therefore calls down "automatically" in redemptive response a complete divine descent into the creation in excess of any *avatar* or phantasmic manifestation of a mere heavenly being. (It is for this reason that Boehme's distortion is indeed a distortion of orthodoxy rather than a mere exaggeration of ancient Gnostic heresy.)

Perhaps, all the same, Hart is in slight danger of over-separating the perspective of faith and that of the historian. After all, historical detachment is impossible and a presumptive and prevailing professional cynicism on the part of most historians has now been given an extraordinary demonstrative critique by Andrew Willard Jones in his book on Saint Louis.[23] Hart himself admits how the Athanasian position, though novel, makes better sense of inherited texts (including, one can mention, a very early lexicographical underscoring of the *nomina sacra* of Father, Son, and Spirit)[24] and practices than did Arian tradition. Nor are the "strange" Pauline elements necessarily just locked in an irretrievable cosmology—perhaps both they and the cosmology can be reworked, repeated differently, in order plausibly to challenge all our current assumptions? After all, Hart himself has drawn attention, in the wake of C. S. Lewis, John Carey, and others, to the way in which, for instance, Paul's half-fallen angels make periodic returns as fairies, *ninfe*, elves, and sprites during the whole long course of the Christian epoch.[25] Equally, the lost "Gnostic" dimensions are not just alien to what has survived but

---

21. See Pickstock, *Repetition and Identity*, 171–92.
22. Parnell, *The Theurgic Turn*.
23. Willard Jones, *Before Church and State*.
24. See Bokedal, *Biblical Canon*, 83–123
25. Carey, *A Single Ray*.

rather are significantly close, in Origen, to all those persisting practices of reading, praying, and teaching that he did so much to establish.[26] But I do not think that any of these qualifications are in any real disagreement with what Hart is saying, with all of which I essentially concur.

4. Balthasar in Question

If Balthasar did not after all consistently identify the right counterfeit, then does that affect the content of his own theology? One can argue that it does. Precisely because Balthasar failed to see that the problem with Hegel is not precisely "Gnosticism," but rather a Lutheran and Kantian mutation of the "Gnostic," rendering it indeed heterodox, his own theology turns out then not to be altogether free of Hegelian or perhaps Schellingian distortions. These significantly show up in his own book-length summary of his Trilogy, *Epilogue*, which is also a bit confusing.

One can mention first the way in which Balthasar does not really allow quite the fluidity between nature and supernature entertained by Henri de Lubac. This is perhaps most strikingly witnessed when he wrongly and surprisingly declares that even the Thomistic doctrine that in God essence, being, and substance coincide falls prey to "ontotheology" as defined by Heidegger. For Balthasar it seems (though he is scarcely consistent in this respect), the real mystery of God is but inauthentically anticipated by reason and its experience must wait entirely on God's own willed revelations of himself.

It is certainly allowed by Balthasar that everywhere there are anticipations of the gospel. And a plausible account is given of the way in which other religions cannot resolve the *aporia* of allowing for the reality of both absolute and non-absolute being in the way achieved by the notion of a trinitarian God who is in himself outgoing, and of a God who himself becomes fully incarnate as a finite creature. Yet at the same time, the intimations in Jewish and Islamic mysticism of a personal and synergic communion with God which this Christian vision entails are strangely reproved by Balthasar. He will not allow any truth to their paradoxical attempts to close the absolute distance between humanity and God while not abolishing this distance. It would seem that it is rather for him the sole job of these non-Christian monotheisms to remain (as they never of course ever purely were) stark experiences of an unmediated God whom we genuinely know of only through his interruptive word. The one real mediation must be freely and absolutely carried out by God in the incarnation. Yet how are we to understand the

26. See again Pickstock, *Repetition and Identity*.

preparation of Israel and Mary to receive and grasp this mediation without the various "mystical" anticipations of this in the Hebrew scriptures and the Intertestamental writings?

It is true that Balthasar offers a compelling account of how Christ surprisingly and unexpectedly fulfils the apparently contradictory aspectual figurative anticipations of his reality in the Old Testament. And yet he will only allow (against the patristic consensus—however qualifiable—that the prophets knew what they were prophesying) that this anticipation works retrospectively. Otherwise, these various *figurae* are stuck in their revealed positivity, which Balthasar also says is *merely* aesthetic. In this respect, they belong curiously together for him with the figures and narrative of myth. In both cases it is declared that such images remain for their devisers and onlookers sheerly at the surface level of their beauty without any intimation of concealed depth whatsoever. Thus, it would seem to be troublingly the case for Balthasar that the interpretative relationship of the New Testament writers to the Old Testament texts is just as *extrinsic* as that of the Stoic and Neoplatonic allegorizers of Homer, whom he mentions. But one should rather question any sheer arbitrariness of imposed significance even in the latter case.

This means that the Hebrew scriptural material is presented as implausibly *frozen*, as lacking in its own inherent dynamism. And this concurs with the way in which Balthasar here summarizes his treatment of the Old Testament. It is alarmingly positivistic and Barthian. Significantly, and surprisingly (one would suppose), Balthasar incoherently sees the actually received grace derived from Christ in advance, which is present everywhere (as the entire Christian tradition has affirmed), as only equivalent to the Rahnerian "supernatural existential," which is the mere grace-given aptitude for receiving grace. In this way, once more, any epigenetic dynamism of emergent meaning is more or less denied, and figurative, never mind natural, anticipations of the supernatural order are given little real role to play. Thus, for Balthasar, in the end, the entire point of the Old Testament would almost seem to be the futility of the mediating role of human reason and imagination—and how very sub-Coleridgean this is! And how lagging behind Eriugena, who saw the scriptures as the supreme work of the liberal arts!

This concurs with the sharp distinction he tends to make (in great contrast to Bulgakov) between natural beauty and supernatural, revealed glory, from which all the "aesthetic" elements of the Hebrew scriptures for him derive. In the end, for Balthasar, natural beauty is seduced by surface form and blind to its beckonings, while conversely the lure of glory tends to surpass form altogether. It is true that at his best, in the first volume of *Herrlichkeit*, he offers fine statements to the effect that beauty consists indissolubly in both surface harmony and symbolic depth—at once in apparent presence and in ineffable call. And this would correspond to an integral unity of the natural with the supernatural. Yet in the entire course of his work and as summarized in *Epilogue*, beauty herself gets undone to the extent that she is ultimately divided between natural and finally deceptive form on the one hand, and supernatural excess over form on the other.

This dubious tendency concurs with the false accusation that Balthasar makes against Romanticism of "reducing" religion to art—perhaps neglecting the point now insisted upon by Olivier Boulnois that in fact "art" is a Protestant invention once the icon has been both rejected and secularized.[27] In that context it would rather seem that the Romantics (whether Chateaubriand or Novalis), by insisting on the religious character of the aesthetic, beyond the Enlightenment substitution of the latter for the former, were re-sacralizing art in a correctly integral gesture that effectively began to restore the iconic and the primacy of the symbolic.

But even the revealed beauty of the Bible is for Balthasar subordinate to the arbitrary drama of willed election, commanding and abandonment of a disobedient Israel (seemingly final for Balthasar in the end). The tone and the idiom cannot be said to be anything other than implausibly legendary and strikingly voluntaristic.

In the second place, there is the question of exactly how Balthasar understands the metaphysics of the transcendentals which organizes his entire trilogy, including the relationship between this metaphysics and his trinitarian and Christological theology. There is a strong and interesting Thomistic dimension in relation to Balthasar's account of reality in general. Not just the Thomistic duality of essence and being is insisted upon, but also the equally Thomistic duality of being and substance, where the former is general but does not subsist, while the latter is self-contained but confined to particularity. It is clear that Balthasar is making a gesture towards a trinitarian ontology here: creation is many substances in one non-subsistent being, rather as God is three hypostases in one non self-subsisting essence.

And the gesture is doubled when Balthasar, in an apparent echo of Klaus Hemmerle (the German *Focolare* theologian influenced as much by Bulgakov as by Balthasar), insists that Being in general is also transcendentally manifestation and relation in general.[28] As with Hemmerle's trinitarian reworking of the *analogia entis*, every individual being only exists by

27. Boulnois, *Au-delà de l'image*, 410–40.

28. Hemmerle, *Thesen zu einer trinitarischen Ontologie*; French translation by Michael Dupuis, *Thèses Pour Une Ontologie Trinitaire*. The book originated as a long letter to Balthasar.

expressing itself through other given realities in which it is paradoxically both itself and not-itself.

However, when it comes to the triple exemplification of the transcendentality of Being in terms of Beauty, Goodness, and Truth, the stress is exclusively on the instance of manifestation in each case and barely on relating, much less on any sort of teleological lure. Beauty is self-showing, Goodness is self-giving, Truth is self-saying. This stands in considerable contrast to the handling of the same three transcendentals by Aquinas. For the Angelic doctor truth was a proportion between things and the mind, fully realized in mind, where it was manifest. Goodness was a reference of things to an end beyond themselves, that in spiritual creatures is consciously willed. Beauty (rarely referred to by name) mediated between the two and was equally related to the understanding and the will. Thus, for Thomas relationality and teleology are involved in this interaction, besides manifestation.

When Balthasar understands the beautiful as luring through form to a depth beyond itself this could fit with a Thomistic sense that Beauty concerns both the manifestation of Truth and the attraction of the Good. Yet in fact it does not so evidently do so. For the Swiss theologian the three transcendental moments stand curiously alone, in a manner that indeed recalls, as he indicates, the Kantian facultative division of theory, practice, and feeling.

And when they do relate it is not in the fully egalitarian manner that their transcendentality should require. Instead, there is a clear progressive advance from the beautiful, through a mediating goodness, towards the truth. Balthasar explicitly associates aesthetic expression with the inorganic level, goodness with the organic that in various ways goes out of itself from within, and truth with spiritual consciousness. He affirms that despite this apparent hierarchy there is really reciprocal equality, but what this actually seems to mean is that the organic obscurely anticipates the inorganic and the organic the intelligent, which is required to complete the cosmic series. The same then applies to the sequence of the transcendentals.

In their case, beauty of form gives way to the sacrificial ecstasy of action and in this respect O'Regan notes that Balthasar's *Theodramatik* is explicitly meant to "correct" the over-Romanticism of *Herrlichkeit*. Indeed, beauty cannot for him be instrumentalized and yet, like the imagination and the "surface" of myth or prophetic and apocalyptic figure, it must be constantly surpassed and left behind. Even the Son's manifestation must be transcended in favor of his indication of the Father—a statement that would seem barely to pass muster as orthodoxy.

In general, the overtaking of form by action encourages the intellect to distil the true essences or specifically spiritual *Gestalten* of things that lurk behind their beautiful appearances, which merely provide an initial access. There are echoes here both of a phenomenological reduction and of a specifically invoked Kantian "apperception" of initially sensory perceptions. The intellectual grasp of truth is a relating of these essences to the self which is also "in tension" with the linguistic expression of truth. Despite the invocation of Hamann here, Balthasar's emphasis is upon the sheer liberty of this expression and the need of words for the achievement of articulation, rather than any inextricable fusion of the cognitive and the sensory as Hamann intended, specifically against Kant.

Thus what appears to be sketched out here in medieval disguise, is a kind of modern idealist advance from substance to subjectivity, such that being first expresses itself, then goes out of itself in action, and finally returns to itself in the mode of self-reflection and self-willing, which indeed renders equally ultimate the Good with the True.[29] But Beauty, no longer playing, as so often it did in both the Arab and the Christian Middle Ages, the role of a "fitting" or *conveniens* mediator, is definitely subordinated by Balthasar. Persisting and insistent Beauty always seems, if one is reading him carefully, to constitute a kind of idolatry. He has far less of a sense of Beauty as analogical harmony performing the work of the Platonic *metaxu* than has William Desmond.

How then, does the triad of transcendentals for Balthasar relate to the Trinity of persons, if he seems to intimate a trinitarian ontology? In a very peculiar fashion. He does not obviously follow Aquinas and Bonaventure in regarding the Son primarily in terms of Truth and the Spirit in terms of Goodness. Instead, once more relegating the dimensions of both relationality and teleology, he sees all three transcendentals, as characterized by manifestation, as mainly exemplified by the divine Son. It is the Son who shows, enacts, and utters the will of the Father. The role of the Spirit here is confined variously to the essence or the enactment of this relationship, or else again to its more ultimate subjectivization, since it is the Spirit who infers the Paternal essence behind the filial form. But none of all this is made sufficiently clear.

Balthasar's somewhat idealist Trinity also echoes the Franciscan legacy in downplaying (by contrast to Bulgakov) substantive relationality—such as when he affirms, with Duns Scotus, that the Father adequately possesses knowledge in his own right and when he speaks of the "handing over" of

---

29. On the idealist and subjectivist elements in Balthasar, see Gonzales, *Reimagining the* Analogia Entis, 107–9.

the entire divine essence from the Father to the Son.[30] But the idealist inflection assumes dubiously Gnostic (in the Behmenist sense) proportions
when it comes to the supreme revelation of the Trinity in the passion. Then
the tendency to render the three persons as three separate locations of loving and responding allows him to envisage a full sundering of the Father
from the Son on the cross and in hell—a division that can only be restored
by the Spirit who repairs this thoroughly Hegelian moment of diremptive
alienation.

Here Balthasar is himself parodying Bulgakov, who instead, and with
considerably greater subtlety, saw that the "shadow" that eternally hangs
over the Father-Son relationship is not one of possible separation, but of
the loneliness of pure substantive relationship, were it to be shorn of its
productive spiritual joy that is involved in a ceaseless re-instigation of the
personal poles as being paradoxically in excess of their constitutive relating,
precisely in terms of their coincidence with the single divine essence, or
(for Bulgakov) personifying *Sophia*.[31] This essence is in turn nothing but
the ceaseless musical chairs of the interpersonal *perichoresis* and as such is
especially linked with the Spirit, who emerges from the Father through the
Son and is the bond of both.

These subtle but crucial complications of trinitarian theology are fully
present in Augustine and Aquinas. Awareness of them allows Bulgakov to
imagine both the Son *and* the Father as experiencing the cross as a momen-
tary sterility of pure relation. This involves no mythical and "Gnostic" separation of what is eternally conjoined, and the numbed suffering derives for
Bulgakov (again in contrast to Balthasar) entirely from the side of Christ's
humanity. Although through the communication of idioms this is somehow
experienced by the divine personhood of Christ, by the same token this
extremity of suffering is also immediately cancelled and surpassed by the
uninterrupted eternal extremity of joy.

By contrast, any absolute sundering of the divine persons suggests
a rather Behmenist or Schellingian hovering of an eternal divine abyss of
ontologized nullity. This is more explicitly affirmed by Balthasar's academic
friend Ferdinand Ulrich in his *Homo Abyssus*. Ulrich accuses modernity of
being defined by a Behmenist and Hegelian "depotentiation" of the Father
in favor of the initially alien work of the Son, yet himself repeats this error
in a more pious guise, by comprehending the mutual kenosis of the persons
as self-obliteration.[32]

---

30. See Milbank, *The Suspended Middle*, 69–84.

31. See Milbank, "Sophiology and Theurgy," in Pabst and Schneider, *Encounter*,
45–85.

32. Ulrich, *Drama of the Question*," 28–36, 255–57.

The thematic of an "is not" as implied by trinitarian difference is handled much more Platonically and traditionally by Piero Coda (in his *Dalla Trinità* and elsewhere) and other Bulgakov-influenced *Focolare* theologians (even if this difference from Balthasar is not always recognized or indicated by them).[33] Here, after Plato's *Sophist*, and the original visionary intuition of Chiara Lubich, *Focolare*'s founder, nothingness is not ontologized save as the mystery of difference, which already for Plato, and more emphatically for trinitarian theology, is grounded in the absolute. The only pure nothing is the truly nothing as absence, from which all was created. The only "ontological nothing" is the impossible degree zero that is never reached of evil, that is yet impossibly touched on by Christ on the cross and in hell. Yet as Coda indicates, this depth beyond any depth we will know or instigate, this "negative real nothing" is immediately transmuted from those sites into the joyful loving nothingness of self-forgetting relational difference in the Trinity. By the same token, self-denying kenosis, even when paradoxically subject to redemptive rupture through the assumption of humanity into the person of the *Logos*, is never for God sacrificial rupture, but always remains a peaceful though constitutive ecstasy that allows and gives way to the other.

One can nonetheless add here that any complete absorption of the *kenosis* of incarnation into the *kenosis* of the passion always runs the risk of a Hegelian distortion, even if modern Catholic theology has been right to stress the continuity of the two, as well articulated by Thomas J. Norris in his excellent little book *The Trinity*. For if one sees the Trinity as *only* first disclosed on the Cross—even though, in a fallen world, this must be the most acute point of disclosure—then there is always the danger of ontologizing the full, but contingent revelation of the Trinity in the instance of its contingent distress (however construed), which will encourage the false idea that the ontological essence of the Trinity lies in alienation rather than in positive manifestation, relating, and desiring.

Instead, as much Anglican thought since the mid-nineteenth century has stressed, primacy must be accorded to the incarnation over the passion, both in terms of its positive completion of the creation and its necessarily positive beginning of the work of re-creation, which is already, with Mary and John the Baptist, who baptizes Jesus,[34] the arrival on earth of the church as both the Sophianic presence of the entire Trinity and especially the presence of the Spirit. Only because humanity has already begun to be restored in the birth and life of Christ, in a particular "beautiful" form (ultimately

---

33. Coda, *Dalla Trinità,*" 533–83.

34. One might interpret the baptism given by John as both already and not yet full ecclesial and Christological baptism—already of water, not yet of Spirit save in anticipation.

downplayed by Balthasar in favor of inter-spiritual "drama") which gives the contentful yet ineffable key to a universal human style that each human person must repeat in her own unique fashion, can Christ then in his humanity both bear and express the full suffering of sin, which actual impairment by sin paradoxically precludes.

In this process, as Balthasar well affirms, lies the negative work of atonement, but its precondition is the positive re-shaping and re-birthing of humanity already begun with Mary's assent. Thus, the only proof of the integration of the necessary negative moment is its immediate surpassing as the resumption of positive re-forming in its completion as resurrection. As Robert Grosseteste argued in the thirteenth century, we are justified, exactly like the innocent Adam, only by the positive perfection of God and of the God-Man, even though this positivity can only reach us through the perfect suffering sacrifice of Christ's humanity in our postlapsarian condition.[35]

Once again, for all his stressing of the passion-Trinity linkage, none of this broader and Mariological-incarnational dimension was neglected by Bulgakov, whom I have implicitly invoked above.

It is clear then that Balthasar somewhat misplaced his anxieties. If he had wished to ward off the Christian parodies engendered by post-Kantian speculation, he should have been much less worried by Romanticism (which was not idealist, but both realist and Platonic, in the case of its most central exponents, Schlegel, Novalis, and Coleridge), and by the Neoplatonic, Gnostic, apocalyptic, and esoteric traditions, and even more worried than he certainly was by the legacy of Scotism, nominalism, voluntarism, and the Baroque sundering of grace from a *natura pura*. Because he was insufficiently worried, he failed to grasp the hidden alliance of an all-too-modern speculation with all-too-modern extrinsicism and himself after all fell somewhat victim to this connection.

Cyril O'Regan has much forwarded our escape from the still often prevailing (even amongst Catholics) Protestant Teutonic captivity of theology. As I have argued, this liberating process needs to be taken still further. However, the thematic of the counterfeit is complex and multi-faceted. Of its very nature it requires us to be constantly on our guard and not to fantasize that we are finally free of deception or have completed the work of its unmasking. Just for this reason there will be constant debate as to how many and how variously decisive are the various sources of misremembering between those committed to a shared project of a true remembrance.

This true remembrance is creative and active mainly on account of its very nature, yet also for the negative reason that it can never be complacently

---

35. Grosseteste, *Cessation of the Laws*, 4:2; 3.1.1–29, pp. 155–73.

certain that it is itself free from all imposture. The quest for a truer orthodoxy continues alongside O'Regan and many others and a debate amongst all of them must also continue, for the same reason of the tentativeness of this quest, despite its ultimate surety. For, as Cyril O'Regan has supremely helped us to see, we have to treat apparent fraudulence with a supposedly inappropriate respect and apparent reliability with a seemingly unwonted suspicion, just because counterfeiting is such a very precise and exacting trade. The Apocalypse of John has already warned us: if we wish to discern the lineaments of Christ, we will have constantly to re-distinguish them from the uncannily similar shapes assumed by the Anti-Christ.

Bibliography

Anonymous [Valentin Tomberg]. *Meditations on the Tarot: A Journey into Christian Hermeticism.* Translated by Robert Powell. New York: Putnam, 1985.

Balthasar, Hans Urs von. *Epilogue.* Translated by Edward T. Oakes. San Francisco: Ignatius, 2004.

Bokedal, Tomas. *The Formation and Significance of the Christian Biblical Canon.* London: Bloomsbury, 2015.

Boulnois, Olivier. *Au-delà de l'image: Une archéologie du visuel au Moyen Âge Ve-XVIe siècle.* Paris: Seuil, 2008.

Carey, John. *A Single Ray of the Sun: Religious Speculation in Early Ireland.* Aberystwyth, UK: Celtic Studies, 1999.

de Lubac, Henri. *La postérité spirituelle de Joachim de Flore.* Paris: Cerf, 2014.

Desmond, William. *Being and the Between.* New York: SUNY Press, 1995.

Gilson, Étienne. *John Duns Scotus: Introduction to His Fundamental Positions.* Translated by James G. Colbert. London: Bloomsbury, 2019.

Gonzales, Philip John Paul. *Reimagining the Analogia Entis: The Future of Erich Przywara's Christian Vision.* Grand Rapids: Eerdmans, 2019.

Grosseteste, Robert. *On the Cessation of the Laws (De Cessatione Legalium).* Translated by Stephen M. Hildebrand. Washington, DC: Catholic University of America Press, 2012.

Hemmerle, Klaus. *Thesen zu einer trinitarischen Ontologie.* Einsedeln: Johannes, 1976.

———. *Thèses Pour Une Ontologie Trinitaire.* Translated into French by Michael Dupuis. Paris: Ad Solem, 2014.

Hoff, Johannes. *The Analogical Turn: Rethinking Modernity with Nicholas of Cusa.* Grand Rapids: Eerdmans,

Libera, Alain de. *Métaphysique et noétique: Albert le Grand.* Paris: Vrin, 2005.

Maspero, G., and J. Lynch. *Storia e mistero: Uno chiave di accesso alla teologia di Joseph Ratzinger e Jean Daniélou.* Rome: EDUSC, 2016.

Milbank, John. *Beyond Secular Order: The Representation of Being and the Representation of the People.* Oxford: Wiley-Blackwell, 2013.

———. "The Franciscan Conundrum." *Communio* 42 (2015) 466–92.

———. "Reformation 500: Any Cause for Celebration?" *Open Theology* 4 (2018) 607–29.

———. *The Suspended Middle: Henri de Lubac and the Renewed Split in Modern Catholic Theology.* Grand Rapids: Eerdmans, 2014.

Norris, Thomas J. *The Trinity: Life of God, Hope for Humanity.* New York: New City, 2009.

O'Regan, Cyril. *Anatomy of Misremembering: Von Balthasar's Response to Philosophical Modernity. Volume 1: Hegel.* Chestnut Ridge, NY: Crossroad, 2014.

O'Regan, Cyril. *Gnostic Apocalypse: Jacob Boehme's Haunted Narrative.* New York: SUNY Press, 2002.

O'Regan, Cyril. *Gnostic Return in Modernity.* New York: SUNY Press, 2001.

Parnell, Jason B. *The Theurgic Turn in Christian Thought: Iamblichus, Origen, Augustine and the Eucharist.* Ann Arbor MI: ProQuest, 2010.

Pfau, Thomas. *Minding the Modern: Human Agency, Intellectual Traditions and Responsible Knowledge.* Notre Dame, IN: Notre Dame University Press, 2013.

Pickstock, Catherine. *Repetition and Identity.* Oxford: Oxford University Press, 2013.

Pabst, Adrian, and Christoph Schneider, eds. *Radical Orthodoxy and Eastern Orthodoxy.* Farnham, UK: Ashgate, 2009.

Willard Jones, Andrew. *Before Church and State: A Study of Social Order in the Sacramental Kingdom of St Louis IX.* Steubenville, OH; Emmaus Academic, 2017.

10

The Banquet of Reading and Being Read
The Gift of Resonance and the Duty of the Question

CYRIL O'REGAN
Huisking Professor of Theology
University of Notre Dame

However niggling the aspiration, moments are rare in life when books turn out to be vehicles of *cor ad cor loquitur* intimacy and enlightenment. It seems altogether too risky and Romantic to claim more than our academic situations can truly bear, even if the urge to speak unimaginably to some imagined responsive and receptive other is what launched writing in the first case. Perhaps the type of this hope is provided by A. S. Byatt's *Possession* (1990), in which writing is a message in a bottle launched on the waves of nowhere to a somewhere and to a someone who truly understands and in understanding can brush the surface hard enough to rid the writer's language of what is dead and recycled, show the capacity to expose deeper layers of meaning, and in some cases grasp and fulfill the intention that was merely inchoate in a work and at best only partially realized. A beautiful idea, but also altogether fantastic and potentially enervating, to which we add our constitutive second guesses that provide reasons for dismissal. Understandable then, the cutback to the disciplinary virtues of evidence and argument and to region-specific protocols that signal expertise. The hope of a responsive reader, one who is touched by and resonates with what

is being said and the saying of it, is simply too unbearable; it demands summary burial and the intercalation of a less poetic disposition satisfied by
the banalities of good reviews, the respect of one's colleagues, and a shift
in one's relative standing in a particular field of humanistic inquiry with
the publication of a new monograph. Until, that is, reality, which truly is
as recalcitrant as our surly asceticism would have it, comes knocking and
says otherwise. My moment of conversion occurred when over two decades
ago I found a somewhat worse for wear envelope in my mail box in the
Department of Religious Studies at Yale. The envelope did not have much to
recommend it; even without the bedraggled appearance one could see that
the paper quality was poor. In addition, all that was there by way of writing
was the scribble of my name and Yale University. The question as to how it
was possible for such a letter to reach its addressee was already boiling over
even before I opened it. When I did, I discovered a short note of one and
half pages, the first half written in pen, the second in pencil. The signee was
Gillian Rose, whom I had never met and who at that time was for me no
less but also no more than the author of the wonderful and influential book
Hegel Contra Sociology (1981).

   This letter was and still remains one of my most prized possessions. It
lay around for years until recently when trying to give it a more permanent
home I secreted it away. As often happens when impractical persons suddenly become practical, I put it in a "safe place." Currently, it is safe but lost,
so I can only do it the injustice of paraphrase. In the first part of the note,
written in pen, Rose wrote that she had been waiting for *The Heterodox
Hegel* (1994) essentially all her entire intellectual life and that she received
it precisely as the fruit of her desire. In the second part of the note, the
part written in pencil and thus presumably later, since there seemed to be
no fade out in the ink, Rose upbraided me for not having paid sufficient
attention to her book on Hegel. I did not know then what I knew shortly
thereafter having caught up with her major work and having read *Love's
Work* (1995), her autobiography, that when she wrote this note she was dying. But even without the added pathos of knowing this, I have rarely been
as moved in my life. Her note to me was like a message in a bottle; it should
have been permanently lost on the high seas of nowhere and never arrived.
But her words did arrive, probably via one of her many willing emissaries
who happened to be passing through New Haven. In any event, her words
transfigured my book into something like a sacrament: by her resounding
it she had sounded it. The reviews of *The Heterodox Hegel* were shockingly
good. There was a lavishness in their praise that was borderline embarrass-
ing and they supplied a canopy of superlatives under which I could recline
and feel fanned. What Rose said and the no-nonsense passion with which

she said it was of an entirely different order: it translated me into the time of an impossible hope in writing of being seen and heard. It did not matter that I was upbraided. In fact, not only did being upbraided have no sting; it seemed to have the quality of the sacred. I thanked her with as much self-control as I could muster, but only after I caught up with her oeuvre, having been sensibly afraid to take the risk of being called out for not giving sufficient attention to another of her books.

The above moment has become a polestar when it comes to reading and being read. Of course, one does not read every piece of writing one comes across with this expectation in view. The bar is usually expertise, competence, and the occasional insight. But one dares to admit that one comes across texts that speak because they say and show and thus speak, just as one dares to excavate the hope that one is read with an understanding that is resonant and thus capable of bringing out strands and inflections that really were latencies. With the group of writers assembled in this book, all of whom I have read with delight, I find myself recalling how I myself was moved to resonance. With this group of writers, I also find that their readings of my own work are resonances, thus appreciations that are at once fulsome and uniquely voiced. I view them as acts of gratitude that also subtly interrogate, or interrogations that themselves are acts of gratitude. I will in due course return to the distinction and relation between these two registers of interrogation, indeed, it functions to structure my entire response. The first half of my response unsurprisingly consists of saying thank you to readers who "illuminate" in the medieval sense not only by making plain some elements of my thought and offering judgments as to its value, but also of making it "splendid" by the shining of their own seeing that unveils as their own hearing resonates.

In order to break the awkwardness of responding to each author in turn, I think it expedient to organize my response to the hearing and seeing of my thought around various themes. The organization of the themes is more or less pragmatic, since a number of pieces play on more than one theme. The three main thematic units covered by the contributors to the volume, gratuitously initiated and marvelously put together by Philip Gonzales, are apocalyptic, Gnosticism, and to a more limited extent the relation between poetry and theology. In different ways Caitlin Gilson, David C. Schindler, and John Betz focus on the theme of apocalyptic, even if other themes are touched on in passing and particular judgments made in my work on philosophical and theological authors called to mind. Gnosticism is an important theme of concern for William Desmond, Christopher Ben Simpson, Aaron Riches and Sebastián Montiel, and David Bentley Hart. Since formally speaking Hart's piece has a more confrontational register, I will not consider him here, but defer him to the second part of my response where I deal with the press of interrogation. With respect to the third theme of poetry and theology, Jennifer Martin's piece on an early two-volume epic poem, "The Companion of Theseus," is at the center. At the same time, other writers implicitly touch on this theme of poetry and its sanction, with Caitlin Gilson and William Desmond being first among equals. Just as there is not an entirely neat division between the treatment of apocalyptic and Gnosticism, since in my own work there are complicated relations between the two, it is also the case that the concept of poetics cannot be segregated from genealogical reflection in which apocalyptic and Gnosticism play a major role. This is because my poetic work can and should be understood as providing the experiential matrix which energizes anti-Gnosticism and the seeing that recognizes and affirms the flesh and its inordinate vulnerability.

Apocalyptic, Gnosticism, and the Poetics of Abjection

I begin with the theme of *apocalyptic*. David C. Schindler and John Betz constitute a unique pairing, since while they could never be confused with each other, it is not hard to see that in their major work they echo, nuance, and deepen each other. Not only are they both Catholic theologians with significant philosophical competence who shuttle effortlessly between Thomism and *nouvelle théologie*, they are similarly committed to rigor of argument and retrieval of necessary Christian voices. The theme they broach in my work is apocalyptic used as a constructive and not simply critical category—although it takes that form in my work also—especially as the category is used to describe the theological oeuvre of Hans Urs von Balthasar and is plausibly extensible to other theologians of *nouvelle théologie* stripe. I myself have suggested the candidacy of Benedict XVI and more than hinted at the candidacy of Henri de Lubac. Schindler, who is an expert on Balthasar, is more than usually aware of the difficulty in using the label with regard to the great Swiss theologian, who not only is normally thought of as the theologian of theological aesthetics, but a thinker of impeccable anti-apocalyptic credentials laid down early in his monumental three-volume *Apokalypse der deutschen Seele* (1937–39). There Balthasar laments the immanentization of the eschaton he thinks typical of modernity and whose form—if not necessarily the source—can be traced back to the twelfth-century Calabrian abbot Joachim de Fiore. Schindler is a powerful and penetrating reader of difficult texts. The sprawl of *Apokalypse* is no match for his clear-sighted grasp that the apocalyptic immanentization takes myriad forms, even if the two main types are those of speculative "Promethean" ascendance and vitalist "Dionysian" descendance. Schindler also sees not only that these deficient forms of apocalyptic make sense only against the backdrop of an apocalypse of "last things" that is truly Christianly adequate, but that Balthasar also wishes to present in general outline what a genuine form of Christian apocalyptic might look like. Here Dostoyevski figures prominently as he does a few years later in de Lubac's *The Drama of Atheistic Humanism*. If *Apokalypse* sets the ground condition for Balthasar's later positive and constructive use of apocalyptic in theology, still the reader of the Swiss theologian can be excused for not having an immediate intuition of this fact when it comes to reading his theological aesthetics, theodramatics, and theologic. It is not simply that the discovery is inhibited by its use in forms of theology that Balthasar rigorously opposes. It is also the case that "apocalypse," even "Christian apocalypse," does not appear to enjoy the same sanction as the language of the transcendentals and the biblical language of glory and love that is so conspicuous in Balthasar's work.

Schindler is persuaded by the argument I prosecuted in *Anatomy of Misremembering Vol. 1* (2014) to the effect that apocalyptic is the fundamental way in which drama is rendered in *Theo-Drama* and that in turn the category of apocalyptic is able to integrate Balthasar's reflections on theological aesthetics and the logic of truth as love and love as truth elaborated in *Theo-Logic*. The acceptance of the fundamental rightness of an apocalyptic designation of Balthasar in Schindler's typically wide-ranging and closely argued essay is fulsome and comes with what in my view is the compliment of compliments, namely, that once some fundamental obstacles are removed, "apocalyptic" becomes an obvious descriptor of the kind of theology constructed by Balthasar. Schindler's perspective here as elsewhere in his work is extrospective. In particular, it is transparent that at no time throughout his well-wrought essay does he draw attention to the fact that in his own reading of Balthasar in *Hans Urs von Balthasar and the Dramatic Structure of Truth* (2004) he uses "drama" to interpret truth and by implication to serve the kind of integrative function I suggest "apocalyptic" plays. This may be a matter of delicacy. Yet I am more inclined to think that Schindler has grasped well that the theological category "apocalyptic" supposes the category of drama and more specifically the dramatic horizon of the play of freedom between the triune God and the responsive and responsible human subject of history. Schindler manages to be a wonderfully generous and resonant reader while being true to his own voice and his own way of proceeding and arriving. It seems to me that our roads which may part in the woods, nonetheless, in the end meet. But there is something conjoint about our *vias* also. The paths of our discourse seem to continually cross and loop around each other and our discourses become deeper and more luminous by doing so.

Like David C. Schindler, John Betz is a writer to whom I turn not only to be instructed in a religious or philosophical topic or a thinker, but to be inspired by a level of intellectual performance that in its coincidence of erudition and freshness, scrupulous interpretive care and yet imaginative excess suggests that the well-springs of Catholic philosophy and theology are not only tapped, but liberally flowing. In John Betz one finds, as one finds in Schindler also, the ascesis of the master translator, in his case the translator of Erich Przywara, in Schindler's case the translator of Ferdinand Ulrich. Although prior to this volume Betz has beautifully engaged my work on Gnosticism, he dialogues with my anatomy of Balthasar's work as apocalyptic indirectly rather than directly. He does so by stipulating its truth value and then proceeding to raise the question whether Przywara, who is the theological mentor of Balthasar (perhaps also in a sense his student), can be seen to articulate in his "later" work what might be called an "apocalyptic turn" or, if not turn, then an apocalyptic specification of analogy or creaturely metaphysics that is the subject of his most famous book, that is, *Analogia Entis* (1932). The texts that Betz submits to penetrating analysis are *Mysterium Crucis* (1939) and *Four Sermons* (1943). By means of *explication de texte* at once incisive, comprehensive, and compelling Betz makes the case that, as with Balthasar, Przywara also articulates a particular form of Catholic apocalyptic theology. Importantly, Przywara's form of Catholic apocalyptic is Johannine rather than Pauline, Christological rather than pneumatological, analogical rather than dialectical. To that extent it both mirrors and anticipates what can be found in Balthasar's triptych. It does so, however—and this is Betz's major point—in a considerably more apophatic register.

As a philosophical theologian who has laid down the opposition between the prophetic and apocalyptic Hamann and the agnostic Kant of the First Critique, Betz grasps well that to affirm an apophatic register is not necessarily the same as affirming unrestricted apophasis, and that Przywara's mode of apocalyptic not only cannot be collapsed into a Benjamin style apocalyptic, but in fact represents a genuine alternative that preserves analogy in a way that Benjamin's messianic apocalyptic does not. Betz ingeniously suggests that one of the ways of thinking the difference between Balthasar's and Przywara's mode of apocalyptic theology, both of which are Johannine and thus fully eidetic, is to underscore the latter's considerably less ambivalent acceptance of Carmelite modes of mystical theology that deal confidently with divine absence, indeed hyperbolic forms of such absence. Undoubtedly, had Betz not been so diligent in presenting Przywara to the reader who is less familiar with him than Balthasar, he might also have pointed to the palpable shift in Przywara's work from thinking that Hegel articulates the apocalyptic form that Catholicism has to oppose (*Analogia Entis*) to thinking in his later work that Nietzsche articulates the Catholic anti-type. This is just the opposite movement traversed by Balthasar from *Apokalypse* to the triptych. It is not only in his reviews of my volumes on Gnosticism, but here also, that Betz shows that to understand a thinker means to "go on." He amply exemplifies this Wittgenstein virtue in making Przywara rather than Balthasar the object of analysis. As he does so, one can see how the essay functions recursively with respect to his own analyses of the aesthetic and the sublime. Indeed, we could say that as there is an aesthetic mode of Catholic apocalyptic (Balthasar), there is a sublime form (Przywara), but in this case the sublime is cataphatically restricted, on the one hand, by the givenness of revelation and, on the other, by the responsive and ecstatic believer who catches sight of but cannot pin down the God who is crucified love.

Caitlin Gilson's response to my work is a delight, as is her work in general, which attracts by being at once the most earth-bound and Platonic, the most quotidian and transcendental writing to be found in contemporary Catholic theology. She elevates, as do Schindler and Betz, the apocalyptic dimension of my thought, but does so by emphasizing the importance of apocalyptic in my work, not so much as a category of analysis, but as a real existential. She throws further light on apocalyptic functioning as an existential category by putting my work in conversation with the hermeneutic philosophy of Paul Ricoeur. Gilson is always surprising, her intuitive leaps entirely convincing. She invariably gets me right, even as I tend to retire behind the categories of genealogical analysis and screen my fundamental commitments and decisions. In addition, she also gets Ricoeur right, but does so not by repeating him, but by creatively extending him in an explicitly apocalyptic direction. Gilson is, however, brave as well as prescient. She is brave because despite having been a longtime reader and teacher of Ricoeur, I have only published a few pieces in which Ricoeur's hermeneutical and narrative thought is the crux of the affair. Gilson proves herself to be a connoisseur of traces. The flimsiest of notices seem sufficient for her to draw out our common resistance to speculative apocalyptic forms and the theodicies that invariably accompany them and our shared commitment to situatedness, finitude, vulnerability, and testimony. Crucially, for Gilson, testimony supposes an "apocalyptic actor" in a drama who gives witness, while following at a distance the archetypal witness of Christ. Gilson builds an apocalyptic bridge between my work and Ricoeur's through a totally individuated voice and an intelligence that is mobile, deft, and resolute.

Gilson's voice is at once poetic and mystic, restrained and ecstatic, unique and irreducibly dialogical. She names and qualifies, she reaches, yet never too far, and is always entirely herself even as she encounters and makes present the authors whom she inserts in a dialogue whose horizon is infinite. She also effortlessly grasps that Hölderlin is a resource who can be relied on to help contemporary philosophers and theologians think through the demands of a fully adequate Christian apocalyptic. Moreover, as with Przywara and Marion before her, she points to "Patmos" being exemplary. Hölderlin is also a figure alluded to by Betz in his argument that Przywara is fundamentally a Catholic theologian of apocalyptic stripe, although his Hölderlin requires rescue from a post-Nietzschean construction in which Christ is displaced by Dionysus. Nonetheless, although the role of invoking Hölderlin in an argument concerning Catholic apocalyptic is similar in both Gilson and Betz, the formal function is different. Gilson performs the porosity of literary, theological, and philosophical discourses by enlisting what she takes to be another apocalyptic poetic voice, this time that of T. S. Eliot, who discloses modernity to be bedeviled by attenuation and trapped between a light that has gone down and a dark that has not arrived, and all the worse for the anticipation. Gilson's great theological talent is her ability to be the site of variation of kinds of discourse and the multiplication of number whereas that of Betz is, after the model of John Milbank and David Bentley Hart, the installation of theology as the regulative discourse that has Christ ever mysterious and the triune God ever fecund as its formal object.

I turn now to another constellation of reflections from my visionary and auditory company. This is a constellation of four responders—William Desmond, Christopher Ben Simpson, and Aaron Riches and Sebastian Montiel—each of whom meditates on, mediates, and extends my reflections on the nature of Gnosticism and the genealogy of "Gnostic return." William Desmond and I are close friends, but it is writing that called this "between" into existence. Although our natality, specifically our Irishness, is important to both of us, we discovered each other through reading each other's work and thus reading through to the other. The degree of overlap between our respective work is as large as it is accidental. Desmond is not wrong to draw attention to the difference in register, in his case the register of the phenomenological and metaphysical, in my case the register of the hermeneutical. He is right to warn, however, that this way of distinguishing between our work is of limited value. As there is plenty in Desmond's work that is hermeneutical and genealogical, so also there are more than a few moments in mine of phenomenological excavation and ontological vehemence. Desmond's meditation on Gnosticism in this volume is paradigmatically dialogical: it is his response to my response to his reflection on

Gnosticism in *God and the Between* (2008) in which he construes Gnosticism less in terms of ontological dualism than in terms of a doubling that destabilizes the distinction between origin and expression and the order within the placial pairs of "in" and "out" and "up" and "down." His response both deepens our understanding of ancient Gnostic texts made available by the Nag Hammadi library, while also showing clearly how modern thought might still be "repeating" Gnosticism while all the time eschewing ontological dualism. Of course, one is made aware in other sites in Desmond's work, for example, in the trilogy of the "Between," but preeminently in *Hegel's God: A Counterfeit Double?* (2003), that Hegel represents the classic case of pulling Gnosticism in a dynamic, developmental, agonistic, and more nearly monistic direction. But this would not mean anything if such a possibility could not also be spied in the ancient texts. It is a central part of my analysis of ancient Gnosticism to uncover precisely such as latency. Desmond is neither affirming nor contesting the details of my "Gnostic return" program, even if his troubling of standard interpretations of Gnosticism are congenial to my reading of Gnosticism and in line with a brilliant suggestion made by Hans Jonas in the 1960s to the effect that the phenomenon of doubling may be what links ancient Gnosticism and German idealism. Desmond is a rigorous arguer, but he is also a font of allusion. One of the more powerful of his allusions is his exposé of *Macbeth* as naming the equivocal and its duplicity as the threat to a would-be solid reality. Desmond does not mean that Shakespeare is Gnostic; indeed, perhaps precisely the opposite. The bard is a watchman diagnosing toil and trouble for the stability of nature and the coherence of being. Here Shakespeare, as elsewhere in Desmond, is not "inventing the modern," as Harold Bloom would have it. Rather, Shakespeare is at the pass, speaking to now but also the whence and whither of our language, our understanding, and our prospects of living in a world both made and unmade by desire and the passions that no longer have an intelligible interpretive horizon. Were we to think in literature at the full arrival of the equivocal and its myriad faces, then my choice would undoubtedly be Kafka's meditation in *The Castle* on the promises of a legible world betrayed by the constant doubling and looping of a reality that refuses to make sense.

Of the three reflections on Gnosticism in the volume, it is that of Christopher Ben Simpson that most concertedly focuses on the technical apparatus of my "Gnostic return" theory. Simpson presents in outline what I have called "Gnostic narrative grammar," which competes with Christian narrative grammar by altering the meaning of each of the latter's major narrative episodes: for example, creation, fall, redemption, and eschaton. Simpson's interest in Gnosticism is more genealogical than taxonomic, and accordingly he is focused on how this grammar can operate in a modern environment that is inimical to the kind of ontological dualism that is a stable part of the vocabulary of ancient Gnosticism. Thus, his attention to the second major concept of my Gnostic return thesis, that is, rules of deformation of classical Gnostic paradigms which underwrite doubling, development, agonism, and monism. It is in light of both of my major concepts, but guided by the second, that Simpson asks the question whether Gilles Deleuze could be thought of as a modern example of Gnosticism and thus an example of Gnostic return. Here Simpson accepts the invitation that is encoded in the theoretical apparatus of the Gnostic return theory to broaden the candidates for Gnostic ascription and submit them to a rigorous criteriological test. In answering his extraordinarily interesting question Simpson proceeds along two tracks, the first genetic, the second structural. Along the genetic axis Deleuze is linked to Martinist theosophical currents in France which, if in one sense are independent, in another sense serve as conduits for the speculative theology of the German Lutheran mystic Jacob Boehme. In exposing this strange linkage Simpson should not be thought to deny the influence of Nietzsche on Deleuze or for that matter a peculiarly vitalist Spinoza who seems anachronistically to have borrowed such features from Leibniz. On the structural axis, Simpson argues that the concept of "rule-governed deformation of classical Gnostic norms" allows one to think of Deleuze's dynamic, differential, monist conjugation of reality as Gnostic, or at the very least, not disqualify it from the outset.

Simpson's brilliant essay is, however, much more than an application of my Gnostic criteriology to an unlikely discourse that wears its modernity or postmodernity on its sleeve. In what has to be the hinge on which the essay turns, Simpson suggests that it is paradoxically in Deleuze's commitment to radical immanence that we can see the appearance of Gnosticism, for the commitment effectively enjoins leaving the world precisely as it is. Gnosticism in Deleuze, then, in Simpson's view, operates *sub contrario*; it is verified precisely in what appears to deny it. This is an important judgment and is hypothetically extendable to other modern discourses. One thinks, for example, of the Christian discourse of the later Michel Henry whose non-representationalism seems more neighborly to the *Gospel of Truth* than to John's Gospel. While Deleuze may abhor Hegel, no more than in Hegel's discourse is there room in his philosophical matrix for testimony. Nor can any encouragement be given for a sacrifice that has no exchange value, and even less recognition of a paradigm of sacrifice such as Christ. As with Desmond, Simpson has not only grasped brilliantly what I say about Gnosticism and Gnostic return, but pays my thinking the respect of seeing it as an invitation both to experiment with it and to go beyond it. In the very depth of his reading, he constitutes himself as a reader to be hoped for but not necessarily expected.

In what represents an extension of a review essay on *Anatomy of Misremembering* that appeared in *Modern Theology*, Aaron Riches and Sebastian Montiel concentrate not so much on the technical details of Gnostic return in modernity as the phenomenon of haunting as diagnosed by Balthasar and illustrated crucially by Hegel. In this sense their elegant essay resembles that of Desmond. Riches and Montiel exploit "haunting" in much the same way as Desmond exploits "doubling" and both express modalities of the return of Gnosticism in modernity under auspices that neither involve mythic figuration nor static ontology. Riches seems to agree with *Anatomy* that Gnosticism is best thought of as a spectral presence in modern religious discourses, a presence that effectively manages to madden them. Astonishingly, like Desmond, Riches and Montiel also recur to Shakespeare as providing an understanding at the threshold of the modern as to what "haunting" really means. The preferred play is now *Hamlet* and not *Macbeth*, and specifically Hamlet's experience of the ghost of his father. In their essay the accent falls on the effect of the haunting, its ability to upset, affright, and derange. These capacities match up fairly exactly with what might be called my hauntology of modern religious discourses, and Riches and Montiel seem satisfied that seeing the effects of the ghastly is a required skill with respect to unmasking discourses such as Hegel's that pretend to be Christian. Interestingly, they put me alongside John Milbank when it comes to interpreting Hegel and modernity more generally. Even more interestingly, given my unusual and yet far from ghastly encounter with Gillian Rose, they put her into play along with Rowan Williams to double down on haunting. In any event, Riches and Montiel emphasize what unites rather than divides us and what we have by way of common cause.

Just as Desmond evinces a keen theological eye while resolutely remaining a philosopher, Riches and Montiel demonstrate considerable philosophical acumen while equally resolutely remaining theologians. As a major theologian in his own right, Riches is rightly obsessed with how it goes with Christ in theology in general and in Catholic theology in particular. He is currently writing a three-volume Christology that aims to make normative claims through an extended historical analysis in the manner of his beloved de Lubac and with the template of Congar's work on the Trinity in mind. For him one of the great merits of Balthasar's wide-ranging theology is to point to the systemic distortion in theology when Christ no longer is thought to be rendered by the Spirit but to be displaced by it. The thinker who paradigmatically lays down this as a possibility is Joachim de Fiore, who if important in the thought of Balthasar, is even more important in de Lubac, whose *La postérité spirituelle de Joachim de Fiore* (1978–80) is the text of texts when considering the track of Joachimite ideas in modern thought. Riches' and Montiel's essay has the added virtue of illustrating that while the concepts of "apocalypse" and "Gnosticism" are formally distinct in my work, in practice they often overlap. On the one hand, the complex concept of "Gnostic apocalypse" is not a contradiction in terms and, on the other, historically speaking, especially in the case of German idealism and Romanticism, the concepts are imbricated.

This brings me to the third category of engagement, what I have christened the *poetics of abjection*, that deals with the way my own poetry both echoes and grounds the taxonomic and genealogical sophistications of my meditations on apocalyptic and Gnosticism. If in one sense this is a category with only one instance, that is, Jennifer Martin's remarkable excavation of *The Companion of Theseus*, a two-volume poem written while I was a graduate student in philosophy decades ago, in another sense the naming power of poetry is a leitmotif threaded throughout the essays of the contributors to the volume. The epigraph to William Desmond's piece is a poem by Czeslaw Milosz, the great poet of testimony who holds speculative thought's feet to the fire of historical experience. Milosz is also for me one of the poets I cannot do without. In any case, neither Desmond's choice of poetry nor the particular poet is accidental. Desmond has made it clear throughout his work that literature can be a touchstone of philosophical and religious thought because at its best it remains in the closest proximity to experience. And, for him, as for Noble laureate Seamus Heaney, the power of Milosz's poetry is vested in its sense that poetry is both a form of seeing in a world that conceals itself in mystification and a form of testimony against the grain of the world, which is the grain of power that pulverizes and historically and materially wreaks havoc. If all of Caitlin Gilson's work moves towards a condition of poetry, poetry is folded in the discourse of her essay from the beginning. Her title of "Heart's Spectacular Silence" is inspired by my requiem poem dedicated to my brother that is the epigraph of the *Anatomy of Misremembering*. In addition, throughout her essay she frequently recurs to poetry in order to light up what Ricoeur and I have in common. Hölderlin's "Patmos" is invoked, Eliot's "The Rock" engaged, and through Eliot's use of the language of "dappled," Hopkins evoked. As we have seen, apocalyptic is the horizon of recall, so Eliot is not only the Eliot of "twilight," but the Eliot of "The Waste Land," and Hopkins is not simply the poet of epiphany, but the poet of disaster, the poet of "The Wreck of the Deutschland" and also the late sonnets that deal with the absence of God. Poetry is not entirely absent from the other contributors either. Like Gilson, in the context of his interpretation of Przywara as an apocalyptic theologian, John Betz gestures towards the importance Hölderlin held for him. Nor should it be ignored that Przywara is himself a religious poet of some note, which makes comprehensible the importance John of the Cross held for him both as apophatic mystic and as one of the greatest poets in the Spanish language.

Still, even if Martin is not alone in her intimating the importance of poetry in the matrix of relationship between philosophy, theology, and literature, her reading of my early and halted epic poem, *The Companion of Theseus*, is a startling and unexpected engagement with my poetry none greater than which can be thought. Her essay constitutes a complement and supplement to Ann Astell's essay in *Apocalypse of Love* (2018) on *Origen in Alexandria*, a volume of poems made up of both published and unpublished poems, imagining a nighttime Origen second-guessing his daytime thoughts which move within the ordinance of the proper and the sedimented tradition. This strangely contemporary Origen is experimental, edgy, and eccentric with regard to mainline Christianity as he digs down and up to a love tolerant of senselessness. Martin has an obvious sympathy for the anti-hero Perithous, who, unlike the real hero Theseus, whom he accompanies into the underworld with a view to stealing Persephone, does not escape. Martin demonstrates a superb grasp of the switching back and forth in the poem between two geographies and mindscapes, the first the geography and mindscape of ancient Greece, the second of a modern Ireland and an even more modern Dublin. She is sensitive to the way language in the poem is used both to disclose and hide grief, vulnerability, and death. Her patience with the poem's dense symbolic texture, its disturbed syntax, and the obscurity of its diction is marvelously forgiving while also purposeful, in that on her extraordinarily resonant reading *The Companion of Theseus* is an apology for flesh, incarnation, and world and a protest against intellect, abstraction, Cartesianism, angelism, a protest that is also voiced by a very non-Platonic Origen in *Origen in Alexandria*. One of the real achievements of Martin as a reader is that she demonstrates that she not only sees the poem as both hymn and requiem to the flesh, but grasps that the language performs this insistence of the sense and flesh, what William Desmond in his eulogies to incarnation calls "singing." More than any poem of mine, the 7,000-word *The Companion of Theseus* needs to be read aloud.

Martin does not make the mistake of casting *The Companion of Theseus* as a Christian poem, even if it is saturated by religious themes such as conversion, redemption, confession, hope, and love. If I were to attempt to place the religiousness of the poem, I think it would occupy a space between unbelief and belief, despair and hope—with the needle pointing to the second in each pair—after the manner of Simone Weil. In a way, Simone Weil functions as source and interpreter for *The Companion of Theseus*, in that first, she is the great thinker of destitution, absolute exposure, of how we are brought into the realm of un-accommodation in which our only agency towards a reality, at once indifferently brutal and brutally indifferent, is that of the suppliant, and second, while she frames her thought as a long conversation between a creative reading of Greek tragedy and a relentlessly honest depiction of the modern human condition as piteously exposed to forces which grind down human beings to nothing. While Martin does not expose Weil as a pervasive presence in the poem, nonetheless, throughout she demonstrates unbelievable archeological skills in bringing to the surface my literary and philosophical debts. While she grasps that there are myriad of poetic echoes—*The Companion of Theseus* is a poem of resonance that creates a community of voices—Martin ingeniously places the accent on Eastern European poets, especially the Russian poets Osip Mandelstam and Anna Akhmatova and the Polish poet Zbigniew Herbert. She marvelously distills that my account of the flaying of Marsyas is in direct conversation with Herbert's "Apollo and Marsyas." She is so good when it comes to un-earthing the major philosophical influences that it becomes impossible to distinguish guesses from apodictic truth. Merleau-Ponty's phenomenology of flesh and perception is presented as an ideological pylon in the poem. This, indeed, is so. Phenomenology was my first venture in philosophy and Merleau-Ponty was my main discovery. Although Heidegger was a close second, with regard to Merleau-Ponty I have never harbored the ambivalence that has been typical of my response to Heidegger from the very beginning.

Martin wonders whether a poem such as *The Companion of Theseus* provides a clue as to my later reflective and systematic opposition to Gnosticism. While it is difficult to avoid somewhat the fallacy of reconstruction, it should be said that even at this stage, as a student of phenomenology, I had begun to steep myself in Gnosticism and Manichaeanism and more broadly Western esotericism. If one were to model the style of opposition, it would be more after the manner of Tertullian than Irenaeus (who later becomes my heresiologist of choice), since for him the whole case of Christianity against Gnosticism rests on the vibrancy and vitality of the flesh of human beings and their archetype and savior Jesus Christ. Speaking about flesh and its absolute vulnerability, which is the main theme of the poem, it is almost impossible not to think of Martin's own work on Julia Kristeva, whom she enlists on behalf of a Christian theology of enfleshment that for her is one of the main deliverances of *nouvelle théologie*. If Kristeva is Christianly enlisted, she is never pared down: the flesh is insistent and suffering, dense and ecstatic. Kristeva's embodied self is the self as abject, a pulsation of desire satisfied only by the infinite which is irredeemably obscured and blocked by finite institution and ideology. Martin's Kristeva is my Weil, Kristeva's abjection, Weil's destitution. Martin's hints to this effect are, like poetry itself, louder than her statements. But she helps me name *The Companion of Theseus* as a poetry of abjection, or better, the attempt to find its language, that is, to find its poetics.

The Duty of the Question and the Modalities of Interrogation

All seven essays discussed so far identify significantly with the saying and said they present and imaginatively appropriate. They also extend what they find there, and do so in voices that are at once resonant and entirely their own. There is, however, no delinquency with regard to questioning, even if the urging is reserved and the insistence mild. First, to write on poetry—whether mine or someone else's—is to write about the questionable and to enter the space of question. Moreover, as deployed in my work and refracted through my undeserved readers, the categories of "apocalyptic," "Gnosticism," and "Gnostic return" are categories of intervention generated in the space of interrogation regarding definition and application in a context in which what is at stake is how it has gone with Christian theology in modernity and what are its future prospects as it suffers like all discourses the centrifugal force of the postmodern condition. A number of readers underscore the "apocalyptic turn" in twentieth-century Catholic theology (although not it exclusively), recommend it as both matching up with the magisterial tradition as well as being biblically adequate and, in addition, are convinced that more than other forms of theology it has the capacity to answer the imaginative and existential needs of the moment. Other readers speak approvingly of my narrative grammar definition of Gnosticism that in turn licenses talk of "Gnostic return." They are aware not only of the conflict of interpretation regarding the definition of Gnosticism, but also of the conceptual roadblocks regarding any talk of Gnostic return which has been in circulation since the first half of the nineteenth century in such figures as August Neander and F. C. Baur and recycled and recalibrated by the likes of Hans Jonas and Gilles Quispel in the twentieth. It is all for the best that no defense is mounted on my behalf. Rather what intrigues my readers are the issues of the definition of Gnosticism and the possibility of its return in a social and intellectual environment radically different from that of the ancient world. My views are entertained as hypotheses that can be tested, confirmed or falsified, and theoretically revised if required.

I will have more to say about the definition of "Gnosticism" and "Gnostic return" when I take up shortly David Bentley Hart's more explicit and bracing line of questioning, supported in some ways and softened in others by John Milbank, but first I want to speak to my readers' shy signifying of an absence or a specter. I am speaking of Heidegger, who though well-covered in essays and with respect to whom I have launched a number of pilot pieces speaking to the relation between him and Balthasar, as yet has not received the kind of comprehensive and fully satisfying coverage that only a book can supply. All I can say is that I am in the final stages of revising the manuscript that is volume 2 of *Anatomy of Misremembering*, and the text should be at the publisher by the time this volume is published. The basic thesis is that in and through a deep reading of Balthasar's critical appropriation of Heidegger one can discern that Balthasar constructs Heidegger as the other great misrememberer in a modernity that facilitates misremembering as well as forgetting of Christian discourses, practices, and forms of life. This is by no means to say that Heidegger is a misrememberer of Christianity of the same order or kind as Hegel, and it is by no means to imply that if Hegel admits of the label of "Gnostic," Heidegger does also. For Balthasar, Heidegger can more obviously be taken theologically on board, and though there are ways in which he undercuts and distorts Christian themes, practices, and forms of life, on Balthasar's account he is far less systematic than Hegel in doing so. The format of the volume repeats in essential ways that of the first volume of *Anatomy*, in that it articulates, first, what features of Heidegger's thought can be enlisted for Christian purposes and, second, what features have to be resisted if Balthasar's project of bringing the Christian tradition forward is not to be scuttled. Of course, given *Anatomy 1* as a template, there is considerable discussion of precursors and successors: in the case of Heidegger, precursors such as Nietzsche and Heraclitus; and in the case of successors, epigonal figures such as Vattimo and Caputo; in the case of Balthasar precursors such as Przywara and Augustine, and successors such as Marion, Lacoste, and Chrétienne, who extend and sharpen Balthasarian criticisms of the German philosopher. The volume does not restrict itself, however, to Balthasar's adoption of key Heideggerian ideas and his resistance to others. One of the ways in which this volume goes beyond *Anatomy 1* is that it considers doublets in Heidegger's texts of discourses such as prophecy and apocalyptic, of Christian practices such as Christian liturgy and prayer, and Christian forms of life deemed to be exemplary and characterized by radical self-emptying and disponibility.

Another way in which this volume goes beyond *Anatomy 1* is that, in getting the measure of Balthasar's critical appropriation of Heidegger, the credits and debits concern the very same features of the German

philosopher's thought: the features that are worth theologically appropriat-
ing in Heidegger are precisely those features that demonstrate flaws, and
contrariwise, precisely those features that need to be resisted have elements
in them that can and maybe even should be appropriated. Put in the positive
light of retrieval, there are five such Heideggerian features: (1) The diagnosis
of modernity as essentially characterized by a rationalism that exhibits its
violent orientation towards reality in a myriad of ways, but most explicitly
in technology that enjoys unimpeachable prestige; (2) Correlatively, a genealogy that inquires into the *longue durée* of the gestation of this rationalism;
(3) The constitutive priority of question over answer; (4) truth understood
as disclosure or *aletheia*, rather than correspondence or correctness; (5) the
essential equivalence of philosophy, religion, and poetry as discourses of
disclosure and the necessity of complex and nuanced intermediation.

Balthasar is not a Christian appropriator of Heidegger who restricts
himself, like Rahner, to explicitly phenomenological works such as *Being
and Time* (1927) and the *Kantbuch* (1929). Many of the features that he is
drawn to in Heidegger find their expression in post-*Kehre* texts that are genre
bending, at once hermeneutic and oracular, polemical and apocalyptic. Be
that as it may, it is extraordinarily interesting that these five features form a
"constellation" of properties that, if they do not essentially define Balthasar
as a Heideggerian theologian, do provide him with a quasi-Heideggerian
identity. The function of the technical term "constellation," which I draw
from Benjamin, is to suggest more than a congeries of accidental properties
without relation to each other, but something that falls short of constituting an essence. Indeed, I argue in *Anatomy 2* that given the importance of
the set of elements recalled, appearances to the contrary, Balthasar can be
regarded as the most Heideggerian of all major theologians of the twentieth
century. The crux of my argument, however, is that as Balthasar adopts the
constellation of five features, he takes issue with what he sees as constitutive
biases in Heidegger's particular formulations that turn out to be inimical to
historical Christianity. With regard to (1), Balthasar refuses to countenance
the view of modernity being a deformation without remainder; nor is he
willing to concede that Christianity is a constitutive part of the problem.
While admitting that the contributions of Christianity have not been entirely positive—the missteps and miscalculations are many—in line with Ro-
mano Guardini, Balthasar remains convinced that Christianity is part of the
solution. With regard to (2), when it comes to genealogy, Balthasar refuses
to go along with Heidegger's damnation of the history of Western thought
as the deepest form of forgetting (forgetting that does not know that it is
forgetting), which seems to him to be an application of a Protestant view
of absolute corruption. In addition, Balthasar vastly extends the very thin

swathe of Heideggerian exception, consisting of the Pre-socratics, Meister Eckhart, Hölderlin, and Heidegger himself. With regard to (3), without demurring about the priority of question over answer and questionability as an existential, Balthasar wonders whether the logic of the question uplifts answerability, if not actual answer, and whether questionability is to be interpreted as a permanent or temporary state. With regard to (4), while Balthasar regards Heidegger's disclosure model of truth to be perhaps his most important single achievement, moreover, one that helps enormously in curing Catholic thought of its addiction to propositionalism, nonetheless, he fears with Przywara and Stein that Heidegger's particular formulation is riddled by finitism and nihilism. With regard to (5), for all his railing against metaphysics and for all his plea for something like a democracy of the discourses of philosophy (non-metaphysical), religion, and poetry, it is not clear that Heidegger does not erect his own post-metaphysical philosophy as the master discourse. Overall, then, for Balthasar, Heidegger is at the very least an ambiguous resource for Christian theology. The constellation of features that can be put to use in refurbishing both the central content and rhetoric of Christianity makes retrieving Heidegger an enormously attractive option. Equally, however, particular inflections of these core features make appropriation of Heidegger an extraordinarily vexed affair that calls for critical acumen and consummate powers of discernment. Heidegger is a dangerous Christian ally, because though he recovers features of Western philosophical, religious, and poetic thought that enable Christian understanding and contribute to its mission, he also distorts them in the process. Thus, misremembering shadows remembering.

Precisely because Heidegger's engagement with the Christian tradition is far less extensive and systematic than Hegel's, which rewrites the entire Christian narrative, the range of distortions is narrower, and the distortions do not run as deep. This has the consequence that, *pace* Jonas and Milbank, Heidegger can in no way be cast as a Gnostic. This in turn means that, relative to Heidegger, Balthasar in his mode of critic cannot be cast as an *Irenaeus redivivus*. This leads fairly naturally to the question of what thinker or thinkers might be thought to foreshadow the kind of constitutive anti-Heideggerianism of Balthasar's trilogy. With due respect given to the roles of Aquinas and the negative theology tradition in Balthasar's construction of Heideggerian misremembering, I suggest that Balthasar's ultimate precursor is precisely that Christian thinker whose early rejection by Heidegger sets the German philosopher on his voyage of naming and unnaming of Being, that is, the myriad-voiced Augustine of the *Confessions, de trinitate, City of God*, and *Elucidation of the Psalms*, or more substantively the proposer and lover of beauty, the connoisseur of ecstasy, the criticizer of the worship of myth and the pride of stand-alone philosophy, the thinker who insists that life is worship and prayer and that both are impossible without Christ and the triune God. According to Balthasar, the reader of the *City of God*, for Heidegger to elevate in society the worship constituted by myth is to inscribe violence. Nor does the so-called "disinterestedness" of philosophy and Heidegger's own transcription of worship into a noetic register guarantee either that it is not itself a form of violence, or at least in collusion with the mythic form that it would both interpret and let stand.

In *Anatomy 2*, giving Augustine the opportunity to answer back is not the staging of an elaborate revenge fantasy against a Heidegger who, both early and late, reads the Catholic tradition with extreme prejudice. With regard to Balthasar as the fabulous orchestrator of the Catholic tradition, the elevation of Augustine is intended to suggest that when it comes to enlisting resources to filter and screen modern philosophy, Balthasar chooses well: it is the multiverse Augustine and not Irenaeus who is better set up to resist an equally multiverse, but also self-consciously post-metaphysical Heidegger who is obsessed with the apocalyptic advent of Being and human being's response to its call. No more, however, than in the case of marshalling the resources of tradition against Hegel should we think that Balthasar provides the only line of defense. Throughout his triptych Balthasar avails of other voices besides that of Augustine. Aquinas is definitely one of these voices, especially as this voice is mediated through the inflections of Gustav Siewerth and Ferdinand Ulrich in which Thomas is already regarded as talking back to Heidegger. In addition, one cannot ignore in Balthasar the purchase of negative theology against the Heideggerian liquidation of the Christian philosophical and theological traditions, even if this is a strand of resistance that needed to be pulled by Marion and Lacoste in order to see its full potential. Still, even if the elements of the tradition that can be harnessed against those features of Heidegger's thought are plural, it is my contention that Augustine is *primus inter pares*. The case for this becomes even stronger when one considers how Augustine functions in Przywara's theological anthropology and the proximity in time of the publication of Przywara's masterful anthology of Augustine and his magisterial *Analogia Entis*. While Augustine in *Anatomy 2* is very much a dependent variable, I confess that he also functions in my work as a whole quite independently of Balthasar as a Christian thinker who capacitates us to respond to a thinker who fascinates and horrifies us at once, a mystagogue who punctures our Christian pieties, a hater of Christianity who, nonetheless, reminds us sometimes of our better Christian selves.

Now, it is true that to the extent to which the seven commentators to whom I responded interrogate, they do so in the kind of muted fashion consistent with the genre of encomium. The discourse of encomium is refused by David Bentley Hart, but importantly more nearly because of redundancy, when it comes to reception of a theological and philosophical oeuvre, than because of deficiency. This is an important distinction, because I think it would be misleading were one to read Hart to suggest that the fundamental obligations of interpretation are met only in and through a comprehensive and lancing line of questioning. I read him as saying that such a line of questioning is one of the responsibilities that needs to be attended to if a body of theological and philosophical work is to be properly and authentically received. I thank him for being willing to accept the role and even more for the panache with which he adopts it and never steps outside. To state that Hart is a brilliant stylist is to state the obvious. His prose moves like water and in its rushes and perceptible hesitations and pauses participates in a cosmic rhythm, even if the artifice cannot be ignored. It would do considerable injustice to Hart, however, to dilate only on his style and rhetorical powers which are all put into the service of extraordinary learning, broad cultural sympathies, and firmness and yet flexibility in theological judgment. I am grateful, even if a little uncomfortable, that all this talent is put to work in a relentlessly deep questioning of my work that never fails to bring out what is essential, indeed, what reaches nothing less than both the well-springs of my thinking and its basic form.

If Hart is a master rhetorician, he is also a maestro of impersonation equally adept with regards to techniques of deflation and inflation. Here deflation is to the fore. One would not misunderstand Hart's relentless questioning of my work on Gnosticism, my figuration of an early modern figure such as Jacob Boehme (1575–1624), and possibly also my view of tradition, were one to construe it as providing a set of *dubia* regarding my work both in fact and in principle: whatever the achievement and level of achievement, neither my conclusions nor methods of analysis have been fully accepted, while in addition there may be specific features of my work that call for immediate critical attention. Still, one should also not ignore entirely the comedic surface. While the questions that Hart asks are deep ones, in a manner that reminds of Aristophanes' desconstruction of Greek literary and philosophical production, Hart asks (im)pertinently whether I have said anything meaningful, for example, about the nature of Gnosticism that would be of any use in constructing a theory of Gnostic return? Here Hart willfully and strategically ignores the entire theoretical apparatus presented in *Gnostic Return in Modernity*, which Desmond supposes in his marvelous account of "doubling" and Simpson deploys to such consequential effect in his analysis of Deleuze. There is no recall of "Gnostic narrative grammar" or "rule-governed deformation of classical Gnostic genres," nor any recall of my designation of the transgressive hermeneutic of Gnosticism vis-à-vis the biblical text. The reason for this is not simply unfairness. The critical posture Hart adopts with respect to my work appears to be at odds with what one finds in his own oeuvre, whose sympathies are manifestly theological and pro-church fathers. Two of the most basic marks of this posture are a distrust of all the heresiologists, not excluding Irenaeus, who make evaluative theological claims and a commitment to a radical historicism which, on the one hand, discourages generalization when it comes to ancient texts, and absolutely forbids even contemplating the prospect that ancient forms of thought repeat themselves in the modern discursive field or fields. That Hart envelops himself in a form of historical positivism, on which he routinely pours his considerable resources of invective, leads one to believe that he is being mischievously ironic. To have read *Gnostic Return in Modernity* is to know that it intended to represent a theoretical alternative to the historicism that Hart dons for argument's sake. Were I forced to make a choice between Irenaeus and Hart on the topic of Gnosticism, I would fairly quickly choose Irenaeus. Still I cannot believe that Hart is forcing such a choice—we have travelled very similar roads for a long time—and that he is asking me to repent of a backbone of a work which is ongoing and to which sooner rather than later I hope to add volumes on German idealism and English and German Romanticism.

But maybe Hart is not being Aristophanic. Maybe he means what he says, even if what he says is curiously out of line with regard to what he has said up until now and the general line of implication of his thought. One might conjecture that his recent translation of the New Testament has led to a fundamental rupture in his thought. If Hart is impeccably urbane in his criticism of "Gnosticism" as a genealogical category and even an analytic category throughout his essay, he is also relentlessly pointed. He places the texts of Nag Hammadi historically in the world of assumption of the New Testament from which strictly speaking they are indistinguishable. Both species of texts suppose a fundamental split between spiritual and material reality and a complex spiritual world in which there are divine and angelic actors in addition to God. Thus, the essential spuriousness of the category of "Gnosticism" in general, which obviously makes impossible a genealogical employment that depends on the category applying to specific band or bands of texts that are different from the texts of the New Testament. In addition, Hart suggests that the figure who might be regarded as the arch-heresiologist, that is, Irenaeus, does not testify to the reality of Gnosticism, but merely speaks of the "Gnostics so-called." Although the above two arguments are quite familiar to me, the only thing that it is out of joint is that it is Hart who would make them. They represent two anti-tradition blocks that characterize the field of Early Christian Studies. That there is considerable echoing of the New Testament in some texts of Nag Hammadi would make sense, for not all the texts of Nag Hammadi are involved in the articulation of a metanarrative that could be regarded as a rival for the Christian story; they are meditations on the quandary of salvation in a world of hostile powers in which the existential and the mythic go hand in hand. Moreover, some of the texts of Nag Hammadi that Hart cites in his footnotes do seem to be early compositions. Crucially, however, some of the texts of Nag Hammadi—for example, the *Apocryphon of John*, the *Reality of the Rulers*, the *Gospel of Truth*, and the *Tripartite Tractate*—do have fully elaborated narratives of the kinds that are contested by the heresiologists and enact a form of biblical hermeneutics clearly intended to cut against standard communitarian readings. Again, for a theologian whose own use of language is as judicious as its elegant, Hart is peculiarly flat-footed in the way that he exploits Irenaeus' locution of "Gnostics so-called." Hart reads it to mean that this group cannot be identified with a particular sect or set of sects. This does the intelligence of Irenaeus an enormous disservice. Irenaeus clearly thinks that there are particular groups who produce the kinds of metanarrative texts which he exegetes, and what he wants to say is that they have arrayed themselves in the mantle of a "gnosis" that properly belongs to those Christians who have the true faith that has been handed on over the decades.

If Hart, the recent translator of the New Testament, is not being Aristophanic, but entirely sincere, then the question has to be asked what is behind his call that I should give up of the category of Gnosticism and his conspicuous sidelining of the heresiologists, Irenaeus included. One is reduced entirely to conjectures. A first observation: more than at any other time in Hart's writing one senses a commitment to the original. Perhaps it is because he feels that the texts of Nag Hammadi are produced not only broadly speaking in the same linguistic and ideological environment, but also more or less during the same period as the production of the New Testament text, that he is emboldened to assert that the texts of Nag Hammadi are far closer to the New Testament than they in fact are. A second observation: one wonders whether the relative unbridled enthusiasm for the speculative Origen in the early church and the speculative Bulgakov in modern Eastern orthodoxy play a role in what looks to be a profound allergy regarding any univocist tendency in Christianity when it comes to the formulation of particular doctrines and the insistence on their centrality. Hart makes a point of insisting that he does not disapprove of doctrine. Yet much of what he says in his essay encapsulates his studied preference for Rowan Williams' far greater openness to plurality and ambiguity than that which can be espied in Newman's *The Development of Doctrine* or *mutatis mutandis* the Neo-patristic School of Eastern Orthodoxy exhibited by Flo-rovsky and Lossky.

Together with a refusal to engage the hermeneutic, taxonomic, and grammatical analyses of Gnosticism articulated by *Gnostic Return in Modernity*, Hart elaborates an alternative captivating vision that effects a recovery in elegiac mood of the religious discourses of the early centuries which demonstrate both extraordinary variety and cross-fertilization. It is to this source or sourcing, characterized by Heraclitean flux, that he invites us to pledge our troth. When Hart is not being quite so lyrical, once again he seems to tarry with the Early Christian Studies establishment in celebrating equivocity. Of course, the irony is delicious: he proposes a very univocal version of the equivocal matrix of early Christianity to which, if we are truly faithful, we would have to be far less tradition-inclined than we have turned out to be. Of course, with Hart one can always hear echoes of more theoretical discourses which one could expect no denizen of Early Christian Studies to have mastered. One wonders, given *The Beauty of the Infinite*, whether Hart does not find productive Deleuze's reflections on singularities that cannot be reduced to unity. Thus, if Simpson can have a Deleuze that speaks for me, Hart has a Deleuze that speaks against me. Although Hart never speaks to my view of Gnosticism as a grammar, it is likely that it would smack too much of univocity, this despite the obvious fact that to speak of grammar is to support an analogical field of discourse and depending on the generosity of the grammar, one can think of the field of discourse as "metaxological" in Desmond's sense and thus more or less resistant to procrustean reduction.

A similar ambiguity seems to characterize Hart's presentation of my construction of Jacob Boehme as the originary site of Gnostic return in modernity. It is not clear whether Hart has adopted the comedic role of Aristophanes or is speaking for himself when he peremptorily rejects "Gnostic" attribution to Boehme, which also cuts off one of the few ways of thinking of how ancient Gnosticism could plausibly make its way into modernity. While again Hart refuses to attend to the complex argument of *Gnostic Apocalypse: Jacob Boehme's Haunted Narrative* (2002), he does cast it aside as itself a Hegelian construction and very deliberately adopts what he takes to be the "commonsense" position that Boehme is a faithful Lutheran, although this gets further specified in terms of both carrying forward medieval theological voluntarism and modifying it. Whereas medieval theological voluntarism speaks of God the creator in terms of divine will, Boehme will speak of divine will as a divine will to self-determination. Leaving aside for the moment that Hart smooths out what should be taken as a *metabasis eis allo genos*, it is puzzling to find a reader of the theological tradition of the caliber of Hart ignoring the fact that Boehme's fidelity to Lutheranism was fiercely questioned in his own day, failing to take account of the influence of Paracelsian alchemy, with its view of *arcana, magia*, will and desire, on Boehme's construction of God, and siding with Hegel's and F. C. Baur's construction of the positive relation between Boehme's theosophy and Luther, which subserves their common construction of German idealism as consistent with Luther's thought, despite the peremptory sidelining of *sola scriptura* and *sola gratia*. There is much in Hart's analysis that is apodictic in the extreme, and seems to call for Paul Valery's reminder in and through his character Monsieur Teste to avoid trying to persuade by your tone when you cannot persuade by your meaning.

For the record, however, there is a whole section in *Gnostic Apocalypse* called "Orthodox Reserves" where I underscore that there are a number of important places where Boehme remains aligned with the mainline theological tradition and where Luther wins out over Paracelsus, for example, in his articulation of creation. So even if Hart were actually disagreeing with me, the disagreement would be far more modest than he thinks. To the degree to which Hart argues against my "Gnostic" reading of Boehme rather than asserts the contrary, one of the planks of the argument is that "theogony" and ancient Gnosticism—although one should keep in mind that "Gnosticism" is not an identifiable religious system, but a particular set of qualities in ancient texts contemporary with the New Testament— are contraries. Hart once again could do with more exegetical finesse. He sidelines the reading of Irenaeus and other heresiologists who attempted not only to describe forms of thought that were alien to a biblical form of Christianity, but to draw out their implications, one of which is "theogony." In addition, while admitting that in the Nag Hammadi library theogony is not a defining ingredient of the heterogeneous, it is observable in the *Tripartite Tractate*, where a developmental twist is introduced into what is the more standard Hellenistic structure of a dualistic contrast between the spiritual and material planes of existence. This is sufficient to establish the negative capability for theogonic construction in Gnosticism and thus represents an argument for continuity between ancient and modern forms of Gnosticism, even if it turns out that that theogony is a dominant feature of modern forms of Gnosticism, whereas it was more or less a recessive feature of ancient and/or classical Gnosticism.

Now, while it remains undecidable whether Hart is really attacking the substance of my Gnostic return thesis or taking on the responsibility of the virtuoso to exhibit what an attack would look like, there can be no doubt that many of the pages of this beautiful and plangent piece constitute a doxology to the teeming variety of symbols and narrative of the New Testament and the texts of the Hellenistic world that were contemporary with them and the hopes and fears embedded in both. The evocation is beautiful enough to wring an amen from any reader capable of being enchanted. I count myself as one of them. Yet, if we can find some way to break the spell, the radical historicism of Hart's position becomes clear. (1) Categories of analysis need to be determinate and determinacy is a function of application to historically discrete phenomena in a world of multiple discourses and plural aims. In the case   of lack of evidence for the reality of discrete phenomena, categories of analysis should be barred. The conclusion is obvious: since it is far from clear that Gnosticism is a historically discrete phenomenon, the category of Gnosticism is barred. (2) To respect history is to proscribe any religious phenomenon returning as such and thus with respect to discourses we should repent of our capacity to claim continuity across history and across the divide between the modern and the premodern in particular. With regard to the latter Hart finds himself in the company of Hans Blumenberg who insists on the novum of the modern age. The negative consequences of this historicist option on any Gnostic return thesis, and not simply mine, are obvious.

Hart makes his affinities for plurality, both synchronic and diachronic, clearer here than in any other text of his that I have read. For him, this affinity and his commitment to analogy are essentially the same thing, for by the nature of the case, analogy is tolerant of variety. These affinities and commitments provide the context of Hart's appeal to the kaleidoscope as the figure of analogy. Hart offers us a gorgeous rendition of the physical structure of the kaleidoscope, a lustrous account of its function, which delivers a ceaseless variety of forms in various degrees of relation. Nonetheless, if the intent is to get us to give up our perennial habit of violent imposition of a unifying discourse, it is far from evident that Hart gives us the middle term one finds either in Przywara's view of analogy or Desmond's view of metaxology. Instead, there is the rave of the plural, an uplifting of an equivocity that will not yield to ordering. Has Hart gone over to the other side? Probably not. But he does seem to have given up significantly on our ability to make sense of our world and to determine what is central and what is peripheral to our faith, as well as, of course, our capacity to make normative claims and to justify distinctions between orthodoxy and heterodoxy. The last is particularly noticeable, as we find a Hart unnerved by multiplicity, paralyzed by the difficulty of choice, which in the final analysis can only be arbitrary. Against his best intentions, the luscious prose of Hart gives the impression that he has succumbed to the very skepticism and nihilism that it has been his vocation to exorcise. Still, even this could be a case of impersonation, calculated to show us what theology and the churches are up against. And maybe one should not be quite as shocked as one is, since the power of diagnosis of intellectual deformations, arguably, is in all members of this colloquy, not excluding myself, in direct proportion to our fascination. Nihilism is the serpent in all our gardens, skepticism its sweet tongue. In this essay Hart mimes a perspectivalism that will order nothing while submitting to everything.

Perhaps there is a hope in what sometimes seems like despair, in that the plurality and ambiguity is such that we are denied easy and reductive forms of analogy that would not be faithful to the *metaxu*. Although the term is Plato's, the sense may well be that of William Desmond, who recommends that we think of far more complex mediations and intermediations than customarily we think under analogy. If this is what Hart intends, then once again we are in agreement. My essays on tradition directly involve a metaxological supplement to the notion of tradition as defined by a grammar, which in my view is just another way of speaking of analogy. I take this view, however, to be continuous with the view of tradition provided Newman, but also the Tübingen School of Möhler and Drey, not forgetting Blondel. A metaxological view of tradition may well be what Hart is pressing, even as his rhetoric sometimes suggests a liquifying of the Christian tradition to the extent that it risks liquidating it. Hart's appeal at the end of his piece to the Romanticist elucubrations in "Lapis Lazuli" of my fellow countryman W. B. Yeats on the inseparability of form and content in literary production seem to serve this agenda. To which it is appropriate to reply by referring to another poem of Yeats, that is, "The Second Coming." This poem catches something of the nightmare of history that comes across in Hart's deep musings, while also in the figure of "the rough beast slouching towards Bethlehem to be born" that underscores the prospect of doubling and counterfeiting so central to my own work.

The final object of challenge in Hart's essay is addressed to my formulation of a "theory" of modernity or lack thereof. Again, I wish to say that the somewhat abrasive form of the challenge is far less subversive than the actual content. This is not to say that there is not a real question being addressed, but simply that Hart knows well that I have reflected throughout my work after the manner of my teacher Louis Dupré on the nature of modernity and its gestation, and that I have also engaged thinkers such as Heidegger, Hegel, Marx, Jacques Derrida, Jean-François Lyotard, Hans Blumenberg, Jürgen Habermas, Alasdair MacIntyre, Charles Taylor, Jonathan Israel, and Thomas Pfau, to give but a few of the more prominent names. Given what I believe to be the difficulties in constructing a theory of modernity that would function as explanation rather than description, what I have presented thus far in publication would doubtless be found wanting from a strictly explanatory point of view. My operative model of modernity functions like all the others, descriptively rather than explanatorily, a heuristic with a large degree of epistemic reserve in which I can account for rupture, which is as much ongoing process as punctiliar event, which leaves behind not only ancient conceptions but specific forms of thinking and feeling, leads not only to forgetting of the past, but to the experience of the present as intolerably empty and flat, and leads to the recycling of more imaginative forms of discourse to the side of the mainline Christian tradition. There is not much in Sartre than I find sustaining after all these years: not *L'Être et Néant* or *Critique de la raison dialectique*. But I have imbibed the lesson of Sartre's four-volume work on Flaubert, *L'Idiot de la famille*, in which—his ambition frustrated—Sartre says that his 2,000-page account of Flaubert fails to explain him. By implication a satisfactory theory of modernity, even a Marxist or Marxian one, will also fail. Sartre's failure tells me that a theory of modernity is essentially eschatological, and what Hart, Desmond, and myself and others are providing are plausible guides to selected aspects of modernity that, if in the short run look as if they are competitive, in the long run might turn out to be complementary. For example, I am by no means persuaded that Hart's emphasis on modernity being in significant respects an explication of the theological voluntarism of the late medieval period is incompatible with my views about Gnostic return and forgetting and misremembering. In any event, a mere survey of both of our work would suggest that while both of us construct modernity as a derailment, we also see that modernity is defined by "folds," to deploy Deleuze's proto-ontological construct in a genealogical manner. Modernity is as much a folding of the premodern as the naming of an absolute gap between the "new" and what went before. Premodern discourses of quite different kinds, my Gnosticism, Hart's theological voluntarism, are pressed in the folds and though they will recall their premodern ancestors, will also look different. With regard to the premodern, modernity is not so much the other as the non-other (*non Aliud*) which contains all forms and ceaselessly combines and offers permutations of them. True, modernity has new things to say, but it make the past disappear not by making it cease to exist, but by plying a grammar of evasion, allusion, and substitution in which the past continues to haunt the present. The existential correlative of this disorientation and haunting is a general sense of vacuity that alternates between muteness and logorrhea, brute insistence and periphrasis, harmonious praising of narrow but clear ways forward and cacophony of circumquaques in which meaning in language has been defeated and all that abides is its sonic register.

As is the case with Hart, indeed, as with all the contributors to this volume, John Milbank and I are fellow travelers when it comes to theology, philosophy, and literature and their relation. Our areas of agreement are huge, our areas of disagreement fairly small, and seem to have about them the air of a family squabble. I am particularly grateful to him for his careful, nuanced, illuminating, and gracious analysis of *Anatomy of Misremembering* in which he perspicaciously elevates, as does Schindler, the theme of apocalyptic. He recommends a great deal and I have no reason to think that he is being disingenuous in doing so. Nonetheless, while appreciative, the overall register of his essay is critical, with interrogation proceeding essentially along two axes. The first involves not so much a critical questioning of my interpretation of Balthasar, nor even of Balthasar's program, but rather a critical questioning of Balthasar's theological performance, which, of course, bears indirectly on my own, given how highly I recommend it. The second essentially repeats criticisms of my Gnostic return genealogy made in this volume by Hart, although Milbank does so with the laudable intention of mediating between us.

I think it best to begin with the second rather than the first line of criticism, since, on the one hand, the outlines of my reply have already been laid down in my response to Hart and, on the other, Milbank's criticisms of Balthasar's theological performance are best understood against the backdrop of Milbank's own genealogy in which theological voluntarism plays an essential role. As one would expect, Milbank agrees with Hart that the transformation to modernity occurs in significant part due to the displacement of metaphysical participation in which the triune God expresses itself in the world and the human subject participates in this God to a sovereign God of arbitrary will who creates a world of nature and human beings. The resulting relation between God and the world is extrinsic in both cases. If what occurred is clear, just when it occurred and who are the essential discursive points of origin continue to be points of investigation. Milbank is as loud as Hart in his rejection of the model of divine sovereignty in Luther and Calvin, but is anxious to push the sea-change as far back into the medieval period as he can: certainly further than the fourteenth century of William of Ockham and Gabriel Biel, and perhaps even further back than Duns Scotus in the thirteenth. Milbank is convinced that anthropological voluntarism is the correlative of theological voluntarism, although in his essay here he merely gestures to it in his positive appraisal of the work of Thomas Pfau. Do I think that Milbank has named an important feature of modernity? Absolutely! Do I think that it explains its genesis? Absolutely not! Even leaving aside for a moment my reservations regarding the prospects of any genealogy proving to be explanatory in the strict sense, I find myself in the company of my teacher, Louis Dupré, who, though he regards theological voluntarism as a fundamental element of a complex process of transition from the premodern to the modern, felt disinclined to think that it captured the entire process.

As indicated previously, Hart thinks that his theological voluntarism genealogy and my Gnostic return genealogy bear a competitive relation to each other. Milbank also appears to be convinced that this is the case. Playing the role of reconciler, he attempts to alleviate the putative zero-sum game struggle between these genealogical models by suggesting that my Gnostic return model is best thought of as the sub-plot of the theological voluntarism genealogical model that he and Hart share. Although this is a well-intentioned offer, it is one I feel obliged to refuse. First, I am not at all convinced that the genealogical models are competitive. I think that the two models are looking at different discursive features of modernity that have displaced and replaced a premodern consensus and that, accordingly, and thus fundamentally, they are complementary and mutually illuminating. Second, it is dangerously presumptive to think that one has come upon the genealogical secret and that one has in one's possession the master narrative that has sufficient explanatory power to make all other genealogical narratives at best functions of the one true narrative. Where this surreption is best illustrated is in Milbank's repetition of Hart's claim that the theogonic metaphysics of Boehme is simply a variant of standard theological voluntarism with the difference that in this case the divine does not so much chose a particular world as chose a pattern of becoming whereby it comes to be all that it can be. But this is to make a basic mistake regarding the grammar of divine sovereignty: as much as the classic Christian tradition, which is not addled by theological voluntarism, the grammar of an Ockham, a Luther, and a Calvin is that God is fully constituted being. It makes no sense to say that God wills to become all that God can be as if there is lack of being. In essence, the theogonic discourse of Boehme breaches the standard grammar, which is still in play in theological voluntarism. Boehme is a widely heterodox thinker. The most that can be said of his putative Protestantism is that he tries to speak as if he is faithful to Luther's circumscribed notion of divine will, even as the saturation of his theological discourse by Paracelsian speculation on cosmic powers and drives makes this impossible. Milbank joins Hart in forcing an interpretation on Boehme that in my view seriously damages the persuasiveness of their theological voluntarism genealogy by requiring it to do more work than it plausibly can.

Similarly, Milbank is guilty of overreach when it comes to the interpretation of Hegel. Having designated Boehme as a mere variant of classical theological voluntarism, the Hegel-Boehme relation inclines Milbank to suggest—evidence to the contrary—that Hegel can be grafted into the overarching genealogy of theological voluntarism. Milbank, thereby, gives Hegel a pass when the German idealist flaunts his Lutheran credentials. Of course, in order to do this Milbank has to ignore Hegel's determined stance against theological voluntarism, indeed any absolute form of separation between God and the world, as well as the incredibly close connection between Hegel and Spinoza, who is the most concertedly anti-voluntarist philosopher not only in modernity but, arguably, in the entire philosophical tradition. My Gnostic return genealogy which positions Boehme as the major transitional figure accounts for far more in Hegel's texts than Milbank's theological voluntarism model does. Moreover, it is built to do so. I admit that Milbank's theological voluntarism model—Hart's also—covers a far broader field of discursive phenomena in modernity than mine. The theological voluntarism model makes up in range what it lacks in perspicuity, just as my model suffers a contraction in range precisely in order to be perspicuous with regard to a limited band of highly influential discourses that look as if they have saved the appearances regarding Christianity, but that in my view constitute counterfeits. To insist that one has articulated a model that covers all the important phenomena of modernity and can track their gestation, generation, as well as identify and recommend the phenomena they replace is not only to risk hubris, it is to effect to prosecute the forensic side of theology in a voice that is as univocal and thus as violent as could possibly be imagined. In other words, it displays precisely a kind of framing that it is the intention to Radical Orthodoxy to oppose.

Milbank uplifts two features of my interpretation of Balthasar. He approves, on the one hand, of my stressing that in many instances Balthasar's criticisms of modern discourses such as Romanticism and idealism are a fruit of his attraction and, on the other, my demonstration of a deep engagement of Balthasar with Bulgakov. If Milbank does not turn the first compliment against me, he does turn the second. Despite the overlaps between the two theologians when it comes to apocalyptic, figuration of the triune God and the question of divine possibility, figuration of Christ, and deification, in the end one has to choose: *either* Balthasar *or* Bulgakov. Balthasar's indication of distance from Bulgakov when it comes to the level of proximity between God and the world, or otherwise put Balthasar's lack of full appropriation of Bulgakov's sophiology, which is indicated in the recurrence to the language of divine freedom, is sufficient not only to make him less theologically compelling than Bulgakov for Milbank, but sanction Balthasar's inscription in the genealogy of theological voluntarism and the resultant extrinsicism of the relations between God and world and vice versa. Apparently, de Lubac is superior to Balthasar on this scale of measurement and thereby—one assumes—nearer to Bulgakov. There are a number of major problems with this assessment besides its rashness and lack of nuance. The first is that Milbank seems to see theological voluntarism everywhere and is prepared to attribute it to a Catholic theologian who more effectively rebutted Barth's theological voluntarism and actualism than any theologian in the twentieth century. The second is that from the perspective of representative Catholic theologians such as Balthasar and Erich Przywara there are two dangers facing any modern or postmodern theology that would be adequate to scripture and tradition: there is, of course, theological voluntarism, which opens up an unbridgeable gap between God and world, but there is also the prospect of identifying the divine so much with the world that God is immanentized and the grace that enables participation naturalized. An adequate Christian theology, for these as well as other Catholic thinkers, has to steer between the Scylla and Charybdis of both. I allow that Bulgakov's sophiology might in the end be exonerated of a dangerous overcorrection of theological voluntarism, but at the very least his brilliant speculative theology invites questioning. It is in this light that one should understand Balthasar's recourse to the language of divine freedom. Again it is a heuristic device not a substantive position in which, unbeknownst to himself, he comes to subscribe to some form of *potentia absoluta* in contradistinction from *potentia ordinata*, where the first suggests that God has the prerogative of the sovereignty to suspend or absolve the intelligibility of the good world that he has created.

Besides these two problems I have a more general worry that in the end is the other side of my worry about the highly univocal nature of Milbank's genealogical model. This has to do with the definition of orthodoxy itself. If Hart compromised "orthodoxy" by equivocating about its possibility, Milbank seems to do just the obverse: not only the usual suspects or villains are named, but now Balthasar and Newman, Bonaventure, Augustine, maybe even Aquinas have become suspect to various degrees. Since Milbank deals generally with theologians rather than councils and popes, as a Roman Catholic to get her markers for orthodoxy, the dark question begins to emerge what precisely of the mainline theological tradition is left. The theological tradition is certainly being seriously trimmed, and the number of those who can really be counted as "orthodox" seriously depleted. Indeed, arguably, it is now made up only of those thinkers, Neoplatonic and otherwise, who support forms of participation none-greater-than-which can be thought. As I see it, Milbank runs the risk of two different (but maybe related) reductions. First, he runs the risk of mistaking radical orthodoxy for hyper-orthodoxy, that is, confusing the defense of the broad-based tradition against its secular despisers with a recommendation of a small slice of this tradition based on what an adequate view of the God-world relationship should look like. At the same time, he runs just the opposite risk of making "orthodoxy" a trope: a theological discourse is orthodox or not depending on his say-so. But this is willfulness *in extremis*, a hyper-voluntarism that goes hand in hand with a tendency towards the univocal in terms of performance if not necessarily in terms of substance.

The founder of "Radical Orthodoxy" is by nature an arguer. He will argue with friends as well as enemies, and perhaps even more eagerly with his friends than his enemies. Thus, I consider that he has paid me the highest of compliments. Here as elsewhere Milbank prosecutes an argument with such verve but also innocence that it gives no sign that argument is simply a function of the fallen world, just one more cacophony to go along with the cacophony of totalization and violence that characterizes historical existence and especially historical existence under modern conditions. One senses in the case of Milbank that paradise is unimaginable without the mischief and beauty of argument. Maybe one could even go a step further: perhaps one might speak of the play of argument, with the accent falling on *play*. Arguing is a mode of being and above all *being with*. And I am grateful for John Milbank's demonstration of being with, which is always a sounding and resounding. What applies protologically has eschatological implication: can we and should we imagine a heavenly symposium in which an eternally productive rhetoric never allows for a harmony that implies satiety? I am also assuming with him, as with Hart, that their pressing is an invitation to press back. I have accepted it and come to think of it as an obligation, a condition, indeed, of robust friendship.

Here(ing) the Banquet in Which We Are a Conversation

Heidegger routinely cites the line in Hölderlin in which the German poet speaks to becoming a conversation with unnamed others to whom he speaks because he hears (and sees), thereby setting up a circle of saying and showing of enormous privilege which compensates for what is banal in life and painfully without issue. What was promised to me in the event of the note from Gillian Rose over two decades ago, and which converted me to think that adumbrations of transparence were possible, has been enacted in these eight essays, just as much in the one essay that is deliberatively non-encomiast as in those essays that more obviously say thank you. The one person whom I have yet to acknowledge and thank is the convener of this symposium, the procurer of the banquet, that is, Philip Gonzales. The fact that I was a reader for his dissertation hardly justifies the time he has put into making this volume a reality. After the manner of Gillian Rose he read and found himself in a state of resonance, just as I have read and found myself put in a state of resonance by Philip's extraordinarily mature work on Przywara, as well, of course, by all the writers gathered in this volume who are every bit as resonant with each other as they are with me. But as his wonderful book on Przywara shows, Gonzales is a consummate orchestrator of voices, which sound and resound. If, only after the fact, it is predictable that he would be the executor of his extraordinary act of charity. I assume that he knows I know that I cannot possibly repay him. But for the record let me say it explicitly. As Gonzales's work over the past decade or so has resonated with Przywara, for an even longer period mine has resonated with that of Balthasar. And it is with him that I bring this response to a simply mind-boggling bouquet of gifts to a close. In Ireland I would be more inclined to say "creel" of gifts, since "creel" is not only a wicker basket in which one places fish, but because of the association of fish with wisdom, the creel takes on the significance of a sacred box of revelation.

What also does not fail to get called to mind is both Eucharist and its eschatological promise of sharing and transparence. The Eucharist is for Balthasar the site where forgiveness and transformation happens, where we are enabled to become who we are meant to be, to be a gift poured out and to be shared. Eucharist, for Balthasar, as for de Lubac before him, and Benedict XVI afterwards, institutes church, which in its fully realized practical form is demonstrated in our transparence with respect to each other. To have found oneself resonating with others, and to have discovered that oneself is a source of the resonance of others is to be provided notice of a state that is not our possession, a state merely glimpsed on this side of the eschaton. As Balthasar scholars know well, when the Swiss theologian speaks of Eucharist, it is not simply the Gospel of John to which he refers but the book of Revelation in which "the one slain from the foundation of the world" finds us and founds us as the community of the gift, which was always our vocation. At least one of the permissible meanings of the image of the heavenly banquet is that it crystallizes the permanence of a reality of transparence in community only glimpses and foretastes of which are available to us *in via*. Balthasar comes to see what Dante came to see, that is, the delight of recognition, and comes to hear what Dante came to hear, that is, the harmony of resonance. There is also a clear sense in both that the conversation is infinite, that mutual transparence is precisely that which does not allow a self to be fixed and thus exhaustively known: conversation has register of delight, surprise, and continually freshness. If real conversation is a notice of heaven, then one might ask: is there a place for disagreement, for remembering otherwise? Even if Dante would proscribe and Balthasar hesitate, I feel bound to say yes. If the banquet is to be revelry, Aristophanes gets his invitation. Still, this leads to one further question: who are the "we" at the banquet? My answer is that we are the fully enfleshed, the fully resonated and resonating responses to Christ and through Christ the triune God; we are the fully ripe "nows" from which before and after have been smoothed out, and each and all superbly "here" so that we can listen with rapt attention, hear the resonance, and see and know only what love knows. Since we are talking about that which we cannot talk about, perhaps we might approach it from another angle and say that to have found oneself listened to, to be seen and known, is to found oneself "here" and to be incarnate. As Gillian Rose once graced me with such a promise, as a recent book on my work, edited by Jennifer Martin and Anthony Sciglitano, has renewed it, this colloquy, orchestrated by the irrepressible Philip Gonzales, finds me amid all the floundering of abstraction, etiolation, and excarnation and participation in the founding of me that is precisely Christ's apocalyptic work and the triune God's indelible aim.

Index

CPSIA information can be obtained
at www.ICGtesting.com
Printed in the USA
LVHW112247010920
664806LV00003B/923